POLITICAL

COGNITION

The 19th Annual
Carnegie Symposium
on Cognition

POLITICAL

COGNITION

Edited by

Richard R. Lau
David O. Sears

LAWRENCE ERLBAUM ASSOCIATES, PUBLISHERS
1986   Hillsdale, New Jersey   London

Lawrence Erlbaum Associates, Inc., Publishers
365 Broadway
Hillsdale, New Jersey 07642

Library of Congress Cataloging in Publication Data

Symposium on Cognition (19th : 1984 : Carnegie-Mellon University)
  Political cognition.

  Includes index.
  1. Political psychology—Congresses.   I. Lau, Richard R.
II. Sears, David O.   III. Title.
JA74.5.S97   1984   320'.01'9   85-7080
ISBN 0-89859-652-1

Printed in the United States of America
10 9 8 7 6 5 4 3 2 1

Contents

Contributors   vii

Preface   ix

PART I INTRODUCTION

1. An Introduction to Political Cognition   3
   Richard R. Lau, David O. Sears

PART II RECENT ADVANCES IN COGNITIVE PSYCHOLOGY AND SOCIAL COGNITION

2. A Primer of Information-Processing Theory for the
   Political Scientist   11
   Reid Hastie

3. Schema-Based Versus Piecemeal Politics:
   A Patchwork Quilt, But not a Blanket, of Evidence   41
   Susan T. Fiske

4. Behavioral Decision Theory and Political Decision Making   55
   Gregory W. Fischer, Eric J. Johnson

PART III APPLICATIONS OF SOCIAL COGNITION TO POLITICAL BEHAVIOR

5. Cognitive Consequences of Political Sophistication   69
   Ruth Hamill, Milton Lodge

6. Political Schemata, Candidate Evaluations, and
   Voting Behavior   95
   Richard R. Lau

7. The Role of Inference in the Perception of
   Political Candidates   127
   Pamela Johnston Conover, Stanley Feldman

8.   A Schematic Variant of Symbolic Politics Theory,
      as Applied to Racial and Gender Equality   159
      David O. Sears, Leonie Huddie, Lynitta G. Schaffer

9.   Partisan Cognitions in Transition   203
      Arthur H. Miller

10.   Presidential Character Revisited   233
      Donald R. Kinder

11.   Justice and Leadership Endorsement   257
      Tom R. Tyler

12.   Emotion and Political Cognition: Emotional Appeals in
      Political Communication   279
      Ira Roseman, Robert P. Abelson, Michael F. Ewing

PART IV COMMENTS FROM POLITICAL SCIENCE

13.   Candidate Evaluations and the Vote: Some Considerations
      Affecting the Application of Cognitive Psychology
      to Voting Behavior   297
      Richard A. Brody

14.   What are People Trying to do With Their Schemata?
      The Question of Purpose   303
      Robert E. Lane

15.   Cognition and Political Behavior   319
      Robert Jervis

16.   Argumentation and Decision Making in Government   337
      Richard A. Smith

17.   The Relevance of Social Cognition for the Study of Elites
      in Political Institutions, or Why It Isn't Enough to
      Understand What Goes on in Their Heads   341
      Paul A. Anderson

PART V CONCLUSION

18.   Social Cognition and Political Cognition: The Past,
      the Present, and the Future   347
      Richard R. Lau, David O. Sears

References   367

Author Index   395

Subject Index   405

Contributors

ROBERT P. ABELSON Yale University, Department of Psychology, New Haven, CT 06520

PAUL A. ANDERSON Carnegie-Mellon University, Department of Social Sciences, Pittsburgh, PA 15213

RICHARD A. BRODY Stanford University, Department of Political Science, Stanford, CA 94305

PAMELA JOHNSTON CONOVER University of North Carolina, Department of Political Science, Chapel Hill, NC 27514

MICHAEL F. EWING Yale University, Department of Psychology, New Haven, CT 06520

STANLEY FELDMAN University of Kentucky, Department of Political Science, Lexington, KY 40506

GREGORY W. FISCHER Carnegie-Mellon University, Department of Social Sciences, Pittsburgh, PA 15213

SUSAN T. FISKE Carnegie-Mellon University, Department of Psychology, Pittsburgh, PA 15213

RUTH HAMILL State University of New York, Department of Political Science, Stony Brook, NY 11794

REID HASTIE Northwestern University, Department of Psychology, Evanston, IL 60201

LEONIE HUDDY University of California, Department of Psychology, Los Angeles, CA 90024

ROBERT JERVIS   Columbia University, Department of Political Science, New York, NY 10027

ERIC J. JOHNSON   Carnegie-Mellon University, GSIA, Pittsburgh, PA 15213

DONALD R. KINDER   University of Michigan, Institute for Social Research, Ann Arbor, MI 48106

ROBERT E. LANE   Yale University, Institution for Social and Policy Studies, New Haven, CT 06520

RICHARD R. LAU   Carnegie-Mellon University, Department of Social Sciences, Pittsburgh, PA 15213

MILTON LODGE   State University of New York, Department of Political Science, Stony Brook, NY 11794

ARTHUR H. MILLER   University of Iowa, Department of Political Science, Iowa City, IA 52242

IRA ROSEMAN   The New School for Social Research, 66 West 12th Street, New York, NY 10011

LYNITTA G. SHAFFER   University of California, Department of Psychology, Los Angeles, CA 90024

DAVID O. SEARS   University of California, Department of Psychology, Los Angeles, CA 90024

RICHARD A. SMITH   Carnegie-Mellon University, Department of Social Sciences, Pittsburgh, PA 15213

TOM R. TYLER   Northwestern University, Department of Psychology, Evanston, IL 60201

Preface

This book joins two major intellectual traditions that have, until now, largely remained interdependent of each other: cognitive psychology and political behavior. The gradual replacement of animal models with information processing models in experimental psychology really began to take hold about 20 years ago, producing a field self-consciously identifying itself as Cognitive Psychology. At the same time, political scientists were accumulating vast amounts of empirical data on the political behavior of both mass and elites, only somewhat guided by the social psychological theory of the day. By the early 1980s, both traditions had developed to a high level of sophistication and had developed a substantial corpus of theory and research that had successfully challenged and altered conventional models of information processing and political behavior, respectively. Just as important, both have been concerned with the same core phenomena—the human individual's perceiving, thinking, judging, and deciding about complex alternatives in complex fields of information.

The time seems ripe for provoking a concerted effort to apply the principles and methods of cognitive psychology to the core phenomena of political behavior. Our goal is to speed up application of cognitive theories to political behavior by provoking assessment of early efforts at application, by the early-appliers themselves, and by cognitive psychologists and political behavior researchers who have not been involved in this bridging effort. We do not wish to produce interdisciplinary contact where none usually exists. However, such applications happen sooner or later on their own, whenever exciting and relevant basic theory exists in neighboring disciplines, just as rational choice theory has been incorporated into political behavior research because of its great heuristic potential.

The volume is organized in the following manner: After a brief introduction, the first major section includes chapters by Hastie, Fiske, and Fischer and Johnson that provide extensive reviews of recent advances in the cognitive, social cognition, and decision making literatures, with suggestions by the authors about how this research might be relevant to political behavior. The next section reports eight empirical papers that all attempt to study political information processing with very different methodologies. The first five of these empirical papers (Hamill & Lodge; Lau; Conover & Feldman; Sears, Huddy, & Schaffer; Miller) try more or less explicitly to operationalize and study political schemas. The remaining three empirical studies (by Kinder; Tyler; Roseman, Abelson, & Ewing) are all quite cognitively sophisticated but deal with political information processing without invoking the schema concept. The fourth section reports the reactions of a set of political scientists to political cognition (Brody; Lane; Jervis; Smith; Anderson).

The applications span a broad range, from quite literal translations of such cognitive concepts as "schema", to the political context, to treatments of candidate perception and political norms that depend implicitly on cognitive concepts. Commentary from our colleagues provides some cautions about the donating science, in this case cognitive psychology, and some wise and far-ranging observations about the regions and boundaries of its value to political behavior theory and research.

The hope of all involved is that publication of this volume helps stimulate further work along the numerous lines suggested at one place or another in these far-ranging contributions.

ACKNOWLEDGMENTS

This volume reproduces many of the papers, comments, and discussions occurring during the 19th Annual Carnegie Symposium on Cognition, held on the campus of Carnegie-Mellon University May 18–20, 1984.We would like to thank the Social Science and Psychology departments at Carnegie-Mellon for co-sponsoring the symposium; Marilyn Becker, Betty Bowl, Debra Colding, and especially Janice Dolnack and Karen Hartman, for tirelessly providing much of the backup support necessary for making the symposium a success; and the National Science Foundation and the Carnegie Corporation of New York, for providing financial support of the conference. We would also like to thank Murray Edelman, Kathy Frankovic, Roger Masters, Warren Miller, Richard Perloff, Michael Ross, Jim Sidanius, Denis Sullivan, and various colleagues from Carnegie-Mellon who attended the conference and provided much intellectual stimulation.

INTRODUCTION

1 An Introduction to Political Cognition

Richard R. Lau
Department of Social Sciences
Carnegie-Mellon University

David O. Sears
Department of Psychology
University of California, Los Angeles

Some years ago, V. O. Key (1961) wrote, "to speak with precision of public opinion is a task not unlike coming to grips with the Holy Ghost" (p. 8). The intervening 25 years of political behavior research has clarified matters considerably, but has also highlighted some central, and persistent, knotty problems. The question of what an ideology is, and who has one, continues to stimulate both methodological and conceptual debate (e.g., Converse, 1964, 1970, 1975; Lane, 1973; see Kinder & Sears, 1985, for a recent review). Similarly, there remain continuing controversies over the rationality of the body politic (Downs, 1957a; Fiorina, 1981; Sears, Lau, Tyler, & Allen, 1980) and the prevalence and character of issue voting (e.g., Boyd, 1972; Brody & Page, 1972; Kessel, 1972; Nie, Verba, & Petrocik, 1976; Pomper, 1972). Moreover, important questions about the perception of political candidates were long ignored or treated only as a surrogate for the vote and are only now beginning to be explored (Abelson, Kinder, Peters, & Fiske, 1982; Kinder, Peters, Abelson, & Fiske 1982; Lau, 1982, this volume).

There have been two distinct psychological theories underlying most research in the area of political behavior. For the past 3 decades, political behavior research has been dominated by a rivalry between the Michigan voting model (e.g., Campbell, Converse, Miller, & Stokes, 1960) and rational choice models (e.g., Downs, 1957a; Fiorina, 1981; Page, 1978). The elegantly simple model of *The American Voter* centers on longstanding party identification as the primary predictor, both affecting the vote directly and acting as a perceptual screen that influences the assessment of specific candidates and contemporary political issues. Party identification is in turn a function of the respondent's background characteristics, including parents' party identification. Rational choice models assume that a rational person votes for the candidate who is closest to the voter on the attributes the voter cares about (Davis, Hinich, & Ordeshook, 1970; Downs, 1957a). These are not meant to be simply normative descriptions of how rational people should vote, but also are offered as reasonable, positive descriptions of actual voting behavior (e.g., Fiorina, 1981; Page & Brody, 1972; M. J. Shapiro, 1969).

Much current research debates the relative merits of the two approaches. Is party identification merely an anachronistic product of preadult socialization, or is it responsive to party performance and other current stimuli? To what extent are issue preferences and candidate perceptions derived from basic party identification as opposed to other determinants? How powerful are economic variables in voting choice? Political behavior specialists have debated these and many other competing predictions between these two fundamentally different viewpoints.

Part of the debate may be traced back to disputes between the psychological theories to which these models owe their origins. Political science has been a borrowing discipline, adopting psychological learning theory to understand political socialization, psychoanalytic theory to understand the careers of political activists, economic theories to understand the public policy process, sociological theories to understand the activities of interest groups, and so on.

Similarly, research on political behavior has borrowed extensively from a variety of traditions in social psychology. The origins and maintenance of party identification were understood in the terms of learning theory. Party identification was acquired early in life, heavily influenced by the rewards and punishments of parental socialization, and maintained by repeated practice (Campbell et al., 1960). The voting choice itself was interpreted in field-theoretic terms borrowed from Lewin (1939). The voter perceived the various short-term forces of the campaign through the lens of his or her underlying party identification and balanced them against each other in arriving at a vote decision (Campbell et al., 1960). As *The American Voter* model evolved through the 1960s and 1970s, it increasingly became viewed as an instance of one major descendent of field theory, namely, cognitive consistency theory (see Sears, 1969). People find perceived inconsistencies to be unpleasant and are motivated to reduce the inconsistency, usually by revising the belief element that is easiest to change (Festinger, 1957; Heider, 1958). Thus, if voters perceive that the candidate they supported in the previous election is now adopting an issue position with which they disagree, the voters will be motivated to change their own stand on the issue, change their opinion of the candidate, or change their perception of the candidate's position on that issue.

The rational choice approach to political behavior (e.g., Davis et al., 1970; Downs, 1957a; Fiorina, 1981; M. J. Shapiro, 1969) is based on more rational theories of human behavior. The emphasis on the thoughtful, calculating nature of the vote decision is quite consistent with psychological theories of people as rational problem solvers. Rational decision-making paradigms, such as expectancy-value theory (Edwards, 1954; Feather & Newton, 1982) or the theory of reasoned action (Ajzen & Fishbein, 1980), describe people as making decisions on quite logical bases. Most errors and biases in the decision process are presumed to come from the intrusion of motivational factors or from inadequate information. Similarly, early versions of attribution theory tested the possibility that people logically deduce the causes of their own and others' behavior (Jones et al., 1971; Kelley, 1967). According to this view, people consider information in a rational, scientific manner and attribute causality to that entity with which an outcome covaries. Thus, if a voter notices that having a Republican President regularly covaries with being laid off from his job, he may rationally come to attribute his unemployment to Republican economic policies and presumably grow to dislike Republicans. The problem with this normative, rational approach, in the view of other psychologists, is that people are rarely so careful and calculating in their thought processes. Even when there is no reason to suspect motivational biases, there are many errors and inconsistencies in human cognition, so that such normative attribution theories may not be very precise descriptions of how people usually behave politically (see Nisbett & Ross, 1980).

Partly in response to such problems, information-processing paradigms have had an increasing impact within social psychology. Cognitive psychology has made considerable progress in recent years in understanding basic human memory and perceptual processes. It has generated a portrait of the human being as having limited on-line information-processing capacities, with extensive long-term storage capabilities. This has implied an information-oriented cognitive view of the human being, a being that produces numerous errors and biases in information processing due to these limits.

Within the past decade, social psychologists have begun to apply what has been learned in cognitive psychology to the study of explicitly social phenomena. As a result, models of social cognition have increasingly proven to be estimable rivals of the more familiar consistency and rational choice theories. These models have implied constraints upon our ability to create consistent attitudes, regardless of whether the consistency was assessed on the basis of logic (as in the rational choice case) or psychologic (as in the case of cognitive consistency theories). The social cognition literature has developed these ideas in a number of ways, usually applying simple principles derived from cognitive psychology. The 11th Annual Carnegie Symposium on Cognition was instrumental in getting the study of social cognition off to a good start (Carroll & Payne, 1976); it is now an important influence upon social psychology (for reviews, see Fiske & Taylor, 1984; Kahneman, Slovic, & Tversky, 1982).

More recently still, a number of researchers have begun to apply the theories and methods of cognitive psychology and social cognition to the study of political behavior. This research has begun to appear piecemeal at professional meetings and in the journals. The first explicit and systematic application of modern cognitive psychology in political science was by Axelrod (1973, 1976). His research focused on the *causal schemata* (Kelley, 1971b) of foreign policy makers: the beliefs of political leaders about why different political events came about. For example, after studying transcripts of the deliberations of the British foreign policy committee considering the continuation of British involvement in Persia, Axelrod (1972) concluded that the decision makers structured the problem cognitively in a way that would make it relatively easy to solve. A similar effort to look at decision making was Herstein's (1981) attack upon the cognitive plausibility of several current voting models. After examining a number of conventional models of the vote decision and finding them all cognitively unrealistic in some respect, Herstein set out to develop a new model in which cognitive plausibility would be a foremost consideration.

Other applications have dealt explicitly with the kind of survey data upon which political behavior research depends. An elaborate application of the schema concept to public opinion data came in Sears and Citrin's (1985) analysis of the California tax revolt of the late 1970s and early 1980s, in which a schema was defined as a coherent set of attitudes toward the various attitude objects in a limited area of political life. Graber (1982, 1984) examined how people follow a presidential campaign through the media, extensively studying the information-search patterns of a small sample of adults in Evanston, Illinois, during the 1976 campaign. Conover and Feldman (1984) have explicitly attempted to study the structure of political schemata, focusing particularly on issue domains (e.g., racial beliefs) and political ideology. Still other such applications have appeared recently (e.g., Fiske & Kinder, 1981; Gant & Luttbeg, 1983; Lau, Coulam, & Sears, 1983; Lodge & Hamill, 1983; Miller, Wattenberg, & Malanchuk, 1982; Sharp & Lodge, 1985).

These examples illustrate how information-processing ideas and terminology are beginning to make their way into fairly diverse areas of political science. No one approach has caught hold; no new paradigm has been established. Still, there is sufficient evidence that researchers in those areas of political science that deal with individual decision making are becoming aware of the most advanced psychological theories of human thinking. We feel the time has come to assess more systematically the value of these new social cognition models in understanding the political decision making of the mass public.

To make this assessment, we organized the 19th Annual Carnegie Symposium on Cognition around the theme of political cognition. Three groups of distinguished behavioral scientists were invited. Some were researchers actively applying the ideas of social cognition to problems of political behavior. Others were well-known contributors to the social cognition literature who had not previously worked on political phenomena. Borrowing concepts from one discipline for use in another always runs the risk of twisting and distorting them in the translation process, and specialists from the originating discipline are perhaps the best judges of such problems. And still other conference participants were political scientists who themselves had not worked with social cognition concepts, but who have applied other psychological concepts extensively in their own research and could be useful commentators on the utility of this new approach. The main contributions of that conference have been extensively edited and are reproduced in this volume.

One of the dangers of being a borrowing discipline is becoming a victim of time lags. Because of rapid changes within each discipline and the time required for new concepts to be fully utilized in a new discipline, by the time the borrower begins using concepts from the originating discipline, they can already be obsolete. Conferences and volumes like this one can speed up the borrowing process. The information-processing idea is a case in point. It made a fundamental impact upon academic psychology in the mid-1960s, and by the early 1970s, it had fundamentally altered the landscape of general experimental psychology. Social psychology, in turn, then borrowed many of the concepts and methods, but with the usual lag. Social cognition began to dominate the study of attitudes in social psychology only by the late 1970s, the central journal had incorporated the term by 1980, and the first major textbook in the area had appeared by 1984 (Fiske & Taylor, 1984). A second purpose of the conference and this volume, then, is to accelerate the application to political analysis of concepts and methods from the area of social cognition.

In short, this book attempts to present a sampling of the various ways in which social cognition concepts and methods can shed light on political analysis. A variety of different ideas are included. Perhaps the most prominent is the notion of *schema*, which interfaces with such older ideas from political behavior as ideology, belief systems, constraint, and so on. Readers unfamiliar with the schema concept would be well advised to turn to our brief review of research on social schemata in the concluding chapter before proceeding through the rest of the book. Another important idea is how cognitive mechanisms deal with large social problems; for example, how do people think about concepts such as justice? Although much of the language in this volume is cognitive, emotion comes in for its share of the limelight as well; one chapter challenges cognitive imperialism by looking at how emotion is used in propagandistic appeals. If there is a single theme, it is the borrowing from psychology of new models that emphasize cognition and how they can be used profitably in political science. Our hope is that this venture will help political behavior specialists to extract quickly and directly those aspects of social cognition that will best illuminate political analysis.

This book is meant to be an early collection of research in political cognition, but it is also meant to play an advocacy role. Political scientists studying political behavior at the individual level should be aware of what we know about basic information processing. Hence, we hope this volume will encourage more political behavior researchers to become familiar with cognitive and social cognition research. We have all been careful to provide plenty of references for more in-depth study.

The objectives of the conference and of this volume, which reports the important conclusions, are ambitious. At bottom, we hope to use principles of human information processing developed in quite abstract and aseptic laboratory situations to illuminate our understanding of how the mass public responds to the blooming and buzzing confusion of public life. To be of significant value, this political cognition approach, if it may be called that, must ultimately prove to illuminate still larger questions of political life, such as why and how reigning authorities are replaced, why people do or do not comply with the wishes of authorities, what allows democratic systems to persist and accommodate to the wishes of the public, and so on.

All of that is a long way from the psychological laboratory. But to use a now overused cliché, every journey begins with a single step. We feel that it is timely to identify the area of political cognition as an entity with common roots, aims, and methods, and to begin testing its value. Judging by the papers, and by the responses which they have drawn, it is a good healthy start. Not surprisingly, it is also one with a good healthy dose of the usual problems in putting a new approach together. Some of these problems will reappear in various forms as the approach is tested. There will be problems of conceptualization: Just what predictions can be made just as easily from other theoretical approaches? There will be problems of operationalization: How can concepts such as schema be measured? There will be problems involved in processing the empirical data: At what point do we decide that these concepts are being clearly verified by the data, and when do we decide that the data are just not supporting the predictions? But these are problems of every approach to social psychology or to political behavior, and they should not be overly distressing. The proof of the pudding is in the tasting, as it is often said; so we now turn the reader over to those who have been developing this area of research. We return later with a final summary essay.

II

RECENT ADVANCES IN COGNITIVE PSYCHOLOGY AND SOCIAL COGNITION

2

A Primer of Information-Processing Theory for the Political Scientist

Reid Hastie
Department of Psychology
Northwestern University

The field of political science is defined by fundamental and enduring questions concerning collective action, political power, justice, and effective government. Sometimes the task of answering these questions can best be performed by developing a theory of the individual actor. Many of the participants in the 19th Annual Carnegie Symposium on Cognition were interested in theorizing about the individual's thoughts or behavior. They are concerned with questions such as: How is a political candidate, party, or ideology represented in the individual voter's mind? What characteristics of candidates or parties determine the individual's voting choices and how is the relevant information represented mentally? How can individual differences in knowledgeability or sophistication about political entities and events be described and measured? What activities does a person engage in when motivated to seek information in order to make judgments or decisions concerning the political world?

Although many participants in the conference had already decided that they were interested in the psychology of individual political actors, others were not so sure that they wanted to include individual psychology in their analyses (see Anderson, this volume; Brody, this volume). Even those who had decided to move to the individual level were uncertain about how to build a theory of individual thinking or what theories to consider from the current psychological literature. Figure 2.1 is a decision tree diagram that summarizes the major choices confronting a political scientist who is planning to theorize about individual behavior and thought. The diagram is probably most useful to political scientists who have already decided to include individual psychology in their theoretical analyses. However, the diagram may help sharpen the thinking of researchers who are simply considering the possibility of including this level of theory in their work.

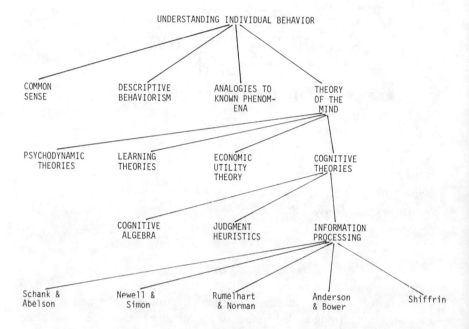

FIG. 2.1   Decision tree summarizing choices confronting a theoretician concerned with individual human behavior.

The basic point of the diagram is that political scientists do not necessarily have to theorize about individual behavior, but if they attempt to do so, they will have to take a position somewhere among the alternatives in the decision tree. The body of this paper argues that information-processing theory is the best alternative among those available.

At the top of the diagram is a fourfold choice among very general approaches to the individual political actor. First is the possibility of simply using common sense concepts and ordinary language to discuss human behavior. For example, Barber (1972) used his intuitions and common-sense concepts of personality to describe the formation of presidential character and to explain the behavior of presidents when in office. In general, I would argue against this alternative because psychological theory is now much more useful and precise than everyday common sense. However, there is a principled argument for staying with common sense and ordinary language which asserts that the essential task of a psychological analysis is to capture the phenomenological material in the subject's mind. I reject this approach because I am dissatisfied with the unsystematic character of current phenomenological, semiotic, and ethnoscientific methods.

The second alternative is to discuss the individual but to stay with behavior, making minimal commitments to concepts involving mental processes or mental representations. Verba and Nie (1972) provide an example of the descriptive approach, and many of its limits are apparent in their analysis of political participation. Strict descriptivist approaches run into difficulties when the task of imposing an economical organization on the plethora of low-level behavioral phenomena is encountered. Without an underlying concept of the mind, it seems impossible to select one simplifying organizational system from the many candidate structures. Again, I am inclined against this approach. In my view, this is simply marking time while waiting for more powerful theoretical concepts to describe the mind. However, it may be prudent to use this vocabulary until suitable theoretical concepts that fit the political scientist's interests have been developed in psychology or elsewhere (see Miller, this volume). My view is that current psychological theories are useful enough that the political scientist will probably want to use those conceptual tools. But it is plausible that more progress can be made on some problems in political science with a descriptive behaviorism.

A third alternative involves reasoning by analogy from intermediate-level empirical generalizations or laws of behavior. Some successful current examples of this approach involve interpreting the behavior of voters with reference to the cognitive judgment heuristics described by Kahneman and Tversky (1974) and by social psychologists interested in causal attribution (Nisbett & Ross, 1980). For example, the theoretician might claim that a diplomat's judgments can be understood as exhibiting an underuse of base-rate information (Jervis, this volume), an availability bias (Schuman, 1983), or a fundamental attribution error (Pettigrew, 1979). Some of the most elegant examples of this method are provided by Jervis's (1980, 1985b) use of findings in social and experimental psychology to interpret the behavior of elite political decision makers.

The fourth alternative, and the one developed most thoroughly in this paper, involves applying a general theory of the mind (usually originating in clinical or laboratory research by psychologists) to the understanding of political science phenomena. This extension is not simple; in many cases the task of extension will require sophistication equal to that required to develop the original theoretical formulation. Furthermore, conclusions reached from the effort to extend the original theory may have important implications for the development of the original formulation. For example, as I note later, cognitive information-processing theories are impoverished in their treatment of emotion and motivation factors in behavior. The effort to apply cognitive theories to nonlaboratory, real-world phenomena such as the behavior of political actors will force the political scientist and the psychologist to develop these aspects of the theory.

Under the general heading of theory of the mind (Fig. 2.1), I have distinguished four theoretical points of view, selecting them primarily on the basis of their current or historical popularity. Two of the alternatives, psychodynamic theories and learning theories, have had their historical heydays, but are no longer popular in social psychology or closely related fields. The other two alternatives, economic utility theory and cognitive theories, are popular now and are frequently cited in the papers in this volume.

It is probably a misusage to label each of the four points of view a theory. What we have in each case is a budget of general principles that is abstracted from a collection of more specific theories. For example, there are 5 or 6 psychodynamic theories all closely related to Freud's formulations (Monroe, 1955); there are 8 to 12 learning theories included under the general rubric (Bower & Hilgard, 1981); and there are several variations on the basic theme of utility theory in economics (Feather, 1982; Shoemaker, 1982). However, the four general headers have a theoretical reality as lists of unifying features that apply to most of their subordinate theories. Although there are counterexamples (discussed later), the political scientist who wants to extend a theory of the mind to his or her problem usually starts with a theory defined at the general principles level. One of the basic goals of this chapter is to summarize the cognitive information-processing theory as a list of features that will be useful in applications to political science.

Most of the psychologists represented in this volume (myself, for example) are social psychologists associated with the social cognition subfield. Social psychology is an interstitial field, which frequently serves to translate results from experimental psychological laboratories into applications to phenomena from related fields. At the same time, social psychologists perform the reverse function of communicating back to experimental psychology about the usefulness, weaknesses, and possible extensions of the laboratory-based theoretical formulations.

The theories I focus on, which I have labeled cognitive information-processing theories, originated outside of social psychology (in laboratories studying perception, memory, and problem solving with nonsocial materials). However, there is a sense in which it is proper to say that the cognitive information-processing theory that is being extended by political scientists originates in social psychology. This is because the theory being discussed is a list of general features that have been abstracted by social cognition researchers from more specific information-processing models and heuristic models developed in the experimental psychology laboratory. The seminal ideas should probably be attributed to experimental psychologists, not to social psychologists. However, their source for political scientists is in the writings of social psychologists.

I would also like to make another distinction, which concerns the alternate forms of cognitive theory in social psychology. In my view, three forms of cognitive theory are important in social psychology: information-processing theory, heuristic judgment theory, and cognitive algebra. All three are cognitive in that they describe the mental structures and processes involved in linking stimuli to responses. Elsewhere (Hastie, 1983), I have described the three approaches and cited the advantages and disadvantages of each. I favor the information-processing approach developed in this paper.

One last point, given that the cognitive information-processing theory presented here is actually an abstraction from more specific theories: What are these theories? First, there are three or four general theories of the mind that aspire to the level of generality associated with a system of psychology; these would include the family of computer program models developed by John Anderson and his colleagues (Anderson, 1983); another system of computer programs developed by Newell and Simon (1972; Simon, 1979b) and their colleagues; the computer programs developed by Norman, Rumelhart, and their colleagues (Rumelhart & Norman, 1984); and the attention and memory models developed by Shiffrin and his students (Gillund & Shiffrin, 1984; Raaijmakers & Shiffrin, 1981; Schneider & Shiffrin, 1977; Shiffrin & Schneider, 1977). There are also a host of less general models for specific information-processing tasks which subscribe to the same general viewpoint (Estes, 1979). Furthermore, the general orientations of the judgment heuristics approach and the cognitive algebra approach are quite close to the information-processing theory model, and there is more overlap than disparity. Essentially, the judgment heuristics approach is a set of generalizations that are close to the empirical phenomena to be explained, but as yet the approach lacks a general theory of mental structure and function. The cognitive algebra approach is a general system, and its major difference from the information-processing approach is the strict commitment to algebraic models that operate on continuous variable representations of information.

ADVANTAGES OF THE INFORMATION-PROCESSING APPROACH

Information-processing theory is truly a general theory of the mind that accounts for most of the mind's characteristics and functions. Like other general theories, it includes conceptual links to other theories at different levels of scientific analysis (e.g., neuroscience and social science) as well as increasing numbers of applications to naturally occurring practical problems in domains involving education (J. R. Anderson, 1981), skilled intellectual performance (Anderson, 1983), motor performance (Kelso, 1982), and so forth. The theory has advantages over competing formulations such as psychodynamic theories and learning theories. It is newer, having developed since the 1950s, and therefore subsumes many of the conclusions from earlier theoretical formulations and accounts for the major empirical phenomena discovered by previous researchers.

The most important reason to choose information-processing theory is because it is popular. It is a simple fact that most of the interesting research in psychology today, including virtually all of its subfields, concludes with theoretical analyses in terms of the information-processing principles that I outline in this paper. This means that the political scientist who uses this point of view will have access to the most current, most complete theoretical thinking in psychology. In addition, it means that the political scientist's conclusions, when they are expressed in the information-processing vernacular, will be available to a large audience of psychologists.

Obviously, popularity by itself is not a sufficient reason to accept a theoretical point of view. I now present a more detailed exposition of information-processing theory which emphasizes substantive advantages of the approach. Eventually, I turn to a comparative appraisal of the approach and acknowledge some of its shortcomings.

One of information-processing theory's most significant advantages accrues from its use of developments in computer science and artificial intelligence. I separate two contributions from those fields: (a) computing machines as a metaphor for the human mind and (b) computing machines as a medium in which to state and explicate a theory of the mind. In the first case, artificial intelligence researchers have developed principles for a general theory of intelligence (whether machine or human) and many examples of machines and computer programs that serve as analogies to the human mind (Boden, 1977). In the second case, computer program languages and the machines on which they run provide a medium with precision, representational flexibility, and enormous deductive power that makes an ideal tool for theorizing in psychology or any other science (Abelson, 1968).

Another advantage of information-processing theory is that it brings with it some methods that have proven useful in identifying its constructs, measuring its variables, and exploring its implications. Two methods in particular have moved to center stage in research on information-processing models. These are the method of using reaction times to draw inferences about the sequencing of mental events occurring between the presentation of a stimulus and the subject's response (Pachella, 1974) and the use of think-aloud protocols (Ericsson & Simon, 1984) produced by subjects while they are performing a cognitive task to infer the nature of mental events occurring during task performance. These methods are not new to psychology, but only with the information-processing approach (in particular, the powerful computer programming language representational medium) have theories that are sufficient to predict empirical patterns in these types of data been available.

CHARACTERISTIC FEATURES
OF INFORMATION-PROCESSING THEORY

This section of the paper is a summary of the essentials of information-processing theory, presented as a list of general principles. This list is typical, and it is designed to be useful to political scientists. There are several excellent texts (e.g., J. R. Anderson, 1980; Lachman, Lachman, & Butterfield, 1979) and survey articles (e.g., Bower, 1978; Estes, 1980; Simon, 1979a) that provide alternate treatments of the same material.

1. The fundamental material in an information-processing analysis is information. Sometimes information is measured or represented in terms of quantitative metrics (N. H. Anderson, 1981; Garner, 1962). However, the most common practice is to represent information as lists of features, English language sentences and phrases, or geometric diagrams. Because the most common experimental stimuli are words, sentences, and pictures, these formats for representation, closely matching the structures of the stimulus materials, are convenient and have proven successful as theoretical symbols. Some special problems have arisen when researchers want to represent the information underlying motor performance, emotional reactions, and musical experience. Motor performance and music are far enough from current political science concerns that I need not cover them in the present chapter. The types of representation that are most useful for political scientists concerned with their respondents' thoughts about political candidates, political events, and general beliefs about the political world should be closest to the theoretical solutions developed by cognitive psychologists interested in text comprehension (Rumelhart & Norman, 1984).

Typical practice would be to represent a concept node as a location in a graph that is described by a word or phrase and associated with a list of attributes. In the case of noun categories, these features are usually properties of the entity referenced by the concept that are useful to verify whether or not an object is an instance of the concept (Fig. 2.2). Relations between idea nodes are symbolized theoretically as links in the network or pointers that connect the nodes. These links are given with labels selected from a short list of quasi-formal relationships that are allowed in the specific representational system. The attribute lists associated with the nodes corre-

PIGEON	CANARY	CHICKEN	COLLIE	DAISY
A_1: animate	A_1: animate	A_1: animate	A_1: animate	A_1: inanimate
A_2: feathered	A_2: feathered	A_2: feathered	A_2: furry	A_2: stem
A_3: flies	A_3: flies	A_3: pecks	A_3: tan	A_3: white
A_4: lives-in-cities	A_4: yellow	A_4: squawks	A_4: barks	
		A_5: lays eggs		
		A_6: cannot fly		
		A_7: edible		

FIG. 2.2   Attribute list representations of concepts (based on Smith & Medin, 1981).

spond loosely to the concept's *reference,* and the links in the network correspond loosely to the concept's *sense.*[1]

The attribute-list approach to concept representation is readily apparent in several papers in this volume. Kinder (this volume) and Lau (this volume) hypothesize that a political candidate is represented in the mind of a subject chiefly as a list of attributes or features. Conover and Feldman (this volume) suggest that political party concepts are represented mentally in a similar fashion, as a list of feature values. Hamill and Lodge (this volume) assume that individual differences in political sophistication are primarily a matter of differences in the extent, complexity, and organization of knowledge structures that are composed of political concepts that comprise features. In each of these examples, it is clear that cognitive psychologists' analyses of the structure of semantic memory, particularly the representation of noun category systems (Rosch, 1975; E. E. Smith, 1979), exerted a strong influence on the political scientists.

The emphasis on semantic attribute representations for stimuli is characteristic of information-processing theory, and it highlights one of its major limitations. How are nonsemantic, nonpropositional types of information (e.g., emotions, sensory experiences such as rare tastes or melodies, dense impressions such as images of works of art, etc.) represented mentally? Of the problematic information types, political scientists will be most interested in theoretical analyses of the relationships between cognition and affect (Clark & Fiske, 1982). The clearest proposal of a representational format for affect is as a set of semantic tags (corresponding to alternate emotional states) that are linked to concept nodes as features or as alter-

---

[1]Figures 2.2-2.9 were selected to illustrate current practice in the information-processing approach. To understand the details of these illustrations and their implications further, the reader should refer to their sources.

nate concept nodes in the same network (Bower & Cohen, 1982). Thus, affect information is treated like any other semantic information in the network. However, there is considerable controversy on this issue, and some theorists (e.g., Zajonc, 1980) argue that the semantic representation solution is inadequate.

The influence of emotional reactions to a candidate or issue on voting behavior has been of interest to political scientists for a long time (Campbell, Converse, Miller, & Stokes, 1960; Lippman, 1922). Recent research by cognitive psychologists has reaffirmed the significance of emotional factors in political choice (Abelson, Kinder, Peters, & Fiske, 1982; Abelson & Roseman, this volume), although specific models of the representation and processing of emotion-provoking political stimuli have not been applied to politically significant stimuli.

2. Information is stored in memory in one of several alternate structures. One of the major contributions of the information-processing reliance on the analogy between human and machine information processing has been an increased sophistication about possible structures for information (Winograd, 1975). These structures usually apply to the relationships between conceptual nodes (discussed earlier), and a small set of structures appears again and again in the cognitive psychology literature. The most common structure is a list of concepts, with each concept linked to one or two adjacent nodes. The list structure is probably popular because many of the stimulus materials in memory research have been presented as lists (e.g., word lists, digit strings, etc.). In addition, the features for concept nodes are typically represented as lists.

The hierarchy, a directed graph, in which some nodes are superordinate to other (subordinate) nodes with the hierarchical ordering extending over several tiers is also popular. These structures are common in theoretical descriptions of long-term conceptual memories (E. E. Smith, 1979; E. E. Smith & Medin, 1981) because of the manner in which many English language nomenclature systems are structured. Linguistic concepts frequently have an embedded character, in which one concept can be used to reference many levels of abstraction. As I noted earlier, these interconcept networks correspond to the sense of the concepts, and the links are usually labeled by a small set of relationships that are fundamental to the meanings of the concepts (see detail of Fig. 2.3). Additionally, many other linguistic entities such as sentences, paragraphs, and narrative texts can be described in terms of hierarchical phrase structure diagrams or text outline hierarchies (J. R. Anderson & Bower, 1973; Kintsch, 1974) (Fig. 2.4). In these cases, comprehension is hypothesized to involve the application of rules that parse texts or events into meaningful units that are stored separately but linked together, often in a hierarchical structure. The hierarchical

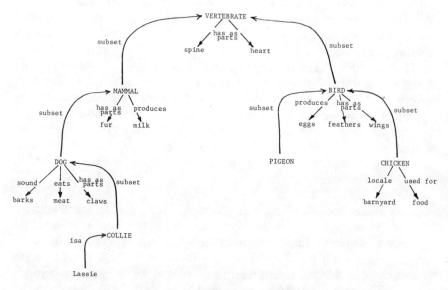

FIG. 2.3   A simple semantic network, chosen to illustrate inheritance relations among concepts (based on Rumelhart & Norman, 1984).

structure is also useful to represent plans for actions that can be described at many levels of specification (J. R. Anderson, 1980; G. A. Miller, Galanter, & Pribram, 1960).

A third type of structure, the undifferentiated network, is frequently used to represent the organization of material where time or semantic constraints do not impose the orderly relations implied by the list or hierarchy. For example, Hastie and Kumar (1979) and Srull (1981) have proposed such structures to characterize the organization of facts in memory that refer to a single casual acquaintance.

Hamill and Lodge (this volume), Miller (this volume), and Lau (this volume) use the theoretical concepts of schema and associative network, although they do not commit themselves to more specific structural assumptions. Conover and Feldman (this volume) imply a hierarchical ordering of concepts with general ideas, such as self-concept and Republican party, linked to specific ideas, such as Ronald Reagan. A more explicit general-to-specific hierarchy, diagrammed as a network, is postulated by Sears, Huddy, and Schaffer (this volume) to describe the relationships between general values (e.g., equality) and specific issues (e.g., right to abortion).

One popular type of structure is often referred to by the label *schema* in social psychology and political science writing. The term raises some problems in usage because its referents are not precisely limited, and

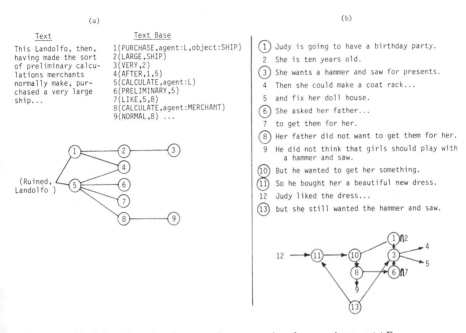

(a)

Text	Text Base
This Landolfo, then, having made the sort of preliminary calculations merchants normally make, purchased a very large ship...	1(PURCHASE,agent:L,object:SHIP) 2(LARGE,SHIP) 3(VERY,2) 4(AFTER,1,5) 5(CALCULATE,agent:L) 6(PRELIMINARY,5) 7(LIKE,5,8) 8(CALCULATE,agent:MERCHANT) 9(NORMAL,8) ...

(Ruined, Landolfo)

(b)

1 Judy is going to have a birthday party.
2 She is ten years old.
3 She wants a hammer and saw for presents.
4 Then she could make a coat rack...
5 and fix her doll house.
6 She asked her father...
7 to get them for her.
8 Her father did not want to get them for her.
9 He did not think that girls should play with a hammer and saw.
10 But he wanted to get her something.
11 So he bought her a beautiful new dress.
12 Judy liked the dress...
13 but she still wanted the hammer and saw.

FIG. 2.4   Examples of structural representations for narrative text. (a) Fragment of an episode of a short story, its propositional text base, and a graph summarizing the hierarchical relations between the propositions (indicated by number), see Kintsch, 1978, for further explication. (b) A fragment of a short story and the corresponding causal chain structure summarized as a graph (Trabasso, Secco, & Van Den Broek, 1984).

different writers seem to refer to different theoretical structures when they use the common label. For example, some theoreticians (e.g., Rumelhart, 1984) use the term schema to refer to almost any mental element, whereas others (e.g., Mandler, 1980a) restrict the usage to one or two specific knowledge structures (e.g., those that describe certain pictorial scenes and certain narrative stories). Recent reviews (Hastie, 1981; Taylor & Crocker, 1981) provide a sampling of the knowledge structures to which the label has been applied and emphasize the breadth and variety of referents. However, papers by Axelrod (1973), Brewer and Nakamura (1984), and Alba and Hasher (1983) give an impression that there is a precisely limited usage of the term schema and that there is a circumscribed theory associated with the concept. This impression is misleading, and the Alba and Hasher paper, in particular, attributes a "prototypical schema theory of memory" to memory researchers, which I believe is too restrictive to apply to anyone. In any case, there is no unitary theoretical entity that deserves the label *schema theory* extant in current information-processing psychology.

Although there is no commonly accepted schema theory, there are a number of theoretical constructs associated with the label schema that are well-defined and in common usage by certain theorists. An enculturated member of any society will have a large stock of schemata stored in long-term memory. When a schema is activated by the occurrence of a relevant event (i.e., when the schema's entry conditions are satisfied), the schema functions as a scaffold for the orderly encoding of incoming information. Relationships among disparate elements of the experienced event are provided by the schema. The perceiver is motivated to seek missing information that has not been experienced, but which is anticipated by the provision of slots in the schema. And sometimes, when information is missing, it is inferred as a default value to fill an empty slot in the schema.

Probably, the best way to describe the notion of a schema is to give some examples from the theoretical literature in cognitive psychology. Figure 2.5 presents a schematic structure for the familiar restaurant script (Abelson, 1981; Schank & Abelson, 1977). This knowledge structure summarizes the entry conditions, settings, roles, props, sequentially dependent stages, and exit conditions for the characters and events that occur in a visit to a typical restaurant in this country. Similar stereotyped action-routine templates have been described for other social events (e.g., flying in an airplane, visiting the dentist, etc.), and it is presumed that such knowledge structures are involved in the comprehension of many everyday activities.

A second example of an abstract knowledge structure is the episode schema that is found in many theories of text comprehension. Figure 2.6 provides a simple summary diagram of the elements of the highly abstract episode schema with the relations among them. A schema of this type is invoked in the comprehension of narrative discourse, and it serves to summarize parts of the explicit text, to indicate the relations among them, and to direct the reader to fill in the blanks by inferring missing information that belongs in the schema structure.

3. Information in memory is available according to simple spreading activation principles. The major role played by knowledge structures in the information-processing theory is to prescribe, and sharply constrain, the patterns of activation of information in the mind. Although phenomenal experience provides an incomplete picture of information activation, the subjective impression that we are aware of only a few ideas at once is a fundamental assumption of all modern psychologies. Information structures provide a metric that measures the amount of ideas that are active and available for use (i.e., to influence behavior) at any point in time. Furthermore, the structure predicts the direction and speed of changes in active mental content, experienced subjectively as movement from idea to idea.

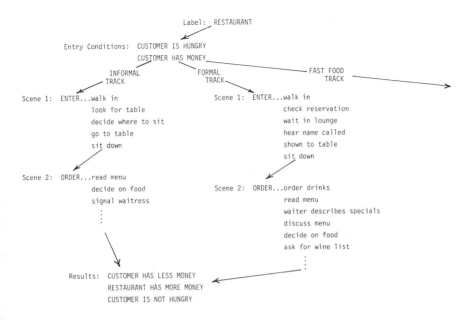

FIG. 2.5   Example "script" structure for comprehension of everyday events (following J. R. Anderson, 1983; Schank & Abelson, 1977).

The most common assumption of information-processing theorists is that activation spreads from a currently active location in a knowledge structure to other nearby locations, that the spread is rapid, that the amount of activation of proximate locations is inversely related to the number of locations (number of efferent links), and that it diminishes sharply with distance from the source of activation.

Additional factors affect the level of activation of ideas in memory. First, ideas that represent the immediate environment being experienced through the sense organs are activated (stimulus-driven activation). The encoding specificity principle (Tulving, 1983) for retrieval of information from memory is an important, closely related conclusion: A stimulus event (cue) will effectively activate an idea in memory if and only if information about the cue and its relation to the idea to be remembered was stored in memory at the same time as the original idea. Second, ideas that are closely linked to goals that have priority in guiding current processing of the system are activated (goal-focused activation). The implications of goal-focused activation depend on the system's rules for goal development and ordering by priority. Goals will be determined by specific requirements of the task the subject performs, but some general rules for the executive are emerging (see sections 4 and 5).

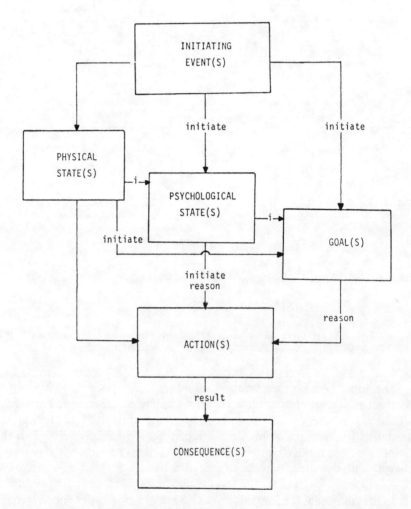

FIG. 2.6   Schema to represent the abstract structure of episodes (following Pennington & Hastie, 1981).

4. The basic processes of thinking involve the transformation of symbolic information from one representation into another. An overview of the information-processing system would show physical signals in the environment converted to sensory feature information and sensory information transformed into intermediate, semantic information. Later stages of processing would involve the elaboration by inference and association of the semantic information (including visual information) and then the transformation of semantic information into appropriate codes to generate responses. The analogy to computer program functions and operators is

strong, and theoreticians have attempted to reduce the complexity of information-processing theory models by agreeing on a limited set of elementary information processes (Chase, 1978; Posner & McLeod, 1982). The elementary operations would include processes such as reading and writing into and out of memories, recoding information from one format or structure into a second format or structure, and comparing and testing two pieces of information to determine the relationship between them (e.g., to return a judgment of similarity or identity). Thus, the economy of the information-processing theory comes from increasing consensus among theoreticians on an elementary set of formats for information, structures for information, and elementary information processes that transform one representation into another.

Probably the most common organization of the elementary processes is in terms of production systems. The analogy to computer programming languages is dominant, and the production-system architecture used to describe many computer programs is accepted as an appropriate characterization of the human organization of a system of elementary information processes. The basic unit of a production system is a two-part *condition-action* pair directly analogous to the stimulus–response (S–R) unit from old learning theories. The condition part of the unit specifies a state of the operating system (the presence of a certain pattern of information); the action part describes an operation or process to occur in the system. Actions are restricted to the basic operations provided by the set of elementary information processes (Fig. 2.7). A set of these basic production units, when coupled together into a larger procedure, is called a

---

1. Discrimination. It must be possible for the system to behave in alternative ways depending on what symbols are in its short-term memory.

2. Tests and Comparisons. It must be possible to determine that two symbol tokens do not belong to the same symbol type.

3. Symbol Creation. It must be possible to create new symbols and set them to designate specified symbol structures.

4. Writing Symbol Structures. It must be possible to create a new symbol structure, copy an existing symbol structure, and modify existing symbol structures, either by changing or deleting symbol tokens belonging to the structure or by appending new tokens with specified relations to the structure.

5. Reading and Writing Externally. It must be possible to designate stimuli received from the external environment by means of internal symbols or symbol structures, and to produce external responses as a function of internal symbol structures that designate these responses.

6. Designating Symbol Structures. It must be possible to designate various parts of any given symbol structure, and to obtain designations of other parts, as a function of given parts and relations.

7. Storing Symbol Structures. It must be possible to remember a symbol structure for later use, by storing it in the memory and retrieving it at any arbitrary time via a symbol structure that designates it.

FIG. 2.7   Elementary information processes (based on Newell & Simon, 1972).

production system. Production systems constitute a general, uniform descriptive language for many types of computer programs, and because information-processing models are usually implemented in the programming medium, they provide a useful vocabulary to describe cognitive processes.

5. At any point in time, the information-processing system is under the control of an executive monitor operating on a series of goals and plans organized into a control structure hierarchy. The development of this executive gives cognitive psychology the characteristics that most sharply distinguish it from traditional learning theory. A clear forerunner of current conceptions of the executive appeared in the Atkinson and Shiffrin (1968) distinction between structural features and control processes in a larger memory system. Newell and Simon (1972) introduced the notion of a hierarchy of goals and subgoals along with an executive that executed plans according to goal priorities. These developments gave cognitive theories an active, planful character that was lacking in previous analyses of learning and problem solving. Furthermore, with the aid of computer simulation methods, the theories of executive control were stated precisely in a "respectable," scientific form that was not susceptible to learning theorists' criticisms of mysterious homunculus models.

The hierarchical organizational principle appears as a description of the relationships between superordinate goals, subordinate goals, and plans that are under consideration or under execution to achieve the superordinate goals (J. R. Anderson, 1983; Figure 2.8). For the most part, simple goal-plan hierarchy structures have been considered as theoretical devices, however, there is speculation about the relations between coordinate, independent, and competing goals, and single and multiple-function plans as characterizations of the logic of the executive (e.g., Schank & Abelson, 1977; Wilensky, 1983).

One application of these theoretical developments to political science phenomena is Carbonell's (1979) description of ideologies as goal-plan structures (see also Schank & Abelson, 1977). Carbonell hypothesized that an ideological belief structure is organized as a goal-subgoal tree with higher level goals such as "communist containment" and lower level goals such as "strong U.S. military" and "elect Reagan" ordered accordingly. The system was implemented as a computer program that could enact the role of a citizen with a conservative or a liberal ideology and evaluate policies or events to assign desirabilities to them.

6. The larger information-processing system is composed of a series of component locations that are referred to as *independent memories*. The typical system (see Fig. 2.9) distinguishes between sensory registers, short-term memory, long-term memory, and sometimes a working memory. The memories are often hypothesized to be associated with separate physical

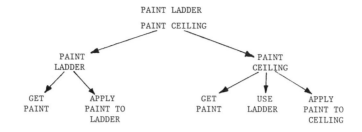

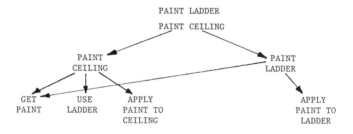

FIG. 2.8   Example goal structures produced in the solution of a planning problem. Sacerdoti (1977) and Anderson, (1983) discuss an example planning problem in which the goals are to paint a ladder and to paint a ceiling. Production system rules operate on the initial goals to produce subgoals (e.g., get paint, apply paint to ladder, etc), to identify goal conflicts (e.g., if ladder is painted first, it would be useless for painting the ceiling), and to reduce inefficiencies (e.g., needless trips for more paint). The upper panel shows the goal structure underlying the paint problem after the initial decomposition productions have been applied. The lower panel shows the goal structure after transformations to eliminate goal conflicts and redundant goals.

structures of the brain. They are characterized by distinctive formats for symbol representation and capacity limits for representation and processing. Many of the important predictions of early information-processing analyses came from the assumption of a limited capacity short-term memory store. A short-term memory limit on the amount of information that could be represented or actively transformed at any point in time implied that information processes would exhibit an orderly sequential character (serial processing). Furthermore, many errors in subjects' performance on perception and memory tasks could be "explained" with reference to the loss of information as it was passed from sensory registers to the limited capacity short-term memory.

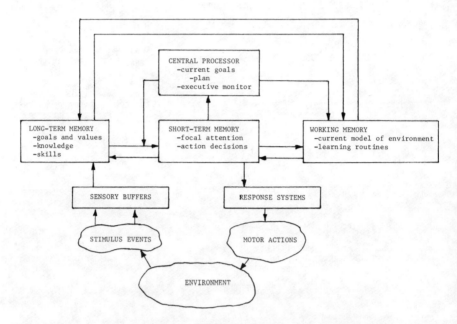

FIG. 2.9   The principal components of the perception and memory system.
Arrows indicate the direction of information flow and control among the
components (based on Bower, 1978).

   The emphasis on the transformation of symbolic information according
to a production system hierarchy of elementary information processes and
the "geographic" organization of the mind into a series of submemories,
with the most active memories (i.e., short-term memory) restricted in
capacity, have given information-processing models the characteristic appearance of organizing complex cognitive performances into a series of temporally
ordered, discrete stages. This organization is most obvious in simple models
for recognition memory scanning (e.g., Sternberg, 1969) and certain perceptual tasks (e.g., Broadbent, 1958). However, the same character can be
discerned in models for much more complicated accomplishments such as
playing chess, logical reasoning, and computer programming (J. R. Anderson,
1982; Newell & Simon, 1972).
   The long-term memory store is assumed to be extremely capacious and
to exhibit great representational flexibility in accepting a variety of formats
and structures for knowledge. Many theoreticians further subdivide the
long-term store into two functionally distinct components: one that represents temporally coded, episodic information (e.g., information about a
specific experience that occurred once in the person's history) and a
generic, semantic memory that is an encyclopedia-like repository for gen-

eral knowledge about the world (including nonlinguistic information, e.g., melodies and motor skill routines; Tulving, 1972, 1983).

7. Principles of limited resources (mental energy and representational capacity) affect the performance of the information-processing system. There is a general tendency for the information-processing system to behave economically to accomplish its goals by expending a minimum of time, processing resources, and strain on its memory systems. For example, in choice and decision tasks, people will typically act to "satisfice" by terminating search when an acceptable, but possibly not optimal, solution has been achieved. Similarly, in memory and judgment tasks, speed of performance and accuracy will be traded off so that when task demands restrict one aspect of the response (e.g., accuracy), the other aspect (e.g., execution time) will be used more liberally. Another example occurs in the typical model for long-term memory search where self-terminating search rules are frequently hypothesized such that the system stops searching for information when any item that is sufficient to render an answer has been obtained.

Some theoreticians (e.g., Lau, this volume; Taylor, 1981) have referred to these properties of the system with the term *cognitive miser*. I am reluctant to use this label myself because it is difficult empirically to determine exactly what resource or commodity the system is "hoarding," and in some cases, it seems that the system is generous rather than miserly. For example, the organization of knowledge structures in long-term memory appears to be relatively sprawling and uneconomical. However, such structures may have other advantages; they may be easy to learn, and perhaps the uneconomical redundancy serves other functions for the larger organism system. In any case, it is difficult to be precise about "cognitive economies" (Navon & Gopher, 1979; Posner, 1978), and I prefer to stay with a list of characteristic "habits" that tend to produce a usually efficient system.

There is a common misconception that the information-processing-theory emphasis on computer simulation models implies that the human mind is as orderly, tireless, and error-free as a well-tested piece of computer software. This impression is completely false. Information-processing theorists use the computer simulation medium to express their theories so that they can be precise and accurate about their theory's implications. However, the theory describes the behavior of humans, and this behavior is frequently errorful, imprecise, and haphazard. The theory, if it is correct, must simulate these properties of human behavior, as well as other more orderly characteristics of human behavior. One of the major conditions that introduces the haphazard and errorful quality (to the extent it is present) to an information-processing model's predictions of behavior comes from the implications of principles of limited resources. For example, a plan for behavior, generated by the model's executive, may be incomplete or may be executed in an inadequate manner because of hypothesized limits on the model's (and the human's) memory capacity. Thus, a considerable portion of the human-like character of an information-processing model will be produced by the limited resource principles.

SHORTCOMINGS OF INFORMATION–PROCESSING THEORY

Information-processing theory is certainly not the final word on the human mind. It has three shortcomings that are of particular significance to a political scientist who is trying to decide whether or not to adopt the information-processing point of view. First, when a theoretician accepts a theoretical position as a list of characteristic features such as those just presented, he or she does not gain much theoretical deductive power. At the level of a list of general features, the theory may be useful to interpret empirical results, to prepare research methods in the expectation that some results will obtain, or to design research to look for certain types of results. However, the list of features does not have the deductive power we associate with specific information-processing models designed to apply to particular tasks or empirical phenomena. For example, the Atkinson–Shiffrin information-processing model (1968) was specific enough to yield deductions of testable empirical hypotheses, some of which were confirmed and some of which were disconfirmed. Similarly, John Anderson's ACT (A Cognitive Theory) model, when specified to account for logical inference task-performance times and error rates, yields deductions of specific hypotheses that can be disconfirmed in empirical research. However, the list of characteristic features of information-processing theory, at a higher level of generality, is unlikely to yield sharp deductive implications that can be disconfirmed. This also makes information-processing theory difficult to falsify at the level of generality at which it will be applied to political science phenomena.

Some political scientists may be interested in going beyond the general features of the information-processing theory approach emphasized in this review to develop a specific information-processing model. This may be fruitful, but there are several obstacles that must be overcome to achieve success. First, it is likely that there is no specific information-processing model currently available that is directly applicable to the political science phenomenon of interest. Information-processing approaches are new and still limited. For example, there are few specific models for judgment, choice, and decision task performance, even in highly controlled laboratory settings. But these are the tasks that would be most pertinent to political science applications. A second obstacle derives from the possibility of selecting an inappropriate information-processing model. Third, once a commitment has been made to a specific model, the task of application requires detailed knowledge of that model. It may be difficult to acquire that knowledge even through careful study of documents produced by its proponents. Direct collaboration with an information-processing psychologist may be necessary for successful application. Fourth, political scientists are doubtless interested in elucidating phenomena from their field. However, they can become embroiled in local quarrels concerning details of a specific information-processing model that are important to psychologists but irrelevant to political scientists.

It may clarify the relationship between information-processing models and political science phenomena if I outline the steps that would be necessary to apply a specific model to deduce testable predictions in a simple cognitive task. I use a simple person-memory task as an illustration because it is central to the cognitive analyses included in several papers in this volume. The task is important because the manner in which information about a political candidate is stored in memory and retrieved underlies important judgments and decisions, including evaluations of the candidate and his or her actions as well as the respondent's voting behavior.

For this example, I use ACT, the information-processing theory that has been developed by John Anderson (1983) and his colleagues at Carnegie-Mellon University. The ACT system is a language in which to write a specific model. The system provides three formats for declarative knowledge representation (temporal string, spatial images, abstract propositions); a production system notation for the representation of processes; and system-wide rules limiting the capacity to activate declarative or procedural knowledge, to execute procedures, and to alter declarative or procedural knowledge structures. Expositions of the ACT approach provide numerous examples of applications of the theoretical "language" in the form of specific models for task performance with an emphasis on learning, skill acquisition, and problem solving. Probably the easiest route to a new application is to find a close analogy between a task to which ACT has been applied (e.g., sentence memory) and a new task that is important in political science (e.g., candidate memory).

I apply the ACT system to describe a respondent's long-term memory for information about Ronald Reagan. Declarative information ("facts") about Reagan can be represented in several formats in the ACT model. The likely representation will include propositional formatted information (most of the entries in Fig. 2.10), image information (information depicted in a picture in Fig. 2.10), goal information (in propositional format in Fig. 2.10), and affect responses (which would probably be represented as propositional information, see Bower & Cohen, 1982, noted by broken-bordered surrounds in Fig. 2.10). The structure of the information in Fig. 2.10 is a sprawling network that Anderson (1983) would call a *tangled hierarchy*. Some instantiations of the ACT system do not specify labels on links in the network, and for simplicity, I use unlabeled links in this example.

Note that in order for the model to be applied to a domain such as political candidate memory, an exact specification (perhaps still a hypothesis) of the memory structure must be provided in the vocabulary of the ACT representation system. This is no simple task, and the ACT theory itself provides only very general guidelines for the structure of specific memory representations. The task of establishing the representation usually involves a back-and-forth bootstrapping process in which the theoretician starts with intuitions about the memory structure, evaluates those intuitions by making assumptions about processes, derives implications, and checks those implications against empirical data. Then the researcher typically has to modify the original assumptions about representation, evaluate again based on predictions assuming certain processes, and so forth until a working representation is in hand. This is a lot of work, but it is not fruitless. There has been considerable success in establishing memory representations for complex lexical (E. E. Smith, 1979), pictorial (Kosslyn, 1980), text (Kintsch, 1974), social (Hastie, Park, & Weber, 1984), and

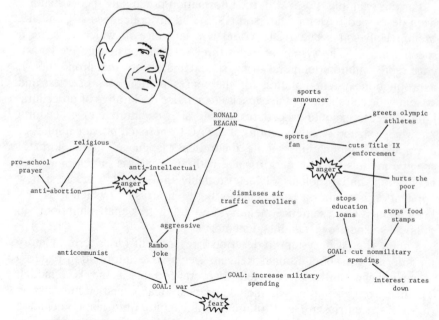

FIG. 2.10   Network structure for a fragment of one subject's memories of Ronald Reagan.

problem-solving (Chase & Simon, 1973) domains (see examples in Anderson, 1983). Nonetheless, establishing the memory representation is a big job, and deductions concerning performance cannot be derived without the representation. Furthermore, the task of providing a representation to the information-processing theorist falls most heavily on the shoulders of the collaborator who wishes to apply the model to a specific content domain. A laboratory psychologist interested in the ACT model would not be able to provide a hypothesized memory representation for political candidates without help from an expert in political science.

Anderson has spelled out explicit spreading activation rules that yield predictions of probability of recall, order of recall, speed of recall, and so on, given a memory representation as a foundation on which to calculate predictions. Anderson has developed explicit production system models that perform the recall retrieval task. Thus, we would be able to derive exact predictions concerning retrieval times and probabilities for a subject's behavior when asked to respond to: Recall what you can about Ronald Reagan; Recall what you can about Reagan's career before he became governor of California; Recall what you can about Reagan's fiscal policies; or Recall what you can about Reagan's family.

Development of a successful model of a respondent's long-term memory for information about a political candidate would be an important achievement. Several papers in this volume provide useful suggestions concerning the form and contents of the memory representation and specific models (e.g., Anderson's ACT) or general principles (e.g., the list in the present chapter) that could be applied to make more progress. A serious effort to model candidate memory would start the bootstrapping cycle of hypothesis-test-revision-hypothesis, which will lead to convergence on representation and process. Political scientists must do most of the work in the application, initiating and sharpening the empirically based picture of the memory representation, but guidance concerning possible representations and methods for their development is available in the information-processing literature.

There are several warnings to be derived from this quick sketch of a specific application of ACT to candidate memory. First, the example foregrounds the large contribution that must come from the political scientist. A theory of the mind based on laboratory analyses of perception, memory, and reasoning processes demands many domain-specific ingredients before a theoretical cake is ready for the deductive oven. Even commitment to a specific model within the information-processing approach does not purchase quick, cheap profits in the form of predictive power; the predictions will still be expensive. Second, I listed some of the many obstacles to successful application; even with commitment and expensive ingredients, the cake can fail. Third, the application is likely to require extensive developments before the theoretical questions of major interest to political scientists are addressed. The candidate memory model would require a large investment from the political scientist, but an account of candidate memory is only a first step toward a major contribution to political science such as a model of voting behavior.

A second limitation on information-processing theory is its impoverished treatment of motivational factors. Although many seminal formulations (G. A. Miller et al., 1960; Newell & Simon, 1972) dealt extensively with goals and plans, modern formulations have tended to downplay motivation (e.g., Nisbett & Ross, 1980; see also the comment by Lane, this volume). Typically, in the experimental laboratory research that provides the empirical grist for information-processing theory, motivation levels are assumed to be relatively constant, and variations in factors that would affect motivation are excluded from the research. One of the most important consequences of efforts to extend the approach to phenomena such as those in political science will be to force the theory to develop explicit principles to characterize the relationship between motivation, affect, and cognition. Signs of this development are already present in the psychological literature, many of them stimulated by social psychologists, clinical psychologists, and educational psychologists who have attempted to extend the theory (Clark & Fiske, 1982; Schank & Abelson, 1977; Zajonc, 1980).

Third, information-processing theory does not include sophisticated measurement theories or scaling techniques. Many of the major products of the field of political science are survey methods used to assess attitudes and to predict behaviors in popular elections. Political scientists are knowledgeable and intent on developing and using measurement instruments. In contrast, information-processing theory is one of the most casual fields in psychology when it comes to measurement and scaling. Although it is probably healthy for the development of the field, the topic of measurement is rarely addressed, and most information-processing theory research is sloppy when it comes to these matters. Granted, information-processing psychology has developed and exploited in a clever fashion many dependent variables, some new and some old (e.g., reaction time measures, think-aloud measures, etc.). However, the scale properties of the most common information-processing-theory dependent variables are unknown, even after decades of research (e.g., percentage correct measures in memory tasks, confidence ratings in perception tasks, etc.).

This may be a major problem for the political scientist who wishes to extend information-processing theory to the phenomena he or she wants to study. For example, at the Carnegie-Mellon Symposium, there was considerable discussion, uncertainty, and discomfort concerning the manner in which a mental schema might properly be measured. In fact, there are no uniform methods used by experimental psychologists to take a "snapshot" of a schema. There are numerous converging operations, varying in precision and utility, that when taken together make a convincing case for the existence of a schema and even for some of its structural properties. However, there are no generally accepted index measurements that are used to define, identify, and measure a schema. This means that a political scientist who accepts the information-processing-theory point of view has not purchased a set of well-developed and agreed upon measurement methods.

Although this section of the review has emphasized imperfection, incompleteness, and the cost of application of the information-processing approach, I do not want to be unduly negative. Earlier sections emphasized the considerable merits of the approach, merits that seem even more important when comparisons are made with alternate theories of the mind.

INFORMATION-PROCESSING THEORY VERSUS UTILITY THEORY

Utility theory, or rational expectations theory, is the general theory of the mind that is most often selected as an alternative to information-processing theory by economists, political scientists, and sociologists who decide to include an analysis of individual thinking in their research. Utility theory has many sources, but in its most common form, it is derived from a formulation published as an appendix to von Neumann and Morgenstern's volume, *Theory of Games and Economic Behavior* (1947; Shoemaker, 1982). Utility theory can be summarized in the same manner as I summarized information-processing theory, as a list of principles or features (see also Tyler, this volume).

1. An individual who is making a choice or a decision is faced with a set of alternative actions. Each action can be described fully, for the purposes of the utility-theory analysis, by stating its relationships to other future events (within or outside of the control of the decision maker) and to outcomes that are associated with the action and each combination of future events.

2. The consideration of events is in terms of their probabilities of occurrence, and these probabilities will follow the rules of consistency prescribed by mathematical probability theory.

3. The outcomes associated with each action-event combination include the costs to the actor for taking the action as well as consequences of the act that may be pleasant or unpleasant. These outcomes can be summarized with reference to a single continuum of utility, frequently described in

a metric of "dollars." Utilities have several scale properties: all outcomes can be compared with one another (e.g., it is sensible to make a choice between a bowl of oatmeal for breakfast or a vote for Reagan for President); a decision maker is infinitely sensitive, and so any two outcomes can be discriminated from one another consistently with reference to their utilities; and utilities for different outcomes will follow certain rules of mathematical consistency, such as transitivity.

4. When an action is evaluated to make a decision, probabilities and utilities will be multiplied for each event-action-outcome combination, and these products will be summed for all combinations associated with a single action to yield the overall utility for that alternative.

5. After considering a set that includes all possible alternatives, a decision maker will always choose the action that has the maximum utility.

Utility theory is a useful framework to summarize the influence of important characteristics of many situations on a decision maker's actions. There is a great parsimony in the analysis that reduces all considerations for a decision to two metrics, probability and utility, and prescribes a clear, incredibly simple algebraic computation as the basic processing rule for choice and decision. Furthermore, there is general acceptance that the theory in its full form prescribes a rational or optimally adaptive calculus for success in our natural and social worlds. Utility theory is also the basis of several theories for aggregate behavior in economic markets that provide close analogies to aggregate behavior in political, legal, and community situations that are the focus of political science analysis (e.g., Becker, 1976). There is no doubt that utility theory is a very useful theory of the mind and that in some applications it is completely appropriate for application to elucidate political science phenomena.

The major problem with utility theory is that it does not provide an accurate account of most empirical results from research on individual human decision making. There is a trivial sense in which all scientific theories, because they simplify and abstract, are false. But utility theory is false in many fundamental ways, and there seems to be little hope for its development as an adequate theory of the mind (Arrow, 1982; Lindblom, 1959; Simon, 1979c). First, the theory is implausible because well-established conclusions about limitations on information processing from the vast literature on perception, learning, and problem solving imply that the human decision maker is incapable of performing the information integration and calculation required by the utility-theory model. Second, careful tests of human behavior in simple choice and judgment situations that are most congenial to the utility-theory analysis demonstrate repeated violations of all fundamental axioms from which utility theory is derived (Maccrimmon & Larsson, 1979). Third, empirical research on the mental processes that humans engage in when performing judgment, choice, and decision tasks rarely, if ever, reveals processes that parallel or are analogous to those prescribed in the utility-theory models (Kahneman, Slovic, & Tversky, 1982; Slovic & Lichtenstein, 1983).

Many economists will shrug off this list of criticisms of utility theory and note that the theory is an as-if model of input–output relationships among factors that affect decision behavior (Friedman, 1953). The model, according to this defense, was never intended to describe the details of individual behavior. My assertion is even stronger than it might appear: I am claiming that utility theory also fails as a model of input–output relationships. The only conditions under which the theory is successful involve its applications to the behavior of aggregates, not individuals. Furthermore, even in these applications, success is usually "purchased" through post hoc model-fitting procedures that involve novel assumptions (not part of utility theory) about the shape of utility functions or about the factors that influence judgments of utility and probability (e.g., by assuming, after the fact, that justice has utility, that information has costs, etc.).

Another naive defense of utility theory is to claim that it complements cognitive theories by providing the account of motivation that is missing from them. Cognition explains the how of behavior, and utility theory explains the why. However, utility theory goes beyond simple motivational principles to require extensive rational analysis in a highly constrained form (the multiplying, adding, maximizing calculations) by any decision maker that it describes. This account of rational analysis by decision makers is an inaccurate characterization of most decision behavior. Furthermore, neither utility theory nor information-processing theory includes a fully developed and thoroughly tested analysis of motivation. Utility theorists frequently cite psychological literature, primarily from animal learning laboratories, when pressed to explain the sources of utilities. Information-processing theory does include speculation about basic goals or the relationship between affect, the conditions that produce it, and motivation, but again, this is a preliminary and incomplete treatment (Roseman & Abelson, this volume; Schank & Abelson, 1977; Wilensky, 1983). I have also mentioned the notion of goal-subgoal hierarchies and their relationships to plans that control behavior, but this aspect of information-processing theory, although present from its beginnings, is not as well developed as portions of the theory concerned with mental representation and mental processes. The point is that neither information-processing theory nor utility theory includes clear specifications of the environmental conditions that will give rise to utilities or goals. No one has a satisfactory scientific theory that tells us where values or desires come from.

There have been many efforts to preserve utility theory as a model of individual judgment, choice, and decision by weakening or altering some of its basic principles, while retaining the basic form of the probability, utility, multiplying, adding, maximizing model. My evaluation is that none of the efforts to develop a weak version of utility theory has demonstrated success as a theoretical account of empirical data describing individual human decision behavior. In my view, the current best candidate of the weak utility-theory models is the Kahneman and Tversky prospect theory (1979). (Interestingly, the most important contribution of the prospect-theory formulation is its treatment of "problem structuring," that is, framing, and this analysis is outside of the utility-theory framework. I should also note that the framing principles included in prospect theory are preliminary and have not proven successful in accounting for empirical data; Fischhoff, 1983.) In any case, it would be silly to claim that all versions of utility theory will be wrong or that there are no decision domains to which utility theory applies as a description of individual thought. My point is that utility theory's "track record" is almost all losses in its application to account for individual decision processes.

What is the value of utility theory to a political scientist who wishes to understand human behavior? One important contribution of utility theory, common with many other normative models, is that it provides a framework to describe the task that subjects perform, and it identifies key features of the task, at least with reference to optimal or high levels of performance. Second, in spite of its multitude of failures to predict individual decision processes, when "fitted" to behavior, the model provides a useful general summary of the relationship between decision alternative characteristics and human decisions. (Again, I would like to emphasize that the success of the utility-theory model as a summary of general features of environment-behavior relationships does not imply that it is a true description of the specifics of subjects' behavior.) Third, often what is needed in a social science theory to account for aggregate behavior is a simple summary of individual behavior, which is not the focus of the larger theoretical analysis and which merely needs to be accurate to some level of approximation, allowing the theoretician to proceed by developing his or her characterization of principles of aggregate behavior. Utility theory is frequently a good choice for this role as a parsimonious summary of the general characteristics of individual behavior. Fourth, the heavy emphasis associated with utility theory on concrete, short-term outcomes is often a useful directive to theorists concerned with developing elaborate information processing or other mentalistic models of behavior. It is a simple fact that human actors are very sensitive to concrete outcomes and monetary consequences of their actions.

To recapitulate, utility theory is a poor description of individual decision processes. Furthermore, I doubt that it can be modified or extended to provide a satisfactory account of individual decision behavior. However, as a general summary of aggregate decision behavior, it is often successful. At this level, as a general summary of environment-behavior relationships, it may be appropriate as an ingredient in a political science theory for aggregate behavior. In my view, information-processing theory is much more promising as a general framework to account for individual decision processes. However, the account of motivation in the information-processing-theory framework is relatively untested, and neither utility theory nor information-processing theory provides hypotheses about the basic sources of utilities, goals, or values of human actors.

CONCLUSION

This paper has attempted to explicate the basic concepts of information-processing theory so that readers interested in application to political science phenomena will be able to make that application. The political scientist who will make progress in understanding individual behavior must make difficult choices among the theoretical alternatives summarized at the beginning of this paper. The best choice will often be information-processing theory. I believe that information-processing theory is the most successful and most promising theory of the mind available in the social sciences today. However, I hope that the presentation has made it clear that information-processing theory is not a universal solution for every theoretical problem. The paper was written to make the reader self-conscious about the gains and losses associated with the application of information-processing theory. Still, I hope the chapter encourages researchers to apply information-processing concepts to political phenomena. The other chapters in this volume provide clear evidence that the confluence of political science and cognitive psychology is off to a strong start.

ACKNOWLEDGMENTS

The author is grateful to Nancy Pennington and Tom Tyler for helpful comments on drafts of this chapter.

3

Schema-Based Versus Piecemeal Politics: A Patchwork Quilt, but Not a Blanket, of Evidence

Susan T. Fiske
Carnegie-Mellon University

Whenever a paradigm threatens to dominate a scientific domain, it is always wise to ask: Compared to what? Many of the papers in this volume tend to follow a single paradigm—or less grandly, a single approach—that draws on a particular idea imported from cognitive and social cognitive psychology. Even the most casual reader will notice that many of the papers rely on the schema concept, as will be illustrated in this chapter. This is not surprising because much social cognition work, from which these papers borrow, also relies heavily on the schema concept. Given the schema concept's current emphasis, if not domination, in both political and social cognition research, it seems useful to raise the "compared to what" question. In that spirit, this chapter describes schema-based processing as only one of two contrasting processes for understanding the political and social world. The alternative process, piecemeal-based understanding, is best viewed in juxtaposition to schema-based processes, and it answers the "compared to what" question.

SCHEMA-BASED PROCESSES

Schema-based understanding, as exemplified in many of this book's chapters, is holistic, category-based, or theory-driven. A schema is a cognitive structure that contains a concept's attributes and the links among those attributes (see chapter 18 of this volume, for a brief review of social schema research; see Fiske & Taylor, 1984, for a more extensive review). When a person responds schematically, the person draws on organized prior knowledge to aid the understanding of new information. A new person, event, or issue is treated as an instance of an already familiar category or schema.[1] Representative Geraldine Ferraro could be viewed as an instance of a northeastern urban Democrat, a typical glad-handing politician, a harebrained female, or a pragmatic feminist. Whichever schema one applies, it enables one to focus on schema-relevant information and to ignore irrelevant information in forming an impression of her.

In social cognition research, the schema concept originally derives from a Gestalt, configural approach to perception. For example, in an approach that anticipated the schema concept, Asch (1946) described a configural model of how people form impressions of others, given a list of personality traits. He posited that the traits become organized around a central trait that determines the perceived root of the personality. The whole system of relations among the traits determines their meaning as a whole, especially with regard to a central or dominant trait. A person described as "warm, practical, and industrious" seems quite different from someone described as "cold, practical, and industrious." One retrospective interpretation of such differences is that the two configurations evoke different schemata. Another early example that, with hindsight, fits into a schematic approach is Allport's (1954) work on stereotyping. He posited that people categorize others to simplify the complex task of understanding them. Once applied, "categorization assimilates as much as it can to the cluster" (p. 20), and "the category saturates all it contains with the same ideational and emotional flavor" (p. 21). Current usage of the term schema fits these configural, category-based approaches to social cognition.

In political cognition, the illustrations of apparently schema-based processing are varied. Consider the examples within this volume. Hamill and Lodge discuss the utility of ideological, partisan, and social class schemata for perceivers structuring political information. Conover and Feldman discuss party, ideology, and self-schemata as generating inferences about candidates' issue positions. Lau discusses issue, group, party, and personality schemata as influencing the vote decision. Miller discusses changes in the richness of party schemata as a concomitant of declines in party identification. Sears, Huddy, and Schaffer discuss affect-laden equality schemata that influence the consistency and direction of political attitudes. Elsewhere, Kinder and Fiske (in press) discuss the role of schemata in understanding and appraising presidential candidates and incumbents.

---

[1]Strictly speaking, it is possible to distinguish between categories and schemata. A category contains instances of the general class, whereas a schema contains the attributes most typical of category members. For a discussion of some useful differences between schemata and categories, see Mandler (1979) and Fiske and Pavelchak (1985).

These efforts (and others) all testify to the heuristic value of the schema concept in political cognition research (cf. Lau & Sears, Chapter 18, this volume).

Work on schema-based processing has arrived for an extended stay in both political and social research. However, an alternative type of cognitive process is neglected by the current wave of schema-oriented research.

PIECEMEAL PROCESSING

There is an alternative mode of processing that describes what people do when they ignore or abandon their schemata. Piecemeal processing is elemental or attribute by attribute; it individuates or particularizes the person, event, or issue, instead of treating it as merely another example of an already familiar category. Piecemeal processing relies only on the information given and combines the available features without reference to an overall organizing structure. For example, a voter might appraise Representative Ferraro solely on the basis of the information encountered by calculating the perceived pros and cons of her issue stands, personal attributes, and group affiliations.

In social cognition research, work on piecemeal processing dates back to a straw model of impression formation proposed by Asch (1946). In this type of process, a social perceiver would combine a list of personality traits by summing or averaging their isolated values. The elements would not be considered in relation to each other, but rather each on its own merits. The elemental approach has been most developed in the algebraic models of N. H. Anderson (1981) and Fishbein and Ajzen (1975). They provide extensive evidence that people can combine the evaluations of isolated elements to form a summary judgment that follows algebraic rules (see Schneider, Hastorf, & Ellsworth, 1979, for a review of piecemeal approaches).

In political research, the elemental approach is well illustrated by voting models that follow an algebraic approach. For example, Kelley and Mirer (1974) predicted 90% of the votes in four elections by summing voters' stated likes and dislikes with regard to each major party and candidate. Fishbein, Ajzen, and Hinkle (1980) show that people's vote intentions can be predicted with considerable accuracy from a summation of their beliefs about the outcomes associated with each candidate, multiplied by their evaluations of those outcomes. Economic models of voting also implicitly follow a piecemeal approach (Downs, 1957b). Such models have been criticized as cognitively unrealistic; that is, they are not concerned with keeping the voter's limits in mind (Herstein, 1981). Nevertheless, their predictive power is impressive.

The research literature currently provides no consensual basis for fully favoring either a schematic or a piecemeal approach to political thinking and decision making. In part, this is because the two approaches have tended to serve different research goals. As a result, the piecemeal approaches have the advantage of specificity and predictive power within a narrow set of tasks, whereas the schematic approaches have the advantage of cognitive realism within a broader range of tasks. No critical tests have been devised to distinguish between them; each approach can be stretched to account for the data of the other (cf. Ostrom, 1977).

AN INTEGRATED VIEW OF SCHEMA-BASED AND PIECEMEAL PROCESSES

Within the literature on social cognition, the two contrasting approaches can be traced back to the historical and philosophical roots of the field (see Fiske & Taylor, 1984); the outlines of this debate are thus recurring. One possible conclusion is that both approaches may accurately describe how people make sense of their social world, but each may hold under different circumstances. My students and I have collected evidence that each process applies under circumstances that favor it. The dual-mode approach to social cognition arguably applies to political cognition as well. After summarizing our approach, this chapter illustrates its applicability to political cognition. It also argues that the different circumstances (perhaps not surprisingly) reflect the standard research settings characteristic of adherents to each approach.

The dual-mode model is relatively straightforward (for readers who wish more detail on the cognitive intricacies of this model, see Fiske & Pavelchak, 1985). The model is category-based; that is, people are presumed to categorize incoming stimuli whenever possible. If the stimulus possesses many critical features that overlap with the most salient and applicable schema, then categorization will be relatively successful. If the stimulus does not possess critical features that overlap with a salient, applicable schema or if the features decidedly contradict the most available schema, then categorization will be relatively unsuccessful, and piecemeal processing will result.

Successful categorization activates a schema in memory. Consistent with the most standard definition (cited earlier), my students and I hypothesize a schema to consist of a concept label at the upper level and associated attributes at a lower level. The attributes are all tightly linked to the label and somewhat more loosely linked to each other (see Fig. 3.1). One implication of this structure is the well-established finding that schema labels are especially good cues for remembering schema-consistent attributes. For example, it is easy to remember that a given northeastern urban Democrat favors spending on social programs. The schema also provides a structure for remembering schema-*in*consistent attributes. This occurs because inconsistent information forges new links to old information in memory. If one learns that a heretofore typical northeastern urban Democrat favors increased defense spending, one may generate an explanation in terms of the factories in that person's district; this new explanatory link (factories) enhances the memorability of the schema inconsistency. The only type of information not favored by schematic memory is schema-irrelevant information, which has the advantage of neither existing nor newly created linkages in memory.

Just as schemata guide memory, they also guide inferences where information is missing or ambiguous. Activating the schema enables one to fill in potential gaps by using the schema-consistent attributes in memory. Thus, given successful categorization and good fit to an existing schema, a large body of research indicates that memory and inference will be schema-based.

In addition to these now standard effects on cognitive responses (inference and memory), our model suggests that affective and evaluative responses

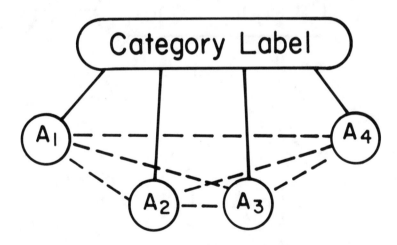

FIG. 3.1   Hypothesized representation of a schema cued by categorization. $A_1 \ldots A_4$ represent the attributes typical of category members. From Category-based versus piecemeal-based affective responses: Developments in schema-triggered affect (p. 171) by S. T. Fiske and M. A. Pavelchak, 1985, in R. M. Sorrentino and E. T. Higgins (Eds.), *Handbook of motivation and cognition: Foundations of social behavior,* New York: Guilford Press. Copyright 1985 by Guilford Press. Reprinted by permission.

also can be schema-based. To add affect to the model, we propose that there are affective tags for each of the schema's attributes and for the top-level label as well (see Fig. 3.2). The top-level affective tag can act as a proxy for the lower level tags; it is a "precomputed" summary of the perceiver's reaction to the schema's attributes as a whole. The implication of this top-level affective tag is that successful categorization provides an immediate basis for an affective response without the respondent examining all the pros and cons associated with the schema's various attributes.

All these schema-based responses—both cognitive and affective—assume successful categorization. If one fails to categorize a stimulus, if it simply does not fit an existing schema, one may be forced to process it piecemeal. That is, one may be forced to think of it as a unique example without reference to prior knowledge about others of its type. In that piecemeal case, the stimulus attributes will be loosely linked to each other in memory without benefit of the strength provided by prior associations. Piecemeal processing provides a weak basis for memory and inference because there is only the one instance on which to draw. Moreover, piecemeal-based affective responses require one to access and combine all the affective tags associated with each of the stimulus attributes. This is a slower process

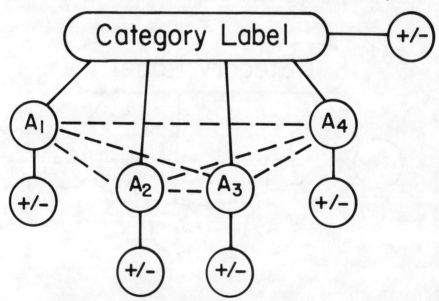

FIG. 3.2   Hypothesized representation of affect within schema structure. Note. From Category-based versus piecemeal-based affective responses: Developments in schema-triggered affect (p. 172) by S. T. Fiske and M. A. Pavelchak, 1985, in R. M. Sorrentino and E. T. Higgins (Eds.), *Handbook of motivation and cognition: Foundations of social behavior,* New York: Guilford Press. Copyright 1985 by Guilford Press. Reprinted by permission.

than schema-triggered affect, but it is more responsive to the merits and demerits of the stimulus as presented.

According to our model, circumstances determine whether schema-based or piecemeal-based processing occurs. The circumstances that favor schematic processing are: (a) those in which a schema is cued by strong assumptions that particular groups of attributes fit a given schema or (b) those in which a consensual schema label is provided to respondents, with or without additional supporting evidence. The circumstances that favor piecemeal processing are: (a) those in which a group of attributes simply do not cue any particular schema or (b) those in which the attributes blatantly contradict the most available schema. Evidence for schema-based and piecemeal-based cognition under these separate conditions comes from research in our laboratory (Fiske, Neuberg, Beattie, & Milberg, 1984). We find that schema-based processing—however elicited—enables rapid, top-level, affective responses and rapid, accurate memory. Piecemeal processing—however elicited—enables slower, attribute-level, affective responses and slower, less accurate memory. Ongoing research seeks to detail the processes and boundary conditions of schema-based and piecemeal-based affective responses.

APPLICATIONS TO POLITICS

Each of these processes, schematic and piecemeal, also occurs in the political domain. As noted earlier, schematic processing is amply illustrated by the research presented in this book, whereas piecemeal processing is illustrated by algebraic models of voting and political decision making. This section further illustrates the two alternative modes of processing in two of the papers from this volume, each of which focuses on one type of processing. But before turning to those papers, another paper, not from this volume, is of interest because it illustrates both types of processing within one setting.

Herstein (1981) presented undergraduates of voting age with information-board displays that depicted two hypothetical candidates for President. Each candidate was depicted by 45 attributes that included issue stands, policy orientations, party identification, and personal information. Each item was available for inspection upon turning over a labeled index card. The subjects' task was to examine enough information to reach a voting decision, thinking aloud the entire time.

Of particular interest in the current context is the manner in which the information was displayed. Some subjects received "candidate-salient" displays, in which each candidate's attributes were organized in two separate sections of the board, with comparable information in the same location on each side. Some subjects received "item-salient" displays, in which the organization was by attribute, instead of by candidate. In an actual campaign setting, a candidate-salient display would occur in campaign literature or in the most common type of newspaper listing, organized by candidate; an item-salient display would occur in a debate context, in which each candidate alternates in presenting an explanation of every issue.

The two conditions are especially pertinent to the two modes of processing political information. Herstein presents evidence suggestive of two somewhat different decision-making processes under these two conditions. In the candidate-salient condition, subjects are more likely to construct an overall evaluation separately for each candidate, but in the item-salient condition, subjects are more likely to construct their evaluations piecemeal. In both conditions, subjects apparently choose by first checking for an overall evaluation of each candidate, which would be a top-level affect tag in our terms.[2] If subjects cannot locate an overall evaluative tag, they choose by making a few comparisons on particular items, which would be lower level piecemeal processing in our terms.

The Herstein data are interesting because they represent a fine-grained analysis of political cognition and choice; moreover, although not designed to test our model, the Herstein data suggest that the dual-mode approach may operate as suggested here. People first attempt an overall (category-based) evaluation and then switch to piecemeal processing, attribute by attribute. Moreover, people are apparently likely to engage in piecemeal processing when attribute-level information is made more salient than is the individual as a unitary entity. Although it constitutes only indirect evidence for our two-mode approach, Herstein's paper also suggests techniques for empirically investigating these two processes in simulated voting decisions.

More direct evidence for the operation of category-based affect, with piecemeal-based affect as an alternative mode, comes from two papers that examine political cognition in more realistic settings.

Affect-Laden Schemata in Symbolic Politics

Sears, Huddy, and Schaffer (this volume) present elegant survey evidence indicating a role for affect-laden political schemata. Sears et al. specifically

---

[2]Herstein finds that only negative overall evaluations determine the vote, which is interesting, but perhaps must be interpreted in light of people's overall tendency to evaluate individual people, including politicians, positively (Sears, 1983b). Hence, the negative evaluations would be more informative (Fiske, 1980; Lau, 1982, 1985). The precise reasons for this asymmetry in the Herstein data are irrelevant for our present purposes.

examine the relationships among equality schemata, specific policy preferences, political sophistication, and group membership. They hypothesize
that: (a) there exist abstract and concrete levels of equality attitudes
organized hierarchically in a schema-like structure; (b) political sophistication and group membership help determine which level of equality schema
any given individual uses to understand the relevant issues; (c) people's
equality schemata determine affective responses to manifestly dissimilar
but cognitively similar political issues.

To test these hypotheses, Sears et al. first demonstrate the importance of
equality as a potent political symbol or affect-laden schema that is independent of more conventional political predispositions, such as political
ideology, demographics, and party identification. Second, they find that
political sophistication plays a role in the relevant level of schematic
organization. Sophistication increases the consistency of affective reactions to manifestly dissimilar but schematically related equality issues. The
assumption is that increased information allows respondents to organize
manifestly dissimilar issues within the same schematic structure. Finally,
they show that group membership also influences the relevant level of
schematic organization.

The Sears et al. paper is a model of modesty, quite properly stating
the caveats necessary when importing fine-grained cognitive theories to
aggregate survey settings. Schemata are quite difficult to establish at the
mass level of analysis, but the Sears et al. data present a nice example with
several lines of converging evidence. The schema-based approach clearly
provided a useful framework for thinking about the interplay between
different levels of conceptually related political issues and their affective
concomitants, as well as for the role of political sophistication.

The research setting they used suits their schematic approach. That is,
the equality issue and the methods used might well favor the discovery of
schema-based processing. This is not to suggest that Sears et al. created
schematic processing where none existed, but merely that their choices
were appropriate to the type of political understanding they wished to
investigate. In particular, their study focused on relatively abstract judgments, which were not drawn directly from citizens' concrete personal
experiences. Respondents were asked to endorse items relevant to equality
in general, equality based on gender and race, or specific national policies
concerning gender and race equality. They were not asked to evaluate their
own experiences in each regard. Moreover, the requested judgments were
probably not novel. That is, people are likely to have preexisting responses
to each of these topics. Both factors, the abstractness and the familiarity of
the judgments, would tend to favor schema-based judgments. I return to
this point later.

Piecemeal Processing in Perceived Political (In)justice

Tyler (this volume) provides a nice example of the alternative nonschematic mode of political cognition. In a scholarly literature review, backed up by his own research, Tyler argues that endorsements of the political system are not only based on economic calculations of benefits received and costs paid. He argues that citizens also judge the justice of the system's procedures and that these are added to system endorsement, along with personal gains and losses. This critical point expands the traditional view of citizens as naive economists to include their propensity to be naive moral philosophers.

In the present context, Tyler serves to illustrate the application of a piecemeal model of political evaluation in a setting that favors that type of processing. Tyler explicitly assumes that fairness judgments are another term in the equation. Fairness judgments combine algebraically with cost-benefit judgments to produce the overall evaluations of political institutions and leaders. In one study, he examines how people's specific experiences in court contribute to their evaluations of the court system as a whole; he shows that people's judgments of how justly they were treated are distinct from the outcomes they received. Moreover, justice judgments contribute to system endorsement beyond received outcomes. In a second study, Tyler makes a similar point regarding federal outcomes (taxes and benefits), perceived fairness, and federal system endorsement. In each study, Tyler makes a compelling case for the distinct contribution of perceived justice in the calculation that adds up to system endorsement.

Tyler's setting is arguably one that would favor piecemeal processing, for several reasons. First, people are generalizing from specific and concrete experiences to their overall system judgments. Thus, their evaluations are explicitly data driven and elemental. Second, the overall judgments were elicited following evaluations of the component judgments. This would encourage a feature-by-feature judgment over a schema-based response. Finally, to the extent that the judgments are novel, they are unlikely to be based on precalculated summary judgments. Hence, Tyler's model suits his domain.

When Are People Schematic and When Piecemeal?

At several points, the foregoing discussion has suggested conditions that favor each mode of processing. It may be useful here to summarize the conditions that encourage each. As noted earlier, schema-based processing is most likely when: (a) an affect-laden category label is available, with supporting information or with nothing additional; (b) the available information strongly cues an affect-laden category; (c) global judgments are required; or (d) the required judgments have been made previously. In addition, we suggest elsewhere that schematic processing is likely when: (e) the judgment is rushed; (f) the respondent's outcomes do not depend on the judgment; or (g) the respondent has a simple view of the judged object (see Fiske & Pavelchak, 1985, for details on these last three points). Conversely, piecemeal processing is favored when: (a) the judged object is category inconsistent; (b) the judged object is a collection of information that does not cue a category; (c) concrete, instance-oriented judgments are required; (d) the required judgment is novel; (e) the judgment is made at a leisurely pace; (f) the respondent's outcomes depend on the judgment; or (g) the respondent has a complex view of the judged object. Not all of these conditions operate in any one circumstance, but each contributes to predicting when piecemeal and schematic processing will occur.

COMMENT ON THE UTILITY OF BORROWING BETWEEN SOCIAL AND POLITICAL COGNITION

It is traditional to close chapters of commentary with exhortations to further effort. The challenges facing both political and social cognition research are considerable, and time will tell how we face the challenges.

For political scientists studying cognitive processes, the challenges include conceptual precision about the schema concept. As noted, the papers in this volume frequently use it. (On a bet, it will have the longest entry in this volume's index.) The schema concept, if used rigorously, is extremely useful in work on complex information processing (Fiske & Linville, 1980). But the caveat "rigorously" is important. Researchers profit the most when they define the term, detail what the schema contains, specify what it does, and articulate alternative models. The future credibility of the schema concept in political research depends on this type of precision. Similar points apply to the nascent interest in affect and politics; terms must be defined precisely, and alternatives considered carefully.

On a more general note, a major challenge for political cognition researchers is to specify the ways that political cognition may differ from other types of cognition. Consider a few of the distinctive, if not unique, features of political understanding. At a minimum, there is the fact of mediated perception. Information about the political world is indirect; it is prepackaged and organized by the media, by politicians, and by opinion leaders. Unlike ordinary understanding in other realms, a double filtering process occurs when the packagers and the citizen each in turn structure the relevant data according to their own cognitive and motivational strategies. One implication of mediated perception is that one must study both types of filtering. The papers in this volume focus more on the citizen's structuring and filtering than on the packager's structuring and filtering, but more attention to the latter would usefully illuminate what political stimuli citizens actually confront (cf. Smith, this volume).

Another distinctive feature of political cognition is that many perceivers are simultaneously understanding the same stimulus. In that sense, political cognition is inherently mass cognition. By the same token, social cognition is only half social. It is social in that the objects of perception are people, but it is not very social in the situation of the perceivers. One implication of the fact that political cognition is a mass activity is that social comparison and social influence processes will play an important role in citizens' understanding. Traditional social psychology research on these topics is neglected by the current burst of research on the voter as an isolated political information processor.

A final illustration of the distinctive features of political cognition is the level of stakes involved. In one way, the stakes are among the highest: The fates of millions depend on some individuals' political understanding. In another way, the stakes are low: Ordinary citizens are apparently less interested and notoriously less informed than some might hope or expect. One implication is that political cognition research must attend to emerging social cognition research on variations in cognitive processes as a function of motivational factors (e.g., Clark & Fiske, 1982; Sorrentino & Higgins, 1985).

All these features of political cognition, and others as well, could be illuminated by a careful task analysis. That is, what is the task of the political understander? What is the stimulus environment, knowledge base, and required response? Specifying these factors would prove useful in the quest for a detailed understanding of political cognition.

Turning to the challenges facing social cognition research, this volume presents some remedies for the perennial problems we face. The shortcomings of social cognition research fall into two categories: its narrowness and its unrealistic viewpoint (see Fiske & Taylor, 1984, for more detail). With regard to narrowness, social cognition research views the person primarily as a thinker, whose overriding goal is efficient (i.e., rapid) understanding. However, people's understanding of the world involves other goals. As Tyler (this volume) so aptly points out, people have moral concerns; the citizen is not just a thinking person, but also a moral person. Citizens also have goals related to their public image, the greater good, and more. Each of these goals—being the moral person, the public person, the altruistic person—influences the process of understanding. Work on political cognition already expands the overly narrow view that dominates social cognition research, namely, that people are solely thinkers.

Besides being narrow, social cognitive theories of people are somewhat unrealistic, even within their narrow focus on thinking. The assumption, as noted, is that people prize efficiency or economy over total accuracy; this assumption is characterized by viewing people as cognitive misers (Fiske & Taylor, 1984). The drawbacks to this portrait of people result from its tendency to become a caricature. The cognitive miser is an exaggerated portrait on several counts. First, people are not in fact maximally efficient, any more than they are maximally accurate. The cognitive miser is not an information-processing whiz kid, but rather someone who often takes wrong turns or even simply stays in place, perseverating. Second, people are substantially constrained by reality in constructing their understandings of the world, and to a greater extent than most current theories suggest. The cognitive miser is caricatured as a fantasizer, having a somewhat lunatic disregard for reality; however, people do indeed respond to the information given. Third, the cognitive miser is isolated from social processes, as noted earlier. This portrait of people as hermits is unrealistic and suggests more attention to social factors in cognitive processes. Finally, the cognitive miser is often portrayed as a blank slate, without variations in the type and amount of information brought to bear on the task of understanding. The work of Sears et al., Hamill and Lodge, and Lau in this volume all demonstrate the importance of idiosyncratic knowledge brought to bear on the understanding of new political information.

Many of the pitfalls in social cognition research are mended in political cognition research by broadening how the thinking person is viewed and by providing converging evidence of similar phenomena across dissimilar settings. Borrowing between the two fields ultimately benefits both.

AUTHOR'S NOTE

The author would like to thank Rick Lau and Jim Sidanius for their comments on an earlier draft of this chapter. The author is presently in the Department of Psychology, University of Massachusetts at Amherst.

4 Behavioral Decision Theory and Political Decision Making

Gregory W. Fischer,
Eric J. Johnson
Carnegie-Mellon University

Decision making is central to most theories of political behavior. Choices between alternatives are the focus of discussions of voting behavior, legislative activity, foreign policy formulation, and the enforcement and execution of laws. Further, the process of making decisions is clearly cognitive in the sense that it involves higher order mental processes. In addition, there are strong parallels between issues in political cognition and current research on decision making.

It is noteworthy, therefore, that decision making per se has received relatively little attention in this volume on political cognition. Although no one discipline has an exclusive claim to decision making as a topic, there is an emerging body of literature that concentrates on the empirical task of describing choice processes rather than the prescriptive task of establishing normative techniques for making choices. This area, which we term *behavioral decision theory* (Einhorn & Hogarth, 1981), is somewhat difficult to define: It lies in the nether world between cognitive psychology, economics, and statistical decision theory. Its central focus is on individual inference, prediction, and decision. The questions addressed by behavioral decision theorists include the following: How do people choose between risky alternatives whose consequences are uncertain? How do people choose between alternatives that involve trade-offs between conflicting decision objectives? How do people use knowledge of past events when making predictions regarding future events? How do people modify probabilistic beliefs in the light of new evidence? How do people mentally represent decision, inference, and prediction problems? What are the determinants of subjectively perceived risk? What are the major shortcomings of intuitive inference, prediction, and choice, and how can these shortcomings be overcome?

Though the field of behavioral decision theory is relatively new, research in this area has already generated a large body of published findings on a wide variety of specific topics. Excellent reviews are provided by Einhorn and Hogarth (1981), Payne (1982), and Pitz and Sachs (1984). Here we make no attempt to review the field as a whole. Instead, we focus on a few key findings and theoretical insights that have relevance to the study of political cognition. Our discussion is organized into two sections. The first focuses on cognitive strategies for combining information in making choices. The second focuses on the role of memory in choice.

DECISION STRATEGIES AND POLITICAL CHOICE

Consider a prospective political candidate who is deciding which office, if any, to run for. The offices differ in their potential costs and benefits, if the candidate should win nomination and emerge victorious in the general election. They also differ in terms of how likely the candidate is to succeed in his or her quest for office. How do prospective political candidates weigh and balance the uncertain costs and benefits of different courses of action in making their choice? How do political decision makers in general—presidents, legislators, bureaucrats, lobbyists, diplomats, and voters—make complex choices involving uncertain costs and benefits? If political decision makers adopt decision strategies similar to those used by the student subjects, physicians, and business officials who have been the prime objects of study by behavioral decision theorists, then behavioral decision theory provides some interesting hypotheses regarding political decision-making processes.

Framing Effects

The principle of *invariance* is central to normative theories of choice (Tversky & Kahneman, 1981). According to this principle, different but logically equivalent representations of a set of choice alternatives should give rise to the same decision. As Tversky and Kahneman (1981) have demonstrated, however, intuitive decisions do not satisfy the invariance principle. The following example, taken from their paper, shows how different verbal representations of a public health policy decision can alter preferences for the alternatives in question.

Problem 1: Imagine that the U.S. is preparing for the outbreak of an unusual Asian disease, which is expected to kill 600 people. Two alternative programs to combat the disease have been proposed. Assume that the exact scientific estimate of the consequences of the programs are as follows: If program A is adopted, 200 people will be saved. If program B is adopted, there is a ⅓ probability that 600 people will be saved, and a ⅔ probability that no people will be saved. Which of the two programs would you favor?

Problem 2: |This problem is identical to Problem 1 up to the point where the alternatives are described.| If program C is adopted, 400 people will die. If program D is adopted, there is a ⅓ probability that nobody will die and a ⅔ probability that 600 people will die. Which of the two programs would you favor? (p. 453)

If you are like most of the subjects in Tversky and Kahneman's study, you prefer A in Problem 1 (72% of their subjects did) and D in Problem 2 (78% of their subjects did). But upon careful consideration, it is evident that policy A in Problem 1 is equivalent to policy C in Problem 2, and policy B is equivalent to policy D. Thus, the modal pattern of choices in these problems violates the invariance principle. Tversky and Kahneman refer to this as a *framing effect*. Logically equivalent but psychologically distinct ways of framing a set of decision alternatives can lead to different preferences among the alternatives.

The notion that preferences can be affected by the manner in which alternatives are described is hardly foreign to political decision makers. But recent developments in behavioral decision theory provide the basis for a more systematic treatment of such information-manipulation strategies. For instance, Tversky and Kahneman offer the following explanation for the preference reversal just described. People display a general tendency to be risk averse for gains but risk prone for losses (Kahneman & Tversky, 1979). In Problem 1, outcomes are described in terms of how many of the 600 potential victims' lives will be saved (a gain), and people choose the low-risk strategy of a small sure gain. But in Problem 2, where the same outcomes are described in terms of how many of the 600 lives will be lost, people tend to prefer the high-risk strategy that offers some hope that nobody will die. This example suggests a general hypothesis concerning how people should frame political arguments regarding public policies designed to avert losses (e.g., health and safety policies intended to avert loss of life). Those who favor novel, high-risk options that offer a chance of completely eliminating the loss in question should frame outcomes in terms of losses. Those who favor relatively low-risk alternatives that offer a high probability of partially eliminating the potential losses should frame outcomes as gains (i.e., losses averted). We do not claim that political actors are implicitly aware of this principle, only that it is likely to operate to the advantage of those who knowingly or unknowingly exploit it.

More generally, research indicates that the distinction between gains and losses plays a pervasive role in intuitive decision making. Kahneman and Tversky (1979) have proposed a theory of choice, *prospect theory*, in which they assume that outcomes are coded as gains or losses relative to some neutral reference point and in which the *value function* that is implicitly used to evaluate outcomes is steeper for losses than for gains (e.g., the disutility of a $100 loss exceeds the utility of a $100 gain). Further, the prospect theory value function is S-shaped around the reference point, indicating that people are more sensitive to changes in the vicinity of the reference point. For instance, the difference between a loss of $0 and $1,000 looms larger than the difference between a loss of $1,000 and $2,000.

Unfortunately for the intuitive decision maker, the neutral point that separates gains from losses is usually ill-defined. Different ways of framing a problem shift the neutral point. (The preference reversal for Problems 1 and 2 can be understood in this way.) Political actors routinely exploit this ambiguity. For instance, budgetary officials will claim to have reduced the deficit (a gain) when in fact the deficit is larger than that for the previous year (a loss). Upon examination, the "savings" turn out to be relative to what the deficit would have been in the absence of any cost control efforts. Similarly, the Reagan administration prefers statistics regarding the "employment rate," a gain which is getting better, rather than statistics regarding the "unemployment rate," a loss, despite the fact that it is getting better. If forced to deal with unemployment rates, they naturally refer to "reductions in unemployment," which can be viewed as a gain. The lability of reference points leads to lability in the evaluation of political outcomes.

Sunk cost effects provide another instance of how the framing of decision alternatives and the redefinition of neutral points can shift political preferences. Economic theory holds that bygones are bygones; only incremental costs and benefits are relevant to decisions about future action. But as Thaler (1980) has shown, if sunk costs are coded as losses relative to the reference point in the prospect theory value function, people will tend to violate the sunk cost principle. That is, once costs have been expended, people will tend to persist with a course of action even after the balance of marginal costs and benefits favors cessation of the project. In support of this hypothesis, Thaler (1980) presents the following example from the congressional hearings on the Teton dam disaster:

> One part of the hearings was devoted to an analysis of the *theory of momentum*—"that is, the inclination on the part of the Bureau of Reclamation to continue dam construction, once commenced, despite hazards which might emerge during the course of construction . . . " The Commissioner of the Bureau of Reclamation denied that such a problem existed. However, when asked to "give an example of any dam whose construction was halted

or even paused or interrupted temporarily once the physical construction processes actually began on the dam itself," the Commissioner came up empty handed. (p. 48)

This example does not prove the point, but it is suggestive. Further, the sunk cost effect can be used to advantage by political actors who understand it. The "foot in the door" strategy of initially funding public programs on a low-level basis is an instance of this strategy. The fact that we have already spent hundreds of millions of dollars on the MX, a weapon of dubious military utility, is an advantage to those who favor the MX because they can use this fact to argue against "throwing away" the sunk costs that were paid for by taxpayers' hard-earned dollars.

These examples only scratch the surface of framing effects. The central point is that recent developments in behavioral decision theory provide a powerful theoretical framework for analyzing framing effects in political argumentation.

Task-Contingent Decision Strategies

Economists generally assume that people take essentially the same approach to all decision-making problems. That approach involves maximizing the utility of the alternative chosen, subject to the constraints on the alternatives available to the decision maker. But as Payne (1982) has argued and demonstrated in his own research, behavioral studies of decision making indicate that people use different kinds of strategies for making different kinds of decisions. Although our understanding of how people "select" strategies is rudimentary at best (it need not involve conscious choice of a strategy), it appears that strategy selection depends not only on the stakes involved, but also on the structure of the decision problem itself.

Judgment Versus Choice.   One important distinction is between what psychologists refer to as judgment and choice. As behavioral decision theorists use the term, choice tasks involve choosing among a discrete set of mutually exclusive and exhaustive courses of action.[1] Evaluative judgment tasks involve evaluating alternatives on an ordered response scale, that is, assigning monetary values to them, rating them on a continuous scale, rating them on an ordered scale with a discrete number of levels, or assigning "utilities" to outcomes using the lottery procedures favored by decision analysts. Classic rational choice theories imply that responses to

---

[1]The choice models used in behavioral decision theory cannot be directly applied to continuous alternatives, as in a allocation task.

both types of tasks should yield equivalent results; for example, if a decision maker is willing to pay more for alternative A than for alternative B, the decision maker should choose A over B in a direct choice. In fact, that is not always the case. There are well-documented conditions under which monetary evaluations of alternatives are inconsistent with direct choices between alternatives (Grether & Plott, 1979; Lichtenstein & Slovic, 1971). Einhorn and Hogarth (1981) argue that such preference reversals result from the fact that people adopt different cognitive strategies for judgment and choice tasks. Further evidence that judgment differs from choice is provided by E. J. Johnson and Russo (1984).

Linear Models of Evaluative Judgment. When the decision task in question involves evaluating a single decision alternative or outcome on some sort of ordered scale, the resulting judgments can almost invariably be explained with great precision by a linear statistical model in which the independent variables are the attributes or characteristics of the alternative or outcome in question (Fischer, 1979; Slovic & Lichtenstein, 1971). There seem to be at least two reasons why this is the case. First, linear statistical models are quite robust. An additive main effects model will often provide an excellent approximation to nonadditive judgment processes (Dawes & Corrigan, 1974). In addition, however, it may be the case that linear models are roughly isomorphic to the actual psychological processes involved in evaluative judgment. As Lopes (1982) has argued, linear statistical models are consistent with a simple *starting point and adjustment strategy* in which the decision maker forms an initial impression by focusing on one attribute of the alternative in question. That impression is then modified in light of the decision maker's evaluation of the second attribute of the alternative. This combined impression is then modified in light of the third attribute and so forth. At any given point in the serial adjustment process, the decision maker need hold in memory only the current overall impression of the alternative and the evaluation of the attribute currently being considered. Depending on the nature of the adjustment process, a starting point and adjustment strategy can be mathematically represented by either an additive or bilinear statistical model (Lopes, 1982).[2]

When linear models are fitted to judgment data, they typically explain between 75% and 95% of the variance in the responses of individual subjects. Moreover, it is usually the case that no more than three to five independent variables are needed to explain the responses of a given

---

[2] A bilinear model involves additive main effects and two-way multiplicative interactions between these main effects.

individual (Slovic & Lichtenstein, 1972). The latter result does not necessarily imply that three to five variables will yield adequate predictions in a survey research setting, however. If different individuals attend to different factors, then cross-sectional models will typically require a larger number of independent variables than the average individual attends to. (See, for example, Lau's chapter in this volume.)

Compensatory and Noncompensatory Choice Rules.   The foregoing discussion of evaluative judgment is potentially relevant to understanding how people form overall impressions of a candidate or make overall evaluations of the performance of the President. But when people make choices between political candidates or when members of Congress choose between alternative versions of a bill, the psychological processes involved may be quite different.

The starting point and adjustment strategy is of course potentially applicable to choices among alternatives as well as to judgments regarding the value of individual alternatives. In making choices with the starting point and adjustment strategy, the decision maker simply evaluates one option at a time, holding in short-term memory the overall evaluation of the current best option and comparing that with the evaluation of each new option considered. If a better option is discovered, it replaces the current best option, and so forth, until all alternatives have been considered. The main drawback to this approach is that it requires substantial cognitive effort to evaluate alternatives in this manner. The starting point and adjustment strategy requires repeated trade-offs between value criteria, and making direct trade-offs is a difficult, sometimes painful, task. Thus, people often resort to simple *elimination strategies* that are easier to employ. One such strategy is the *satisficing rule* suggested by Simon (1957). With this strategy, the decision maker considers one option at a time, searching for an option that is satisfactory with respect to every value criterion of concern. Search terminates once such an option is found. Another elimination strategy is the *elimination by aspects* (EBA) process proposed by Tversky (1972). With EBA, the decision maker considers one criterion at a time, eliminating all alternatives that are unsatisfactory with respect to this criterion. The process continues until the choice set is narrowed down to one alternative. Though many elimination strategies are possible, they share one important feature: All avoid the cognitively difficult task of making trade-offs between decision objectives. Alternatives are simply eliminated if they are unacceptable with respect to a criterion considered. This is in contrast to the starting point and adjustment process, which is *compensatory* in the sense that it implies that people make trade-offs (possibly quite crude) between objectives.

Compensatory and noncompensatory strategies are not mutually exclusive.

Payne (1976, 1982) has argued and demonstrated empirically that people sometimes use *phased rules* in which they begin by using noncompensatory elimination strategies to narrow down large sets of alternatives and then switch to compensatory strategies (e.g., starting point and adjustment) to make a final choice between the best two or three options. Payne's findings suggest that voters (like laboratory subjects) may use both simplified, noncompensatory (i.e., "heuristic") choice strategies and the compensatory strategies posited by more "rational" spatial models (e.g., Shapiro, 1969).

Finally, the comparison of compensatory and noncompensatory choice rules is complicated by the recent finding that some noncompensatory rules can perform almost as well as a compensatory rule under certain conditions (Johnson & Payne, 1985). Because of this, it is not clear whether detailed process considerations such as these have substantial relevance to the study of political behavior. Does it matter, for instance, whether voters use elimination strategies or cast their ballots on the basis of an overall impression derived from a compensatory trade-off process? One detailed model of voting choice (Herstein, 1981) suggests that it does. Herstein developed a model of voting choice using a detailed process analysis. The model represented a phased rule and had a strong resemblance to models developed for choice in other domains. Herstein then applied the model to survey data to predict the choices made by voters in a gubernatorial election. The model predicted these choices as accurately as most linear models and also provided insight into the information used by these voters in making their decision. In addition, the model underlined the distinction between judgment and choice. The best predictors of the vote were not the overall evaluations of the candidates, but rather the comparisons of the candidates on each issue. Although these results are encouraging, they have not been pursued by subsequent research, and the ultimate value of such analyses can be established only by further attempts to apply the process tracing techniques to political decision processes.

MEMORY, KNOWLEDGE, AND POLITICAL CHOICE

We are optimistic that behavioral decision concepts can contribute to our understanding of political cognition, but we should acknowledge our concerns as well. In the typical laboratory experiment, college students make choices among hypothetical alternatives that they know little about. There is typically little feedback, and the interaction between decision maker and topic could be described as brief, at best. Real-world decisions, such as deciding to vote for one candidate, occur over an extended period of time, and unlike subjects in our laboratory studies, real decision makers often have a large store of prior knowledge, feelings, and impressions to draw upon in making these choices.

The impact of prior learning—whether we characterize it as a schema, frame, script, or simply as knowledge—is a central theme not only of this volume, but of much of cognitive psychology as well. Until recently, however, behavioral decision theory has paid little attention to the influence of knowledge upon decision making. In this section, we concentrate upon three areas of impact: (a) prior knowledge and the ability to process new information; (b) prior knowledge and the selection of decision strategies; and (c) prior knowledge and the evaluation of alternatives.

Prior Knowledge and Learning New Information

How does old knowledge impact upon new knowledge? A very robust finding, appearing in a number of studies, suggests that prior knowledge of a domain facilitates learning new information. The classic work of Chase and Simon (1973) started a decade of research demonstrating that individuals initially rich in domain-specific knowledge get richer. Experienced people can learn new information about a domain more easily than those who lack that knowledge. Recent work by Fiske, Kinder, and Larter (1983) provides a particularly relevant example. They examined the recall of political experts and novices who had read an article about the political institutions in a country previously unknown to them. As hypothesized, Fiske et al. found that the knowledgeable individuals used their greater encoding abilities to recall more information than did the novices. Specifically, the more knowledgeable subjects recalled more information that was inconsistent with their prior expectations.

These findings suggest that it is important to specify more carefully a notion, quite popular in this volume, that people are *cognitive misers* who carefully monitor their expenditures of mental resources. The finding that knowledgeable people encode information more easily suggests an important modification: Not all mental resources are equally dear for all people. If the notion of a relatively impoverished information processor is to be useful, we need to identify exactly which mental capacities are limited and how people can overcome these limitations. Although processing capacity in some very real sense is limited, some of these limits are, in a practical sense, not fixed, and it is important for theories that use the concept of a cognitive miser to specify these limits closely.

Prior Knowledge and Decision Strategies

Although more knowledgeable people can in many ways process more information, it is not necessarily the case that they will. Knowledge can help in encoding, and knowledge can also help in deciding which information is relevant. E. J. Johnson and Russo (1984), for example, showed that consumers who were more familiar with automobiles actually remembered less information about a set of new cars than did those who were moderately familiar with cars. This, they hypothesized, was because the more familiar consumers immediately identified much of the information as irrelevant, knowing which attributes were more predictive of product performance. This key finding that more knowledgeable people can separate relevant information from irrelevant information appears in a number of studies, including work in physics problem solving (Larkin, McDermott, Simon, & Simon, 1980), and in the study of expert decision makers, such as physicians and stock analysts (E. J. Johnson, in press).

This raises rather interesting implications for the study of political sophisticates. Theirs is an interesting balancing act, which must apply enriched ability to process information while using knowledge to search information carefully. However, researchers should not be surprised to find that more knowledgeable individuals may actually search less information than those less knowledgeable, letting previous knowledge and a good sense for relevant information replace extensive search.

Prior Knowledge and Evaluation

Finally, to complicate our survey of the effects of knowledge further, there is evidence that the complexity of decision makers' knowledge structures about a domain is related to the extremity of their evaluations of events in that domain (Linville, 1982; Linville & Jones, 1980). In this research, two factors contribute to the "complexity" of a decision maker's knowledge structure: (a) the number of features or attributes used in representing the domain and (b) the degree of redundancy among these features. The more features used and the less redundant these features, the more complex the decision maker's knowledge structure. Evidence from studies of how people evaluate other people indicates that those with a more complex knowledge structure are less extreme in their evaluations of events in the domain. That is, those with simple knowledge structures tend to be more positive about events that they like and more negative about events that they dislike. This is consistent with the observation that the most strident and vociferous letters to the editors of local papers seem to come from those individuals who seem less knowledgeable about the subject of their letter. The implications for political behavior are apparent, if the complexity-extremity effect generalizes to this domain. In fact, unpublished findings by Linville and Fiske (1985) suggest that it does.

In summary, it is apparent that the presence of prior knowledge can have a number of quite different effects upon a decision maker. These effects are not necessarily mutually contradictory. Rather, knowledge of a domain seems to affect many aspects of decision processes, ranging from an individual's ability to encode information to the extremity of the final judgment. Any confusion stems not from contradictory effects, but from our lack of knowledge about how these effects combine. Exploring these issues presents a major challenge to those who study decision making, and the domain of political cognition seems to be a fruitful area for such research.

CONCLUSION

Although the marriage (or at least the courting relationship) between political cognition and behavioral decision theory is just beginning, there seems to be some potential. But the mapping is not an easy one, and in many ways, evaluation of a political candidate is more similar to choosing a new car or brand of soap than to choosing among hypothetical stimuli such as apartments. Thus, the marriage would benefit behavioral decision theorists, forcing them to examine decisions carefully under conditions more typical of real-world circumstances (i.e., decisions that unfold over time, in a changing environment, about which the decision maker has considerable prior knowledge.). As suggested in this paper, we also believe that the marriage can be advantageous to students of political cognition. The concepts and models of behavioral decision theory provide potentially powerful tools for understanding how people evaluate and choose among political alternatives.

APPLICATIONS OF SOCIAL COGNITION TO POLITICAL BEHAVIOR

5 Cognitive Consequences of Political Sophistication

Ruth Hamill
Milton Lodge
Laboratory for Behavioral Research
Department of Political Science
SUNY, Stony Brook

The citizen, whether portrayed as rational voter or *Homo not so sapiens,* must of necessity develop some schema for making sense of the world of government and politics. Confronted with a blizzard of facts, figures, and images on which impressions are formed and judgments made, the individual must somehow selectively attend to some stimuli and disregard others, group together and categorize events that share common attributes, encode and store in memory some representation of the event, and then retrieve and utilize this information to interpret and structure new stimuli. Whatever the terminology adopted, whether frame, script, or schema—we use the concept schema—the basic notion is quite simple: One's prior knowledge about some particular domain is organized in memory in a coherent structure that influences what one sees and remembers and how one interprets reality. A schema is, as Axelrod (1973) says, a "shorthand device" for making sense of the world and guiding behavior.

Given the complexity and ambiguity of things political, there are many ways to think about leaders, issues, and political events (Hamill, Lodge, & Blake, 1984). One could (apparently many people do) interpret information about government and politics in terms of political parties and partisan conflicts. Leaders sometimes say what they say and do what they do because they are Republicans or Democrats. Another possibility, which by all counts is more commonly used by elites than the general public, is to organize one's beliefs and constrain one's preferences along ideological lines. For citizens sophisticated enough to structure the world this way, there are liberal and conservative politicians, ideologically discernible people, groups, and policies. Other schemata are possible as well. One could—as Karl Marx was wont to do—see politics as the expression of class conflict, the bourgeoisie versus the workers, or in vulgar terms, the rich versus the poor. Other possibilities are to see the world as race against race, blacks versus whites, or to organize one's thinking about politics in terms of religious or sexual cleavages. All of these ways of making sense of the world, as well as others, are viable schemata in contemporary America for understanding the news, putting what leaders say into perspective, and anticipating what is likely to come next.

The cognitive sciences have made significant progress in recent years using the schema concept to explore the effects of different knowledge structures and varying degrees of their sophisticated use on the processing of new information (Fiske & Taylor, 1984). In the first part of this chapter, we describe methods and procedures for operationally defining knowledge-based measures of partisan and ideological sophistication which are similar to the measures employed in the cognitive sciences to discriminate experts from novices in nonpolitical domains. In the second part, we summarize the results of two laboratory experiments designed to apply contemporary theories of information processing to the study of political cognition, testing the effects of sophistication on the recognition, verification, and speed of political information processing. Next, we propose a more elaborated causal model of political sophistication and test this model via LISREL measurement and structural equation techniques. We conclude by discussing the problems and prospects of this approach to the study of political behavior.

THE MEASUREMENT OF SOPHISTICATION

Recent advances in the cognitive sciences (J.R. Anderson & Bower, 1973; Kintsch, 1974; Loftus & Loftus, 1976; Norman & Bobrow, 1975; Tulving & Donaldson, 1972), particularly in the application of information-processing models to social cognition (Abelson, 1976; Bobrow & Norman, 1975; Cantor & Mischel, 1979; Mischel, Ebbesen, & Zeiss, 1976), provide welcomed theoretical guidance and tested methods for determining the meaning of concepts and their function in social cognition. This research effort, seen by Simon (1980) as central to the development of the social and behavioral sciences, demonstrates that the cognitive processes involved in the encoding, storage, and retrieval of information are structured semantically (i.e., meaningfully) by concepts (Collins & Quillian, 1972; Rips, Shoben, & Smith, 1973; Rosch, 1975). A schema is a cognitive structure that contains knowledge about the attributes of a concept, specific instances and examples, and their interrelationships.

To help place our studies in perspective, let us emphasize some of the characteristics of schemata described in the summary chapter by Lau and Sears (this volume). The hallmark of a schema is knowledge. Declarative knowledge provides the basic facts, and procedural rules govern the way things typically fit together and characteristically behave. As Tesser (1978) notes:

> When we apply a particular schema for thinking about some stimulus object it does two things. First it tells us what to attend to. Like a scientific theory it makes some attributes relevant, that is, salient, while allowing others to be ignored. Second, a schema contains the network of associations that is believed to hold among the attributes of the stimulus and thereby provides rules for thinking about the stimulus. (p. 209)

Declarative and procedural knowledge, in conjunction, structure the information about a concept and provide hypotheses about how some particular aspect of the world characteristically works and why. Attitudes, evaluations, and actions are made on the basis of the knowledge contained in the schema that is activated when some decision or behavioral response is required.

In a recent critique of schema models of memory, Alba and Hasher (1983) identify four critical assumptions of schema theories, namely that schemata influence the selection, abstraction, interpretation, and integration of new information. In turn, these processes determine what is stored and ultimately retrieved from memory. Following these lines, our studies focus on cognitive dependent measures, looking at how political schemata affect the processing of politically relevant information (for more complete reviews of schematic processing consequences, see Fiske & Taylor, 1984; Hastie, 1981; Taylor & Crocker, 1981).

Individual Differences
in Schema Content and Structure

Whatever the domain—whether music, politics, sports, or some other realm of human endeavor—people range from those intensely concerned and knowledgeable about some aspect of the world to those who have little interest or knowledge in that particular domain. In political science, virtually every descriptive statement about the behavior of citizens and elites must be qualified by their "level" of sophistication, and almost all attempts to model political behavior introduce one or another measure of sophistication as a control or intervening variable (Norpoth & Lodge, 1985). The literature of cognitive psychology makes similar distinctions, often in terms of expert and novice. In social psychology, those individuals who possess a rich knowledge structure about a particular domain are termed *schematics,* whereas those who have not developed an elaborated knowledge structure—whether for lack of interest, ability, or experience—are said to be *aschematics* (H. Markus, 1977). Whatever the terminology—experts, sophisticates, or schematics—individuals differ not only in the amount of knowledge available, but also in the way this information is structured and organized in memory (Fiske, Kinder, & Larter, 1983). As Conover and Feldman point out in this volume, such differences in the structure of a schema, as well as the amount of knowledge stored in memory, affect a variety of decision-making tasks.

Differences between experts and novices in the amount and complexity of domain-related information have been demonstrated in such far-ranging areas as computer simulations of problem-solving tasks (Larkin, McDermott, Simon, & Simon, 1980), memory structures about dinosaurs (Chi & Koeske, 1983), physics (Chi, Feltovich, & Glaser, 1981), medicine (P. E. Johnson et al., 1981), baseball (Chiesi, Spilich, & Voss, 1981), chess (Chase & Simon, 1973), and person perception (H. Markus & Smith, 1981). In politics, as in each of these domains, some citizens are more knowledgeable and more sophisticated users of their schemata than are others (Conover & Feldman, 1984; Hamill, Lodge, & Blake, 1984; Lau, Coulam, & Sears, 1983).

Whereas some individuals may not be interested enough, experienced enough, or wise enough to have developed a schema for organizing political information, others may develop and use one or perhaps many different schemata to think about politics and guide their political behavior. We start with the assumption that partisan, ideological, class, and racial schemata are the most general political schemata available today to put contemporary American politics into perspective. An individual may be more or less sophisticated with respect to each (Hamill, Lodge, & Blake, 1985). For example, a person may have a well-developed class schema, but a much less sophisticated partisan schema. And some individuals are likely to be sophisticated with respect to several domains. The key point is that if a schema exists, if it is activated, and if the incoming information is seen as relevant to the existing schema, then the cognitive effects on political information processing should be similar to those found in the social and cognitive literatures.

We follow the lead of social cognition researchers in using the terms schematics and aschematics to organize our work in political cognition. Underlying the application of the human information-processing approach to the study of political behavior is an analogy that the very same memory processes governing social judgments operate on political decisions as well. Accordingly, in political cognition as in social cognition, knowledge matters; it affects how new information is interpreted and used to guide behavior. This may be too robust an assumption for some of our colleagues to accept, arguing instead that the political realm, more than others, is represented by ill-defined, nonconsensual concepts (e.g., Republican, Democrat, liberal, and conservative) and by far more abstract instances (e.g., Reagan, labor unions, and welfare programs) than commonly studied in psychology and that for most people, government and politics exerts a less perceptible impact on their lives than does, say, their occupation.

Acknowledging these significant dissimilarities between the stuff of politics and the elements of cognitive psychology, we cannot be certain that the analogy holds. This being the case, some basic questions need to be asked: Are political concepts defined and structured in semantic memory like other concepts? Do the same patterns of facilitation effects and liabilities found for how "experts" process information in nonpolitical domains hold for the processing of political information by political sophisticates?

On the Nature of Political Schemata

Whereas most cognitive and social-psychological studies differentiate experts from novices (or schematics from aschematics) by some consensual or positional measure (e.g., by comparing beginners to chess masters), in the absence of an "objective" measure of political sophistication, we must rely on indirect indicators of expertise and then attempt to validate the measures on such schema-dependent information-processing tasks as the recognition, verification, and structuring of political information. Because our procedures for defining a schema and measuring degrees of sophistication are the same whatever the political schema (schemata are thought to differ in content and structure), let us focus first on the measurement of ideological sophistication, leaving the validation tests and comparisons with other political schemata to the section on experimental evidence.

Ideological Sophistication.   Our strategy is to analyze political concepts in much the same way as contemporary theories of semantic memory model other concepts. Whatever the concept—whether animal or mammal, bat or bird, corner bank or river bank, liberal or conservative—a concept is defined by its content, by its prototypical examples, instances, and attributes, and a schema is known by the concepts it subsumes. Graphically, we see the representation of political knowledge in memory as semantic networks.

Following Lasswell's (1936) lead, we treat political leaders, groups, and policies as the basic stuff of politics. Leaders and groups are the "who" in

Lasswell's formulation, and policies are the "what."[1] Relying on Rosch's (1975) method for defining the semantic meaning of a concept, the requisite first step for ascertaining the content and structure of a schema is the collection of all those examples, instances, and characteristics that potentially make up its meaning. Over the past 3 years, we have collected more than 300 words and phrases from open-ended questions in the 1976 and 1980 CPS/SRC election surveys, which ask respondents for their likes and dislikes of the presidential candidates, as well as from the CPS questions asking respondents to define the terms liberal and conservative and from news articles summarizing candidate positions in the 1980 election. After redundant items were dropped from this pool, respondents in local area surveys were asked to indicate which of the words and phrases were characteristic of, typical of, or part of the concepts liberal or conservative. Virtually all the items with high levels of consensus among respondents relate to either leaders (e.g., Reagan, Kennedy), groups (e.g., labor unions, black people), or issues (e.g., defense spending, federal spending for social programs). Several pretests confirm the obvious: Some people can, but others cannot, categorize the leaders, groups, and policies as instances or attributes of the concepts liberal or conservative, Republican or Democrat (Bastedo & Lodge, 1980; Sharp & Lodge, 1985).

At this juncture, let us simply describe the current version of the three-component model of declarative ideological knowledge and the general measurement procedures, leaving a discussion of other schemata as well as conceptual and methodological problems to later. Embedded in a conventional CPS-type survey instrument tapping political interest, activity, and party identification are three sets of questions asking subjects to categorize political leaders, groups, and policies as liberal or conservative.

The Classification of Political Leaders.   One set of questions calls on subjects to categorize a number of contemporary political leaders as politically liberal or conservative (or don't know/not sure). Among them are Ronald Reagan, Ted Kennedy, Barry Goldwater, Walter Mondale, and Tip O'Neil, as well as such less known figures as Robert Dole, Christopher Dodd, Jack Kemp, Robert Michel, George McGovern, Jesse Helms, and Alan Cranston, who only the most knowledgeable subjects can correctly identify.

---

[1]The reader should be aware that our definition and operationalization of sophistication in terms of one's knowledge of the cognitive content of schema labels is in contrast to work presented elsewhere in this volume. Obviously, this reliance on the declarative knowledge component of schemata to the exclusion of procedural rules for integrating such information into a plan of action is insufficient, as is our failure to take affect into account. These problems are discussed in our conclusion.

Although each of the leaders has an Americans for Democratic Action (ADA) rating above 75% or below 25% liberal, we lack a truly objective measure of liberalism or conservatism. Thus, the coding of responses as correct or incorrect ultimately depends on what Converse (1964) calls a *social definition* of liberal-conservative ideology. To be included in this sophistication index, a leader, group, or policy must satisfy two criteria: consensus and discriminability. Here, the consensual answer across the sample identifies the correct answer: Reagan is a conservative because a majority of subjects type him as such, whereas Kennedy is a liberal because consensus opinion says it is so. The second criterion test for including a leader in this component of the knowledge index involves an analysis of the distribution of responses for each item. After dividing the sample at the median index score, items that do not discriminate those scoring high from those scoring low on this knowledge of leaders index are dropped from the component. Some of the casualties from various pretests were: John Anderson, Jimmy Carter, Henry Kissinger, Henry Jackson, and Patrick Moynahan. This coding scheme awards a +1 to subjects who share the common usage of the ideological term, assigns a 0 to those who don't know or are not sure, and subtracts 1 point from those who guess wrong or perhaps have an idiosyncratic or anachronistic view of contemporary language use. (Not surprisingly, the ADA ratings confirm consensus opinion on all the leaders.)

The Classification of Groups.   The survey questionnaire also calls upon subjects to decide whether liberals or conservatives are more likely to favor one or another group. Those groups achieving a high degree of consensus and discriminability in the item analyses include: corporations, the rich, labor unions, poor people, Republicans, Democrats, minorities, and the unemployed. Although The Moral Majority can be consensually defined as conservative and the National Organization of Women as liberal by the most sophisticated half of our adult samples, and are therefore included in the index, other groups (e.g., the military) generally fail to discriminate ideological schematics from aschematics and are summarily dismissed from this knowledge of groups index.

The Classification of Issues.   The 20 policy positions used by the SRC/CPS to define the end points of the 10 issue questions in the 1980 national election survey are also included in the questionnaire. Subjects are asked whether liberals or conservatives are more likely to favor each policy position. Some of the issues that pass the two criteria tests and are incorporated into the issues component of the sophistication index include: favor abortion, more support for social security, increased federal spending for education, increased military spending, opposition to school busing, cuts in federal spending for social services, and opposition to a government health insurance plan. Whereas the policy of favoring the Equal Rights Amendment (ERA) can be consensually defined as liberal by those scoring high on the sophistication index, and is therefore included in this issues component, support for prayer in the schools is not consensually defined by sophisticates and is dropped from the index.

Were a researcher to incorporate this sophistication measure into a model of political behavior (Norpoth & Lodge, 1985), an additive index of ideological sophistication could be constructed by summing the scores for leaders, groups, and policies. Assuming nine items for each component, the index of ideological sophistication could theoretically range from −27 to +27. Empirically, the scores generally traverse the full range of the index, with approximately 25–30% of the sample typically falling below zero and statistically significant differences discriminating low, medium, and high levels of sophistication.

Two obvious problems come to the fore: Is knowledge of political leaders, groups, and policies a necessary (albeit not sufficient) component of an ideological schema? And if so, is the ability to categorize leaders, groups, and policies correctly in liberal–conservative terms an adequate measure of ideological sophistication? As with all questions of validity, the criterion test is prediction to behavior. Different cognitive structures and varying degrees of their sophisticated use should produce predictable effects if our measures are appropriate.

EXPERIMENTAL EVIDENCE

Although schema effects have been demonstrated for the social domain, few studies have examined the impact of political sophistication on cognitive performance. Most of the work in political science focuses instead on such affective dependent variables as candidate and policy preferences (exceptions include work by Bolland & Cigler, 1984; Fiske et al., 1983; J. T. Johnson & Judd, 1983). The studies described in this section adapt for use in the political domain several cognitive performance measures that have been shown to produce reliable information-processing consequences predicated on expertise or sophistication. The first study examines the effects of ideological sophistication on the recognition of political words and the speed and accuracy of verifying political statements. The second study looks at partisan sophistication and its consequences on memory for information contained in a political message.

At this juncture, neither study includes the categorization of leaders and groups and policies. The studies reported here have been conducted over a 3-year period, and our measure of sophistication evolved over time. Nonetheless, one constancy has been the emphasis on declarative knowledge as a defining attribute of a sophisticated person and on categorization of leaders and/or groups and/or issues as indicators of such knowledge. To avoid the laborious task of detailing the construction of the sophistication measure used in each of these studies, let us simply report the results in terms of schematics versus aschematics differences regardless of the precise measurement of sophistication used in any given study and then present a more complete model of sophistication in the next main section.

Recognition of Schema-Relevant Information

The first study conducted in this program of research (Lodge & Hamill, 1983) analyzed the effects of ideological sophistication on two of the most basic aspects of information processing (viz., the recognition and verification of political information) and served as an initial validation test of our sophistication measure. Based on responses to an in-class survey 2 to 3 weeks prior to the experimental session, 75 undergraduates were categorized as ideological schematics or aschematics. In addition, a special "elite" sample of 8 professors and 8 graduate students of political science agreed to participate in this study. In the laboratory session, each subject was seated at a table before a 19-in. high resolution monitor and computer keyboard. Positioned at the subject's dominant hand was a button box, with one button labeled "yes" and the other labeled "no." Subjects first completed two tasks designed to give them practice making fast, accurate decisions using the button responses.

Subjects next completed a standard keyword recognition task, first for the well-learned concepts *furniture* and *vegetables* and then for the political concepts *liberal* and *conservative*. The instructions explained that a series of simple, declarative sentences would appear on the monitor one at a time. The first set of sentences referred to pieces of furniture or types of vegetables. Each sentence contained a blank. Subjects were told that the missing keyword would be the name of a piece of furniture, the name of a specific vegetable, or something irrelevant to either furniture or vegetables. Furniture and vegetable represent well-learned concepts that have been studied extensively in the psychological literature on human information processing (Rosch, 1975). Thus, they provide comparison data for the political concepts. The same format was used for all trials: A context sentence such as, "A _____ is a vegetable," stayed on the screen for 5 sec, was followed by a ready signal, and then a very brief (50 msec) exposure of a keyword.

The subject's task was to recognize the keyword, signaling yes or no by the button response. If the yes button was pressed, the computer program asked the subject to type in the keyword. For the furniture-vegetable trials, there were 24 randomly presented keyword-in-context sentences. One third appeared in a congruent context (e.g., "A *chair* is a piece of furniture), one third were incongruent (e.g., "A *sofa* is a vegetable"), and one third were irrelevant (e.g., "A *canoe* is a vegetable").

Following the furniture-vegetable recognition task, subjects were randomly assigned to either the control or experimental condition. For subjects in the experimental condition, the political recognition task was procedurally identical to the furniture-vegetable task, but the concepts liberal and conservative replaced furniture and vegetable.

All the political keywords had been consensually defined as liberal or conservative earlier.[2] There were four basic variants of the political context statements: "Liberals (or Conservatives) favor _____," when the keyword related to a political leader or group, or "Liberals (Conservatives) favor more (less) government support for _____," when the keyword referred to a policy.

Each subject in the experimental condition read 30 sentences, 10 of which placed keywords in an ideologically congruent context and 10 in an ideologically incongruent context, with the 10 remaining words irrelevant to the concepts liberal or conservative. Subjects in the control condition were presented with the same 30 keywords but without a context sentence. Their responses provided a base-line measure of the simple recognizability of keywords independent of ideological context.

Results.   The literature on information processing led us to make several predictions. First, Alba and Hasher's (1983) review of the literature suggests that during the initial encoding or acquisition of incoming information, people are likely to make inferences, especially if they need to fill in vague or missing data. When dealing with attributes of well-learned concepts, subjects are prone to "see" and process information that matches their expectations. Thus, in the furniture and vegetable task, we predicted a type of item context effect such that congruent information should be recognized more accurately than incongruent information, which in turn should be recognized more easily than irrelevant information. Predictably, these results should hold for all subjects, who it is assumed have equally well-developed schemata for the concepts furniture and vegetable.

---

[2]The political keywords used were: Goldwater, Kennedy, Mondale, Reagan, corporations, Democrats, labor unions, poor, Republicans, rich, abortion, education, environmental protection, health care, military, minorities, social security, social services, unemployment, welfare. Twenty irrelevant control words were also included.

Second, ideological schematics, aschematics, and elites should do equally well in the political control condition, which is a simple word recognition task that should not activate the relevant schema.

Third, for the political statements presented in the experimental condition, however, one's level of ideological sophistication should affect the number and type of political keywords recognized. Sophisticates (referring to both the student group scoring high on the ideological knowledge measure and the elite sample) should correctly recognize more of the political keywords than should aschematics, should recogize more congruent than incongruent political words, but should also systematically err in the direction of making ideologically congruent errors because their schemata activate congruent information.

Taking each of these hypotheses in order, as expected all subjects performed equally well on the first recognition task related to the concepts furniture and vegetable, with an overall average of 44% correct recognition, and all individuals recognized more congruent than incongruent or irrelevant keywords. As predicted, analyses of the error responses showed that on the average subjects are three times more likely to make congruent than incongruent errors, that is, to impute erroneously a keyword that made the context statement congruent. This context effect holds for political elites, schematics, and aschematics, as it should, because the task is irrelevant to ideological sophistication.

The results of the political recognition task are summarized in Table 5.1 and only partially corroborate the furniture and vegetable findings. Let us first examine the performance of the control group, which was presented with the political and nonpolitical keywords without a liberal or conservative context statement. These results appear in the left-most columns of Table 5.1. In this simple word recognition task, we neither expected nor found a schema effect. Because the keywords were not presented in a context that would activate an ideological schema, sophisticates did no better than aschematics. All subjects were more or less equal in their ability to recognize the political words and phrases used in this experiment.

Turning now to the experimental condition in which the keywords did appear in a liberal–conservative context, we find support for a schema effect. Sophisticates correctly recognized more political keywords than did aschematics in both the congruent and incongruent contexts, and did about the same (viz., poorly) when presented with politically irrelevant keywords. Our type of item hypothesis was in the right direction but is not statistically significant. Within each level of sophistication, recognition accuracy is about the same for both congruent and incongruent items.

Statistically significant type of item schema effects show up more clearly in analyses of the number and type of errors made in this political information-

TABLE 5.1
Recognition of Political and Nonpolitical Keywords in Control Condition (No Context) and Ideologically Congruent, Incongruent, and Irrelevant Words in Context by Level of Ideological Sophistication

	Control Condition			Experimental Condition			Context Effects		
	% Recognition of			% Recognition of Keywords in Context			Experimental Group One-tailed Probability of t-test differences		
	Nonpolitical Keywords	Political Keywords		Congruent (C)	Incongruent (In)	Irrelevant (Ir)	C vs. In	In vs. Ir	C vs. Ir
Aschematics (n = 16)	23.1	25.2	Aschematics (n = 19)	34.2	29.5	7.9	NS	.001	.01
Schematics (n = 22)	18.8	28.6	Schematics (n = 18)	56.9	56.9	10.6	NS	.001	.001
Elite (n = 0)	na	na	Elite (n = 16)	61.9	56.3	14.4	NS	.001	.001
All Subjects (n = 38)	20.6	27.1	All Subjects (n = 53)	50.3	46.5	10.8	NS	.001	.001
ANOVA F probability <	NS	NS	F probability <	.01	.01	NS			

processing task. Nearly two thirds of all recognition errors turned irrelevant and incongruent keywords into ideologically congruent information. But contrary to expectations, schematics and elites were no more prone to this bias than were aschematics. Aschematics did, however, make twice as many errors overall.

Sentence Verification

A distractor test intervened between the recognition phase of the experiment just described and a sentence verification task in which subjects read 60 statements, half placing the keywords in a liberal sentence and half in a conservative sentence. Each of the political keywords appeared twice in counterbalanced orders, once in a congruent context (making the statement true) and once in an incongruent context (making the statement false). The irrelevant words appeared once each, half in the liberal context and half in the conservative context. The subject's task was to indicate "as quickly as possible without making errors" whether the sentence was true or false by pressing the true or false button. The primary dependent variables in this information-processing task are percentage correct and reaction time.

Results. One measure frequently used as an indicator of cognitive processes is reaction time (RT), that is, the amount of time it takes an individual to reach a decision, recall an event, or make a prediction. Reaction time is a standard measure employed extensively in experimental psychology to measure the ease of information access and retrieval (Pachella, 1974). Given that RT is an indicator of the strength of association between a concept and its attributes, we reasoned that sophisticates and aschematics should produce reliably different RTs to sentences containing the concepts liberal and conservative. Specifically, we believed that schematics and elites: (a) will be more accurate than aschematics in verifying ideological statements and (b) will respond faster than aschematics when verifying or disconfirming ideological statements.

As predicted, schematics and elites were significantly more accurate, $p < .01$, than aschematics when verifying ideologically congruent statements or disconfirming incongruent statements, but as expected, they did not differ in rejecting context-irrelevant information. Aschematics averaged 78% correct verification for the congruent and incongruent items combined, whereas schematics scored 93% correct and elites 94% correct.

Table 5.2 reports the mean RTs in thousandths of a second for each group to classify correctly an ideological statement as true or false. The RT results confirm the hypothesized schema effect. Looking first at the lower left panel of Table 5.2, F ratios comparing the mean response time of the three groups show a statistically significant decrease in the time required to verify ideologically congruent information and to disconfirm incongruent and irrelevant information. Aschematics find it difficult to deal with ideological information, whether in a congruent, incongruent, or irrelevant context, taking more time to respond in each case than do the schematics or elites.

These results generally validate our sophistication measure and confirm expectations. When ideological sophistication is operationally defined in terms of one's declarative knowledge of the instances and attributes of the concepts liberal and conservative, the same type of predictable information-processing consequences emerge as when subjects deal with the better learned and objective concepts used in cognitive psychology. Ideological sophisticates outperformed aschematics in recognition, verification accuracy, and speed of processing, demonstrating three facilitation effects of schematic processing. On the other hand, subjects showed a bias for "seeing" more ideologically congruent than incongruent information in this study, with no particular liability for sophisticates. We explore the differential processing of congruent and incongruent information further in the next study.

That we find ideological sophistication effects in such basic political information-processing tasks, but not for processing information about furniture and vegetables, implies that our knowledge-based indicator of

TABLE 5.2
Reaction Time to Correctly Verify Ideologically Congruent,
Incongruent, and Irrelevant Information in Sentences
Related to the Concepts Liberal and Conservative
by Level of Ideological Sophistication (in msec)

	Keywords in Context			One-tailed probability of t-test differences		
	Congruent	Incongruent	Irrelevant	C vs. In	In vs. Ir	C vs. Ir
Aschematics (n = 37)	2687	3146	3357	.01	.01	.01
Schematics (n = 38)	2292	2333	3168	NS	.05	.05
Elite (n = 16)	1531	1569	1866	NS	.05	NS
All Subjects (n = 91)	2311	2515	3005	.01	.01	.001
ANOVA F probability <	.001	.001	.01			

ideological sophistication represents a necessary component of an ideological schema.

Memory of Information from a Political Message

A second study (Hamill & Lodge, 1984) examined the effects of a partisan schema on memory for information in a complex political message. This quasi-experimental study proceeded in four stages and involved interviewing a nonprobability sample of 603 residents of Long Island, New York. The first stage consisted of a conventional survey questionnaire that included, along with the standard array of CPS/SRC questions, our measure of partisan knowledge. Based on subjects' ability to correctly classify leaders, groups, and policies as Republican or Democrat, we trichotomized our sample into high, medium, and low partisan schematics.

In Stage 2, 503 of the subjects were randomly assigned to one of two experimental conditions and were told that they were taking part in a large project whose aim was to design a booklet giving voters information about the policy positions of their representatives in Congress. Each subject then read a short biography of a fictitious Congressman Williams from distant upstate New York who was described as a lifelong partisan and party leader. Half the subjects were told he is a Republican; the other half was told he is a Democrat. All experimental subjects then read a series of 40 policy statements attributed to the Congressman.

For those in the Republican condition, 30 of the policies were congruent (i.e., based on pretest evaluations of the statements as Republican) and 10 were incongruent (i.e., selected from the set of policies previously characterized as Democratic). An example of a policy congruent with the Republican party label is, "Congressman Williams calls for major cuts in federal spending on social programs," whereas an incongruent policy stand is, "Congressman Williams favors federal programs to create more jobs." For subjects in the Democratic condition, told that Congressman Williams is a Democrat, the mix of policies was reversed—75% Democratic, 25% Republican. Subjects read and characterized as Republican or Democratic all 40 statements.

Eighty subjects were randomly assigned to the control group, which read and characterized as Republican or Democratic all 100 statements used in both experimental conditions and in all subsequent phases of the study. This task served primarily as a reliability check to determine the extent to which the 100 policy statements were consensually defined as characteristic of the Republican or Democratic parties by this sample.

Stage 3 consisted of a vocabulary test and provided us with both a measure of subjects' verbal ability and a distractor task prior to Stage 4, the recognition memory stage of the experiment in which 40 policy statements were presented. Half of these statements were "old," that is, policy statements actually attributed to Congressman Williams in the earlier phase of the study. Of these old statements, 10 were selected from the set of policies congruent with the Congressman's party label and 10 were incongruent. The other 20 statements were all "new" items, not previously attributed to Congressman Williams in the booklet, 10 of which were congruent with the ascribed party label and 10 of which were incongruent. Participants were to decide for each statement whether or not Congressman Williams actually made the particular policy statement.

Based on the social cognition literature, we fully expected that, overall, schematics would be more accurate than aschematics in recalling whether a statement was or was not actually made by the Congressman because schematics possess the relevant knowledge structure to integrate information packaged in partisan terms. We also expected a type of item effect for congruent versus incongruent information. Schematics are likely to recall information that is congruent with their schema, whether or not it was actually presented in the message. Those policies congruent with Congressman Williams' partisan affiliation and actually presented earlier (old congruent) should, predictably, produce higher levels of accurate recognition by schematics than by aschematics. On the other hand, those schema-congruent policy statements not in the original message (new congruent) should produce a relatively high rate of false recognition (errors) for schematics. Because schematics are knowledgeable about the policy positions of the prototypical Democrat, then even when the Congressman does not make a public statement supporting increased federal spending for education, for example, schematics may erroneously attribute such congruent statements to him.

Relatedly, schematics should be able to reject new incongruent policy statements because such statements do not fit their expectations of partisanship. The evidence concerning memory for previously presented incongruent information is, however, mixed in the social-psychological literature, with some researchers (Hastie & Kumar, 1979; Hemsley & Marmurek, 1982; Srull, 1981) concluding that because schema-incongruent information is out of character, it is more salient and more memorable; other researchers (C. E. Cohen, 1981; J. T. Johnson & Judd, 1983; Rothbart, Evans, & Fulero, 1979) find that incongruent information is not remembered as well. Poor memory for incongruent information may result because it is not initially encoded (see Alba & Hasher, 1983, for a detailed explanation and review of the evidence) and/or because insufficient time is allowed for encoding incongruent information (Berman, Read, & Kenny, 1983; Hastie, 1981; Sentis & Burnstein, 1979). Another possible explanation

(R. C. Anderson & Pichert, 1978) for the loss of incongruent items is that such information is encoded but, because of insufficient or irrelevant retrieval cues, it is not available for recall. The puzzle has not yet been solved.

Thus, for partisan schematics, we expect to find both a facilitation effect, as evidenced by more accurate recognition of congruent information, and signs of information-processing bias. A well-developed schema should facilitate the recognition of old policies that are congruent with the partisan schema as well as help sophisticates reject new policies that are incongruent with their schematic expectations. A congruency bias would be demonstrated when subjects erroneously attribute new congruent policies to the Congressman and recognize more of his old congruent than old incongruent policy statements. Aschematics, in contrast, lacking a well-developed partisan schema, should evidence neither facilitation effects nor strong biases but will, predictably, perform at about chance levels for all types of policy statements.

Results. Of the 20 old policy statements, 10 were congruent and 10 incongruent with the Congressman's partisan label, just as 10 of the new policy statements were congruent and 10 incongruent. Responses were coded as correct if the subject answered "Yes, Congressman Williams said that" to an old item that was actually presented earlier or if the subject answered "No, he did not make that policy statement" to a new item. All correct answers received a score of +1; all incorrect and don't know answers received a zero.

Focusing first on the test for schema effects, we find that schematics did indeed correctly recognize more policy statements than did aschematics. The schematic group averaged 60.3% correct recognition and the middle group 53.4%, followed by the aschematics who did no better than chance with 49.7% correct recognition.

A schema effect for different types of information can be examined when the recognition scores are broken down by the four distinct types of policies: old congruent, old incongruent, new congruent, and new incongruent. Considering first the old information, a separate, one-way analysis of variance on the percentage correct recognition scores shows a schema effect only for old congruent policy statements. Here, levels of sophistication are ordered as expected: The aschematic group exhibited the poorest performance (57.2% correct recognition), the middle group performed better (62.4% correct), and schematics demonstrated the most accurate recognition (69% correct).

For the old incongruent items, none of the schema groups did better than chance, a consequence, we believe, of different factors. The inability of sophisticates to recognize incongruent statements actually made by the Congressman is a liability of their partisan schema. Given the avowed partisanship of Congressman Williams and the theory-driven nature of a partisan knowledge structure, schematics failed to recognize 50% of his incongruent statements, yet remembered 69% of his schema-congruent policies. The low recognition level by schematics for the incongruent items could result either from faulty encoding stategies and/or insufficient retrieval cues. Conversely, the failure of aschematics to recognize old incongruent information is in keeping with their general inability to use partisanship as an organizing principle for processing political information. The aschematic group produced low recognition scores for all types of items.[3]

Turning now to the new policies (i.e., positions never expounded by the Congressman), we expect schematics to make more false recognition errors on the congruent than on the incongruent items, whereas aschematics should demonstrate little difference between the two. Aschematics did indeed show a nonsignificant difference in error rate: 56% errors for the congruent items and 52% for the incongruent. Schematics, however, evidenced a strong congruency bias, committing 46% errors for the congruent items and only 31% for the incongruent items. As expected, the middle group is in between, with 54% errors for recognition of the congruent policies and 46% errors for the incongruent policies.

A summary measure of recognition accuracy can be computed by comparing the number of "hits" to "false alarms" for each type of policy. Hits refer to the correct identification of previously read statements as old, whereas false alarms occur when subjects respond "Yes, he said that" to a new item. By then subtracting the false alarm score from the hit score, a measure of accuracy corrected for guessing old is obtained. Scores near zero indicate relatively equal numbers of correct responses and errors, presumably a consequence of random responding or guessing; positive scores reflect the ability to differentiate between presented and nonpresented information.

The aschematic group produced mean scores close to zero for both the

---

[3]One possible explanation for the difference in accurate recall among the three groups is that schematics, having more verbal ability than aschematics, find the initial encoding and therefore the subsequent recognition of policy statements an easier task. The research design allowed us to examine this possibility using each subject's score on the Civil Service vocabulary test. A median split on the vocabulary index produces six subject groups: high and low verbal ability crossed with the three schema levels. Separate two-way ANOVAs, including both level of verbal ability and level of sophistication as factors, yield a main effect of verbal ability for the old congruent, new congruent, and new incongruent items, but in each case, the schema effect is maintained; that is, within each level of verbal ability, schematics score higher than the middle group, who in turn do better than aschematics. Thus, although verbal ability enhances recognition performance, schematics consistently outperform aschematics regardless of their vocabulary score.

congruent (0.50) and incongruent (−1.90) types of policies, thereby confirming predictions of their chance level performance. The middle and high groups exhibited significantly more positive scores, p < .01. The overall accuracy scores for the middle group were 7.90 for congruent items and 5.50 for incongruent items; for the schematics, these scores were significantly greater, 23.10 and 18.20, respectively.

A number of breakdowns of the recognition scores were examined using both schema level and verbal ability as factors to compare the Republican versus Democratic conditions, self-identification as a liberal, moderate, or conservative, and self identification as a Republican, Democrat, or independent. The pattern of results is consistent within each comparison: The high schema group produces the most accurate recognition scores, followed by the middle and then the low schema groups. In other words, one's own partisan or ideological identification does not affect these basic schema processes.

These findings again parallel schema effects found in the social cognition literature and demonstrate the similarities between processing political and nonpolitical information. Our results make evident that the processing of political information is dynamic, at least for sophisticates, who are not passive collectors of information but theory-driven processors. Their prior knowledge about political parties provides cues as to what information to attend to (congruent) and what to ignore (incongruent) and, as a consequence, systematically helps but at other times hinders their ability to process schema-relevant information.

A COGNITIVE MODEL OF SOPHISTICATION

The results of the two experimental studies lend construct validity to our measures of sophistication, whether partisan or ideological. In each case, we can discriminate knowledgeable from unknowledgeable individuals and then show that what is encoded and retrieved from memory is heavily determined by the amount of their previously acquired knowledge. Yet a model of sophistication, whether ideological, partisan, or other, must include more than measures of the amount of domain-relevant declarative knowledge stored in memory. For example, schema theory specifies that cognitive structures are premised on interest and schema-related experience (H. Markus, 1977), both of which may reasonably be thought of as precursors of sophistication.

Figure 5.1 displays a general measurement and structural equation model of ideological sophistication in the LISREL format developed by Joreskog (1973, 1977) and his associates (Joreskog & Sorbom, 1979), and described in English by Bentler (1980) and Long (1983a, b). The results are based on a

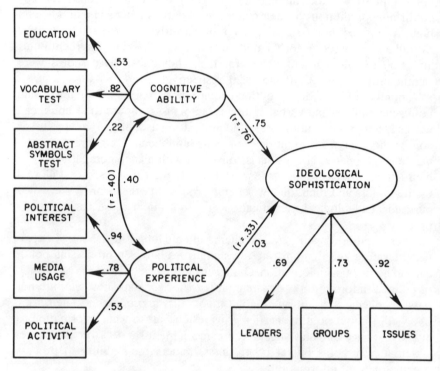

FIG. 5.1   LISREL Estimates of a Model of Ideological Sophistication.

third study (Hamill, Blake, Finkel, & Lodge, 1984) in which we interviewed 180 Long Islanders. The survey included the full array of indicators used in the current measurement model of ideological sophistication (i.e., categorization of leaders, groups, and issues) as well as demographic information, questions tapping political interest and activity, and measures of verbal and abstract ability.

Combining confirmatory factor analysis and structural equation methods, LISREL estimates the linkages between theoretical unobserved variables (e.g., ideological sophistication) and observed variables, which are thought to be indicators of it (e.g., the categorization of leaders, groups, and issues), while simultaneously estimating both the causal effects in structual equations and errors in measurement. LISREL estimates how much of the variance in each observed variable is accounted for by the latent variable and how much is error, whether error of measurement or error caused by the observed variables' relation to one or more factors outside a given model. This task is aided by the production in LISREL of a statistical test of the model's overall goodness of fit to the observed data, thereby providing a method for evaluating the measures of an ideological (as well as partisan, class, or racial) schema and the proposed causal analysis of sophistication.

The right side of Figure 5.1 displays the basic three-component measurement model, where we ask whether the categorization of leaders, groups, and issues as liberal or conservative is a reliable and valid indicator of the ideological sophistication concept. The left side of the figure displays what we call the precursors of sophistication. One set of variables is posited as indicators of *cognitive ability,* the other as indicators of *political experience.*

Employing multiple indicators, cognitive ability is measured by education (years of formal schooling), verbal ability (the score being the number of words correctly defined in a 38-item multiple choice version of the 1975 Civil Service Commission Vocabulary Test), and abstract ability (the score obtained from six items in the Civil Service test, which ask subjects to compare geometric shapes in terms of their similarity). Cognitive ability is incorporated into this model to test hypotheses relating cognitive limitations to sophistication. The argument is that those who do not have the basic wherewithal to handle the ambiguity of political information using the abstract concepts liberal and conservative will, predictably, score low on the ideological sophistication measure (Converse, 1964). We suspect that such individuals may prove able to use other, less abstract schemata (e.g., race and class) to structure their political beliefs (see Hamill, Lodge, & Blake, 1984). The assumption here is that one's general level of cognitive ability is a prerequisite for using the concepts liberal and conservative, as they are more abstract, less "concrete," and less directly experiential than the concepts defining a class schema (rich and poor) or racial schema (black and white).

The second set of precursors of ideological sophistication incorporated in this model includes those indicators of political experience commonly employed by the CPS to explain political behavior, measured here by the standard survey questions asking respondents to rate their interest in public affairs, attention to politics in the media, and participation in such conventional political activities as voting, attending political rallies, and contributing time or money to a campaign. Preliminary evidence from other research (Hamill, Lodge, & Blake, 1984) indicates that such factors do correlate with ideological knowledge. Thus, ideological sophistication—measured by three indicators, each of which is an index score based on the number of leaders, groups, and issues consensually categorized by the sample as liberal or conservative—is hypothesized to be a function of one's cognitive ability and political experience, with both of these precursor variables also measured by three index scores.

In Figure 5.1, the coefficients shown are the standardized correlation coefficients, with the simple correlations noted within parentheses. The reliability of an indicator can be obtained simply by squaring the coefficient from latent variable to that indicator. The overall fit of the proposed model is adequate, X^2 (24, N = 180) = 60.59, but certainly in need of improvement.

Looking first at the components of ideological sophistication, we see that all three indicators are indeed measuring the latent variable, with the ability to categorize policies as liberal or conservative being the most reliable of our measures and the characterization of groups and leaders somewhat less so. Although each of the measures can be strengthened, analyses show that if either the leader or group component were dropped from the measurement model, the effect would be to weaken the overall model. Apparently, then, each of the three measures taps some aspect of the declarative knowledge component of ideological sophistication.

Turning to the precursors of ideological sophistication, we find that cognitive ability (as indicated by education, the Civil Service Vocabulary and Abstract Symbols Tests) exerts a more powerful effect on ideological sophistication than do the indicators of political experience. Political experience, as measured in terms of political interest, activities, and attention to the media, proves at best to have only a marginal impact on one's ideological sophistication. This is not to say that political experience is unrelated to sophistication. The simple product moment correlation is moderately strong at .33, but within the overall causal model, the partial effect drops to a mere .03.

The insignificant effect of political experience on ideological sophistication is at odds with the theoretical literature of both political science and social psychology. Our best guess for this null effect is that these CPS/SRC indicators of political experience (general political interest, participation in conventional political activities, and keeping up with the news in magazines, newspapers, and TV), although reliable, do not capture the kinds of experience that inculcate ideological knowledge.

A word or two about the individual measures defining the latent cognitive ability variable. The vocabulary test score is by far the most reliable indicator, .68, years of schooling a weak second, .29, and the abstract symbols test the least reliable, .05. That education is not a particularly good indicator of cognitive ability is consistent with the findings of Converse (1980) and Abramson (1983). The failure of the abstract symbols test is, perhaps, more a consequence of the test itself (too little variance) than a conceptual deficiency or lack of relationship to cognitive ability. We are in the market for better measures of one's ability to deal with abstractions so as to test the hypothesis that cognitive limitations preclude citizens from learning to use the abstract concepts liberal and conservative and, perhaps to a lesser extent, use the labels Republican and Democrat. Taken together, cognitive ability and political experience explain 58% of the variance in ideological sophistication, once again signaling the need to strengthen the indicators and investigate other variables left out of this model.

CONCLUSIONS: PROBLEMS AND PROSPECTS

Our model of ideological sophistication, though theoretically grounded and empirically validated, is obviously incomplete. As noted earlier, we see the need to develop a measure of the heuristic rules that schematics use to integrate their declarative knowledge about leaders, groups, and issues within one or another political schema. One simple measure of procedural knowledge that we are actively exploring asks subjects which leaders and groups would likely favor or oppose various bills before Congress (e.g., increasing unemployment benefits, providing aid to nonpublic schools). Predictably, ideological schematics will anticipate the likelihood of conflict involving those leaders and groups that are central to the concepts liberal and conservative. They also should provide more possible consequences in greater detail, in a shorter period of time, and with higher levels of confidence than aschematics.

A second, perhaps more serious, deficiency in this model is the absence of a measure of affect. If one is to model political preferences and evaluations, then affect is obviously central. But even here, when dealing with the "purely" cognitive processes of recognition and categorization, affect is likely to be critical. Recent provocative findings in the cognitive literature suggest that one's likes and dislikes influence what and how information is encoded and retrieved from memory (Fiske & Taylor, 1984; Zajonc, 1980). Should this be the case, affect—perhaps measured simply by tapping subjects' positive and negative evaluations of schema labels and the exemplars of each concept—will provide a dramatic improvement in the measurement model of ideological sophistication.

Thus far, we have purposely, and successfully, avoided using the term *belief system*. Yet at this point, it seems necessary to acknowledge and clarify the relationship between schemata, as operationalized here in terms of declarative knowledge, and the more conventional levels of conceptualization measure of political sophistication used in the National Election Survey (Campbell, Converse, Miller, & Stokes, 1960; Converse, 1964).

On a theoretical level, there are many similarities between the two concepts as Lau indicates in his chapter in this volume. Both provide for cognitive economy; both see ideology, parties, groups, and issues as possible reference points for evaluating political stimuli; both recognize that relative expertise influences the way we handle new political information. Yet the levels of conceptualization approach is not grounded in schematic theories of memory, which specifically emphasize cognitive limitations and concomitant effects on information processing. We believe that in order to model political behavior, we must learn how to deal more effectively with the cognitive processes involved in political decision making, including the processes involved in the expression of opinions. The schema concept is explicitly directed toward these goals.

Another major distinction between the belief system and schema approaches is that the levels of conceptualization measure erroneously orders sophistication, ranging from those classified as "ideologues" to those with "no issue content," and a person is considered to be in one group or another. In contrast, schema theory does not assume that there is one overarching dimension called ideological (or political) sophistication along which all members of society must be judged; rather, it clearly postulates that there are a number of schemata available for making sense of the world of politics. Because a citizen cannot use one framework (e.g., ideology) does not necessarily imply that the individual has no "judgmental yardstick" for handling political events and should therefore be relegated to the ranks of the uninformed. On the contrary, recent evidence (Hamill, Lodge, & Blake, 1984) indicates that individuals who cannot use partisan or ideological schemata frequently can use other less abstract schemata (e.g., class and race) to deal effectively with the arduous task of political information processing.

We believe that the incorporation of the schema concept into a general theory of political cognition has great potential for the study of broader substantive questions of interest to political scientists. For example, we plan to continue to investigate the possibility that some, perhaps many, individuals who are not ideologically sophisticated may be partisan schematics. If true, what are the consequences of having one political schema rather than another? Is a partisan schema more limiting than an ideological schema, or can it deal effectively with the political information needed to participate "rationally" in electoral politics? Multiple schemata are also possible, perhaps especially among the most sophisticated who, depending on the situation, may be able to apply an ideological, partisan, racial, class, or other schema to the interpretation of political events. If so, under what conditions will the individual use one or the other? These questions have important implications for actual political behavior inasmuch as political leaders apparently "frame" official actions in ways that activate individual schemata and promote popular support (Bennett, 1975). For example, when President Reagan speaks of "outside influences" in Central America, is he attempting to activate the "communist" schema in the typical citizen so as to influence the way citizens take in and evaluate information about conflicts in the area? Are schematics in this case more or less susceptible to the priming of schemata by political leaders? Research on these questions is just beginning (Fiske & Kinder, 1981).

Clearly, the view of an individual as an active information processor focuses on many aspects of political behavior largely ignored by the discipline. Instead of the emphasis on frequencies (i.e., who is and who isn't an ideologue), the information-processing model is a dynamic one that alerts us to the cognitive and behavioral consequences of the content and structure of a particular schema. What kinds of political schemata exist for what kinds of individuals is one important question, but equally important is how individuals seek out, take in, and organize information given their prior knowledge structures.

ACKNOWLEDGMENT

The research reported in this paper was funded by the National Science Foundation, Grant # SES8025069.

6

Political Schemata, Candidate Evaluations, and Voting Behavior

Richard R. Lau
Department of Social Sciences
Carnegie-Mellon University

The current state of knowledge about the limitations on human information processing, or more appropriately, the limits of cognition about social objects, has been described in earlier chapters of this volume. As Herstein (1981) has argued, most of the conventional political science models of the vote decision are, at least in part, cognitively unrealistic because they fail to take these information-processing limitations into consideration. In this chapter, a new and cognitively more realistic model of political information processing is presented. Research that tests and confirms the proposed model (to as great an extent as is possible with the traditional survey-based data of American electoral behavior) is described. Finally, new insights which the model brings to some classic political questions are discussed.

This new model rests heavily on the notion of cognitive *schemata*. Briefly, a schema is a knowledge structure, based on experience, that organizes people's perceptions of the world. Schemata are hierarchically structured, containing a schema label, particular instances of the schema, and generic information relevant to all or almost all of those specific instances. Schemata organize the processing and storage of incoming information, and they guide the recall and interpretation of information already in memory. Readers less familiar with the schema concept are urged to turn to the review of the literature on social schemata in the final chapter before reading on.

A SCHEMATIC MODEL
OF POLITICAL INFORMATION PROCESSING[1]

I have integrated what we have learned about schemata (see chapter 18, this volume) into a model of political information processing that guides the research presented here. Based on past studies of voting behavior, I expect people's schemata for politicians to emphasize some limited combination of issues, group relations, party identification, and/or candidate personality factors. I call each of these four *political schemata*. Any individual may have one or more (but because of cognitive limitations, not many) political schemata. These political schemata should guide the formation of person schemata for specific politicians. Now the elements (i.e., the specific issues, groups, or traits) associated with each candidate will differ, but the same general dimensions or schemata should be applied by an individual to all politicians.

A rather formal political information-processing model is depicted in Figure 6.1. People live in a given (political) information environment. They have little control over this environment; it is set by politicians, world events, and the media. Of course, no individual is exposed to every bit of information in the political environment. But even the most interested and persistent voter cannot learn a candidate's position on an issue if the candidate refuses to reveal his or her position. On the other hand, no one is aware of (i.e., can remember and understand) all the political information to which he or she is exposed. Certainly some exposure to politics is self-selected, but a good deal of it is random or haphazard. When a person is presented with some political information (for whatever reason), the individual tries to "fit" that information into a preexisting political schema. If the information is irrelevant to the schema, it is unlikely to be recalled. If the information is relevant to and consistent with a schema, it is very likely to be remembered. Whether information that is relevant but inconsistent will be remembered depends on the level of expertise or development of the schema.

Thus, the information that an individual holds about any politician or any political event is jointly a function of the information to which the individual is exposed (which is, for the most part and for most people, beyond the individual's control) and the individual's political schemata, which facilitate the processing, storage, and later recall of that information.[2] I also assume, following Fiske (this volume) that each schema, and every bit of information in the schema, has affect associated with it. For example,

---

[1]Richard Smith and I have worked together in developing this model.

[2]I leave aside, for the moment, the question of how political schemata develop in the first place.

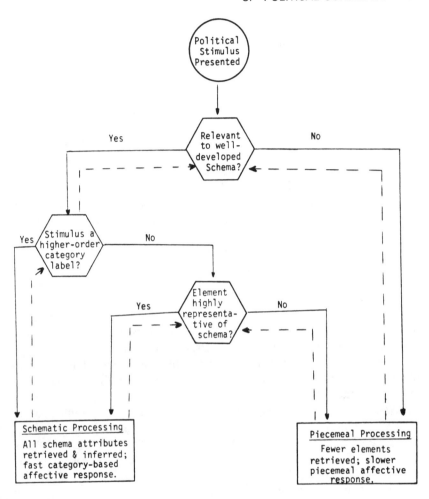

FIG. 6.1   A Schematic Model of Political Information Processing.

learning that a particular politician favors abortion also means automatically associating a certain affect, either positive or negative, with that
politician. Now, if the person holds a well-developed issue schema, learning
that a politician favors abortion will probably lead to a quick category-
based affective response because one's stand on abortion is very diagnostic
(or highly representative) of a liberal or conservative. If the person does
not hold a strong issue schema but does hold a strong party schema, say,
then information about a politician's stand on abortion will contribute little
or nothing to affective evaluations of that politician, as long as party
information is available about that candidate. Finally, if the individual
holds no strong political schema or if available information does not allow

categorization of the politician into a well-developed schema, then affective evaluations will be piecemeal. The overall evaluation of the politician will be a "running total" of all the affect associated with every individual bit of information known about that politician.

The reader will note that I have defined political schemata by topics (issues, groups, parties, personalities) rather than by roles. If the only type of political judgments people made were about politicians, then the most efficacious way of thinking about political schemata would be in terms of different types of typical politician-role schemata. For example, individuals might hold some combination of role schemata such as liberal politician, conservative politician, big city machine politician, "our group" politician, "their group" politician, Democratic politician, Republican politician, charismatic politician, and so on. I have chosen to talk about and operationalize political schemata, rather than politician schemata, because I think they are more general. If we talk about politician schemata, we are limiting ourselves to considering information processing about politicians. Thinking about more general political schemata, on the other hand, allows one to consider the processing of information about politicians, but it is also relevant to processing information about other countries or governments, about specific government policy actions, about Supreme Court decisions, about political tolerance, and so forth. Processing information about these other political topics is not addressed in this paper, but I have tried to define (and operationalize) political schemata in a way that will facilitate their consideration at some later time.

How can one best study and test such a model of political information processing? One way, and perhaps the best way, is to adopt the methods and procedures of cognitive psychology. This is the path that has been taken by Hamill and Lodge (this volume). Reaction time, false recognitions, and the like become the prime indicators of schematic processing in laboratory studies. Another procedure is to focus on the organizational properties of schemata, using Q-sorts or similar technologies to study cognitive structure. This is the route taken by Conover and Feldman in some of their work (1984). Again, fairly elaborate, time-consuming procedures are required. A third route, and the one which I have followed in this research, is to be as innovative or opportunistic as one can in measuring schemata with traditional survey data. This route is inevitably less precise than other routes, in which the procedures are specifically designed to measure political schemata. On the other hand, by utilizing traditional survey data, one can more easily integrate one's findings into the existing political behavior literature. The remainder of this paper describes the examination of political schemata to which I have been led by this third route.

MEASURING POLITICAL SCHEMATA

What indicators of political schemata are available in the standard Center for Political Studies (CPS) election study? If one eschews closed-ended questions because it is too easy for anyone to pick a number between 1 and 7 irrespective of schema content, one is left with the handful of open-ended questions asked in the surveys. The most appropriate and useful open-ended questions are a series asked in the preelection survey concerning respondents' likes and dislikes about the major parties and candidates in that election. These particular open-ended questions have the advantage of being asked near the beginning of the interview, before potential responses have been contaminated by other questions. They are asked about multiple attitude objects in a similar manner, thus allowing an examination of consistency in responding across attitude objects. These questions are also useful in that they have been asked in almost precisely the same way in every election study since 1952. Thus, if the validity of employing these items as indicators of schema content can be established here, the same procedure can be employed on prior and presumably future election studies.

I have utilized the 1972 and 1976 CPS National Election Studies for my analysis.[3] The 1972 study was a representative sample of U.S. citizens in the contiguous 48 states. Due to a complicated design, the crucial open-ended questions were only asked of a random half of this sample (Form I), thus reducing the potential n to 1,372. As many of the respondents from 1972 who could be followed over 4 years were reinterviewed in 1976. These respondents make up the 1972–1976 panel study, which figures prominently in the analyses that follow. I am only interested in the Form I panel subjects, however, or 671 respondents. Because there is a rather severe (although by no means unexpected) subject loss over the 4 years, these panel respondents should not be considered a random sample. Additional (nonpanel) respondents were interviewed in 1976, yielding a total sample of 2,561 for that year.

The precise wordings of these crucial open-ended questions were: "Now I'd like to ask you what you think are the good and bad points about the parties. Is there anything in particular that you like about the Democratic Party? (If yes:) What is that? . . . Anything else?" In 1972, up to three "likes" were recorded about the Democratic party. The respondents were asked if there was anything they didn't like about the Democratic party, followed by likes and dislikes about the Republican party. Next respondents were told: "Now I'd like to ask you about the good and bad points of the two major candidates for president. Is there anything in particular about McGovern

---

[3]As always, neither the consortium nor the original collectors of the data bear any responsibility for the analysis and interpretations presented herein.

that might make you want to vote for him? (What is it? . . . Anything else? . . .)
Is there anything about McGovern that might make you want to vote
against him? (What is it? . . . Anything else?)." Again up to three likes and
three dislikes were recorded. Identical questions about Nixon followed
those concerning McGovern. These questions were asked in precisely the
same way in 1976, although the two candidates were of course different. Up to
five likes and dislikes about the parties and candidates were recorded in 1976,
but for comparability, only the first three likes or dislikes were examined.

By utilizing open-ended questions as indicators of schema content, I am
employing "cued free recall," one of the most popular but, alas, least
precise measures of schema content (Taylor & Fiske, 1981). Now certainly,
the responses given to these questions are partially a function of recent
(and therefore easily remembered), haphazard exposure to politics, through
a conversation with a friend or through some political propaganda. As
such, they probably have little to do with political schemata. But just as
certainly, these responses partially reflect some underlying cognitive structure,
some readiness to process, store, and have available for recall certain types
of political information. This measure can be further refined by weighting
items according to the order in which they are recalled. Presumably, the
first items recalled about any attitude object are the most readily available
and are therefore the most indicative of schema content. Inevitably, this
variable must include a good deal of random noise, which will decrease the
power of the analyses to find significant effects. Whether there is enough
"true score" in this measure of political schemata to find reliable effects is
the question to which I now turn.

CONSISTENCY AND RELIABILITY
OF SCHEMA MEASURES

If political schemata exist and if they can be measured with open-ended
questions in a survey, then one should observe some underlying consistency in the type of information processed (and therefore recalled) about
different attitude objects. The various responses to the open-ended questions were categorized into items relevant to groups, parties, issues, candidate personalities, and other (see Appendix to this chapter for exact
coding). The first four categories were the hypothesized political schemata.
Then a weighted proportion of the total number of likes and dislikes about
each attitude object (Democrats, Republicans, and the two major presidential candidates) that fell into each of the crucial four categories was
computed. The weighting procedure counted the first response 3, the
second response 2, and the third response 1. The count started over for
each open-ended question (i.e., for the likes and dislikes about all four

attitude objects). These weighted counts of the number of responses falling into the four crucial categories were then divided by a similarly weighted count of the total number of responses offered about each attitude object. For example, suppose a respondent said she likes George McGovern because "he would get us out of Vietnam once and for all," because "he wants to help poor people," and because "his negative income tax plan would straighten out welfare"; she dislikes him, however, because "he seems somewhat indecisive." This respondent would have a total count of 9 (3 + 2 + 1 for the three likes, + 3 for the one dislike) as a base for McGovern. The first and third likes fall into the issues category; hence, this respondent would have a score of .444 (|3 + 1|/9) on the issues schema measure for McGovern. The second response is group-related, resulting in a score of .222 (2/9) for a groups schema. The one dislike is personality related; it would receive a 3, and the candidate personality schema score for McGovern would therefore be .333 (3/9). Finally, no responses were party relevant, and thus, the party schema score would be 0.

This scoring procedure controls for the total number of responses offered about each attitude object, thus eliminating simple verbosity and the things associated with it (e.g., education) from the operationalization. Consequently, every respondent received a score ranging from 0 to 1.0 for each relevant schema dimension for the four attitude objects. The scores represent a weighted proportion of all responses offered about a given political attitude object which fell into each of the four schema dimensions or categories. Respondents who had nothing to say about any of the four attitude objects were coded 0 on all schema measures (as long as the questions were asked). Thus, four separate measures of the groups dimension and of the issues dimension were available in each election year, one for each major party and candidate; only two measures of the party and candidate personality dimensions were available because these involved relevant responses only for the two major candidates.

The intercorrelations among these various measures of schema content are presented in Table 6.1 for the 1972 and 1976 samples. If schemata do indeed guide the processing of political information and if they are being measured with some reliability, then the correlations of the two to four measures of each political schema should be positive. The items in Table 6.1 have been grouped to facilitate these comparisons. As one can easily see by viewing the table, this first hypothesis is strongly supported. Of the 28 relevant (i.e., schematic) correlations in the two samples, 26 are significant, and all are positive. There is a built-in dependency among the different schema measures from a single attitude object; that is, the more group-related responses one gives about Democrats, the less issue-related things one can say about them. Most of these "intraobject" correlations are significant and negative. For example, the proportion of group-related

TABLE 6.1
Consistency of Schema Measures

	1.	2.	3.	4.	5.	6.	7.	8.	9.	10.	11.	12.
Groups												
1. Democrats	—	.44*	.09*	.12*	.02	.02	-.15*	.03	.01	.05	.08*	.01
2. Republicans	.41*	—	.07*	.17*	.05	.04	.08	-.11*	.05	.06*	.06	.02
3. McGovern/Carter	.23*	.08	—	.19*	-.03	.00	-.00	-.03	-.05	.07*	-.28*	-.10*
4. Nixon/Ford	.13*	.18*	.11*	—	-.01	-.03	.03	.02	.08*	-.06	-.04	-.21*
Party												
5. McGovern/Carter	.09*	.14*	-.06	.04	—	.29*	.06	-.01	-.07*	.00	-.18*	-.09*
6. Nixon/Ford	.04	.09*	.04	-.04	.22*	—	.02	.03	-.06	-.08	-.05	-.18
Issues												
7. Democrats	-.11*	.05	-.01	.05	.06	.04	—	.38*	.08*	.12*	.07*	.03
8. Republicans	.08	-.11*	-.06	.04	-.01	.03	.40*	—	.06	.09*	.10*	.04
9. McGovern/Carter	.07	.07	-.11*	-.01	-.09*	.00	.13*	.12*	—	.17*	-.38*	-.06
10. Nixon/Ford	.06	.03	.09*	-.09	-.01	-.08	.18*	.20*	.24*	—	-.04	-.35
Personality												
11. McGovern/Carter	-.08	.04	-.21*	-.03	-.11*	-.03	.01	-.02	-.34	-.11*	—	.31*
12. Nixon/Ford	-.03	-.00	-.04	-.19*	-.07	-.07	-.10*	-.06	-.08	-.51*	.29*	—

Note. Table entries are Pearson correlations. Correlations in the lower quadrant are from 1972 ($n = 2,561$). Correlations in the upper quadrant are from 1976 ($n = 1,372$).

*$p < .001$.

responses about the Democratic party in 1972 correlates $-.11$ with the proportion of issue-related statements about the Democrats. There are 24 of these dependent correlations. But there is no such built-in dependency across attitude objects. Of the 80 remaining nondependent correlations, only 20 are significant, and 8 of these significant correlations are negative. Hence, it is clear that the 26 out of 28 significantly positive schematic correlations are not simply a function of the large sample size.

On the other hand, although these relevant schematic correlations are all positive and mostly significant, the size of the correlations (mean = .20) is hardly overwhelming. The relatively small size of the relevant correlations reflects: (a) that 16 of the 28 (and both nonsignificant) schematic correlations are between moderately distinct attitude objects—a political party and a politician (the eight schematic correlations between two parties or two candidates averages a more respectable .30); and (b) that the operationalization of schemata is far from exact, as I argued it would be. The internal consistencies (coefficient alpha) of the two to four measures of each schema dimension, one indicator of how reliably each dimension is being measured, range from .36 to .52. These reliabilities are moderately low, even given the small number of items figuring in each reliability estimate, confirming that the measures of schema content include a good deal of random error.

The items measuring each political schema were combined to form a summary scale. The intercorrelations among these summary measures of political schemata, both within and across election years, were computed using the smaller panel sample. To the extent the operationalization of political schemata is tapping some enduring cognitive structures rather than ephemeral memory traces, these schema measures should be stable over time. The only significant cross-temporal correlations are those between the measures of the same schema dimension in 1972 and 1976. These correlations range from .14 for the party schema, .19 for the candidate personality schema, .31 for the issues schema, to .39 for the groups schema. Of course, all correlations are attenuated due to measurement error (which, as we have already seen, was substantial).

In order to get more accurate estimates of the actual stability of the four schema measures, all 24 individual correlations from Table 6.1 (from the panel sample only) were entered into a LISREL analysis (Joreskog & Sorbom, 1978). LISREL examines the underlying structural relations among a set of unobserved or "latent" constructs. The program simultaneously tests the hypothesized structural relations and a measurement (or factor analytic) model for the latent constructs. For present purposes, the most important aspect of a LISREL analysis is that measurement error is removed from the estimates of the structural paths.

A very simple structural model was posited, in which each political schema was treated as a latent construct, imperfectly determining its two to four manifest indicators. The political schemata in 1976 are "caused" only by the comparable schema in 1972. The results from testing this model are shown in Figure 6.2. The coefficients in the figure are standardized LISREL estimates. Paths from the latent constructs to the observed variables are in essence factor loadings. The square of these loadings is the reliability of each manifest indicator. The important paths are those between the political schema measures in 1972 and 1976. Because of the simple structure of this model, these paths can be thought of as stability correlations. All four of these stability coefficients are highly significant. The arrows pointing to the latent constructs in 1976 are residual variances, the amount of unexplained variance in the construct. Conversely, 1 minus the residual variance is the amount of variance in each construct explained solely by that same construct measured in 1972. This explained variance runs from 10% for the party schema to 64% for the candidate personality schema. The data provide a very good fit to the model: X^2 $(223, N = 677) = 450, p < .001$. For readers familiar with fit indices (Bentler & Bonet, 1980), rho = .90, delta = .86.

Validity of Political Schema Measures

The operationalizations of political schemata are thus reasonably reliable and reasonably stable over time. The validity of these operationalizations has not been established, however. In order to determine whether or not these operationalizations are actually measuring political schemata, we must examine associations between them and other variables with which, theoretically, they should correlate. The theory is rather informal and quite general: Schemata guide the processing of related information. Thus, each schema measure should correlate with other measures of related political information. Validity tests for each schema dimension are described in the following subsections.

Groups Schema.   If a political schema for groups guides the processing of group-related information, then a person with a highly developed groups schema (i.e., an expert) should: (a) be consistent in his or her affective evaluations of groups involved in politics, (b) have tightly constrained attitudes about different groups, (c) be able to locate or place a variety of different groups on issues relevant to those groups, and (d) be reasonably accurate in stating which candidate or party is better off for each group. It is possible to examine each of these different validity criteria.

Holding a well-developed political groups schema should result in more stable, affective evaluations of groups. The logic behind this prediction is simple: People with well-developed group schemata will make category-based affective responses. Any new information about a group will not

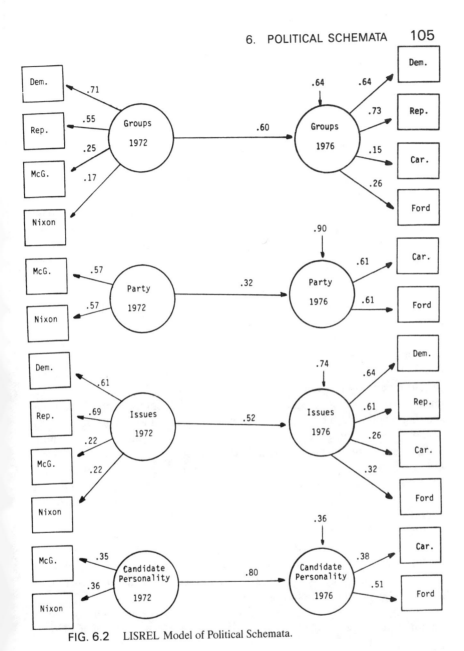

FIG. 6.2 LISREL Model of Political Schemata.

radically change one's evaluation of that group unless it invalidates or changes the initial categorization. If one does not hold a groups schema, however, evaluations of a group will be piecemeal. Any new information about the group (with its associated affect) could easily change the running total average rating of the group.

Respondents evaluated a variety of groups involved in politics on affective "feeling thermometers" in both 1972 and 1976. Respondents with a well-developed political groups schema (or schematics), operationally defined as respondents who gave more than one quarter group-related responses to the eight open-ended questions from which the political schema measures were constructed (21% in 1972, 18% in 1976), were contrasted to respondents with no group schema (or aschematics), operationally defined as respondents who gave no group-related responses to the eight open-ended questions (46% in 1972, 48% in 1976). Stability coefficients for affective ratings of 16 groups involved in politics during the 1970s were computed separately for the two groups of respondents. The 1972 group schema measure is employed. Because one might expect more educated or otherwise "advantaged" people to hold more stable attitudes quite apart from schemata, education and income are partialled out of the stability correlations. The hypothesis is strongly supported. The stability correlations are significantly higher for respondents with a well-developed groups schema for 12 of the 16 groups.[4] On the average, the stability coefficients are 14 points higher for the schematic group.

One of the functions schemata serve is to organize information in a particular domain. The more developed the schema, the more information should be associated with the schema, and the more interconnections there should be among the elements associated with the schema. This reasoning leads to the prediction that people with well-developed political group schemata will hold more tightly constrained beliefs about a group or about two closely related groups compared to people without group schemata. Besides evaluating groups on feeling thermometers, respondents were also asked whether each group had too much, about the right amount, or too little power in society. The more information one holds about a group, and the more stable that information is, the stronger should be forces toward cognitive consistency or constraint among these different group-related attitudes. When one holds little or no knowledge about a group, on the other hand, and when one's beliefs and attitudes toward a group are mostly in the form of "nonattitudes" (Converse, 1964), as should be the case for people without group schemata, one may not even notice inconsistencies among related beliefs about a group.

Strong support for the hypothesized differences is found when the constraint in group-related beliefs of the two groups of respondents in 1976 are

---

[4]The 16 groups were: liberals, radical students, marijuana users, conservatives, the military, policemen, big business, middle class people, workingmen, labor unions, poor people, women's liberation movement, whites, blacks, black militants, and civil rights leaders. Affective evaluations of poor people were significantly more stable among aschematics; there was no difference between groups in the stability of evaluations of middle class people, workingmen, and whites. Evaluations of all the remaining groups were significantly more stable among schematics.

contrasted. Only the 1976 data were examined because: (a) the "group power" list was more complete and (b) the group affect and group power items were separated from each other during the interview, thus reducing any artificially inflated correlations due to continuity in item placement (see Sears & Lau, 1983). Closely related groups (e.g., big business and businessmen; labor unions and workingmen) were combined for this analysis.[5] People with highly developed group schemata held more tightly constrained beliefs about eight of the nine groups (or group "clusters") examined. On the average, the constraint of the schematic group was 12 points higher than the constraint of the aschematic group; 36 of the 38 individual comparisons were higher in the schematic group compared to the aschematic group, a pattern significantly different from chance, $p < .001$.

The 1972 and 1976 surveys contained a set of 7-point issue items on which respondents were asked to list their own positions. For example, in both 1972 and 1976, respondents were asked:

> Some people are primarily concerned with doing everything possible to protect the legal rights of those accused of committing crimes. Others feel that it is more important to stop criminal activity even at the risk of reducing the rights of the accused. Where would you place yourself on this scale, or haven't you thought much about this?

Respondents were handed a card with the numbers 1 to 7 on it. "Protect rights of accused" was written next to the number 1. "Stop crime regardless of rights of accused" was written next to the number 7. If respondents had a position themselves, they were also asked to place the two major candidates, the two major parties, and occasional groups (whites and blacks in 1972; whites, blacks, liberals, and conservatives in 1976) on this same scale. There were 10 such issue scales in each survey. It is simple to compute the proportion of groups that a respondent can locate on these issue scales.[6] It is important to note that there is no criterion of accuracy in this measure, just willingness to place a group on the 7-point scale. Nonetheless, this measure correlates significantly with the measure of group schemata in both 1972 and 1976.

In 1976, respondents were asked whether each of 16 different groups would be better off, worse off, or the same if Carter or Ford were elected.

---

[5]Besides the two already mentioned, the group clusters included: liberals, conservatives, middle class people, people on welfare and poor people, women's liberation movement and women, whites, and blacks and black militants. Whites were the one group in which constraint was no higher among schematics compared to aschematics.

[6]The denominator is the number of issues on which a respondent places him- or herself, not the total number of issues, because respondents are not asked to place groups on issue unless they have a position themselves.

By comparing responses to the paired questions, one can construct indices of "better with Carter," "better with Ford," or "neither" for each of the 16 groups. Now one could simply count the number of items answered here, as was previously done with the placement of groups on issues. But here it was fairly easy to determine "correct" responses to these questions. I hypothesized that respondents with group schemata would be more accurate in naming the groups that would be better off with either candidate. Several different criteria for accuracy were employed: the normative response, the normative response of those with more than a high school education, the normative response of those "identified with" each group.[7] Each of these criteria resulted in slightly different definitions of correct answers to which candidate's election (if either) would be advantageous to each group, but the results were all very similar: The higher the group schema measure, the more accurate the respondent in reporting which groups would be helped by the two candidates, rs vary between .18 and .22, $p < .001$.

Issues Schema.   There are two types of validity criteria available for a political issues schema. The first type is the proportion of issues on which the respondent has a position and the proportion of issues on which the respondent can place the two major candidates, the two major parties, and a variety of different groups (this last variable was also used as a validity criterion for the groups schema). Simple correlations between these four criteria and the measure of issue schemata from both 1972 and 1976 were computed. All correlations are highly significant, if not terribly impressive (mean $r = .20$, range .12-.26). Recalling the less than perfect reliabilities of the schema measures and undoubtedly of the four validity criteria, these simple correlations were recalculated and corrected for attenuation due to measurement error. The reliabilities of the four validity criteria were estimated from their stability across the 4 years of the panel; these estimates ranged from .30 for placement of groups on the issues to .55 for placement of candidates and parties on the issues. When these corrected correlations are employed, the validity coefficients appear much more substantial, ranging from .30 to .43 in 1972 and from .42 to .48 in 1976. Most impressive are the validity correlations which involve the schema measure from 1972 and the validity criteria from 1976. The corrected validity correlations range from .32 to .53. These last validity correlations are most impressive because the schema measure was obtained 4 years prior to the validity measures; therefore, no artificial inflation of associations due to the measures being obtained during the same interview is possible.

---

[7]Respondents were shown a list of 16 groups and asked which of the groups they felt particularly "close to." For purposes of this paper, "identifying with" a group means "feeling close to" it (see Lau, 1983, for a more thorough description of group identification).

The second validity criterion for an issue schema is constraint among issue stands. The reasoning behind this criterion was given earlier: The more highly developed an issue schema a person has, the more information about issues he or she holds, and the more interconnections exist between that information. Respondents were categorized into those with no evidence of an issue schema (i.e., those who did not mention any issues in response to the eight open-ended questions; 27% in 1972, 37% in 1976) and those who held a well-developed issue schema (more than a quarter of all responses to the open-ended questions were issue relevant; 35% in 1972, 24% in 1976). Issue constraint was calculated separately for each of these groups, vis-à-vis their own attitudes and their perceptions of the positions of the two major presidential candidates and the two major parties. In 8 of the 10 comparisons (all but the respondent's own positions in 1972 and perceptions of the Democratic party's positions in 1976), constraint was higher in the schematic group than in the aschematic group. These differences are not large, but given the number of individual correlations on which they are based, most of them are significant.[8]

Candidate Personality Schema.   There was one good validity criteria for a candidate personality schema. In both election surveys, respondents were asked the extent to which they would ascribe a number of different traits to each presidential candidate. In 1972, these traits included "could be trusted," has the "kind of personality a president should have," "would control crime," and "would bring peace in Vietnam." In 1976, the traits included "trust," "presidential personality," "bring moral and religious standards to government," "reduce unemployment," "make government run better," "reduce power and size of government," and "reduce inflation." If one has a well-developed candidate personality schema, one should be quite willing and able to attribute these different traits to the two candidates. If one does not notice, process, or attend to such personality-relevant information about candidates (i.e., if one does not hold a candidate personality schema), such trait attributions would be harder to make. The number of trait ascriptions made to all candidates in each election year were counted (regardless of how strongly the trait was ascribed), and this count was correlated with the measure of candidate personality schemata. These correlations were highly significant, $r = .15, p < .001$ in 1972 ($r = .39$ when corrected for attenuation due to measurement error); $r = .26, p < .001$ in 1976 (corrected $r = .66$). These validity correlations are of similar magnitude to those reported for the other political schema types.

---

[8]The null hypothesis for the significance tests was an equal proportion of larger correlations in each (schematic and aschematic) sample. I calculated the binomial probability of observing, say, 30 out of 45 larger correlations in the schematic sample. Because these correlations are not all independent, however, such a significance test is not strictly appropriate.

Party Schema.   The last political schema type to be validated was the party schema. The most obvious validating criterion for a party schema is party identification. Clearly, noticing and processing information about parties should be conducive to holding a strong party identification, but the opposite causal direction must also be considered. It is quite plausible that holding a strong party identification leads to the development of a strong party schema. As we know, party identification develops as early as any political attitude (Sears, 1975). The issue of what causes political schemata is addressed later. For purposes of validating the party schema measure, one must only hypothesize an association between that measure and strength of party identification. To be consistent with earlier analyses, the party schema is treated as the independent variable, and strength of party identification is considered the dependent variable.

Respondents were divided into those with some evidence of a party schema and those with no such evidence. In contrast to the other schema measures, the operationalization of party schemata produced very skewed distributions. In 1972, only 6% of the respondents mentioned anything relevant to party in the four open-ended questions about the two candidates. In 1976, the numbers rose slightly to 8.5%. These skewed distributions certainly limit the magnitude of any correlations between the party schema measures and any other variables and help explain the noticeably lower reliability estimates for this measure. Given the theoretical importance of party identification to American voting behavior research, the limited variance of the operationalization of a party schema is a serious drawback. Be that as it may, respondents who made any mention of party in the four open-ended questions were called schematic, and the strength of their party identifications was contrasted to that of the remainder of the sample. The standard 7-point CPS party identification scale was folded at its midpoint, with independent-independents coded 0 and strong Democrats or Republicans coded 3. Consistent with the hypothesis, people with party schemata had stronger party identification in both 1972 (2.23) and 1976 (2.26) than those without party schemata (1.75 and 1.68, respectively), $t(133) = 5.27, p < .001$ and $t(275) = 9.69, p < .001$. This relationship still holds when the 1972 party schema measure is used with strength of party identification in 1976 as the criterion (2.30 vs. 1.77), $t(81) = 4.31, p < .001$.

A second criterion available for establishing the validity of the party schema measure is constraint among placement of the parties on the issues. In both 1972 and 1976, constraint in placement of both the Democratic and Republican parties on the issues averaged about .04 higher in the schematic group compared to the aschematic group. Only once was this difference significant, however.

Discriminant Validity.   So far, criterion or predictive validity has been established for the political schema measures. Each of the criteria has involved some combination of responses to close-ended questions. The discriminant validity of the four schema measures has not been established, however. That is, although it has been shown that all four schema measures are individually associated with criteria with which, theoretically, they ought to be associated, it has not been shown that they are not similarly associated with criteria with which they should not be correlated. One last validity analysis attempts to establish discriminant validity for the schema measures. Respondents to the 1976 survey were asked two sets of open-ended questions in addition to those on which the schema measures were based. First, respondents were asked for their impressions of the differences between the Democratic and Republican parties. Up to five responses were recorded. Most of the responses fell into either group-related or issue-related categories. Simple counts were made of the proportion of all responses falling into these two categories, weighted by the order in which responses were given. Later, in the postelection interview, respondents who had watched any of the presidential or vice-presidential debates were asked what, if any, impressions they had of the debates and what, if anything, they had learned from them. Up to three responses were recorded for each question, limited of course to those respondents who had seen at least one debate. These responses fell into three categories: (a) those involving some group in society; (b) those involving issues; and (c) those involving impressions of the candidates themselves (including the candidates' physical appearance, personalities, performance in the debate, and qualifications for the presidency). Proportions of all responses falling into these three categories were also calculated, again weighted by the order in which the response was given.

Correlations were calculated between all four political schema measures and these five criteria. The measure of a political groups schema correlates positively with perceived group-related party differences, $r = .15, p < .01$, and with group-related impressions from the debates, $r = .06, p < .05$, but with none of the other criteria; the measure of an issues schema correlates positively with perceived issue differences between the parties, $r = .09$, $p < .01$, and with issue-related impressions from the debates, $r = .11, p < .01$, but with no other criteria; the candidate personality schema correlates positively with candidate-related impressions from the debates, $r = .18$, $p < .01$, but with no other criteria; and finally, the party schema measure does not correlate with any of the five criteria. The one significant positive correlation that was not predicted is the association between the candidate personality schema and perceived issue-related party differences. Despite this one exception, the discriminant validity of the four schema measures is considerable.

POLITICAL SCHEMATA
AND LEVELS OF CONCEPTUALIZATION

Many readers may be wondering about the differences between political schemata, as operationalized here, and the more conventional levels of conceptualization. First introduced in *The American Voter* (Campbell, Converse, Miller, & Stokes, 1960; see also Converse, 1964, 1970, 1975), the levels of conceptualization are a categorization scheme meant to distinguish respondents who hold broadly different frames of reference or "belief systems" for evaluating political stimuli. One's belief system aids the interpretation of new information by supplying "a manageable number of ordering dimensions that permit the person to make sense of a broad range of events" (Campbell et al., 1960, p. 193). As such, belief systems also provide for cognitive economy. Respondents are placed into one of four categories: ideology or near ideology, group benefits, nature of the times, and no issue content. This categorization scheme is meant to be ordinal, running from the most to the least politically sophisticated. Moreover, the categorization is accomplished by examining responses to the same open-ended questions that were used to operationalize political schemata. Hence, on the face of it, there are many similarities between political schemata and levels of conceptualization.[9]

The similarity is not accidental because schemata capture the same sense as levels of conceptualization or belief systems. There are important theoretical and empirical differences between the two, however, which should be pointed out. First, the levels of conceptualization are based on attitude theory; any cognitive economy that results from a grouping of attitudes is coincidental. Schemata are based on research in psychology, which recognizes definite limitations on information processing; political schemata, therefore, begin with the idea of cognitive economy. A second difference is that the levels of conceptualization place respondents into one of four categories. A person is an ideologue, or a group benefits person, or a nature of the times person, or a no issue content person. Four separate political schemata have also been operationalized, but with the schema approach, every respondent gets a score on all four political schemata. Mathematically, it is possible to be schematic (by the previously defined cut-points) on all four schema, although theoretically one would not expect anyone to hold all four political schemata because of cognitive limitations. Holding two separate, well-developed political schemata is quite feasible, however.

A third distinction between the approaches is that the four levels of conceptualization are explicitly ordered. The most politically sophisticated

---

[9]See Lau and Erber (1985) for an alternative view of political sophistication.

people, the political elites, are ideologues; the least sophisticated people are the no issue content respondents. The idea of ordering is so strong in the levels of conceptualization that the term is often used synonymously with political sophistication. Without questioning the ordering implied by the levels of conceptualization, the political schema measures do not assume any ordering between, or make any value judgments about, the different schema types. People are viewed as more or less sophisticated or more or less expert in their utilization of any given political schema, but all schemata are equally effective in serving their primary purpose, which is guiding the processing of political information.

The last distinction between levels of conceptualization and political schemata is an empirical one. A four-category ordinal variable (at best) is difficult to utilize empirically, whereas the four political schema measures approximate continuous variables. Moreover, various operationalizations of levels of conceptualization have been criticized for having virtually no temporal stability (E.R.A.N. Smith, 1980), even though theoretically the levels are an enduring construct. This is a serious drawback to using the levels of conceptualization for anything but cross-sectional analyses. The measures of political schemata, on the other hand, although far from perfectly stable over time, do have sufficient temporal stability to be employed in panel studies.

The distribution of the American public across the four levels of conceptualization is fairly well known. According to the Hagner and Pierce (1982) coding of the levels of conceptualization for the 1972 and 1976 studies, there are 21–22% ideologues, 26–27% group benefits people, 30–34% nature of the times people, and 17–24% no issue content people. For comparison, the proportion of people who are schematic vis-à-vis the four political schemata was also calculated. My definition of schematic is totally arbitrary: More than a quarter of all responses about parties and candidates must be group- or issue-relevant to be considered schematic in terms of those two schemata (21% and 35% for groups and issues, respectively, in 1972; 19% and 25% in 1976); more than half of all responses about the candidates must be personality-relevant to be considered schematic in terms of that measure (29% in 1972, 51% in 1976); and any party-relevant response about the candidates was sufficient to be called schematic in terms of the party schema (6% in 1972, 8.5% in 1976). This arbitrary coding does allow an examination of the different schema types in each election year. Slightly less than half of all respondents held only one type of political schema (6–7% held only a groups schema; 10–21% held only an issues schema; 20–30% held only a candidate personality schema; and 2–3% held only a party schema); 19–24% were schematic in terms of two different types of political schemata, and only 2–3% held three well-developed political schemata. Over a quarter of all respondents did not hold any well-developed political schemata. These percentages must of course be taken with a grain of salt, for they are based on somewhat arbitrary cutoff points. They do, however, give an idea of the relative distribution of the schema types across the population.

ORIGINS OF POLITICAL SCHEMATA

I have discussed political schemata as enduring cognitive structures that influence the processing of political information across multiple election years. This is an accurate view of cognitive structures in general. People are not born with any particular political schema, however; these schemata develop through experience with the political world. If most political information involves party, issues, groups, or individual candidate personalities (and it is my impression that it does), then individual cognitive structures must mirror this information environment. Although we certainly have no precise measure of the political information environment to which an individual has been exposed over the course of a lifetime, one can make very rough estimates of that environment based on obvious background characteristics and measures of current involvement in politics.

Informal hypotheses linking these surrogate measures of political information environments to the different political schemata can then be tested. To examine these hypotheses, the four measures of political schemata in each election year were regressed on six background characteristics (sex, race, age, education, income, parents' interest in politics) and four more current measures of exposure to politics (political knowledge, involvement in the current campaign, print media usage, and electronic media usage; see the appendix to this chapter for details of scale construction). The data are shown in Table 6.2. Only results that are consistent across election years are discussed.

It is stereotypic, and sexist, to believe that men are more interested in issues when it comes to politics and that women are more interested in the personalities of the candidates. But, the data come alarmingly close to supporting this hypothesis: Males are much more likely to hold well-developed issue schemata; females, on the other hand, do not consistently hold stronger candidate personality schemata. I expected nonwhites to hold strong group schemata because their minority status makes reference groups very salient (see Lau, 1983) and strong party schemata because the Democratic party has been a traditional ally to minorities. Both of these hypotheses are supported. In addition, nonwhites are more likely to hold strong issue schemata and less likely to hold strong personality schemata. In other words, nonwhites do not care about the personalities of the candidates who run for President, but they do care about their party, group relations, and issue stands. Two significant effects are found for age: Young people hold stronger issue schemata; older people hold stronger candidate personality schemata.

Both education and income, as indicators of an advantaged background, were hypothesized to be positively related to a strong issue schema, but they are not, at least in the context of other variables that undoubtedly correlate with them. Education is associated with a strong candidate personality schema, however. Parents' interest in politics, political knowledge, and involvement in the current campaign were expected to be positively related to all four political schemata. The parents' interest provides weak and inconsistent results, but the other two variables are strongly associated with all political schemata except party.

Finally, reliance on different media for one's political information was expected to have differential impact on the various political schemata. Patterson and McClure (1976) have shown how television news focuses on the hoopla of campaign crowds and baby kissing at the expense of detailed information about candidates' stands on the issues, which is much more the strength of newspapers. Hence, I hypothesized that reliance on electronic media for one's political news would be associated with well-developed candidate personality schemata, whereas reliance on print media would be associated with a strong issue schema. Disappointingly, neither one of those media variables produces consistent effects.

In order to examine possible interaction effects, $2 \times 2 \times 4$ ANCOVAs were performed on the four schema measures. The three factors were sex, race, and age, with education and income as covariates. Age was recoded to distinguish four political cohorts: those socialized (i.e., having the opportunity to vote in two presidential elections) before the depression, those socialized during the depression and the formation of the New Deal coalitions, those socialized during World War II and the cold war, and those socialized during the 1960s and early 1970s. I hypothesized that those socialized during the New Deal would have strong group schemata, and the data suggested they did, $F(3, 1284) = 4.12, p < .01$ in 1972; $F(3, 2331) = 12.28, p < .001$ in 1976.[10] It was also hypothesized that those socialized during the 1960s and early 1970s would have unusually strong issue schemata. As already indicated by the regressions, they did, $F(3, 1284) = 4.28, p < .01$ in 1972; $F(3, 2331) = 2.08, p < .10$ in 1976. The only interaction effect that was significant in both election years was a three-way Sex $\times$ Race $\times$ Age effect on the party schema, $F(3, 1284) = 4.18, p < .01$ in 1972; $F(3, 2331) = 3.09, p < .05$ in 1976. In both years, older nonwhite males held particularly strong party schemata.

---

[10]In 1972, mean values of the groups schema across the four age groups were .50, .52, .69 (New Deal cohort), and .51. In 1976, the means were .52, .56, .66, and .58.

TABLE 6.2
Origins of Political Schemata

	Group Schema		Issue Schema		Candidate Personality Schema		Party Schema	
	1972	1976	1972	1976	1972	1976	1972	1976
Background Characteristics								
Sex (Female)	.00	.01	-.12****	-.11****	.05*	.02	-.00	-.07***
Race (Nonwhite)	.13****	.12****	.07**	.07***	-.11****	-.12****	.06**	.08***
Age	.01	.00	-.06*	-.04*	.12****	.06***	.08**	.00
Education	-.02	-.02	.04	-.00	.08**	.19****	-.04	-.09***
Income (Logged)	-.01	.00	-.01	.02	.09****	.02	.01	.01
Parents' Interest in Politics	.00	.03	-.04	.04*	.05	-.03	.04	.01
Individual Characteristics								
Political Knowledge	.19****	.06**	.07*	.09****	.01	.09****	.04	.03
Involvement in Campaign	.13***	.19****	.19****	.26****	.09**	.08***	-.01	.06*
Print Media Usage	-.03	.05*	-.05	-.05*	.05	.05*	-.10**	-.02
Electronic Media Usage	-.03	-.01	-.08**	-.01	.06*	.00	.05	-.04
R^2	.07	.08	.06	.11	.10	.12	.02	.02

Note. Table entries are standardized regression weights. *n* in 1972 is 1,072; *n* in 1976 is 2,067.

*p < .10. **p < .05. ***p < .01. ****p < .001.

POLITICAL SCHEMATA AND VOTING BEHAVIOR

The ultimate test of the usefulness of political schemata to voting behavior research is whether they can shed some light on how the vote decision is reached. Theoretically, if schemata guide the processing of political information, they should also determine the type of information on which candidate evaluations are based. That is, if a person holds a strong party schema, his or her evaluation of a political candidate should be strongly based on the party affiliation of the candidate; if a person holds a strong issue schema, candidate evaluations should be strongly influenced by the perceived policy stands of that candidate and so on. To test this theory in the most conservative way possible, political schemata measured in 1972 were used to predict candidate evaluations in 1976. In this manner, no questions about simultaneity in measurement (i.e., measuring the independent variable schemata and dependent variable evaluation at the same time) can arise; no one can wonder whether we have observed the funnel of causality after the vote decision has been reached.

The dependent variable is differential affect for Jimmy Carter and Gerald Ford, a variable that runs from -97 to 97 (the thermometer for Carter was subtracted from that of Ford). Brody and others have argued that such differential affect is tantamount to the vote (Brody & Page, 1973), and it certainly provides more variance to explain than a dichotomous vote decision.

The major independent variables were constructed as follows:

Party Identification: The standard 7-point CPS measure, reduced to 5 points by collapsing together independent leaners and weak partisans; this variable was centered around 0, with "strong Republican" high.

Issue Distances: The difference between a respondent's position on an issue and his or her perceptions of a candidate's position on that same issue was calculated for 10 different issues. The absolute values of these distances were then averaged together as an indication of how "close" the candidate was to the respondent on the issues. The case was counted as missing unless pertinent data from at least four of the issues were available. The issue distance to Ford was subtracted from the issue distance to Carter as a measure of differential issue distance.

Group Benefits: As previously discussed, respondents were asked which of 16 groups they felt "close to." The were also asked whether any of these groups would be better off with Carter or Ford as President.

The group benefits variable was initialized at 0 and altered by adding 1 for every group a respondent felt close to that would be better off with Ford than Carter as President and by subtracting 1 for every close group that would be better off with Carter rather than Ford.[11]

Candidate Integrity: Respondents were asked the extent to which each candidate "could be trusted as President," has "a presidential personality," and "would bring moral and religious standards to government." These integrity ratings were averaged together, with two missing values allowed. Then the integrity rating for Carter was subtracted from the integrity rating of Ford.

Political Schemata: The four political schema measures from 1972 were dichotomized, with schematic respondents coded 1 and everyone else coded 0. Schematic was defined here as it was earlier, when the validity of the measures was established.

Interaction Terms: Simple interaction terms were created by multiplying each of the first four independent variables by the appropriate schema measure.

The first four independent variables were coded such that they should correlate positively with the dependent variable. The four schema measures should not be associated one way or the other with differential candidate affect. But if the crucial schema hypothesis is correct, each of the four interaction terms will be positively related to the dependent variable.

The data are shown in the first three columns of Table 6.3. They provide striking support for the schema hypothesis: Three of the four interaction terms are significant, and the fourth, Party Schema X Party identification, is marginally significant. Of even greater importance is the magnitude of the interaction terms. The first three are of roughly the same size as the accompanying "main effect." For example, the regression weight associated with party identification is 4.33, and the Party Schema X Party Identification interaction term is 4.42. This means that party identification was

[8]By hypothesizing a major influence of group identifications and group benefits on candidate evaluation and the vote, I am diverging from more conventional models of the vote decision (e.g., Markus & Converse, 1979). The notion that the group memberships are important to American politics is an old one, however (Lazarsfeld, Berelson, & Gaudet, 1944), and the theoretical work necessary to link group identification to a political response is beginning to appear (Lau, 1983; Miller, Gurin, Gurin, & Malanchuk, 1981).

TABLE 6.3
Differential Candidate Affect and Political Schemata

	Schema from 1972			All possible IVs from 1972		
	b	SE	Beta	B	SE	Beta
Party identification	4.33	.86	.14****	3.24	.83	.10
Issue distances	4.24	.96	.15****	1.02	.03	1.11
Group benefits	.97	.27	.10****	1.77	.39	.13****
Candidate integrity	8.83	.53	.52****	11.09	.52	.64****
1972 Political Schemata						
Party	3.85	3.64	.02	3.67	4.44	.02
Issues	− .78	1.69	−.01	.08	1.87	.00
Groups	1.60	1.93	.02	1.13	2.08	.01
Personality	−2.90	2.73	−.02	− 2.52	3.04	−.02
Interactions						
Party Schema × Party Identification	4.42	2.34	.04*	2.71	2.86	.03
Issue Schema × Issue Distances	3.88	1.15	.09****	4.35	1.40	.10***
Groups Schema × Group Benefits	1.02	.45	.06**	1.97	.73	.07***
Personality Schema × Candidate Integrity	2.43	1.06	.05**	2.41	1.20	.05**
Constant	1.55			1.21		
R^2	.80			.78		
n	506			469		

Note. The dependent variable is differential affect for Carter and Ford.
****$p < .001$. ***$p < .01$. **$p < .05$. *$p < .10$.

approximately twice as important in predicting differential candidate affect among those with a strong party schema compared to those with no apparent party schema. The Personality Schema X Candidate Integrity interaction term was not this large, but it still had a significant impact on differential evaluations of the candidates.

As an even stronger test of the crucial schema hypothesis, the voting model was respecified using as much data from 1972 as possible. Thus, in addition to the political schema variables, the measure of party identification came from the 1972 survey; issue distances were calculated using the respondents' own positions on the issues in 1972 and their perceptions of the candidates' positions in 1976; and group benefits were calculated from group identification measured in 1972. Thus, to as great an extent as is possible, questions of reciprocal influence have been eliminated. The data, shown in the last three columns of Table 6.3, basically replicate those just presented except that the Party Schema X Party Identification interaction term is no longer marginally significant.[12]

SUMMARY AND IMPLICATIONS

My purpose in writing this paper was twofold. First, I hoped to convince political scientists that they should pay attention to some of the newer ideas coming out of cognitive and social psychology. There is no doubt that humans are limited information processors. Those limits apply whether one is talking about language acquisition, solving physics problems, or learning about politics. Therefore, it is incumbent on political scientists developing theories about individual political behavior to be aware of and to account for or model those cognitive limitations.[13] My second purpose was to convince more psychologists that politics is an interesting arena in which to test and apply their ideas. Schemata for politicians are inherently more interesting than schemata for furniture; they are probably more complex, and they are definitely more difficult to study. But we will certainly learn more about basic information processing by studying complex social interactions.

I have hypothesized the existence of four different types of political schemata: a groups schema, an issues schema, a candidate personality schema, and a party schema. Each has been operationalized with items available in the traditional CPS surveys. As a group, the measures were reasonably reliable, reasonably stable over time, and reasonably valid. This is not to suggest that the current operationalization of political schemata is the best one could do, or even that it is sufficiently valid to preclude future measurement work. Such measurement work must be done, and it is by Hamill and Lodge, (this volume), and others. Hopefully, improved methods of measuring political schemata can be developed in a format conducive to survey research so that they can be employed by more political scientists.

---

[12]The results in Table 6.3 do not change much when the analyses are restricted to respondents who claimed to have voted in 1976. The standard errors increase somewhat due to the smaller sample size. The coefficient for the candidate integrity predictor is far and away the largest in Table 6.3. The magnitude of this coefficient is probably a result of candidate integrity being both a cause and an effect of the dependent variable that violates the assumptions of ordinary least squares regression (OLS). If such mutual causality between candidate integrity and the dependent variable does indeed exist, then this coefficient would be biased upward. Procedures like two-staged least squares are designed to handle just such situations, but in this case, no instrument was available which theoretically predicts candidate integrity but not the dependent variable. Hence, the simple OLS coefficients are reported in Table 6.3, but the reader should be aware that the coefficient for candidate integrity is undoubtedly biased upward.

[13]Cognitive limitations are also quite important in studying groups and organizations, as Simon (1947) and others have argued (P. A. Anderson, 1983).

The most exciting results presented in this paper, and the reason I am advocating pursuing this line of research, are the influence of schemata on the vote decision. As previously noted, this effect was quite dramatic. The candidates' party, issue stands, and group relations were each roughly twice as important in determining candidate evaluations among people who held a political schema conducive to processing that type of information compared to people who held no such schema. That is a big effect, and finding such a big effect, with admittedly imperfectly operationalized constructs measured 4 years before an election, underlines the importance of studying different political information-processing proclivities.

Why should we care about political schemata? There are several reasons, and surprisingly, greater accuracy in predicting the vote is not one, at least if we are talking in the aggregate sense. The field of political behavior already has several models that can predict the vote with greater than 90% accuracy (e.g., Kelly & Mirer, 1974; Markus & Converse, 1979), and it is difficult to imagine doing much better than that. These models are all probabilistic statements of cause and effect across many instances. But measuring political schemata allows us to be much more specific on an individual level in explaining the vote decision. If I know how a person typically processes and structures political information, that is, if I know what political schemata a person holds, I can predict what type of information that person will remember about a candidate, I can predict what sort of information that person will seek out about candidates, if it is not readily available, I can predict what sort of information will be used by the person to categorize and evaluate candidates, and I can predict what sort of political news or campaign propaganda will sway that person. Notice that I am not simply saying that Democrats like Democratic candidates and conservatives like conservative candidates. Rather, someone with a party schema, for example, and no other political schema, will evaluate candidates chiefly in terms of their party membership, irrespective of issue stands, personality characteristics, and group attachments.

The claim about susceptibility to campaign propaganda is particularly intriguing.[14] Politicians adopt widely varying campaign styles (e.g., Fenno, 1978). Some stress their issue stands, others stress constituent service, others their personal characteristics or experience, and still others their party or group memberships. How effective a particular campaign style is in influencing any given voter is not simply a function of how well the candidate plays the part, however. Whether or not the voter holds a type of political schema that allows or encourages the voter to receive or process the type of information provided by the candidate is also going to strongly

---

[14]Richard Smith and I are beginning to explore this idea.

influence how successful any campaign style is in persuading any given voter.

Of course, one can extend this analysis to aggregates. No politician can amend his or her campaign style to fit every voter (even though some try). But if one could estimate the distribution of people holding different types of political schemata in some constituency, one could gauge what type of persuasive communication would be most effective in influencing the greatest number of people. Likewise, the political analyst who knows the distribution of schema types in a constituency can use that information to help in understanding or interpreting the outcome of the election.

Let me attempt such an analysis for the 1976 election. The model presented in Table 6.3 views the vote as a function of group relations, issues stands, candidate personalities, and party identification. Each of these factors is much more important among people holding a concordant political schema. But was either Carter or Ford disproportionately helped by voters holding one type of political schema or another?

To answer that question, I examined the four major factors influencing the vote separately for those who held or did not hold each of the four political schemata. The relevant data are shown in Table 6.4. On the average, Carter benefited slightly (-0.43) from the group benefits variable among those who did not hold a groups schema, but he benefited significantly more (-1.37) among those who did hold a groups schema, $t(675) = 2.64$, $p < .009$. This translates into a boost of about 2.3 points on the dependent variable in Carter's favor among the 24% who held a group schema.[15] Similarly, Carter benefits slightly by a plurality of Democrats over Republicans among those who do not hold a party schema, but he benefits much more strongly by a preponderance of Democrats, particularly strong Democrats, among those who do hold a party schema. This translates into a 5.3 point advantage for Carter from those with a party schema, although this is less than 7% of the sample.

Ford, on the other hand, was helped by those who held a candidate personality schema. On the average, the candidate integrity variable was trivially in Carter's favor among those who did not hold a candidate personality schema (-0.13), but significantly in Ford's favor (0.58) among those who did hold a candidate personality schema, $t(574) = 2.39$, $p < .02$. This difference resulted in more than a 7.7 point advantage for Ford among the 18% who held a candidate personality schema. Neither candidate was disproportionately advantaged by the existence of issue schemata, however, for there was no difference between those with and without an issue schema in the differential issue distance to the two candidates.

One could conclude, therefore, that Carter's strategy of running as a

---

[15] $-0.43 \times 0.97 = -0.42$ among the aschematics; $-1.37 \times 1.99 = -2.72$ among schematics.

TABLE 6.4
Which Candidate Was Helped by Schemata in 1976?

	Proportion Schematic[a] (1972 Schema Measures)		
	None	32.8%	
	Groups	23.8%	
	Issues	39.3%	
	Personality	18.0%	
	Party	6.5%	
	Dependent Variable	Schematic	Aschematic	Difference
Group Schema	Group Benefits	−1.37	−0.43	−0.94**
Issue Schema	Issue Distances	0.00	0.03	−0.03
Personality Schema	Candidate Integrity	0.58	−0.13	0.71*
Party Schema	Party ID	Schematic	Aschematic	Difference
	Strong Democrat	34.1%	14.0%	20.1%
	Weak Democrat, Independent leaner	36.4%	35.0%	1.4%
	Independent-Independent	2.3%	11.4%	− 9.1%
	Weak Republican, Independent leaner	15.9%	29.1%	−13.2%
	Strong Republican	11.4%	10.5%	0.9%

[a]Percentages do not add to 100% because respondents could be schematic for more than one type of schema.
**$p < .01$. *$p < .05$.

traditional Democrat, stressing his support for groups in the New Deal coalition, was inordinately successful in helping him win the election among the 25–30% of the electorate who respond to such cues. On the other hand, his strong morality and religious values, which were directly measured in the candidate integrity variable, were not enough to overcome Ford's calm leadership abilities. Ford benefited strongly among the almost 20% of the population who respond to candidates' personalities.

Because political schemata are relatively stable, their demographic correlates have strong implications for what types of political appeals will be successful as the electorate changes with time. Nonwhites and people receiving their early political socialization during the depression and New Deal period are the people with the strongest group schemata. Minority political participation is steadily increasing, which can only help Democrats in the future as long as they maintain their appeal to blacks and Hispanics. The New Deal cohort is already beginning to age and will become a decreasingly important part of the electorate over the next three or four elections. These two forces (increasing minority participation and the disappearance of the New Deal cohort with time) are countervailing, and on balance, group appeals in politics should remain about as important in the foreseeable future as they were during the 1972–1976 period.

Issue voting, or rather the proportion of the electorate ready to respond to ideological candidates, should increase with time. The two strongest demographic correlates of holding an issue schema (i.e., being nonwhite and young) are both becoming an increasingly important part of the electorate. These same two factors have an opposite effect on holding a candidate personality schema, however, which should lead to a shrinking in the proportion of the electorate particularly responsive to candidate personality cues. The surprising effect of education on holding a candidate personality schema works against any decrease in the size of the electorate available for personality appeals, however, because overall levels of education are rising in the country.

Finally, an analysis of political schemata suggests that party appeals will become decreasingly effective in American politics as time goes on. Minorities do respond to party appeals, and as already discussed, minority political participation is increasing in America. But the youngest cohort does not respond to party cues. A decrease in the importance of party identification has already been noted by several investigators (G.B. Markus, 1983; Nie, Verba, & Petrocik, 1976; Norpoth & Rusk, 1982) and has been strongly (though not exclusively) linked to age. The absence of strong party schemata among the young can help explain the decline in importance of party identification to American politics, although of course one must then explain why party schemata are not strong in the younger cohort. Such an explanation is well beyond the scope of this paper, except for the few speculations about the influence of the political information environment on political schemata. Nevertheless, an analysis of political schemata leads to the clear prediction that over the next 20 years the size of the electorate cognitively ready to process and respond to issue appeals from candidates will become increasingly large, whereas the size of the electorate responding to party cues will shrink. If politicians pick up on this change, and they probably will, we could see a series of increasingly issue-based presidential campaigns. Indeed, the 1984 election pitted against each other the two most ideologically distinct candidates since Roosevelt and Hoover.

APPENDIX

This appendix describes the construction of the various measures utilized in this research in greater detail than was possible in the text. Wherever possible, I refer to variable numbers and code numbers from the codebooks of the CPS *1972 and 1976 National Election Studies.*

Political Schemata. In 1972, the crucial open-ended questions were M31.1–M46.3 ("M" for OSIRIS's multiple response format). In 1976, the variables were in the series V3088–V3132. The following response codes were counted as evidence for the existence of each of the following schemata in both 1972 and 1976:

- *Groups:* 162–165, 535, 536, 811–824, 1201–1297;
- *Issues:* 509–534, 553, 554, 605, 606, 805–810, 900–1197;
- *Personality:* 201–497, 601–797;
- *Party:* 101, 102, 121–151, 167, 197, 500, 501, 506, 507, 597.

The first response (e.g., M31.1) to each open-ended question was counted three times, the second response (M31.2) twice, and the third response (M31.3) once. Total counts were computed by summing the two counts (one for likes, one for dislikes) for each attitude object (parties and candidates). These total counts were turned into proportions by dividing them by a similarly weighted count of all responses (codes 1–1297) given about each attitude object. Thus, each of the 24 variables (12 in each election year) shown in Table 6.1 range from 0–1. The total schema scores were computed by simply summing these individual measures. Therefore, the groups schema and issues schema measures ranged from 0–4; the candidate personality schema and party schema measures ranged from 0–2.

Validity Measures. All of the validity measures are described in sufficient detail in the text except the open-ended criteria measures used in the discriminant validity analysis. The party differences measures came from the open-ended questions about "important differences between the parties" (V3185, V3187, V3189, V3191) and questions about whether one party is "more conservative" than the other (V3196, V3198, V3200). The codes were as follows:

- *Group-related:* 210–390;
- *Issues:* 1–190, 400–405, 500–505, 600–891.

The impressions from debates questions involved what (if anything) respondents had learned about the issues or candidates from the debates (V3611, V3613, V3615), favorable or unfavorable impressions of the candidates (V3617, V3619, V3621), and any memories concerning Ford (V3623, V3625, V3627) and Carter (V3629, V3631, V3633). These questions were only asked of respondents who had watched at least one debate; hence, V3606 is a screen. The codes for the different criteria were:

- *Group-related:* 60–69;
- *Issues:* 70–89;
- *Candidate:* 1–59.

The responses to the party differences and debate impressions questions were weighted inversely by the order of response, and then each count was turned into a proportion by dividing it by a similarly weighted total count of all responses to each set of questions.

Other Variables. The construction of a few other variables used in the origins of political schemata analysis (Table 6.2) should be described in more detail.

- *Parents' Interest in Politics:* An average of responses to V152 (father's interest in politics) and V154 (mother's interest) in 1972; V3201 (father) and V3203 (mother) in 1976. These measures came of course from the respondent rather than from his or her parents.
- *Political Knowledge:* A count of correct responses to all factual questions asked. In 1972, these included V943 (How many times can a person be elected President?); V944 (How long is the term of a U.S. senator?); V945 (recalling either congressional candidate from the race in Respondent's district); V949 (length of congressperson's term); V950 (which party had a majority in Congress before the election); and V951 (which party had a majority after the election). In 1976, the political knowledge variable only involved V3683 (which party had a majority in Congress before the election) and V3684 (which party had a majority after the election).
- *Campaign Involvement:* An average of responses to four questions: (a) caring about which party wins the election (V29 in 1972, V3030 in 1976); (b) reported interest in the campaign (V163, V3031); (c) whether or not R generally follows politics (V476, V3599); and (d) a count of the number of media used to follow politics (V456, V459, V461, and V463 in 1972; V3600, V3602, V3604, and V3645 in 1976).
- *Print Media:* The extent to which R read about the election in newspapers and magazines (V457 and V462, respectively, in 1972; V3646 and V3603 in 1976).
- *Electronic Media:* The number of radio and television programs R listened to about the campaign (V460 and V464 in 1972; V3601 and V3605 in 1976).

7 The Role of Inference in the Perception of Political Candidates

Pamela Johnston Conover
University of North Carolina, Chapel Hill
Stanley Feldman
University of Kentucky

In recent years, students of voting behavior have come to appreciate the important role that candidate perceptions play in the vote choice process.[1] Voters have been found to differ significantly in their assessments of candidates' issue positions (Aldrich & McKelvey, 1977; Page, 1978), and such judgments have been identified as some of the key determinants of vote choice in recent elections (Markus & Converse, 1979; Page & Jones, 1979). Yet, political scientists have seldom systematically considered the origins of such assessments. Instead, most studies that involve some consideration of candidate perception typically do so as a byproduct of their concern with some other element of the vote choice process (e.g., the impact of issues). As a consequence, we know relatively little about the processes underlying candidate perceptions.

One way of filling this void is to apply what psychologists have learned about social cognition to the study of candidate perception. Unfortunately, in many ways, this is easier said than done. The experimental methods embraced by social psychologists have traditionally been spurned by voting behavioralists. Furthermore, questions that are central to the study of social cognition may hold little practical relevance for the political scientist and vice versa. Thus, even though it is an inherently natural union, any marriage between the study of social cognition and candidate perception will require adjustments from both sides if it is to succeed. With this in mind, using recent theory and empirical work in social cognition as a basis

---

[1] We use the term *perception* very loosely and interchangeably with the terms *judgments* and *assessments*.

127

for our examination, we explore the processes underlying the evaluation of candidates' issue positions.

THE NATURE OF THE POLITICAL ENVIRONMENT: THE VOTERS' DILEMMA

Any study of the processes underlying candidate perception must take into account the nature of the political environment that voters operate in. It is particularly important to consider the type and amount of information that typically is available to the average voter. In that regard, both theoretical arguments (Downs, 1957a; Page, 1976, 1978; Shepsle, 1972) and empirical evidence (Graber, 1980; W. E. Miller & Levitin, 1976; Page, 1978; Page & Brody, 1972; Patterson, 1980) suggest that most elections are conducted within a political environment that is quite ambiguous, in which information is unclear, sometimes contradictory, open to a variety of interpretations, and often hard to get.

Such ambiguity stems from both the candidates' campaigns and the media's coverage of the election. With respect to the candidates, issue ambiguity is seldom a simple reflection of their failure to take positions on the issues; indeed, as Page (1978) has shown, most candidates do adopt concrete positions on a wide variety of issues. Rather, candidates contribute to ambiguity by not devoting much time to presenting the details of their positions to the public, a campaign strategy which is rational for maximizing votes (Downs, 1957a; Page, 1978; Shepsle, 1972). In contrast, candidates may often provide a considerable amount of information directed toward bolstering their images (Page, 1978).

Ambiguity may also be created by the media's coverage of the campaign. The media tend to focus on the "horse race" or "game" aspects of a political campaign—who is likely to win or lose, strategies for winning, logistics, campaign appearances, and hoopla (Graber, 1980; Patterson, 1980; Patterson & McClure, 1976). For example, Patterson (1980) found that during the 1976 presidential election campaign, about 60% of the news coverage dealt with the campaign game; only about 30% dealt with any substantive concerns (see also Graber, 1980). Moreover, when the media do deal with substantive concerns, they are more likely to focus on the candidate's qualifications (i.e., image) than on policy issues (Graber, 1980; Patterson, 1980). In effect, then, the candidates' campaign strategies and media election coverage together create an environment in which information concerning issues is often ambiguous and difficult for the public to obtain.

COPING WITH AMBIGUITY:
SEEKERS OF COGNITIVE CONSISTENCY
AND RATIONAL INFORMATION PROCESSORS

Presumably, voters need information about the candidates' issue positions in order to make a choice. Yet, the ambiguity of the political environment makes it difficult to obtain such information. How do voters deal with this ambiguity? How do voters ascertain the candidates' issue positions?

The empirical evidence addressing this question is abundant, if not particularly enlightening. The starting point for many studies has been the often reported correlation between the voters' own issue positions and the perceived stands of the candidates. Much of this evidence has been accumulated through the use of simple recursive models and cross-sectional data (e.g., Brent & Granberg, 1982; Brody & Page, 1972; Bruner, 1978; Conover & Feldman, 1982; Granberg & Brent, 1974; Kinder, 1978; A. H. Miller, Miller, Raine, & Brown, 1976). Virtually all of these studies have found some relationship between voters' issue positions and their perceptions of the candidates' stances, although there is a pronounced asymmetry: The relationship is much stronger (in the positive direction) in the case of the preferred candidate than it is for the nonpreferred candidates (where the relationship is in the negative direction). From a theoretical perspective, how can such findings be explained? What do they reveal about the processes underlying candidate perception?

In addressing such questions, political scientists have often borrowed from social psychology. In particular, although other viewpoints have come to dominate social psychology (see Lau & Sears, chapter 18, this volume), cognitive consistency theory remains the most prominent approach to understanding candidate perceptions (see, e.g., Berelson, Lazarsfeld, & McPhee, 1954; Brent & Granberg, 1982; Kinder, 1978; G. B. Markus & Converse, 1979; Martinez, 1984; Nimmo & Savage, 1976). As applied to the voting situation, cognitive consistency theory suggests that voters will strive to avoid cognitive imbalance in their judgments of the candidates. Voters may "project" their own issue position onto their preferred candidate (and the opposite position onto their nonpreferred candidate), or they may be "persuaded" to adopt the issue position of their preferred candidate. In effect, both projection and persuasion represent internal mechanisms that minimize the gap between the voter's own issue position and those of the candidates, thereby enabling the individual to achieve cognitive balance. Thus, in explaining the empirical findings concerning candidate perceptions, cognitive consistency theory has played a dominant role.

Despite the dominance of cognitive consistency theories in studies of candidate perception, some political scientists have adopted a rational, information-processing approach (see Lau & Sears, Chapter 1 this volume).

Although this approach is often based on economic "rational actor" models, its assumptions are nonetheless similar to those characterizing the psychologists' "naive scientist" perspective. From this perspective, because information is costly, voters are expected to limit the amount they use and to cut costs whenever possible. Thus, in perceiving and evaluating candidates, voters may use political cues as a substitute for more costly information (Conover, 1980, 1981). For example, voters might infer the candidates' issue stances from their party affiliations. Seen in these terms, the shortcuts that voters might use in candidate perception (i.e., projecting their own issue positions onto the candidates) are reasonable and rational responses to the costs of information in an ambiguous political environment (Downs, 1957a; Page, 1978; Popkin, Gorman, Phillips, & Smith, 1976).

Thus far, although a few studies have taken a rational information-processing approach to candidate perception, the vast majority have been from the perspective of cognitive consistency theory. In adopting such perspectives, political scientists have followed—sometimes quite unintentionally—the lead provided by social psychologists. Yet, as social psychologists and some political scientists have begun to recognize, there are problems with both of the foregoing perspectives (see Lau & Sears, Chp 1 this volume, for an elaboration). Consequently, when applied to the specific area of candidate perception, it is not surprising that both of these viewpoints fall short and leave us with a less than adequate explanation of how voters judge candidates. Clearly, the door is open for a different approach.

COPING WITH AMBIGUITY: VOTERS AS COGNITIVE MISERS

Happily, social psychologists recently have suggested an alternative to both the heavily motivational interpretation of candidate perception provided by consistency theory and the complex, calculating interpretation implied by the naive scientist perspective. As Lau and Sears explained earlier, social psychologists have gradually developed a third perspective on human perception of people as *cognitive misers* (Taylor, 1981). From this viewpoint, cognitive structures (schemata) play a key role in information processing. Although schemata perform many functions in political cognition, it is their role in the inference of new information that is most crucial to our treatment of candidate assessment. In essence, we argue that voters cope with ambiguity in the political environment by making inferences. Therefore, let us elaborate on how schemata guide inferences.

Generally, when data are missing from the stimulus information received, a person may fill in those missing data using a schema. In effect, the schema generates a "best guess" or "default value" (Minsky, 1975) as to what those data should be (Taylor & Crocker, 1981). For example, if you were told that you were going to meet an United States Senator, your best guess would also most certainly be that you were going to meet a man. For most people, male is the default value for a Senator schema. People can make inferences on several different levels (Hamilton, 1981; Harris, 1981; Higgins & King, 1981). Once a stimulus has been identified as an instance of a schema, the other attributes in that schema might be inferred, or inferences might be drawn from a second schema that is implicationally related to the first. Thus, the inferences made on the basis of relatively little information may be far-ranging and extensive in nature.

As applied to person perception, the inference process can be thought of as one in which the stimulus information allows the perceiver to categorize the target person as an instance of a particular schema (Hamilton, 1981; Higgins & King, 1981). Once the target person has been identified as a member of a particular category, the related schema can be used as a basis for drawing inferences, which are then incorporated into the perceiver's cognitive representation of the target person. In essence, voters use their various schemata to structure the processing and inference of information about particular candidates, with the result being the gradual development of a specific schema of that candidate (Hamilton, 1981). For instance, knowing only that a candidate is a member of The Moral Majority, voters might infer that the candidate is a white, male, Protestant, conservative Republican who favors high defense spending, school prayer, and a human life amendment. Over time, then, as the voter gains information about the candidate, more and more schemata will be instantiated and thus represented in the specific schema associated with that candidate.

As applied to candidate perception, we need to address more fully three key questions about such inference processes. First, what sorts of schemata are voters likely to use in making inferences about candidates? Second, what types of contextual factors will influence the inferences voters make about candidates? Finally, to what extent do individual differences affect the inferences voters make?

The Nature of Political Schemata

What types of information give rise to inferences about candidates' issue positions? Certainly, as suggested by much of the literature on candidate perception, voters might use their own issue positions as a basis for judging where the candidates stand. Traditionally, projection effects have been explained as stemming from a "need" for cognitive balance. Yet, such effects may also be interpreted from a "mental economy" perspective. Generally, over time, people may learn that certain aspects of the political world really are constructed in a consistent fashion. In particular, voters might learn that candidates whom they like on other grounds (i.e., party or ideological affiliation) usually also share issue positions similar to their own. Based on this learned pattern of co-occurrence, voters might infer a candidate's issue positions from their own. In effect, projection effects may be interpreted as resulting from a process of cognitive "inference" rather than cognitive "balance" (Feldman & Conover, 1983; Page & Jones, 1979).

An inference interpretation of projection effects can be carried even one step further by placing it in a schematic context. Specifically, an individual's issue positions might be described as loosely constituting part of his or her political self-schema. Generally, in addition to structuring the processing of information about oneself, self-schemata may also be used to organize information about others and as frames of reference for judgments and evaluations of others (see H. Markus & Smith, 1981). In particular, people often judge others in terms of the same dimensions or within the same categories that they use to describe themselves. Thus, for example, a strong partisan might concentrate on a candidate's party identification; alternatively, an extreme conservative might focus on a candidate's ideological identification. Moreover, some generalization from the self to others might occur. In effect, we might not only judge others "on the *same dimensions* we use for our own behavior," we might also "assign them the *same values* on those dimensions . . . i.e., if I cheat a little bit, you must cheat a little bit, too" (H. Markus & Smith, 1981, p. 257). Such inferences from one's own self to another person are most likely to occur when information about the other person is minimal or when the other person is similar to the perceiver (H. Markus & Smith, 1981). In essence, then, voters might infer a candidate's issue positions from their own simply because of the centrality of self-schemata in information processing.

Thus, numerous empirical studies have demonstrated that voters' own issue positions are one source of information that is used in determining the candidate's issue positions. But, why voters project their issue positions onto candidates is not altogether clear.[2] Projection could be prompted by a need for cognitive balance; it could be based on the learning that such consistencies actually exist; or along the same lines, it could be a product of the involvement of the voter's political self-schema in information processing. Further empirical work is needed to determine which of the three explanations is most viable. Consequently, although we discuss projection in schematic terms, we do so cautiously and with the understanding that other explanations may also have some validity.

Voters' own issue positions are not the only basis for candidate inferences

---

[2]We thank Donald Kinder for pointing out the difficulties in determining why projection effects occur.

or even necessarily the most likely source. Various role or "social group" schemata also are likely to play a significant part in guiding the inferences voters make about candidates. In particular, many studies suggest that party cues are important in the perception of candidates (e.g., Brent & Granberg, 1982; Downs, 1957a; Granberg & Brent, 1974; Hamill, Lodge, & Blake, 1984; Kinder, 1978; Miller, Wattenberg, & Malanchuk, 1982; Shively, 1979). Along the same lines, voters may have developed schemata that they associate with various ideological labels (e.g., liberals, conservatives, etc.). Finally, a number of ostensibly nonpolitical categories (e.g., the race and the sex of the candidate) may be associated with schemata that guide the inference of information about candidates (Boles & Durio, 1980; Popkin et al., 1976; Sapiro, 1982). Thus, schemata associated with different social categories (party, ideology, race, and gender, to name a few) may help structure the perception of candidates.

"Point-of-view" (Hastie, 1981) or "issue" schemata (i.e., those organized around a particular policy question; see Graber, 1984) may also influence the perception of candidates. For instance, a candidate's discussion of unemployment might evoke the voters' unemployment schema, which in turn could lead the voter to infer that the candidate is empathic (for an elaboration on the content of various issue schemata, see Graber, 1984). Alternatively, various person prototypes may have an effect on the inferences that people make about candidates. For example, Kinder, Peters, Abelson, and Fiske (1982) found that an "ideal President" prototype influenced how the incumbent President, Jimmy Carter, was perceived, but it had relatively little effect on perceptions of his opponents, Ford, Reagan, and Kennedy. Overall then, there are a number of different types of schemata that may influence the perception of candidates and structure the inferences that voters make.

Not only must we identify the types of schemata that are likely to structure candidate perceptions, but we must also consider their content, that is, the specific elements encompassed by the schemata. We anticipate that there will be variation across political schemata in terms of the nature and breadth of their content. As a consequence of such variation, schemata will vary in the type and amount of inferences that they produce.

Contextual Variation

Contextual factors are likely to exert a considerable influence on both which schemata voters use and on how they use them in making candidate inferences. First, the political environment "primes" voters to use certain schemata in their perception of candidates. In effect, there is contextual variability in the "accessibility" of different politically relevant categories and their related schemata (Higgins & King, 1981; Wyer & Srull, 1981).

Generally, accessibility (the individual's readiness to use a schema) is determined by a variety of factors: expectations, motivations (i.e., goals, values, needs), how recently the schema has been activated, how frequently it is used, and its salience (Higgins & King, 1981). Over the course of a campaign, recurring situations may involve the same expectations (e.g., the candidate will make a speech) or salient objects (e.g., political parties), thereby creating chronic differences in the accessibility of different schemata. In particular, at a very fundamental level, the media and candidates themselves appear to continually prime the voters to use partisan (e.g., Republican, Democrat) and ideological (e.g., liberal, conservative) categories in their perceptions. Alternatively, chance happenings may momentarily increase the accessibility of a particular schema. At a campaign rally, for example, an antiabortion heckler might jeer "baby killer," thereby priming bystanders to use a schema that they almost certainly would not have employed otherwise. Yet, although the increase in accessibility may be quite transitory, the schema could nonetheless have a lasting impact on the voter's impression of a candidate (Higgins & King, 1981; Wyer & Srull, 1981). Thus, there is contextual variation in the long-and short-term accessibility of various political schemata, and this might substantially influence the inferences voters make.

Second, it is expected that there will be significant variation across candidates in terms of the schemata voters use and the number of inferences they make. This variation may have a number of sources. Contextual factors such as the minority status of one candidate (be it ideological, partisan, racial, or sexual in nature) could prime voters to use a particular schema in their perceptions of a specific candidate (Taylor, Fiske, Etcoff, & Ruderman, 1978). In 1984, for instance, Jesse Jackson's candidacy no doubt prompted voters to rely on racial schemata that typically remain inactive in the perception of white candidates. Similarly, voters are likely to make more inferences from party schemata for a candidate known as a stalwart of the party than for one that has been identified by the media as a "deviant" from the party line. Variation across candidates may also be a function of prior knowledge. The better known a candidate and the longer he or she has been on the political scene, the more likely it is that voters will have well-developed specific person schemata of that candidate (Hamilton, 1981); consequently, new inferences are less likely.

Third, there may be variation in the sorts of issues that are typically involved in candidate inferences. In effect, certain issues may not be part of the schemata that are used most frequently in the perception of candidates. To some extent, such variation might be due to individual differences. Yet, it also might stem from contextual factors that condition whether certain issues are incorporated as elements within specific schemata. If, for example, politicians and the media alike structure public debate over an issue in nonpartisan terms, it is less likely that the issue will become part of voters' party schemata and, subsequently, their party-based inferences. Thus, for instance, party schemata are more likely to produce candidate inferences on the issue of welfare spending than on the issue of child abuse. Overall, fewer inferences should be made involving specific issues that commonly are not part of the schemata that voters are most likely to use.

Individual Variation

Most of the social cognition literature has dealt with consensual schemata, that is, knowledge structures that people are expected to share. As a consequence, relatively little attention has been devoted to the individual differences that may characterize the content, structure, and use of particular schemata (major exceptions to this include, Fiske & Kinder, 1981; Fiske, Kinder, & Larter, 1983; Lau, Coulam, & Sears, 1983; H. Markus, 1977). However, such individual differences are likely to have a substantial impact on how people judge political candidates. Therefore, we consider three distinct, though related, sources of such variation: schema accessibility, availability, and development.

As noted previously, schema accessibility is determined by a variety of factors (i.e., expectations, motivations, salience) that may differ individually as well as contextually (Higgins & King, 1981). For example, in anticipation of an ideological clash at a candidate debate, some voters' ideological schemata might become more accessible; others may view the confrontation as a partisan one, and consequently, their party schemata might become more accessible. Similarly, variations in the motivations of voters might generally influence the accessibility of political schemata: Those voters who are highly involved in the campaign and who care about the outcome of the election should have more readily accessible political schemata and thus should be more capable of making candidate inferences. Finally, voters are likely to perceive candidates in terms of those political schemata that are especially salient to them, and this in turn determines the types of inferences that voters are likely to make. For instance, feminists tend to perceive candidates in terms of a women's rights schema (Conover, 1984), and therefore, they should be more likely to make candidate inferences on issues such as abortion and the equal rights amendment than on an issue such as inflation.

People are likely to differ not only in the accessibility of various political schemata, but also in their availability, that is, whether such schemata are even stored in memory (Higgins & King, 1981).[3] As H. Markus and her colleagues suggest in their work on self-schemata (Markus, 1977; Markus, Crane, Bernstein, & Saladi, 1982; Markus & Smith, 1981), with respect to a particular domain people who have schemata (i.e., schematics) process relevant information differently than people who lack a schema in that area (i.e., aschematics). In particular, schematics tend to process and evaluate new information more quickly and confidently (H. Markus, 1977). Moreover, because they can immediately bring a great deal of information to bear on the subject, schematics can potentially make many more inferences from the information that they receive (H. Markus & Smith, 1981).

Related to the differences in availability, voters are also expected to vary in the development of their political schemata. In conceptualizing such developmental differences, a novice–expert distinction is particularly useful (Fiske & Kinder, 1981; Fiske et al., 1983; Lau et al., 1983). First, with regard to content and structure, experts undoubtedly have more knowledge than novices. Moreover, that knowledge is structured differently: As expertise in an area grows, the knowledge becomes more tightly organized. Second, variations in schema development are reflected not only in the content and structure of information but also in terms of information processing. The schemata of experts should be more easily activated than those of novices (Lau et al., 1983). Furthermore, because they have a broader store of more tightly knit knowledge, experts should be capable of making more inferences and a wider range of inferences (Miller et al., 1982). Finally, experts and novices employ different strategies in processing inconsistent information and therefore in making inferences. Novices tend to use "confirmatory" strategies, whereas experts are more likely to adopt "disconfirmatory" strategies. As a consequence, novices make greater use of consistent information in making inferences; in contrast, experts are more likely to take into account inconsistent information, and therefore, they are more likely to make moderate inferences (Fiske et al., 1983). Thus, individual differences in schema development are likely to play a crucial role in explaining candidate inferences.

Summary

From our perspective, voters act like cognitive misers: When faced with the adverse conditions created by an ambiguous political world, they use their schemata (their existing store of knowledge) to make inferences about the candidates. Although such inferences may sometimes be biased or inaccurate, they represent a reasonable response to the political environ-

---

[3]As Higgins and King (1981) point out, recently the terms *accessibility* and *availability* have often been used interchangeably. Nonetheless, like Higgins and King, we think it is useful to maintain the conceptual distinction.

ment that enables the voter to proceed with the vote choice process. Given our assumption that voters act like cognitive misers in their perceptions of the candidates, several factors become crucial to the study of candidate perception. First, it is essential to identify the nature of the voters' political schemata. Second, it is crucial to recognize that contextual factors play a key part in determining whether voters make inferences, and when they do, what kinds of inferences they make. Finally, individual differences are also expected to have a significant effect on candidate inferences. Taken together, these three factors suggest a number of fruitful paths for future research. We cannot begin an in-depth pursuit of all these lines of inquiry here, but we can present some preliminary analysis of each area, which should help structure future research on candidate inferences.

DATA AND METHODS

We base our preliminary examination of candidate inferences on survey data in part because of our interest in contextual variability, which is difficult to simulate realistically in the laboratory. Most previous attempts by political scientists to assess the processes of candidate perception have also relied on survey data; however, they primarily employed simple cross-sectional designs that failed to address the question of causality. In studying candidate inference processes with survey data, it is essential to recognize two aspects of the inference process: the operation of perception across time and the role of political schemata or prior information. Both these factors dictate that the measurement of the resulting judgments must be preceded by the measurement of the prior beliefs that helped to structure them, and even then, any inferences made on the basis of correlations between dependent and independent measures do not provide conclusive evidence about the underlying process (Taylor & Fiske, 1981). Given such conditions, nonrecursive models are inappropriate because they imply simultaneous relationships among the variables. Therefore, our model is based on a series of lagged recursive equations. Consequently, estimation of the model requires the use of panel data.

Accordingly, we use Patterson's panel study of the 1976 presidential election as the basis for estimating the parameters of the model (for a detailed description of the data, see Patterson, 1980). In the panel, 1,236 eligible voters were interviewed several times during the course of the campaign. In making use of these data, an initial issue is the specification of the time lags to be considered. In this regard, there is no "right" or "wrong" time lag to be identified based on the expected duration of perceptual activity because the latter is variable. Instead, we must select time lags that provide interesting vantage points from which to view the evolution of people's assessments of political candidates. Based on this criterion, we focus on that period of time encompassing the early part of the electoral process. Specifically, our analysis draws on the first three waves of the Patterson data. The first wave of interviews (1,002 respondents) was conducted in February 1976 before the New Hampshire primary; the second wave occurred in April at the time of the early primaries (772 respondents were reinterviewed); the third wave occurred in June after the late primaries (720 respondents were reinterviewed) (Patterson, 1980).

This time frame is very interesting in several respects. First, it allows us to concentrate on the early stages of the campaign when many voters are just beginning to learn about the candidates and, therefore, are likely to be making inferences. Second, it enables us to consider a number of candidates: Jerry Ford, Ronald Reagan, Jimmy Carter, Hubert Humphrey, Edward Kennedy, and George Wallace. These candidates vary on a wide range of dimensions (e.g., party, ideology, personality, and prominence), and thus we can consider the inference process in a variety of candidate contexts. Finally, potential variations across issues in these processes may be examined with these data because questions about a number of issues (e.g., busing, guaranteed defense spending, welfare, abortion, and taxes) are included in the survey.

In our empirical analysis, we focus on how three types of cues (self, party, and ideology) trigger inferences about candidates' issue positions. Yet, to this point, there is no clear consensus on how schemata ought to be measured (Fiske & Linville, 1980; Taylor & Fiske, 1981). Some have employed open-ended questions to measure schema content and structure; others have tied the measurement of schemata to some aspect of information processing (for a review of some of these methods, see Ostrom, Pryor, & Simpson, 1981; Taylor & Fiske, 1981). For our part, we need to assess the policy dimensions of self, party, and ideology schemata that are relevant to making inferences about candidates' issue positions. We do this in a manner that is not common in experimental studies of social cognition (see Hamill, Lodge, & Blake, 1984, for another use of this method in measuring political schemata). Specifically, in the case of party and self-schemata, we base our measures on the voters' placements of the parties and themselves on a number of 7-point issue scales that we have recoded so that they range from −3 (very conservative) to +3 (very liberal). In effect, whether and where the voters place themselves and the parties on these scales are taken as rough indicators of the presence and content of a policy dimension in the voters' schemata. Unfortunately, the respondents were not asked where they perceived the various ideological groups (liberals, moderates, and conservatives) to stand on the issues. Therefore, we have no way of measuring the voters' ideology schemata. Consequently, our analysis of candidate inferences from ideological cues is based on the direct relationship of the voter's placement of a candidate on the liberal–conservative continuum with the voter's assessment of that candidate's issue position. In effect, we assume that such a relationship results from the linkage of the liberal label with a particular issue stand. Specifically, it is assumed that the liberal label is associated with the following issue stands: guaranteeing jobs, welfare spending, school busing, the right to an abortion, lower defense spending, and higher taxes rather than cuts in social spending.[4]

Obviously, our measures of party and self-schemata and our "nonmeasure" of ideology schemata are not without problems. In particular, one potentially serious criticism is that our measurement strategy creates schemata where none exist. This may be true to some extent, but at the same time, it should be noted that our respondents had ample opportunity, which many made use of, to refuse to place themselves and the parties on the issue scales. Thus, even though there may be some problems with this measurement strategy, we feel that it is a justifiable and useful approach, given our earlier decision to use survey data.

In measuring the inferences that voters make about candidates' issue positions, we employ 7-point issue scales analogous to those used in the assessment of the voters' party and self-schemata. Specifically, our respondents were asked to place each of the six candidates on each of the six issues. Once again, these responses were recoded to range from -3 (very conservative) to $+3$ (very liberal). Such candidate placements can be interpreted as resulting, in part, from inferences structured by the voters' schemata. Specifically, to the extent that there is a relationship between the particular schema (as measured at Time 1) and the candidate placement (as measured at Time 2), an inference is assumed to have occurred.

FINDINGS

The Nature of Political Schemata

Many of our respondents appear to have well-developed policy dimensions in their political self-schemata. The vast majority is quite willing to take a stand on most of the issues presented to them; over 90% of the people place

---

[4]We do not regard the assumption underlying this measure as being too unrealistic because this does not require that all voters be able to identify correctly the liberal and conservative sides of each issue. All we require is that some people are able to connect ideology and issues in order that they might use ideological labels as cues. In this regard, Levitin and Miller (1979) find evidence that the well-educated in particular are able to distinguish liberal from conservative sides of the issue. As we see later, these same people are also most likely to use ideological cues as a means of inferring issue positions.

themselves on at least five of the six issues that were asked about.[5] Thus, as suggested earlier, political self-schemata are sources of candidate inferences that are available to a substantial portion of the electorate.

With respect to the content of such schemata, Table 7.1 presents the mean issue positions for the entire sample as well as for Democrats, Republicans, and independents. The sample as a whole is fairly conservative on the issues of busing and welfare, relatively liberal on the issue of taxes, and moderate on the remaining issues. When broken into partisan groups, expected patterns of differences emerge (see Page, 1978). Compared to the Republicans, the Democrats take relatively more liberal positions on every issue except abortion, though for some issues (e.g., welfare and busing), both groups have basically conservative positions. The independents have moderate stands on most issues, with their mean positions falling between those of the Democrats and Republicans on all the issues except abortion and defense spending.

Let us turn now to a consideration of the voters' party schemata, which we define as knowledge structures pertaining to information about the parties. Over the years, political scientists have devoted a great deal of research to the concept of party identification and its effects on candidate perception and vote choice (for a review of this literature, see Asher, 1982; Shively, 1980). It is surprising, therefore, that researchers have seldom dealt with the structure and content of the knowledge that people have about political parties. Pomper (1972), for example, has examined voters' perceptions of where the parties stand on the issues. Similarily, Bastedo and Lodge (1980) have probed the meaning of party labels. And most relevant to our own work, Hamill, Lodge, and Blake (1984) recently have begun to explore the nature of party schemata. But beyond that, relatively little research has considered what we would call party schemata.

In studying party schemata, we are immediately confronted with a complex conceptual dilemma that cannot be resolved without substantial empirical testing, namely, the nature of party schemata. In addressing this issue, several specific questions need to be asked. First, do people think of Democrats differently than they think of the Democratic party and its leadership? Second, do individuals tend to have a single integrated schema that encompasses both the Republican and Democratic parties, or do they have a separate schema for each party? A third and related question is what is the relationship of party identification to the development of party schemata? Do Republicans, for example, have a well-developed schema

---

[5]Such findings should be viewed with some caution. The question filters used in the Patterson study were not as stringent as those typically employed in the CPS National Election Studies. Consequently, these data suggest higher levels of opinion holding. Whether such attitudes are "real" (as opposed to non-attitudes) is open to some question.

TABLE 7.1
Issue Locations for Partisan Groups

	All		Democrats		Independents		Republicans	
Issues	mean	sd	mean	sd	mean	sd	mean	sd
Busing:								
Self	−1.95	1.8	−1.70	1.9	−1.91	1.8	−2.50	1.2
Democratic party	0.57	1.7	0.29	1.8	0.59	1.7	1.13	1.5
Republican party	−0.45	1.7	−0.44	1.9	−0.34	1.7	−0.52	1.5
Jobs:								
Self	0.26	2.3	0.81	2.2	0.31	2.2	−0.84	2.1
Democratic party	1.35	1.5	1.42	1.5	1.16	1.4	1.47	1.4
Republican party	−0.71	1.7	−0.65	1.8	−0.71	1.5	−0.79	1.6
Defense Spending:								
Self	0.02	2.2	0.14	2.2	0.39	2.3	−0.65	2.0
Democratic party	−0.15	1.7	−0.32	1.7	0.04	1.6	0.04	1.7
Republican party	−0.61	1.6	−0.57	1.7	−0.53	1.6	−0.79	1.3
Welfare:								
Self	−1.08	2.0	−0.80	2.0	−1.03	2.0	−1.66	1.6
Democratic party	0.78	1.6	0.69	1.7	0.60	1.5	1.17	1.4
Republican party	−0.71	1.6	−0.69	1.7	−0.73	1.6	−0.73	1.4
Abortion:								
Self	0.27	2.5	0.20	2.6	0.34	2.5	0.31	2.5
Democratic party	0.36	1.6	0.49	1.6	0.36	1.7	0.11	1.5
Republican party	−0.02	1.6	−0.22	1.6	0.06	1.5	0.35	1.5
Taxes:								
Self	1.00	2.8	1.36	2.1	1.05	2.2	0.43	2.3
Democratic party	0.86	1.7	0.91	1.8	0.80	1.6	0.80	1.6
Republican party	−0.64	1.6	−0.86	1.8	−0.44	1.6	−0.41	1.4

about the Republican party but an ill-defined one about the Democratic party? Are independents essentially aschematic, having little organized knowledge about either party, or are they equally schematic with respect to both parties? It is essential that such questions be answered if we are to understand fully the role of party schemata in candidate evaluation. Having said that, let us hasten to add that we cannot begin to answer all these questions in this analysis. Nonetheless, our analysis is suggestive.

Let us first consider the availability and development of party schemata, which we measure according to the number of issues on which the respondent can place each party (see Hamill, Lodge, & Blake, 1984, for the use of a similar measure). Almost 30% of our respondents cannot place either party on any of the issue scales; another 20% or so are able to place the parties on half or less of the issues; and only around 44% are able to place either party on five or six of the issues. Thus, policy-oriented party schemata are not as readily available or well-developed as they were in the case of self-schemata. Moreover, the correlation between the Republican party measure and the Democratic party measure is .98; if a person can place one party on an issue, he or she can place the other. In effect, there is little differentiation between parties in the availability and development of party schemata. On the face of it, this suggests that people may tend to have a single schema that encompasses both parties rather than a separate schema for each party. However, such an interpretation should be made with some caution. Because the questions asking respondents to place the parties on the issues were together on the surveys, question-order effects may account for the high correlation between the two schema measures.

What accounts for variations in the development of party schemata? To answer this question, we regressed a combined measure of party schema development (the sum of the separate Republican and Democratic party measures) on a variety of measures.[6] This analysis reveals that, in terms of background characteristics, the more educated, the young, and the males in our sample are more likely to place the parties on the issues. With respect to political characteristics, people who are concerned about the election, who talk about politics, or who identify with a party are more likely to place the parties on the issue scales. Such findings suggest that well-developed party schemata are found primarily among general political experts and not among novices. Thus, as Hamill, Lodge, and Blake (1984) concluded, we find that party schemata are not available to everyone in the electorate.

Next, we can consider the content of party schemata, that is, where exactly the parties are placed on the issues. As indicated in Table 7.1, to the extent that people have perceptions of the parties, they see them as being relatively distinct on most issues. In particular, the sample as a whole sees the Democratic party as being more liberal on every issue. Finally, it is

---

[6]The results of this regression—beta weights—are listed below (* = significant at .05 level):

Schema Development = .19* Gender + .15* Education + .05 Race + .06 Income
- .09* Age + .13* Concerned with Outcome
+ .08* Attention to Network News + .05 Read News Magazine
+ .05 Read Newspaper + .19* Talk About Politics
- .003 Watch Local TV News - .04 Enjoy Politics
- .03 Direction of Party Identification
+ .11* Strength of Party Identification

Attention to the Network News, Watch Local TV News, Read News Magazines, and Read Newspaper were provided in this data set, computed from a series of questions on media use and political discussion over the five waves of the panel. Concern with Outcome is a scale made up of agree–disagree items focusing on the perceived importance of this election and voting in general. Enjoy Politics was constructed in a similar way from items dealing with enjoyment of the presidential campaign. Direction of Party Identification is coded Republican, independent, Democrat, and Strength of Party Identification ranges from independent to strong identifier.

interesting to note that the mean placements of the parties are often quite different from the mean positions of party identifiers. Democrats see themselves as more moderate than their party on every issue except taxes. Moreover, for some issues, (e.g., busing), the disparity is substantial. In contrast, Republicans view themselves as more extreme (i.e., more conservative) than the Republican party on most issues, particularly busing and welfare.

Finally, we can consider possible differences in the nature and use of party schemata as they relate to particular candidates and issues. With respect to issues, voters may be more inclined to make party inferences on issues where the candidates are particularly ambiguous, therefore making it difficult to ascertain their positions. In this regard, during the first wave of the panel, the respondents had the most difficulty in placing the candidates on the abortion issue and, after that, on the jobs issue. Also, party inferences can be most useful in differentiating between candidates from opposing parties on those issues where the parties are most polarized. In 1976, for example, voters saw the parties as most polarized on economic issues (jobs, welfare, and taxes).

With regard to the candidates, voters are expected to make more inferences from party schemata for those candidates most clearly associated with the party in question. Conversely, voters should make fewer inferences from party cues for candidates that have been labeled as "mavericks" from their party. Although we have no direct way of measuring the strength of the association between a party and a particular candidate, some sense of the linkage may be gained by considering the difference between the parties' and the candidates' perceived positions on an issue as measured during the first wave. In the case of the two Republican candidates, Ford and Reagan, there is relatively little difference in terms of which one is perceived to be closer to the Republican party's stands. On most issues, Ford is perceived as being only slightly closer to the party than Reagan. Across all issues, the mean difference between Reagan and the Republican party is 0.92, whereas for Ford it is 0.86. In contrast, there are more substantial variations between the Democratic candidates. Generally, Humphrey is the clear standard-bearer of the Democratic party (mean difference = 0.83), and Kennedy (mean difference = 0.96) is seen as only slightly more distant from the party on all the issues except abortion, where he is perceived as deviating substantially from the party line. The other two Democratic candidates, Carter and Wallace, have more of an "outsider" status. As a newcomer to national politics in 1976, Carter's standing as a traditional Democrat was ambiguous, as reflected in the distance separating him from the Democratic party in the voters' mind (mean difference = 1.07). In contrast, Wallace's long tenure in the national limelight had solidified his position as a true deviant from the traditional party line (mean difference = 1.98). Taken together, this suggests that inferences from party cues should be strongest for candidates such as Humphrey, Ford, and Kennedy and weakest for Carter and especially Wallace.

In summary, our analysis suggests that many of our respondents have positions on the issues, and thus they should be able to use their own issue stands readily as a basis for making inferences about the candidates' issue positions. Fewer of our respondents have a good sense of where the parties stand on the issues. Nonetheless, a sufficient number have some sort of party schema to suggest that party cues may be an important basis of candidate inferences. With this in mind, let us consider what type of inferences voters made about the candidates in 1976.

Political Inferences: Candidate and Issue Variation

In studying political inferences, two different aspects of the process might be considered: whether or not a voter makes inferences and, if so, what kinds of inferences are made. It is important to recognize the theoretical differences in these two aspects of the inference process. Whether or not voters make inferences about the candidates' issue positions depends largely on the availability and accessibility of relevant schemata. In contrast, the kinds of inferences that are made depend on the content of a person's schemata and the use of those schemata in information processing. Empirically, these questions translate into whether a voter can place a candidate on an issue scale (if not, it is assumed that no inference has taken place) and, if the candidate is placed, whether the placement is related to the party's, ideology's, or voter's own issue position (if they are correlated, it is assumed that the judgment about the candidate has been influenced by the schema's content). For our part, we focus on the second of these questions: the strength of the inferences made from party, ideology, and self issue positions (for an empirical analysis related to the first question, see Wright & Niemi, 1983). The basic model to be estimated is as follows (for an earlier test of this model, see Feldman & Conover, 1983):

$$C_1\text{'s stand }_{i(t)} = b_0 + b_1 C_1\text{'s stand}_{i(t-1)}$$

$$+ b_2 (\text{R's stand}_{i(t-1)}) C_1 \text{ Pos}_{(t-1)}$$

$$+ b_3 (\text{R's stand}_{i(t-1)}) C_1 \text{ Neg}_{(t-1)}$$

$$+ b_4 C_1\text{'s Pty's stand}_{i(t-1)}$$

$$+ b_5 C_1\text{'s Ideo stand}_{i(t-1)}$$

$$+ b_6 \text{Netnews} + b_7 \text{Paper} + u_1$$

Each of the terms in this equation represents a process that contributes to the assessment of a candidate's issue position on issue i at time t. The first term—C_1's $stand_{i(t-1)}$—represents the candidate's position at time $t-1$; it indicates the stability remaining in such perceptions once the other processes have been controlled.

The second term models inferences from the voter's own issue position (i.e. projection) for a candidate that is positively evaluated, whereas the third term describes the same process for negatively evaluated candidates. It is expected that the relationship between the voter's and the candidate's position will be positive for favorably evaluated candidates and negative for those that are disliked.

The fourth and fifth terms both represent inference processes in which the voter uses political cues in order to determine a candidate's issue position. The fourth variable—C_1's Pty's $stand_{i(t-1)}$—represents inferences based on the voter's estimate of where the candidate's party stands on a particular issue. A voter may infer, for example, that because the Republican party is probusiness, the Republican's candidate is also probusiness. The fifth term—C_1's Ideo $stand_{i(t-1)}$—deals with a similar inference process, only this time the relevant cue is the candidate's ideology as measured by his or her placement on the liberal–conservative continuum. In effect, it is expected that a candidate labeled conservative will be attributed issue positions typically associated with conservatives.

Finally, the last two terms indicate the impact of watching the network evening news (Netnews) and regularly reading the newspaper (Paper) on assessments of a candidate's issue position. These terms allow us to see whether the well-informed have substantially different placements of the candidates than those who do not pay attention to the media. Moreover, the inclusion of these two terms allows us to control for the possibility that the media are giving people both pieces of information involved in making inferences: the candidate's relationship to the political cue and the information associated with the cue itself. Thus, controlling for media attention helps to eliminate a major source of spurious effects.

Using two-stage least squares, this model was estimated for each of the six issues for each of the six candidates.[7] As instruments for the lagged endogenous term—C_1's $stand_{i(t-1)}$—we used the following variables: (a)

---

[7]Candidate evaluation was measured on a 7-point scale running from favorable to unfavorable. For this analysis, scores of 1, 2, 3 were considered positive, and scores of 5, 6, 7 were considered negative. There seemed to be no obvious indication of positivity bias in these ratings. The issue variables were all coded -3 to $+3$, and Netnews and Paper were coded 0 to 1, with 0 representing minimum attention to the network news and newspapers and 1 maximum attention. In order to make the coefficients for Netnews and Paper roughly comparable to those for the issue and ideological terms, the coefficients for the media variables should be divided by 7.

the respondent's party identification, liberal-conservative identification, age, education, income, gender, and race (all measured at time $t - 1$); and (b) the respondent's placement at time $t + 1$ of the candidate's party on the specific issue and of the candidate on the liberal-conservative continuum. Throughout our discussion, we report unstandardized coefficients because they are unaffected by differences in variances and are directly comparable both within and between equations. The absolute size of the estimates should be viewed with some care because they are likely to be systematically depressed by stochastic error in the measurement of the issue variables (Achen, 1975). Finally, with respect to the interpretation of the inference estimates, it is important to note that missing data for the candidates' ideological placements as well as the respondents' and the parties' issue positions were set equal to the mean values for those variables in the sample. Thus, the estimates for the various inference terms reflect the strength of inferences only for those people who are able to make the related placements, despite the fact that the other respondents are not actually eliminated from the analysis. Essentially, then, we are estimating the strength of candidate inferences for those people for whom the schema is available. With this in mind, the full set of estimates for all 36 equations is presented in the appendix to this chapter. For ease of presentation, we focus on the average set of estimates across all issues for each candidate. However, these averages should be viewed with some caution because they are each based on six regression estimates that are subject to the effects of sampling error. These averages are presented in Table 7.2.

Considering first the average stability of assessments of the candidates' positions over the 3-month period, we find that on the whole the coefficients are relatively strong. At the same time, however, there are sizable variations across candidates and, for any one candidate, across issues. In

TABLE 7.2
Mean Estimates of the Inferences Model for Each Candidate

	All	Ford	Reagan	Humphrey	Kennedy	Carter	Wallace
Stability	.66	.72	.80	.52	.76	.45	.69
Self-Positive	.13	.07	.09	.13	.12	.22	.14
Self-Negative	−.03	−.09	−.09	−.06	−.03	.07	.03
Liberal-Conservative	.13	.10	.14	.16	.10	.12	.14
Party	.16	.17	.21	.20	.20	.13	.05
Netnews	−.12	−.15	−.09	−.03	−.08	−.12	−.25
Paper	.06	.08	.22	.01	.00	−.12	.16

particular, Reagan and Kennedy have relatively high stability coefficients, whereas Carter and Humphrey have low ones, though in the case of Humphrey the average is depressed by the very low stability of perceptions of his stand on the abortion issue (stability for Humphrey on abortion = .17; average stability without abortion = .59). With respect to within-candidate variation across issues, perceptions of Carter are the most variable; his coefficients range from a high of 1.30 on the jobs issue to a negative 1.03 on the abortion issue. The relative instability in evaluations of Carter's issue positions is quite understandable, given that early in 1976 he was probably the least known of all the candidates. Moreover, because very few people were able to place Carter on any of the issues in the first wave of the panel, estimates based on placements of Carter in the first wave have large standard errors and therefore should be viewed with some caution. Overall, then, there is enough variation over time in evaluations of the candidates' issue positions to suggest that as the campaign wore on voters may have revised their initial estimates of where the candidates stood. To what extent might such adjustments reflect the operation of inference processes?

To answer this question, let us begin by examining the degree to which voters infer the candidates' issue positions from their own stands (i.e., projection). In this regard, four key points are suggested by the findings in Table 7.2. First, because projection effects vary substantially across issues, the average projection effects for each candidate should be interpreted cautiously. Again, this is especially true for Carter. Second, for many candidates on a number of issues, there is evidence of significant inferences from the voters' own issue positions. Moreover, there is an asymmetry in the effects: Respondents make considerably stronger inferences for positively evaluated candidates than for negatively evaluated ones. In fact, 20 of the 36 positive projection terms are significant (.05 level), whereas only 3 of the 36 negative projection estimates are significant. Such asymmetry is consistent with the findings of a considerable amount of research in the balance theory tradition (see, e.g., Bruner, 1978; Granberg & Brent, 1975; Kinder, 1978). Yet, at the same time, this pattern of findings is congruent with a schematic interpretation. People should be able to make more inferences about candidates that fit into categories for which they have schemata than those that do not. With regard to inferences from self-schemata, this suggests that individuals will be able to make more inferences about people perceived to be similar to themselves. Voters have less organized conceptions of people different from themselves, people they dislike, and thus can make fewer inferences about such individuals.

A third point to note about the projection coefficients is that they vary across candidates. For one thing, positive inferences are lowest and negative ones are highest for the two Republican candidates, Ford and Reagan. Why this should be the case is not immediately obvious. More understandable are the projection effects among the four Democratic candidates. Positive projection effects are about the same for Humphrey, Kennedy, and Wallace, the three relatively well-known candidates. But they are considerably stronger for the newcomer Carter, averaging .22 as compared to the .13 to .14 range for the other Democrats. The strong positive projection effects for Carter are not surprising, given what an unknown entity he was early in the campaign. Few voters were certain of his standing in the Democratic party or his ideological placement; party and ideology cues, therefore, were not easily ascertained in Carter's case. This left most voters with one key source for making inference about Carter: their own issue positions.

Fourth, for any one candidate, projection effects tend to vary across issues. For example, in the case of both the mainstream, well-known Democratic candidates (Humphrey and Kennedy), projection effects are insignificant on the jobs issue, but significant on most other issues. Because the parties were perceived as being quite polarized on the jobs issue and both candidates were perceived as stalwarts of the Democratic party, many voters appear to have used party cues rather than self-cues to infer where Kennedy and Humphrey stood on the jobs issue (see the appendix to this chapter). To take another case, for George Wallace positive inferences from the voters' own issue positions are insignificant for most issues; however, on defense spending they are quite substantial (.31). Although Wallace was generally perceived as an extremist, his image as a hawk on national defense issues possibly may have been similar to a number of voters' self-images, and therefore, people may have been more likely to infer his specific stand on defense spending from their own position. In summary, our respondents demonstrate a clear willingness to infer the candidates' issue positions from their own, but at the same time, the strength of the inferences that voters make varies substantially across candidates and issues.

People's own issue positions are not the only basis from which to make inferences about the candidates' stands. Our respondents relied just as much on ideologically based inferences; as indicated in Table 7.2, across all candidates and issues, the ideological inference term averages .13. Moreover, as in the case of projection effects, there are considerable variations across candidates and issues in the strength of such inferences. In particular, ideological inferences are on the average, strongest for Reagan, Wallace, and Humphrey. This might be expected for both Reagan and Wallace because they are usually depicted as ideological extremists. In the case of Humphrey, the relatively strong ideological inferences may be traced to standard economic issues such as jobs, welfare, and the more recent social issue of busing.

With regard to the other candidates, ideological inferences are surprisingly weak for Edward Kennedy, a longtime spokesperson for the liberal Democrats. Moreover, ideological inferences about Kennedy are the weakest on traditional economic issues (the average coefficient for the jobs, welfare, and taxes issues is .06). But on the same issues, party inferences are quite strong, thus suggesting that in Kennedy's reputation as *the* liberal Democrat, the emphasis ought to be on Democrat and not liberal, at least for economic matters. On noneconomic issues such as busing and defense spending, voters do make stronger ideological inferences about Kennedy, a finding more in keeping with his strong identification with the liberal label. Ideological inferences are also relatively weak for Gerald Ford and Jimmy Carter. In Ford's case, this might be attributable to his general middle-of-the-road image; voters may have less well-defined schemata of moderates and thus find it more difficult to make ideological inferences about such candidates. In Carter's case, ideological inferences may have been depressed by his ambiguous standing on the liberal–conservative continuum. Most respondents could not make an ideological placement of Carter, and therefore, it was impossible for them to use their ideological schemata to infer his positions. Thus, we see that the inferences voters make depend on how well a candidate fits the ideological category and the extent to which an issue is viewed in ideological terms. Ideological inferences are strongest for extremist candidates (i.e., Reagan and Wallace) or those with prominent ideological reputations (i.e., Humphrey). They are also strongest for traditional liberal–conservative economic issues (e.g., jobs) or relatively clear-cut liberal–conservative social issues (e.g., busing).

The party inferences made by our respondents are even stronger than their ideological inferences. Over all candidates and issues, party inferences average .16 (.18 minus Wallace, for whom party inferences are quite weak). Thus, in general, party inferences are also stronger than projection effects. And again, as in the case of inferences from ideological cues and the voters' own positions, there are substantial variations in party inferences across candidates and issues. Party inferences are relatively strong for both Republican candidates (though especially for Reagan). With respect to the Democratic candidates, as predicted earlier, party inferences are strongest for the two established stalwarts of the party (Humphrey and Kennedy); they are considerably weaker for the newcomer (Carter) and the known party renegade (Wallace).

In terms of the variation across issues, party inferences are surprisingly strong on the abortion issue. Although the parties were not perceived as being particularly polarized on the abortion question, party cues were apparently seen as more reliable than ideological ones for sorting out candidate stands on this issue. Across all candidates, the average abortion coefficient for party inferences was .21, and for ideological inferences it was .09. Party inferences also tended to be high on economic issues.

Conversely, party inferences were relatively weak on defense spending. Only for the incumbent (Gerald Ford) were party cues used to make strong inferences about defense spending. Thus, as anticipated, party cues are a critical element in shaping voters' assessments of where the candidates stand on the issues.

Finally, we can briefly consider the impact of media attention on the placement of the candidates. Remembering that the Netnews and Paper coefficients are not directly comparable to the other inference coefficients (they must be divided by 7 to be comparable), we can see that media attention has virtually no effect on how voters evaluate the candidates' issue positions. Of the 72 coefficients involving these two variables, only 2 prove statistically significant, which could merely be due to chance. In effect, early in the campaign, well-informed voters have not learned enough from the media to place the candidates any differently than the poorly informed. Thus, despite Wright and Niemi's (1983) finding that attention to the media encourages the placement of candidates on issue scales, we find no evidence that the media provide people with information that is useful in knowing where the candidates stand.

To review, our findings lend substantial support to the idea that voters act as cognitive misers. Early in a campaign, when confronted with sparse and ambiguous information, voters use their prior information (their schemata) to infer where the candidates stand. Moreover, in making such inferences, voters draw on a variety of sources: their own issue positions, ideology schemata, and party schemata. Contextual factors (e.g., the candidates and issues involved) also contribute to variation in the strength of inferences. Candidates and issues are differentially related to the schemata that voters use to make inferences; consequently, people make stronger inferences about some candidates and issues than about others. Thus, the cues and the related schemata underlying candidate assessment are rich and varied in their nature.

Political Inferences: Individual Variation

To this point, we have concentrated on modeling the inference process for the public as a whole. As a result, it appears as if we are assuming that inferences from party, ideological, and self-schemata are made equally well by all people. However, even though the model we have used does not explicitly include interaction effects, we have already taken into account some individual differences in schema use. Our decision to set missing data for the respondents' own issue positions, their placements of the parties' issue stands, and the candidates' ideological positions equal to the mean values for those variables in the sample results in estimates for the inference terms that reflect the strength of inferences for people who make those placements (even though others are not actually excluded from the analysis). Thus, on the average, 40% of those respondents included in a particular equation did not place the party on that issue and therefore are not able to use party cues to infer the candidate's stand. By the same logic, somewhat more people are able to make inferences from the candidates' ideological positions, and still more are able to make inferences from their own issue positions. Even though it is implicit in the coding of the variables, our estimates do take into account individual differences in schema availability.

In the case of the party schemata, we have previously shown that the ability to locate the parties on the issue scales is a function of general education and political involvement (concern about politics, discussion of politics, and strength of party identification). Thus, those people that have party schemata, and therefore are capable of making party inferences, can be considered high in political expertise (see also Hamill, Lodge, & Blake, 1984). To investigate individual differences in the use of party schemata further, we looked for interaction effects of party inferences with a variety of measures of political involvement (data not presented here). This analysis produced no evidence of interaction effects, which is consistent with our argument that those with party schemata are to a great extent political experts. Further differences in political involvement do not seem to influence the making of party inferences; those who have party schemata appear quite capable of using them to infer where candidates stand on the issues.

The situation is very different for our estimates of inferences from the candidates' ideology largely because, unlike the case of party schemata, we have no measure of ideology schemata. Although the ideology estimates represent inferences only for those people who are able to locate the candidates ideologically, we have no direct evidence that those who can place the candidates on the liberal–conservative dimension also have schemata containing information about the issue positions of liberals and conservatives. In fact, evidence shows that a large number of people who can place themselves and candidates on the liberal–conservative continuum cannot place liberals and conservatives on issue scales (Levitin & Miller, 1979; see also Hamill, Lodge, & Blake, 1984). Therefore, it is likely that many of the people in our analysis who placed the candidates on the liberal–conservative continuum did not have sufficiently well-developed ideological schemata to make inferences of issue positions. Thus, the model we have been employing probably underestimates the extent to which those people with ideological schemata use them to infer issue positions. In addition, it is possible that there are individual differences in the ability to link a candidate strongly with the liberal or conservative label and hence to use that cue to infer issue positions.

Although we have no direct measures of ideological schemata (the source of our current predicament), we do know that political experts are more likely to have such schemata than novices (Hamill, Lodge, & Blake, 1984; Levitin & Miller, 1979). Therefore, we hypothesize that as political involvement (expertise) increases, inferences from ideological cues should grow stronger. To test this, we first constructed a measure of political involvement from two component measures: the extent to which the respondent discusses politics with others and the respondent's concern with the election and electoral process. The resulting involvement measure is almost normally distributed and was scaled from a minimum of −1 to a maximum of +1. An interaction term was then formed by multiplying the respondent's ideological placement of each candidate by the involvement measure. This new interaction term was then added to our basic inference model. As coded, the simple liberal–conservative term reflects inferences made by people who are about average in political involvement. The interaction term shows how the strength of the inferences varies by involvement. In estimating this new model, it was quickly apparent that too few people could locate Carter's ideological position in the first wave of the panel to permit stable estimates of ideological interaction effects for Carter. Thus, we estimated the new model for the other five candidates on the six issues.

As is often the case, the estimated standard errors of the interaction term were large, and therefore, very few of the parameter estimates achieved conventional levels of statistical significance, $p < .05$. However, out of the 30 estimates of the interaction term, only 4 were negative (i.e., in the wrong direction) and only 2 of the negative estimates were at all large. Interestingly, both of the large negative coefficients appeared in estimates of the abortion issue. Thus, 26 of the 30 estimates were in the predicted direction, and most of these estimates were big enough to produce substantively large interaction effects. Rather than presenting all 30 of the new parameter estimates, Table 7.3 shows the estimates of the liberal–conservative term and the ideology-involvement term averaged over each candidate (Part A) and each issue (Part B). Because the abortion issue was the one deviant issue in the estimates, averages of the coefficients across the candidates are shown with and without the abortion issue.

As shown in Table 7.3, the estimates of the interaction of ideological inference with political involvement vary to some extent across issues. The interaction effect is largest for the busing issue and smallest for the traditional economic issues of jobs and welfare. This suggests that it may be easier for people not highly involved in politics to associate positions on the latter two issues with liberals and conservatives and relatively harder in the case of busing. There is also substantial variation in the estimates across the candidates. Involvement seems to be less important in making ideological inferences about George Wallace and substantially more important in

TABLE 7.3
Mean Estimates for the Liberal–Conservative
and Involvement Interaction Terms

A. Mean Estimates for Each Candidate

	with abortion		without abortion	
	ideology	*interaction*	*ideology*	*interaction*
Ford	.028	.026	.081	.090
Reagan	.121	.093	.140	.086
Humphrey	.128	.115	.136	.123
Kennedy	.081	.081	.092	.156
Wallace	.123	.062	.129	.030
mean	.110	.075	.116	.097

B. Mean Estimates for Each Issue

	ideology	*interaction*
Taxes	.077	.104
Busing	.155	.133
Defense	.104	.093
Jobs	.132	.083
Welfare	.110	.072
Abortion	.084	−.033

C. Estimates of the Ideology Inference Term for Levels of Involvement

percentile involvement	*ideological inference*
95	.194
90	.174
75	.142
50	.119
25	.093
10	.067
5	.051

making inferences about Ted Kennedy. The variation across candidates suggests that involvement may be important not simply in determining the development of liberal–conservative schemata, but also in the ability to make the connection between the category and certain candidates.

In order to better appreciate differences in ideological inferences associated with various levels of political involvement, we computed the estimated ideological inference coefficients for seven different levels (percentiles) of involvement (see Part C of Table 7.3). These coefficients are based on the means of the liberal–conservative and interaction terms for the five candidates over all issues except abortion. As can be seen, the extent to which people make inferences based on the candidates' ideological positions varies considerably across levels of political involvement. At the top 10% of the involvement scale, ideological inferences are about as large as inferences from party. At the lower ranges of involvement, ideological inferences shrink to a third or less of those made by the most involved.

CONCLUSIONS

In this paper, we have elaborated and tested a model of how people make inferences about the issue positions of political candidates. Based on schema theory, we argue that in an ambiguous political environment voters will rely on inferences from schema-based knowledge of the issue positions of various categories of public officials in order to determine where specific politicians stand on the issues. Our empirical analysis dealt with three sources of such inferences: party, liberal–conservative, and self-schemata. Estimates from analysis of panel data collected early in the 1976 presidential campaign show that each of these is an important source for the inference of candidate issue positions. In particular, for those relatively high in political involvement, inferences from party and liberal–conservative schemata contribute strongly to the development of judgments of candidates' issue positions. Even for people who are not political experts, self-schemata are readily available for making inferences. On the other hand, there was no evidence that attention to the media made any significant contribution to where people saw these candidates standing on the issues.

More generally, our analysis shows that people do a reasonably successful job of coping with the ambiguity of the political environment. Developed from continued observation, party and ideological schemata are likely to be relatively accurate global assessments (for those who have such schemata) of Democrats and Republicans, liberals and conservatives. Moreover, people seem to be able to make distinctions across issue and candidates in ways that should increase the likelihood that appropriate inferences will be made. On the other hand, there are reasons to believe that inferences from schemata will not always lead people to accurate judgments about candidates. Specific issue positions often vary considerably across candidates within the same political party or ideological category. Therefore, a dependence on schema-based inferences is likely to limit people's perceptions of potentially significant differences in politician's issue stands. Voters are likely to believe that all Democrats or all conservatives are more alike than is actually the case. Alternatively, candidates must work that much harder to convince voters that they are not just a typical liberal.

The limitations of our analysis provide a good indication of where future research in this area could profitably go. First, we need considerably more information about the nature and content of political schemata. In this analysis, we have focused on party, liberal–conservative, and self-schemata, but these cannot possibly exhaust the schema-based knowledge people can draw upon. We need to know what other cues (and hence, schemata) people may use to make inferences. For example, Ted Kennedy is seen to be much further from the Democratic party on the abortion issue than on any other issue considered here. Could it be that people have a schema for Catholics that includes being conservative on the abortion issue? Certainly, Kennedy's identification as a liberal Democrat does not explain why so many people see him as conservative on this issue.

Second, our analysis shows that contextual variations may be an important aspect of the inference process. More attention is clearly needed to the ways in which the political environment helps to structure inferences to politicians. At the most basic level, interaction with the political environment will help shape the schemata that are used in the inference process. For example, the schema a southerner holds about the Democratic party may very well be significantly different from one held by a New Englander. Inferences to a Democratic politician will then vary according to differences in the contents of people's schemata. The political environment should also play a major role in priming different schemata. Some evidence that the media may be particularly influential in this respect has been presented by Iyengar, Peters, and Kinder (1982).

Finally, greater attention should be paid to individual differences in the inference process. Although we did not examine this in the analysis presented here, it is likely that people vary in their motivation or inclination to make any judgment of candidates' issue positions. Given the vast differences that have been documented in political information holding, political involvement, and attention to the media, it would be surprising not to find substantial differences in the number, nature, and content of political schemata across the public. Individual differences are likely to be substantial in schema availability and access, and in the strategies people use to process political information (see Kinder & Fiske, in press; Graber, 1984). Unfortunately, except for some quite general hypotheses, we know little about how these differences may influence the judgments people make about politicians.

APPENDIX
Estimates of the Inference Model for Each Issue

A. ABORTION

	Ford	Reagan	Humphrey	Kennedy	Carter	Wallace
Intercept	.44 (.21)	.02 (.24)	.02 (.19)	.04 (.30)	.01 (.28)	.33 (.33)
Stability	.75 (.25)	.70 (.20)	.17 (.19)	1.07 (.19)	-1.03 (.96)	.66 (.25)
Self-Positive	.13 (.05)	.13 (.07)	.16 (.05)	.10 (.06)	.26 (.10)	.06 (.10)
Self-Negative	-.04 (.06)	-.09 (.07)	-.14 (.07)	.07 (.08)	.10 (.17)	-.10 (.08)
Liberal-Conservative	.12 (.08)	.05 (.07)	.11 (.06)	-.03 (.09)	.16 (.18)	.14 (.02)
Party	.22 (.09)	.36 (.09)	.25 (.08)	.21 (.09)	.23 (.09)	.01 (.10)
Netnews	-.33 (.28)	.05 (.31)	-.12 (.26)	-.03 (.33)	.16 (.33)	-.23 (.31)
Paper	.06 (.25)	.03 (.27)	-.00 (.22)	-.03 (.29)	-.33 (.29)	-.23 (.31)
R^2	.12	.21	.20	.18	.07	.14

B. BUSING

	Ford	Reagan	Humphrey	Kennedy	Carter	Wallace
Intercept	-.13 (.19)	-.26 (.22)	-.19 (.18)	-.17 (.28)	-.12 (.28)	-.09 (.58)
Stability	.78 (.21)	.77 (.15)	.33 (.15)	.55 (.19)	.76 (.65)	.85 (.26)
Self-Positive	-.01 (.05)	.07 (.06)	.18 (.05)	.14 (.05)	.19 (.09)	.04 (.06)
Self-Negative	-.15 (.06)	-.14 (.06)	-.08 (.06)	-.08 (.07)	-.05 (.13)	-.03 (.05)
Liberal-Conservative	.15 (.06)	.14 (.06)	.29 (.05)	.25 (.07)	.24 (.13)	.08 (.05)
Party	.15 (.06)	.24 (.06)	.18 (.06)	.18 (.06)	.03 (.07)	.09 (.06)
Netnews	-.07 (.24)	-.31 (.26)	-.10 (.21)	-.20 (.25)	.02 (.28)	-.24 (.22)
Paper	.12 (.22)	.56 (.23)	.01 (.18)	.05 (.23)	-.33 (.24)	.12 (.20)
R^2	.10	.21	.23	.16	.03	.05

APPENDIX (Continued)
Estimates of the Inference Model for Each Issue

C. TAXES

	Ford	Reagan	Humphrey	Kennedy	Carter	Wallace
Intercept	-.27 (.20)	-.17 (.27)	-.05 (.24)	-.02 (.27)	.50 (.51)	.07 (.39)
Stability	.48 (.12)	.59 (.15)	.65 (.15)	.58 (.15)	1.02 (.54)	.97 (.26)
Self-Positive	.11 (.05)	.11 (.06)	.17 (.05)	.16 (.05)	.21 (.10)	.13 (.07)
Self-Negative	-.10 (.05)	-.10 (.06)	.03 (.07)	.05 (.06)	.12 (.14)	.08 (.05)
Liberal-Conservative	.16 (.06)	.19 (.06)	.20 (.06)	.06 (.06)	.09 (.14)	.01 (.06)
Party	.13 (.06)	.21 (.06)	.21 (.06)	.19 (.06)	.12 (.07)	-.06 (.06)
Netnews	-.35 (.21)	-.32 (.24)	-.20 (.23)	-.10 (.23)	-.15 (.29)	-.07 (.23)
Paper	.11 (.19)	-.05 (.21)	-.06 (.21)	.09 (.20)	-.00 (.26)	.05 (.22)
R^2	.15	.20	.25	.19	.05	.07

D. WELFARE

	Ford	Reagan	Humphrey	Kennedy	Carter	Wallace
Intercept	.05 (.17)	.14 (.24)	-.13 (.19)	.00 (.22)	-.13 (.23)	.11 (.45)
Stability	.48 (.12)	.59 (.15)	.65 (.15)	.58 (.15)	1.02 (.54)	.97 (.26)
Self-Positive	.11 (.05)	.11 (.06)	.17 (.05)	.16 (.05)	.21 (.10)	.13 (.07)
Self-Negative	-.10 (.05)	-.10 (.06)	.03 (.07)	.05 (.06)	.12 (.14)	.08 (.05)
Liberal-Conservative	.16 (.06)	.19 (.06)	.20 (.06)	.06 (.06)	.09 (.14)	.01 (.06)
Party	.13 (.06)	.21 (.06)	.21 (.06)	.19 (.06)	.12 (.07)	-.06 (.06)
Netnews	-.35 (.21)	-.32 (.24)	-.20 (.23)	-.10 (.23)	-.15 (.29)	-.07 (.23)
Paper	.11 (.19)	-.05 (.21)	-.06 (.21)	.09 (.20)	.00 (.26)	.05 (.22)
R^2	.15	.20	.25	.19	.05	.07

APPENDIX (*Continued*)
Estimates of the Inference Model for Each Issue

E. JOBS

	Ford	Reagan	Humphrey	Kennedy	Carter	Wallace
Intercept	.28 (.18)	.42 (.26)	- .47 (.27)	- .58 (.37)	- .24 (.41)	.28 (.30)
Stability	.70 (.15)	.85 (.17)	.81 (.19)	.86 (.25)	1.30 (.57)	.60 (.27)
Self–Positive	.01 (.05)	.06 (.07)	.05 (.05)	.04 (.05)	.24 (.09)	.18 (.08)
Self–Negative	- .10 (.06)	- .12 (.07)	- .02 (.07)	.01 (.07)	.12 (.14)	.07 (.07)
Liberal–Conservative	.18 (.07)	.16 (.07)	.13 (.06)	.05 (.06)	- .03 (.14)	.22 (.07)
Party	.14 (.06)	.19 (.07)	.15 (.07)	.18 (.07)	.14 (.07)	.16 (.09)
Netnews	- .30 (.23)	- .29 (.28)	.17 (.22)	.33 (.21)	- .08 (.22)	.53 (.30)
Paper	.23 (.21)	.27 (.26)	.33 (.20)	- .08 (.20)	- .10 (.24)	.16 (.27)
R^2	.16	.19	.15	.11	.06	.12

F. DEFENSE SPENDING

	Ford	Reagan	Humphrey	Kennedy	Carter	Wallace
Intercept	.25 (.19)	- .44 (.25)	.14 (.17)	- .33 (.20)	.09 (.19)	.47 (.34)
Stability	.72 (.17)	1.00 (.22)	.69 (.17)	.85 (.15)	1.01 (.49)	1.04 (.27)
Self–Positive	.04 (.05)	.12 (.07)	.11 (.05)	.13 (.06)	.26 (.09)	.31 (.08)
Self–Negative	- .06 (.06)	- .06 (.07)	- .13 (.07)	- .09 (.09)	.17 (.15)	.07 (.07)
Liberal–Conservative	.06 (.06)	.11 (.07)	.10 (.05)	.18 (.07)	- .08 (.13)	.17 (.07)
Party	.29 (.06)	.06 (.08)	.18 (.06)	.17 (.07)	.10 (.06)	.12 (.07)
Netnews	.01 (.22)	- .06 (.28)	.28 (.23)	- .03 (.26)	- .42 (.25)	- .11 (.29)
Paper	- .17 (.20)	.26 (.25)	- .21 (.20)	.14 (.23)	- .07 (.23)	.07 (.26)
R^2	.16	.12	.19	.22	.08	.15

Note. Entries are unstandardized regression coefficients with standard errors in parentheses.

8

A Schematic Variant of Symbolic Politics Theory, as Applied to Racial and Gender Equality

David O. Sears
Leonie Huddy
Lynitta G. Schaffer
University of California, Los Angeles

A series of empirical investigations in recent years has begun to develop evidence for a theory of symbolic politics (e.g., Kinder & Sears, 1981; Lau, Brown, & Sears, 1978; Sears & Citrin, 1985; Sears, Hensler, & Speer, 1979; Sears, Lau, Tyler, & Allen, 1980; Sears, Tyler, Citrin & Kinder, 1978). These studies have focused in particular on contrasting a theory of symbolic politics with a theory that emphasizes the role of self-interest. Because self-interest is by itself a complex and multifaceted matter, these studies have given less attention to developing the implications of a symbolic politics theory. For the most part, they have simply suggested that the public responds to political symbols with relatively longstanding conditioned affective responses, generally described as *symbolic predispositions.* To add somewhat more cognitive complexity to this idea, Sears and Citrin (1985) suggested that these responses might on occasion be organized in "schemata," but they did not pursue this notion very far. If a symbolic politics theory is to have value as a more general theory of the mass public's political thinking, however, it would seem necessary to develop it more fully.

It might be useful to start by placing this symbolic politics theory in a more general context. Theories of the mass public's political information processing range from those primarily emphasizing affective reactions to those that presuppose more complex cognitive structures. At the former extreme would be a simple symbolic politics theory that views the public's policy issue positions and voting preferences as based primarily on affective responses to political symbols such as "liberals," "blacks," or "women's liberation" (Sears et al., 1980). At the other extreme would be theories

159

invoking complex ideological structures, with certain central attitudes organizing an abstract conceptualization of political stimuli and constraining a variety of more specific beliefs (see the descriptions in Campbell, Converse, Miller, & Stokes, 1960; Converse, 1964). The appeal of the simpler, more affective models lies partly in extensive evidence that most members of the general public do not seem to possess complex ideologies in this form (Converse, 1964, 1970, 1975; Kinder & Sears, 1985). Even when some apparent indicators of ideology prove to be quite widespread (e.g., self-identification as liberal or conservative), they often prove in reality to reflect fairly simple affective responses rather than complex cognitive structures (Conover & Feldman, 1981).

Still, it seems unlikely that the political attitudes of most people are as devoid of cognitive structure as this implies. A central theme of contemporary social psychology is that information processing about social objects is heavily influenced by cognitive processes (e.g., Fiske & Taylor, 1984; Kahneman, Slovic, & Tversky, 1982). Political objects are probably no exception. It seems likely, therefore, that the mass public's political thinking would be described most faithfully by a more cognitive version of a symbolic politics theory. This might fall somewhere between the extremes of the simplest, most affect-dominated symbolic politics theory and a portrait dominated by full-blown ideologies. The main purpose of this paper is to begin developing this more cognitive variant. But we begin by elaborating the implications of a simple symbolic politics theory because, as indicated earlier, it has previously been presented only in rather rudimentary form.

A SYMBOLIC POLITICS APPROACH

The symbolic politics approach (hereafter referred to as *simple* symbolic politics) assumes that political attitudes mainly reflect the affects previously conditioned to the specific symbols included in the attitude object. When an object includes multiple symbols, the net affect toward the total object should reflect some simple linear combination of the affects toward the constituent symbols.[1] For example, attitudes toward "forced busing" to integrate whites and blacks would depend on affects toward such symbols as "force," "busing," "integration," and "blacks."

---

[1]The combinatorial principle might be additive or some weighted average. This assumption rests on substantial evidence that evaluations are normally combined in some such linear manner (N. H. Anderson, 1981). The frequency of linear combinations of evaluations should not lead us to overlook the fact that more complex combinatorial principles are sometimes used, presumably mainly when the connotative meaning of a combination is substantially different from that of its constituent parts.

These affects may vary in strength depending on the strength of prior learning (Sears, 1983a). The strongest have been called *symbolic predispositions* to connote their particular persistence and power (Sears & Citrin, 1985). Among the most basic and longstanding are such attitudes as party identification, racial prejudice, and nationalism. Others might include liberal or conservative self-designations, evaluations of various groups (Conover & Feldman, 1981), and ostensibly nonpolitical values such as individualism (Feldman, 1983; Lukes, 1973), egalitarianism (Rokeach, 1969, 1973), and postmaterialism (Inglehart, 1977, 1979).

Treating such orientations as symbolic predispositions is appealing because it allows us to recognize their widespread use by the mass public without assuming that many people hold abstract ideologies in the forms familiar to political elites. Indeed, in its simplest form, a symbolic politics formulation would assume that affects are tied quite closely to the manifest symbolic content of a particular attitude object, without detailed consideration of underlying or latent meanings. If so, attitudes toward objects of different manifest content but shared underlying meanings might be quite compartmentalized.

Yet, there are several problems with interpreting such predispositions solely from this simple symbolic politics point of view. These difficulties suggest that it may be necessary to combine the simple symbolic politics viewpoint with some notion of cognitive structure to get a more satisfactory view of public thinking.

One problem is that attitudes with similar latent meaning are often quite affectively consistent even when they have quite different manifest symbolic contents. The symbolic politics expectation would be that affective consistency across attitudes depends on similar manifest symbolic content of their attitude objects. Thus, there would be no reason to expect high correlations between responses to manifestly dissimilar symbols. Indeed, pairs of objects with quite different manifest content but much shared underlying meaning do frequently evoke very different marginal distributions of opinion, for example, "busing" versus "school integration" (Sears & Allen, 1984), "politicians" versus "your congressman" (Sears, 1982, 1983b), or "smaller government" versus "cutting spending for the police" or other such specific programs (Sears & Citrin, 1985). Despite these grossly different marginal distributions, however, these pairs of attitudes are often highly correlated. Moreover, such pairs often load on the same factor in factor analyses, and share antecedents and consequences in more elaborate causal models (Sears & Citrin, 1985). Hence, there is reason to believe that such manifestly disparate symbols evoke fairly consistent affects, despite attracting quite inconsistent marginal frequencies. This would seem to imply a degree of underlying cognitive structure that a simple symbolic politics theory cannot predict.

The second problem concerns abstraction. The public often seems to evaluate abstract and concrete versions of a given attitude object very differently, even at the opposite extremes of a favorable–unfavorable dimension. For example, in one typical survey, a two-thirds majority wanted "less government," but an equally large majority wanted "more spending" on concrete public services (Sears & Citrin, 1985). Similarly, "politicians" are usually strongly disliked even when specific individual officials receive general approval (Sears, 1983b). A symbolic politics theory might explain such seeming contradictions as due to the somewhat different manifest symbolic content presented at each level of abstraction, with these different symbols then evoking different conditioned associations. For example, most people have quite different evaluations of such concrete symbols as "the Los Angeles busing plan," "Thomas Jefferson," and "the police" than of such related abstract symbols as "racial segregation," "politicians," and "big government," to use examples from the aforementioned pairs. This could simply be due to having learned different affects for them over the years. But it is also possible that these systematic differences in evaluation are due to differences in the level of abstraction, in and of themselves. Such a possibility calls at least for consideration of a more cognitive theory.

The third problem emerges from the effects of information. A simple symbolic politics theory would predict that increased information would do no more than enhance consistency between affects associated with symbols that are themselves frequently paired in the information environment. And there is considerable evidence that information does in fact increase consistency. Media exposure usually increases the consistency of even manifestly dissimilar attitudes, such as policy preferences and voting intentions (Klapper, 1960; Sears & Chaffee, 1979). Greater media exposure, or more information, is associated with greater consistency of voting or policy preferences with basic symbolic predispositions (Converse, 1962; Sears et al., 1980). But greater information is also correlated with outcomes that could not be achieved by the simple passive pairing of symbols, such as more abstract conceptualizations and the use of abstract ideologies (Campbell et al., 1960; Converse, 1964). Such findings also suggest the exploration of possible underlying cognitive structures.

A Schematic Version

The need for notions of cognitive structure, especially hierarchical structures that embody variations in abstraction, leads us to general models of social cognition as developed in social psychology. One is the concept of a schema. Fiske and Taylor (1984) have defined a schema as:

a cognitive structure that represents organized knowledge about a given concept or type of stimulus. A schema contains both the attributes of the concept and the relationships among the attributes . . . the schema concept specifically maintains that information is stored in an abstract form, not simply as a collection of all the original encounters with examples of the general case. (p. 140; see also the review of research on social schemata in chapter 18, this volume).

The schema concept thus would add some new elements to a symbolic politics theory. It provides for the structure or organization of diverse cognitive elements about a political object.[2] And more specifically, it introduces the notion of hierarchical organization. A schema is supposed to incorporate concrete instances and abstract concepts alike. It is also supposed to involve "top-down" or "theory-driven" processing, in which specific responses are derived from general concepts.

However, introducing the schema concept into empirical analyses of public opinion raises some problems, as well. Most obviously, the role of affect, the key element of symbolic politics, has been quite unclear in schema theory. Most schema research has been generated out of cognitive theories that are unconcerned with affect, and it has been conducted on content areas that evoke little affect (the work of Fiske & Pavelchak, in press, is a recent exception).

Variations in schematic thinking can be treated in two very different ways. Content domains may vary in the frequency with which they elicit schematic thinking from the public as a whole; for example, Sears and Citrin (1985) found that Californians frequently thought schematically about their tax revolt, but presumably few Americans think schematically about whether utilities should be publicly or privately owned (Converse, 1970). Alternatively, individuals may differ in whether or not they think schematically about a given content domain, yielding (at the extremes) "schematic" or "aschematic" individuals. Some people plainly thought more schematically about the tax revolt than others did (Sears & Citrin, 1985). Work on self-schemata (e.g., H. Markus, 1977) has generally used this second approach, as do the other empirical papers in this volume (see the chapters by Conover & Feldman, Hamill & Lodge, and Lau).

Finally, a key implication of this hierarchical notion is that processing may be more efficient at one level of abstraction than at others. The exact nature of the relationship between level of abstraction and processing efficiency remains somewhat in dispute, however. Much social cognition research argues that the greater abstraction involved in schematic thinking

---

[2]This does not assume infinite scope. Presumably, most political schemata are more limited in scope than a full-blown ideology (Sears & Citrin, 1985), instead being analogous to what Converse (1964) called a belief system.

simplifies processing compared to the more costly processing at a detailed, concrete, nonschematic level. Hence, people try to simplify processing by grouping concrete instances together into more abstract categories (e.g., "government regulations are just attempts by power-hungry bureaucrats to hamstring private enterprise"). However, such abstraction can lead to all the perils of oversimplification by precluding recognition of important distinctions, as amply documented in the literatures on (and critiques of) racial prejudice and stereotyping (Hamilton, 1981). Similarly, Rosch (1978) has developed the idea that there is a "basic level" of abstraction that provides for the optimal level of categorization, and therefore, the level of abstraction at which people process information most readily.

Processing efficiency may also differ by level of abstraction across individuals. Variations in processing efficiency across levels of abstraction can be investigated by comparing the cognitive processes of novices and experts. On the one hand, experts are thought to have schemata in their area of expertise, whereas novices do not (Chase & Chi, in press). As experts develop their schemata, they become more abstract (Abelson, 1976). Some supportive evidence for experts' greater cognitive abstraction comes from Stimson's (1975) finding that political sophisticates use fewer dimensions to organize political issues.

On the other hand, the schemata of experts are thought to be more complex than those of novices (Linville, 1982; Linville & Jones, 1980), and experts are found to prefer more detailed information in making political judgments (Fiske, Kinder, & Larter, 1983). This suggests that on occasion the schemata of experts allow for greater differentiation between schema elements and, therefore, for more concrete, specific thinking. For example, an experienced government bureaucrat might process information about government in terms of specific agencies and programs, whereas ordinary citizens might more often think at the more abstract level of "big government." The nature and direction of these relationships are not fully resolved at this time.

Combining these ideas leads to the two core propositions of a schematic variant of symbolic politics theory. One is that a given level of abstraction is optimal for information processing (it could be called the basic level, in line with Rosch's terminology, but it need not). This is the level at which people feel most comfortable and fluid in their information processing. As a result, affective consistency, and the power to influence more concrete attitudes, should be greatest at this optimal level. Second, variations in this optimal level of categorization exist across domains and individuals alike, dependent on information level. Which level is optimal would tend to vary with the person's expertise, knowledge, and interest levels in the domain under investigation. However, there appears to be little consensus in schema theory about the direction of this relationship (i.e., whether expertise makes the optimal level more concrete or more abstract).

Where does all this leave us? The consensus of political behavior researchers is that most members of the mass public do not have elaborate hierarchical cognitive structures about politics. In response to that, we have described a symbolic politics theory that portrays people as responding to political symbols in terms of relatively noncognitive, compartmentalized affects. As useful as this simple version of symbolic politics theory may be, it seems wise to entertain the possibility of adding to it some assumptions about hierarchical cognitive structure. Our primary goal here, then, is to explore the implications of expanding a simple symbolic politics theory to include notions of cognitive schema and optimal levels of abstraction.

VALUES ABOUT SOCIAL EQUALITY

This schematic approach to symbolic politics could potentially be tested empirically in any content area in which substantial numbers of people are likely to have political schemata. In particular, our data concern values about political equality and policy preferences concerning women's and blacks' rights. Equality for women and equality for blacks are potent contemporary political issues, and central to current debates over national policy. Values are thought of as relatively stable and as having considerable predictive utility (Feldman, 1983; Rokeach, 1973).[3]

Values about equality also fit more narrowly the particular requirements for an appropriate test of symbolic politics theory. A value can be described as an affect associated with a particular symbol; for example, a person who values equality can be said to have a positive evaluation of the symbol "equality." Many equality-related symbols (e.g., "busing" or "women's lib") evoke strongly affective reactions. Moreover, values have the potential for schematic organization. This organization might be hierarchical; values concerning equality can potentially be quite abstract and may or may not be related to concrete issues (e.g., equality for specific groups such as blacks, women, or Palestinians). Similarly, a schematic organization might be horizontal; valuing equality for one group (e.g., blacks) may or may not be perceived as interdependent with valuing it for others (e.g., the retarded). Thus, the use of equality values in our empirical work has considerable

---

[3]Conceptually, values are usually treated like attitudes, with the usual affective, cognitive, and behavioral components. But they are usually thought of as more general than, and causally prior to, attitudes on specific issues; for example, the value of equality might produce support for proequality policies (e.g., the ERA). The question we raise here is whether or not such values and policy attitudes are generally schematically organized, and if so, with what consequence.

potential for the exploration of our theoretical concerns, providing an issue domain with substantial affective and political vitality as well as the proper potential for schematic thinking.

What would a simple symbolic politics approach to values be? Assume that the elements of a value structure are affectively loaded symbols. Presumably, these can be quite abstract (e.g., "equality") or quite concrete (e.g., "equal access to public accommodations for blacks and whites"). A simple further assumption is that the basic symbols are modular in the sense that the affective loading of more complex ones is a simple function of the affective loading of their modular components. Hence, the evaluation of "equality for blacks" might be a simple function (presumably, usually a weighted average) of the separate evaluations of "equality" and "blacks" (N. H. Anderson, 1981; Osgood & Tannenbaum, 1955).

This simple symbolic politics approach to gender and racial equality is portrayed in Figure 8.1. The two primary constituent symbols are group affect and general political equality. Hence, equality values for women (gender equality values) should be a simple function of affect toward "women" and toward "equality." So should support for women's equality in terms of public policy issues such as equal pay or the ERA. These latter two—gender equality values and support for women's issues— should be related, but only because each is determined by affect toward the simpler symbols they share: evaluations of "women" and of "equality" in general. Figure 8.1 shows that exactly the same analysis can be applied to racial values and racial issues. Thus, the gender and racial systems are connected only by their shared origins in the symbol of general political equality. Otherwise they are not connected, reflecting the compartmentalization assumed to exist between two areas otherwise dissimilar in symbolic content.

This simple symbolic politics approach predicts that level of abstraction is irrelevant; attitude objects in a more specific context, whether that context be group-specific or that of a particular issue, should produce some weighted average of evaluations of the abstract object and of the context. Thus, constraint across the levels of abstraction shown in Figure 8.1 should simply be a function of similarity in manifest symbolism across levels. Indeed, there is evidence that the impact of values changes considerably when they are considered only in terms of blacks as stimulus persons (Feldman, 1983).

A schematic variant of this simple symbolic politics theory would add the notion of a hierarchical value structure, with differing levels of abstraction. The form of the structure might be pyramidal, with the top being most abstract. Four levels of a hierarchical equality schema might be distinguished:

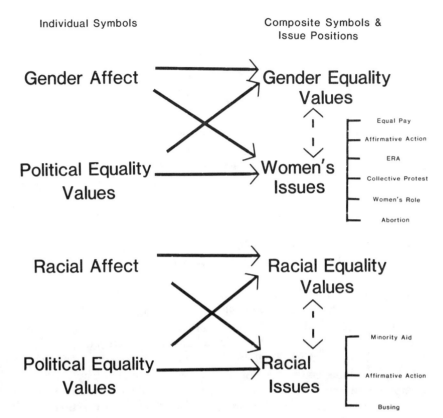

FIG. 8.1   A Simple Symbolic Politics Approach to the Influence of Values on Issue Positions.

1. General values. A general belief in equality, independent of context, might be the most abstract level. This is essentially the level measured by Rokeach (1969) as one of a number of basic *terminal values.*

2. The next most abstract level assigns values to a more specific context. One might distinguish between *general personal* and *general political values,* as advocated by Marsh (1975) and as implemented by Conover and Feldman (1984); equality for various groups in society might be treated quite differently from the question of equality for oneself. Other examples of political values would include Inglehart's (1977) postmaterialist values (e.g., maintaining order in the nation). One could imagine still other types of distinctions at this level of abstraction, for example, equality values during wartime versus peacetime or in the old days (as in the old South) versus today.

3. Various content domains, producing domain-specific values, mark the next level. In the case of political equality values, which is our specific concern here, these might be called *group-specific values* because they might vary across target groups. An individual might have one set of political equality values concerning blacks and quite another concerning women, for example.

4. The specific policy context adds still another level: *issue positions.* For example, racial equality values might be linked to a variety of different issue positions, such as equal access to public accommodations, busing, or affirmative action. Each could pose different, though possibly related, symbols.

This schematic variant, as operationalized in the present study, is shown in Figure 8.2. The most abstract level of general equality values was not measured in this study, nor were personal equality values. Rather, we worked within the bottom three levels and solely within the political context.

Although group affect plays a prominent role in the simple symbolic politics approach, it is noticeably absent from Figure 8.2. This is primarily because the role of affect within schema theory is unclear. Many schematic theories completely ignore affect. Those that incorporate it differ widely in its assigned role (Fiske & Taylor, 1984). One line of research, for example, highlights the dependence of affect on cognitive complexity, with more complex structures leading to more moderate affect (Linville, 1982). A second suggests that tight organization leads to affective polarization (Tesser, 1978), and a third that schema evocation per se triggers specific, associated affects (Fiske & Pavelchak, in press). Given such lack of consensus, then, affect is not incorporated in the schematic theory shown in Figure 8.2. Nevertheless, its role in an equality schema is empirically investigated and discussed later.

The equality schema in Figure 8.2 is further simplified by emphasizing vertical, but not horizontal, connections between elements. Discussion of "tight" schematic organization is common within schema research, particularly in reference to the knowledge structures of experts (Chi & Koeske, 1983; Fiske et al., 1983). It usually implies strong vertical and horizontal connections between elements (i.e., both across and within different levels of abstraction). We presume that the hypothetical equality schema depicted in Figure 8.2 does contain horizontal connections, even though they are omitted from the figure; they are analyzed and discussed subsequently.

A schematic variant of symbolic politics theory, then, implies that people frequently have schemata about political content areas; these schemata are more narrowly defined than is ideology as it has usually been

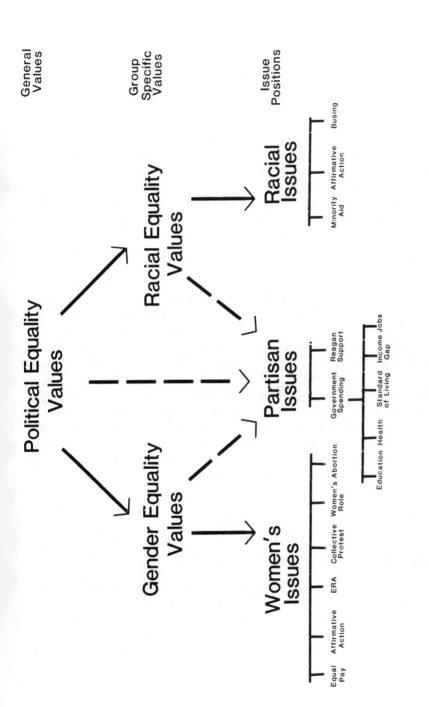

General
Values

Group
Specific
Values

Issue
Positions

Political Equality
Values

Racial Equality
Values

Gender Equality
Values

Racial
Issues

Partisan
Issues

Women's
Issues

Minority
Aid

Affirmative
Action

Busing

Government
Spending

Reagan
Support

Education

Health

Standard
of Living

Income
Gap

Jobs

Equal
Pay

Affirmative
Action

ERA

Collective
Protest

Women's
Role

Abortion

FIG. 8.2   An Equality Schema.

described; they are strongly controlled by the affects that people have toward the symbols within the schema; these schemata are to some extent hierarchically organized; and stable, consistent responses to political symbols may be contingent upon processing occurring at the most appropriate level of abstraction. Hence, stable and consistent political responses may depend on the individual's having some schema about the symbol, even if a rather local one.

The major purpose of this chapter, then, is to elaborate and test the differences between a simple symbolic politics theory and a schematic variant of it. How would we be able to detect these difference empirically? There are probably a number of crucial contrasts, but we focus here on three. First, in a simple symbolic politics theory, affect toward political symbols, with even minimal cognitive support, should have a major political impact, in the vein suggested by Zajonc (1980). In the schematic variant, affect only influences political attitudes among schematics, those that have a schema containing both the issue and the relevant symbol. Second, the simple symbolic politics theory would suggest that differences in the abstraction of various attitude objects are unimportant; one's reactions to highly abstract symbols (e.g., law and order) can be just as immediate and emotional as reactions to very concrete symbols. In contrast, schematic processing implies that processing occurs differentially and in different ways at different levels of abstraction (e.g., a particular arrest described on television). Third, level of political sophistication should matter relatively little in a pure symbolic politics theory because all the individual needs to do is match manifestly similar symbols or determine that two symbols do not match. However, it should be an important contributor to consistency (or the quality of political information processing in general) in the schematic variant; higher levels of sophistication should make it easier to evoke political schemata.

METHODS

Sample

The data come from the 1983 National Election Studies (NES) pilot study. Of a panel originally interviewed as part of the 1982 National Election Study, 314 surviving members were reinterviewed in the summer of 1983. The sample contained more women than 1982 population gender estimates (59% vs. 53%) and similar percentages of minorities; it was better educated, slightly older, and more politically involved. The sample was interviewed in two different subgroups that were given slightly different series of questions.

Equality Values

An additive scale of general political equality values was created from six items, one dealing with equality of treatment, two with equality of opportunity, and three with leadership ability (hereafter referred to as *antielitism*) (these items are shown in the appendix to this chapter). Equality of opportunity and treatment were strongly supported, antielitism was not, and the final scale mean represented an item average of just above the midpoint. The six-item scale did not have high internal consistency (α = .44), although a shorter three-item scale from which the antielitism items were dropped was more consistent (α = .55).

To obtain measures of group-specific equality values, the six general political equality items were minimally reworded for the gender and racial contexts, generally by substituting the symbols "woman" or "blacks" for "people," as shown in the appendix. The gender equality scale exhibited greater internal consistency than did the general political equality scale (α = .71) and had a higher overall scale mean. The reason for this was that elitism was supported at an abstract level, but not when the issue was gender elitism. The racial equality scale was also reasonably consistent internally (α = .64). The antielitism items again lowered the reliability of the scale, but in this instance because these items were so overwhelmingly supported. Gender equality items were asked only of respondents in the first subgroup (n = 143) and racial equality items only of respondents in the second subgroup (n = 131).

Issue Position Scales

The main dependent variables consist of four equality issues: three affecting women (government aid to women, beliefs about women's roles in society, and the desirability of collective action to attain women's rights) and one on blacks' rights. Two additional dependent variables were included because they involve more distal potential political consequences of support for equality and do not share manifest symbolism with either group or equality symbols: support for greater spending on government services and opposition to Ronald Reagan. All issue position scales were constructed by standardizing and adding relevant items. Factor analyses were used to help guide item selection.

Positions on three sets of issues relevant to women were measured. A government involvement scale was formed from two items on affirmative action, one on government involvement in women's issues, and one on equal pay (α = .77). A second scale measured approval of collective political action by women, consisting of two items that correlated significantly but not extremely highly (r = .32). Four items on nontraditional beliefs about women's roles (the Equal Rights Amendment, abortion, and gender differences in drive and ambition) were standardized and added, yielding a scale that was moderately consistent internally (α = .58).

A racial policy preference scale was based on four items: aid to minorities and endorsements of the government's role in improving the position of blacks and in promoting school integration and affirmative action. The scale had high internal consistency (α = .80). A government social spending scale was constructed from six variables: an additive scale measuring preferences for spending on health, education, and other social services; and government action on improvement of the standard of living, jobs for the unemployed, and minimizing the income gap. This scale had high internal consistency (α = .81). The five-item opposition to Reagan scale included an evaluation of Reagan's job performance, the Reagan feeling thermometer, and the respondents' vote intentions pitting Reagan against Mondale, Glenn, or Kennedy; it yielded high internal consistency (α = .89).

Group Affects

Thermometer ratings (on a 0–100 scale) of affective reactions to 14 groups were obtained. Group ratings were standardized with respect to the respondent's reactions to all 14 groups. For example, evaluations of blacks were subtracted from the individual's mean rating across all 14 groups and divided by the standard deviation of these 14 scores. On the basis of factor analyses, two scales relating to women were formed. One summed affects toward women and toward working women; the other, feminists and supporters of women's liberation. Affective reactions to blacks were also used in the analysis.

Information

A general political information scale was based on three subscales: (a) familiarity with national political candidates (Anderson, Bush, Mondale, and own 1982 Republican and Democratic House candidates); (b) familiarity with their congressional candidates' positions on four issues: the number of issues on which the respondent expressed knowledge of at least one candidate's position (54% knew at least one candidate's position on all four issues); (c) knowledge of which party was in the majority in the House and the Senate before the 1982 election. All three subscales were then standardized and combined to form the overall information scale.

A scale was also constructed to measure information about women's issues in particular. Respondents indicated whether they knew the stances taken on women's issues by the Democratic party, the Republican party, the nonpreferred party's House candidate, and the federal government (46% knew the positions of all four).

Political Orientations and Demographics

The standard NES measures for assessing liberal-conservative ideology, party identification, and basic demographic variables were also used. Information about current working status for either respondents or their spouses was collected, and from this, an index was constructed for the presence of a working female in the household.

In all these areas, most items came from the 1983 pilot study, but some were from the earlier 1982 study. These latter included the women's role, ERA, and abortion items in the scale measuring nontraditional gender beliefs, the aid-to-minorities item in the racial policy issues scale, the specific program spending and guaranteed jobs items in the government spending scale, and all items in both political information scales.

VALUES AS PREDICTORS OF ISSUE POSITIONS

The general plan of the analysis is first to show the political importance of values concerning equality by demonstrating that they are significant predictors of domestic policy preferences above and beyond the effects of such standard predictors as demographic variables, party identification, and ideology. Second, we assess the evidence for a simple symbolic politics theory. Third, we turn to evidence suggesting the need for a schematic variant of the symbolic politics approach.

The contributions made by demographic variables and conventional political orientations to our policy preference dependent variables are on the whole rather predictable. Table 8.1 presents separate multiple regression equations for each dependent variable. These analyses show modest demographic effects, mainly for age and education. As is usually the case, gender has little effect on women's issues. Ideology influences positions on most issues, whereas party identification influences only the most explicitly partisan dependent variable (opposition to President Reagan). These results assure us that in general our dependent variables are predictable at expected levels and in expected ways.

Group-specific values had significant effects in almost all cases, especially on issues concerned with equality for a specific group. Support for government action to promote equality for women was influenced by gender equality values (beta = .34), whereas government action to help blacks was strongly influenced by racial equality values (beta = .47). On

TABLE 8.1
The Effects of Demographic Variables, Political Orientation, and Values on Issue Preferences

	Government Involvement		Women's Issues Nontraditional Beliefs		Collective Action		Racial Issues		Government Services		Opposition to Reagan	
Group-Specific Values	Race	Gender	Race	Gender	Race	Gender	Race	Gender	Race	Gender	Race	Gender
Demographics												
Age (old)	.21**	.19*	-.04	-.15*	.10	.14	.26**	.18	-.05	.10	-.01	-.04
Education (high)	-.24**	-.14	.02	.13	-.26*	.15	.07	.04	-.24**	-.33**	-.04	.08
Gender (female)	.22**	.08	-.01	.00	-.03	-.04	.11	-.02	.12	.05	-.08	-.07
Race (black)	.03	.05	-.05	.06	.15	.13	.17**	.14	-.01	.12	-.10	-.18*
Income (high)	-.03	-.11	.12	-.01	.09	-.05	-.17*	-.20*	.09	-.12	.06	-.11
Political Orientation												
Ideology (liberal)	.12	.22*	.33**	.34**	.14	.20*	.15*	.13	.30**	.32**	.22**	.19*
Party Identification (Democrat)	.05	.03	-.09	-.14	.05	-.05	.10	-.06	.13	.09	.54**	.30**
Equality Values												
General	.10	.16	.17	-.06	.07	-.06	.16*	.32**	.13	.24**	-.15	.07
Group-specific												
Gender	—	.34**	—	.55**	—	.45**	—	.21*	—	.04	—	.22**
Racial	.41**	—	.23*	—	.27*	—	.47**	—	.19*	—	-.01	—
Adjusted *R²*	.426	.326	.226	.532	.160	.233	.641	.258	.373	.414	.577	.394

Note. Gender values measured only in subsample 1, and racial values only in subsample 2. Entries are standardized regression coefficients.
*p < .05. **p < .01.

the other hand, general equality values had significant effects in only three of the twelve instances.[4]

These equality values have effects that are to a great extent independent of those of general liberal–conservative ideology. The univariate correlations of general, gender, and racial equality values with ideology were .25, .26, and .41, respectively, scarcely strong enough to argue that values are simply subsumed in ideology. Second, equality values add significantly to ideology in explaining issue positions. This can be seen by subtracting the R^2 for regression equations with ideology and party identification (and demographics) as predictors from equations that also include these variables and the equality values as well. The equality values (general equality plus the relevant group-specific values) add an average of 21% to R^2 on the four issues most directly concerned with equality (women's and racial issues) and modest amounts on the two partisan dimensions (an average of 4% on each; see Table 8.2, row 9). The effects of group-specific equality values on equality issues are statistically significant in all cases, even with ideology included in the equation, as shown in Table 8.1. Thus, equality values have strong effects on policy preferences independent of those of general political ideology. These data are consistent with a symbolic politics approach to equality values in that "equality" seems to serve as a potent symbol quite independent of the more conventional political predispositions.

Finally, the group-specific values turn out to be much more potent predictors of issue preferences than do the general political values. The appropriate test is the unique contribution each makes to R^2 above and beyond the shared variance they contribute. Considering all three women's issues, gender values add 8%, 23%, and 15% to variance explained (in Table 8.2, row 13), whereas general political equality values add only 1%, 0%, and 0%, respectively (subtracting row 3 from row 4). Racial values add 14% to racial issues, whereas general values add but 2%. All of this does not mean that "equality" has no effect as a symbol in and of itself. The general equality values had some strong effects, as can be seen by comparing rows 1 and 2 in Table 8.2. But clearly, the more potent effects occurred from the

---

[4]The direction of causality implied here, from values to issue positions, is of course simply an assumption. A symbolic politics theory could as easily assume the opposite because level of abstraction is assumed not to be crucial. For example, the issue of "busing" could have influenced racial equality values in the 1970s, as Sears and Allen (1984) argue happened in the North.

TABLE 8.2
The Effects of Equality Values and Group Affect: Adjusted R^2

			Women's Issues												
Group-Specific Values:			Government Involvement		Traditional Role		Collective Action		Racial Issues		Government Spending		Opposition to Reagan	
			Race	Gender	Race	Gender	Race	Gender	Race	Gender	Race	Gender	Race	Gender
Regression Equations														
Predictors:	General Values	Group Affect	Group-Specific Values													
1				.262	.161	.143	.269	.100	.070	.402	.088	.322	.358	.565	.334
2	X			.318	.244	.197	.302	.118	.082	.499	.232	.353	.448	.581	.360
3			X	.423	.313	.211	.533	.165	.237	.625	.192	.367	.377	.565	.395
4	X		X	.426	.326	.226	.532	.160	.233	.641	.258	.373	.414	.577	.394
5		X		.259	.201	.141	.494	.115	.174	.399	.103	.318	.380	.570	.359
6	X	X		.319	.284	.220	.520	.139	.190	.496	.258	.348	.430	.584	.378
7		X	X	.433	.315	.217	.642	.194	.282	.621	.193	.362	.388	.569	.396
8	X	X	X	.437	.335	.234	.639	.191	.276	.638	.272	.367	.426	.580	.396
R^2 Uniquely Contributed by:															
9 All equality values (4–1)				.164	.165	.083	.263	.060	.163	.239	.170	.051	.056	.012	.060
10 Group-specific equality values (8–6)				.118	.051	.014	.119	.052	.086	.142	.014	.019	.000	.000	.018
11 General values (8–7)				.004	.020	.017	.000	.000	.000	.017	.079	.005	.038	.011	.000
12 Group affect (8–4)				.011	.009	.008	.107	.031	.043	.000	.014	.000	.012	.003	.002
R^2 Contributed Beyond General Values:															
13 By group-specific values (4–2)				.108	.082	.029	.230	.042	.151	.142	.026	.020	.000	.000	.034
14 By group affect (6–2)				.001	.040	.023	.218	.021	.108	.000	.026	.000	.000	.003	.018

Note. Rows 1–8 present the adjusted R^2 for equations with the categories of predictors indicated. All contain demographics, ideology, and party identification in addition to the variables noted. Rows 9–14 present the increment in R^2 contributed by the categories of variables shown, computed by ... in addition to the use of the adjusted R^2, the entry is given as group-specific values, in which the symbols of specific groups were paired with the symbol "equality."[5]

EXPLORING A SIMPLE
SYMBOLIC POLITICS THEORY

In the interests of parsimony, let us begin by exploring the ramifications of a simple symbolic politics theory. Any data that fit such a simple theory might also be consistent with a more complex schematic variant, though the reverse would not necessarily hold. This initial exploration of the landscape can help to identify data that require a more complex theory.

Symbols at the Same Level of Abstraction

First of all, a simple symbolic politics theory would expect people to respond with consistent evaluations whenever they are presented with a given symbol, at least with symbols such as those used throughout this study: "equality," "women," and "blacks." Among other things, this should result in high levels of consistency across items with common symbols at the same level of abstraction. This can be tested with the interitem reliabilities in each of these areas. These were presented earlier but can be summarized here to make this different point. Group-specific equality values attracted quite consistent evaluations. The Cronbach's alpha reliabilities for the two six-item gender and racial equality value scales are .71 and .64, respectively. The same underlying affective consistency emerges from the two scales dealing explicitly with equality policies for women and blacks: government involvement with women ($a = .77$) and racial issues ($a = .81$).

Consistency of affect toward a single symbol, whether "equality" or a specific group, was lower. The reliability for the general equality value scale is .44, using the full six-item scale; with the weakest three items deleted, it is .55. The reliability, as measured by a Spearman-Brown coefficient, between evaluations of "women" and "working women" on thermometer scales was .74, as was that between "supporters of women's liberation" and "feminists." The Spearman-Brown coefficients between the

---

[5]This less predictive power of the general domain-specific values is not solely due to their lower reliability. When the more reliable three-item scale is substituted for the six-item general equality values scale, the results are very similar. For example, the R^2 estimates for row 2 in Table 8.2 are .294, .290, .107, and .493 for the four equality issues in order, yielding an average increase of 1.4% in R^2 with the more reliable shorter scale (considering just the subsample given the group-specific value items relevant to the issue in question). The average improvement in unique R^2 contributed by the general values (row 4 − row 2) when the more reliable three-item scale is used was 1.2% and, by group-specific values (row 4 − row 3), −0.2%.

other pairs of these four thermometer evaluations, presumably sharing less common symbolic content, were considerably lower: .26, .17, .44, .45. All this represents evidence for consistent affects toward the symbols of equality, women in general, the women's movement, and blacks. Later we consider the greater consistency in responses to two paired symbols (equality for women or equality for blacks) than to either symbol alone.[6]

Single Abstract Symbols and Concrete Composites

A bare-bones symbolic politics theory would hold that consistency across different levels of abstraction is a simple function of the degree of overlap in manifest symbolism. Support for "free speech for college professors" should be quite strongly, but not perfectly, consistent with support for "free speech," because the symbols overlap only partially. Presumably, attitude objects at adjacent levels of abstraction share more manifest symbolism than do objects at very different levels of abstraction. Hence, evaluations of symbols at adjacent levels of abstraction should be more strongly correlated than those of symbols at nonadjacent levels of abstraction. Indeed, general equality values are highly correlated with the two sets of group-specific values (mean correlation = .55), which in turn are highly correlated with positions on the four group equality issues (mean correlation = .50), but general equality values are not as highly correlated with issue positions (mean correlation = .34).

What happens when this reasoning is applied to the customary assumption that general values determine specific attitudes? The simple symbolic politics theory predicts that attitudes toward any given object will be a function of affects toward its separate constituent symbols. Hence, evaluations of symbols at different levels of abstraction that share some symbolic elements should be a function of evaluations of those shared elements.

In the present context, this reasoning suggests that general equality values and affect toward a particular group (e.g., women) ought to determine group-specific values regarding that group (e.g., gender equality), as depicted in Figure 8.1. To test this proposition, separate multiple regression equations were employed for gender and race, predicting from general equality values and the appropriate group affect to group-specific equality values. The data were quite supportive with respect to gender. Gender values were influenced quite strongly by general political equality (with a beta of .46) and gender affect (the composite "feminism" scale contributed

---

[6]This greater consistency of responses to paired symbols than to single symbols can be shown in another way. The mean interitem correlation for the paired-symbol group-specific values was .27 and .22 for equality issues, as against .12 for the single-symbol general equality values.

a significant beta of .26, and "women," a nonsignificant .12). The full model yielded a respectable, though not overwhelming, R^2 of .31.

However, the data were only partially supportive in the case of race. Racial equality values were strongly influenced by general equality values (beta = .43), but race affect made little contribution (a nonsignificant beta of .11). Thus, the R^2 for the total model (general equality values and race affect) predicting racial equality values was a disappointing .20.

A second proposition would be that general equality values and affect toward a particular group should determine issue positions on policies affecting equality for that group. To test this, regression equations were conducted in which the two issue scales most tangibly concerned with group welfare (government involvement with women and racial issues) were regressed on general equality values and group affect. The results were modest. General equality values had fairly strong effects (betas = .35 and .44), but group affect did not (betas for feminism = .13, women = .01, and blacks = .06), and the overall R^2s were unimpressive (.14 and .19).

A third proposition that can be derived from this symbolic politics reasoning is that the effects of general values and group affect upon issue positions ought to be fully mediated by the group-specific values because the symbolic content of the former is fully represented in the latter. For example, affect toward blacks plus general equality values should determine racial equality values, which in turn should determine support for government policies designed to achieve racial equality.

However, contrary to this expectation, group-specific values retain their predictive power even with these supposedly prior predictors in the equation. Table 8.2 (row 10) shows that the R^2 contributed to equality issue positions by the appropriate group-specific values (gender for women's issues and racial for race issues), above and beyond the contribution of the relevant group affect and general equality values, averages 10.0% across these four issues. These additional contributions are highly significant, F = 9.82, 35.60, 15.10, and 41.20, respectively; on 1 and 105 or more df in each case, $p < .005$. By comparison, attitudes toward both of the presumably constituent symbols (general values and group affect) had much smaller effects above and beyond those contributed by group-specific values. Row 11 of Table 8.2 shows that the R^2 uniquely contributed by general values averaged only 0.9% across the four issues, significant only in predicting to racial issues, $F (1,105) = 4.93$, $p < .05$. Row 12 shows that the R^2 uniquely contributed by group affect averaged just 4.0% across the four issues. Hence, group-specific values continued to have a strong, unique influence on issue positions, above and beyond the influence of attitudes toward their constituent symbols. This suggests that level of abstraction, not just symbolic content, is an important factor in determining the impact of values on issue positions.

The Specificity of the Group Symbol

A further proposition from a simple symbolic politics view would be that affects and group-specific values regarding one group should not influence attitudes toward policies affecting other groups, or policies that do not involve groups explicitly, because the symbols are not the same. This point is illustrated in Figure 8.1 by the separation between the systems of attitudes concerning gender and racial attitude objects. Operationally, the question here is what unique contribution a particular group symbol makes to positions on issues that vary in evoking that group's symbol. Hence, the appropriate statistic is the contribution to R^2 made by group-specific values (or group affect) above and beyond the contribution made by predictors that do not invoke the group symbol (i.e., general equality values, general political orientations, and demographic factors).

On this point, group-specific values behave quite as expected. As already indicated, they have strong, unique effects on policies affecting their own group's well-being. They contribute 15.1% to R^2, averaging across the four issues (Table 8.2, row 13) a statistically significant contribution in each case. In contrast, they contribute much less to positions on issues affecting the other group. Gender values contribute but 2.6% to racial issues, and racial values contribute but 6.0% to gender issues on the average, though three of these four latter effects are significant.

By the same reasoning, group affects should influence issue positions concerning the group in question, but not issue positions focusing on other groups. Here again, the picture is supportive for gender but not racial affect. As shown in Table 8.2 (row 14), gender affect makes a significant contribution to all three gender issues (averaging 12.3%), and does not significantly affect racial issues ($R^2 = 2.6$%).[7] However, race affect failed to make a significant contribution to either racial issues ($R^2 = 0$) or gender issues ($R^2 = 0.8$%, on the average).

Finally, consistent with the symbolic politics view, group-specific values have only weak effects upon issue positions not explicitly invoking any group symbols. As also shown in Table 8.2 (row 13), group-specific equality values added very little to the explanation of the composite scale on government spending or opposition to Ronald Reagan, averaging 1.4% in variance explained in the four cases (statistically significant in just one of the four). As also would be expected, affect toward these group symbols contributed nothing to the two issues that have nothing to do with groups: government spending and opposition to Reagan (see Table 8.2, row 14; the average R^2 is 0.5%, nonsignificant in all four cases).

---

[7]The feminist scale produces highly significant betas, averaging .29, whereas "women" does so only in the former case, averaging .10 (see Sears, Huddy, & Schaffer, 1984).

The foregoing data suggest some difficulties with the simple symbolic politics theory. One problem is that racial affect did not always have the simple effects predicted for it, but this may reflect nothing more than well-known difficulties with its measurement. We return to this later. More interesting was that level of abstraction seems to have had effects that cannot be explained in terms of symbolic content. More concrete attitude objects, embodying two symbols, evoke more consistent affects than do more abstract objects embodying just one symbol. This held both when the more specific object was a group-specific value and when it was an issue position. Second, the more concrete group-specific values had an influence on issue positions above and beyond that contributed by evaluations of their more abstract constituent symbols: general values and group affect. Although these findings might have various explanations, in a later section we pursue the notion that level of abstraction, in and of itself, is responsible.

INFORMATION FLOW

Thus far we have considered the symbolic politics approach largely in a static fashion, with the central point being that values should determine issue positions only when both share the same manifest symbolic content. However, voters are not isolated and suspended in time and space; they operate in the midst of an informational environment that is constantly changing. How should information flow affect the consistency of responses to different symbols? In particular, how should it affect the influence of values on issue positions?

A simple symbolic politics theory might yield two propositions. Independent of exposure to information, attitudes toward objects that are highly similar in manifest symbolism should be more closely associated than attitudes toward objects that are very dissimilar in manifest symbolism. Attitudes toward fair treatment for blacks in jobs and in housing ought to be closely associated because they share a common attitude object (viz., blacks). However, attitudes toward keeping American soldiers abroad should not be closely associated with attitudes toward increased federal aid for housing because the two attitude objects are quite dissimilar (see Converse, 1964, for the specific data). Second, information flow ought to increase consistency between attitudes whose objects are regularly associated in the informational environment. Ronald Reagan and the Republican party are regularly associated; thus, exposure to high levels of information should increase the consistency of their evaluations. Robespierre and nuclear power are rarely associated in today's informational environment; hence, high levels of exposure should not affect the (presumably low) correlation between evaluations of them.

A schematic variant departs from this simple symbolic politics view in that information flow can prime the use of more complex cognitive structures such as schemata. There is evidence that schema use can be primed by recent and frequent activation (Higgins & King, 1981; Wyer & Srull, 1981). When the constituent elements (e.g., a value and an issue position) are consistent within the schema, priming should increase consistency in expressed attitudes (Herr, Sherman, & Fazio, 1983). In short, political information flow should enhance schema use through frequent evocation of the schema, thereby making attitudes toward elements more consistent.

To arrive at the predictions these two theories would make, we must consider the two attitude objects upon which the value and issue positions are focused. These pairs of attitude objects may vary both in their manifest symbolic similarity and in the likelihood that widespread underlying schemata exist linking them. There are three major possibilities.

At one extreme are pairs of attitude objects whose manifest symbols are so similar that the priming of some underlying schema should not be required to link them. An example would be gender equality values and women's equality issues. The similarity in manifest symbolism ought to produce generally high levels of consistency in attitudes toward them, which repeated association might enhance modestly, according to a simple symbolic politics theory. Priming the underlying schema that probably links very similar symbols might produce some further increase in consistency, though even for the poorly informed the simple association of obviously similar symbols ought to promote considerable consistency. In this case, then, both theories would predict fairly high levels of consistency even with poor information, only modestly enhanced due to information flow.

At the other extreme are pairs of attitude objects that share no manifest symbolism and that are not schematically linked in most people's minds. To continue our earlier example, Robespierre and nuclear power share no obvious manifest symbolism, and most members of the general public probably do not have schemata that would link them. In such cases, both theories would predict relatively little consistency irrespective of information level.

Intermediate cases would be those in which the attitude objects are manifestly dissimilar, but where some underlying schema links the attitude objects in the information environment and/or within considerable segments of the general public. For example, beliefs about racial equality values and gender equality issues might be linked together in many people's minds by a fairly common schema, even though dissimilar at a manifest level. In such cases, a simple symbolic politics theory might again suggest that greater information flow would modestly enhance consistency to the extent that the two objects are paired in the information environment. Exposure to that association should increase the respondent's attitudinal consistency. However, a schematic variant would predict more dramatic increases in consistency resulting from higher information flow because it should evoke whatever underlying schemata link the two objects. That is, priming those schemata would be necessary to produce consistency between the attitudes toward the two objects. Without evoking such linking schemata, consistency between dissimilar objects is likely to be low.

In short, the simple version of a symbolic politics theory would suggest that information flow will produce modest increases in consistency between attitudes toward objects that are manifestly similar in symbolism or that are manifestly dissimilar but likely to be paired in the information environment. The schematic variant would expect major effects of information flow primarily in the latter case, when widespread underlying schemata might be evoked and symbolic similarity does not exist to produce consistency among the poorly informed.

To test these ideas requires comparing consistency at high and low levels of information flow with regard to attitude objects that vary in manifest symbolic similarity and in the ubiquity of linking schemata in the general public. In this context, we use the term *information flow* only to describe crudely the information to which the individual has been and is being exposed. This could be indexed directly by measuring the flow itself (e.g., media exposure or interpersonal communication) or indirectly by measuring its product (e.g., the individual's store of political information). Here we have chosen the latter alternative. Another assumption that should be noted is that we are viewing schemata as fixed structures that are widely present in the general public with regard to some attitude objects but not with regard to others. People differ in the extent to which they are exposed to political information flow, and that flow can activate schemata when they are widely present. This view of schemata has its parallel in person perception research in which the structure and content of schemata do not vary greatly between individuals, but frequency of activation via priming does (Higgins & King, 1981; Wyer & Srull, 1981).

The relevant data are respondents' levels of consistency between attitudes at different levels of abstraction, especially values and issue positions, as a joint function of: (a) high versus low information level, (b) the manifest symbolic similarity of attitude objects, and (c) the probability of underlying schemata linking them. Four separate regression equations are presented for each dependent variable, one each for respondents high and low in general political information within each of the two subsamples in the study. The data are presented in Table 8.3 in terms of unstandardized regression coefficients because the key comparisons are between high and low information respondents.

TABLE 8.3
The Effects of Political Information on the Determinants
of Issue Positions (Unstandardized Regression Coefficients)

	Subsample 1		Subsample 2	
	(Group-specific = gender equality)		(Group-specific = racial equality)	
	hi info	lo info	hi info	lo info
WOMEN'S ISSUES				
Government Involvement				
Political orientation	.50 (.19)*	.03 (.22)	.34 (.18)	.11 (.21)
General political equality	.12 (.11)	.22 (.17)	.20 (.12)	.01 (.14)
Group-specific equality	.29 (.08)**	.28 (.12)*	.33 (.08)**	.17 (.08)*
Adjusted R^2	.382	.196	.504	.263
Traditional Roles				
Political orientation	.13 (.13)	.01 (.26)	.48 (.20)*	−.29 (.26)
General political equality	−.01 (.07)	−.26 (.15)	.28 (.13)*	.14 (.17)
Group-specific equality	.47 (.05)**	.40 (.10)**	.15 (.09)	.21 (.10)*
Adjusted R^2	.694	.177	.236	.097
Collective Action				
Political orientation	.12 (.11)	.01 (.13)	.19 (.11)	.07 (.14)
General political equality	−.03 (.06)	−.05 (.09)	.20 (.07)**	−.11 (.09)
Group-specific equality	.17 (.05)**	.27 (.07)**	.02 (.05)	.18 (.05)**
Adjusted R^2	.221	.177	.244	.282
RACIAL ISSUES				
Political orientation	.07 (.20)	−.31 (.25)	.39 (.14)**	.45 (.25)
General political equality	.40 (.12)**	.23 (.18)	.21 (.09)*	.06 (.16)
Group-specific equality	.16 (.08)	.20 (.13)	.40 (.06)**	.25 (.09)**
Adjusted R^2	.351	.112	.720	.476
GOVERNMENT SPENDING				
Political orientation	.40 (.17)*	.39 (.18)*	.63 (.19)**	.45 (.22)
General political equality	.33 (.10)**	.09 (.14)	.27 (.12)*	−.03 (.15)
Group-specific equality	.01 (.07)	.09 (.10)	.20 (.08)*	.05 (.08)
Adjusted R^2	.411	.171	.433	.190
OPPOSITION TO REAGAN				
Political orientation	1.36 (.27)**	.19 (.26)	1.44 (.22)**	1.56 (.33)**
General political equality	.00 (.16)	.07 (.19)	.06 (.14)	.32 (.22)
Group-specific equality	.27 (.11)*	.20 (.14)	.16 (.09)	−.04 (.12)
Adjusted R^2	.423	.186	.594	.374

Note. For each issue, four separate regressions were conducted: within each of two subsamples, separately for the high and low informed. The entries are unstandardized regression coefficients, with standard errors in parentheses. Political orientation includes ideology and party identification. In subsample 1, the group-specific values were gender equality; in subsample 2, racial equality.

*p < .05. **p < .01.

Similar Manifest Symbolism

One class of manifestly similar attitude objects in our data (see Fig. 8.2) is general and specific values. These are more strongly linked among the highly informed than among the less informed for both gender values (r = .56 and .24, respectively) and racial values (r = .55 and .31, respectively).

A second class of manifestly similar attitude objects are group-specific equality values and issue preferences regarding that particular group's equality. For this case, there is a high level of consistency irrespective of information flow. The top three panels of Table 8.3 show that the effects of gender equality values on gender equality issues are strong and significant in all cases, whether or not the respondent is well-informed. Similarly, racial equality values have a strong impact on racial issues irrespective of respondent information level, as shown in the fourth panel of Table 8.3. For the highly informed, these unstandardized coefficients average .33 (.29, .47, .17, and .40); for the less informed, they average .30 (.28, .40, .27, and .25). In short, in this case of shared symbolism between the two attitude objects, specific values invariably have a significant effect on issue positions, an effect almost identical among the well-informed and the poorly informed.

These two sources of data yield conflicting results: Information flow considerably enhances consistency between general and group-specific values, but not between the latter and issue positions regarding the group's equality. The former resembles what we would expect if information was evoking a schema, whereas the latter resembles the modest increment in consistency that would be expected from repeated association of already very similar objects. We return to this puzzle later.

Dissimilar Symbolism, Probable Schema

The expectations of a simple symbolic politics view deviate most from those of a schematic variant when the manifest symbols of the predictor attitude differ from those of the dependent variable and when it is plausible that there is an underlying schema that can be activated by a strong information flow. The schematic variant predicts a considerably more powerful impact of information on consistency.

Our data provide four tests of this contrast. First, other evidence shows that people spontaneously tend to link ideological labels with equality issues (Conover & Feldman, 1981), which suggests that underlying schemata linking the two are fairly common. Here, in line with the schematic view, the highly informed do seem to link general political orientations much more closely to equality issues than do the poorly informed, supporting the schematic variant. Our data provide eight such comparisons, shown in the top rows of each of the top four panels of Table 8.3. In seven of the eight cases, the highly informed show greater consistency than do the less informed. The average regression coefficient for the highly informed is .28, with three of eight significant; for the poorly informed, the average is .01, and none are significant. Therefore, general political orientations have their strongest effects upon issue positions among the well-informed.

Second, it seems likely that widespread schemata exist linking general political equality values to issues involving equality for specific groups, even though the general values items do not mention any specific group and the issue items do not explicitly mention equality. Again in line with the schematic view, general political equality values have strong effects upon issue preferences, but only on issues that themselves focus on group equality (and therefore probably have equality-linked schemata) and only among the highly informed. As can be seen in the top four panels of Table 8.3, the unstandardized coefficients for general equality values on the women's and racial issues are more positive for the highly informed than for the less informed in seven of eight cases. Half of the coefficients for the highly informed are significant; none of those for the poorly informed are. In absolute terms, the effect is perhaps somewhat weaker than in the prior case; the average regression coefficient is .17 for the highly informed and .03 for the poorly informed. In other words, general political values significantly influence preferences on women's and racial issues, even though the value and issue attitude objects are quite dissimilar, but only among the highly informed. Presumably this reflects a fairly common underlying schema, linking notions of general political equality to special government aid to disadvantaged groups, which is only evoked by higher levels of information.

Third, domestic spending levels are not manifestly similar to equality values. Nevertheless, it seems plausible that many people have schemata linking them; all federal administrations since Hoover's have advocated federal programs as a mechanism for insuring an equal minimum level of nutrition, housing, health care, and so on for all people and groups. Again supporting the schematic variant, general equality values have greater impact on support for government spending among the highly informed than among the less informed. The relevant data are shown in the fifth panel of Table 8.3. The effect of general political equality is much stronger among the highly informed (.33 and .27, p < .01 and p < .05, respectively) than among the less informed (.09 and −.03, neither significant).[8]

[8]Part of the explanation for the greater effect of general equality values on issue preferences among the highly informed may be due to greater internal consistency of the value scale for this group. We cannot rule this possibility out. The Cronbach's alpha for the highly informed group was much higher than for the less informed (.57 vs. .19) suggesting a less coherent position on abstract equality among the latter.

Fourth, many people may spontaneously link equality values regarding one group with policies that explicitly promote the well-being of another group, even though the two attitude objects share no manifest symbolism. For example, many people may have an underlying schema linking values of racial equality (e.g., if blacks and whites were treated more equally in this country, we would have many fewer problems) to the issue of affirmative action for women (e.g., how much effort and resources should the government put into promoting affirmative action programs that help women get ahead?), even though the two objects share no manifest symbolism. The data on this final point prove to fit the schematic variant in all but one case. Racial values significantly affect positions on government involvement for women more for the highly informed than for the less informed (b = .33 vs. .17, both significant). Gender values do significantly affect positions on racial issues for the highly informed (b = .16). However, the one exception is that they do not do so any less for the less informed (b = .20).

In all these cases, then, the manifest symbolism in the two sets of attitude objects is not the same, but one can imagine that some common underlying schema could be evoked. Thus, according to the schematic variant, consistency should be greater among the highly informed than among the poorly informed, whereas the simple symbolic politics theory would not predict so much difference in consistency. The data do seem to indicate that information flow produces greater consistency: an average regression coefficient of .18 for the well-informed (50% significant) and .04 for the less informed (5% significant). This provides some support for the schematic point of view. These findings were not always very strong in absolute terms, and some have alternative explanations.[9] But they were quite consistent. To repeat, our interpretation is that in these cases of weak manifest symbolic overlap of attitude objects but probable widespread underlying linking schemata, heavy information flow evokes the schemata and hence enhances consistency.

---

[9]Perhaps most obviously, the simple symbolic politics theory does have an escape clause here. It could be that the information environment systematically pairs two quite dissimilar attitude objects over time. If so, massive exposure to that information flow would ultimately lead to a linking of the two objects, even in the absence of preexisting schemata. Such was the case, for example, with Lyndon Johnson and a Vietnam/warmonger image. Prior to the Vietnam War, he was not seen as a very hawkish or warlike politician. In this way a simple symbolic politics theory could account for a finding that those two attitudes were most consistent among the best informed in the late 1960s.

Dissimilar Symbolism, No Probable Schema

A final expectation shared by both theories is that even high information flow would not enhance consistency when attitude objects share neither manifest symbolism nor widespread schematic links. For example, equality values probably should have little effect upon opposition to President Reagan no matter what the respondent's information. There is no clear manifest similarity between "disapproving of President Reagan" and "making sure that everyone has (or women, or blacks, have) an equal opportunity to succeed." We assumed, furthermore, that most members of the general public did not perceive Reagan as closely linked to equality issues (the wishes of feminists, black activists, and other Democrats notwithstanding). Thus, in the absence of either manifest symbolic similarity or widespread schemata, even high information flows should not have produced great consistency. This proved to be the case. The bottom panel of Table 8.3 shows that all but one of the eight terms for the effects of general or group-specific values on Reagan opposition are nonsignificant, with no evidence for greater effects among the informed.

Similarly, racial equality values had no manifest similarity to issues of traditional gender roles or to those bearing on whether women should act collectively. We doubted that schemata linking racial equality to these two gender issues were very widespread in the general public either. Therefore, both theories should predict low levels of consistency between racial equality values and these two gender issues, among high and low informed alike. This too was supported: Only two of the four pertinent regression coefficients were significant, and the low-information respondents actually showed somewhat greater consistency than did the high-information respondents. In the absence of either symbolic similarity or prior schemata that can be activated, then, even high levels of information flow did not produce high levels of consistency.

In short, this examination of the effects of information flow also yields some evidence that is better accounted for by the schematic variant than by a simple symbolic politics theory. Information flow produces its strongest effects upon consistency between two attitudes when their objects are manifestly dissimilar in symbolic content, but probably linked by widespread schemata in the general public that can be evoked by heavy information flow. Repeated association of manifestly similar symbols does not produce such large increments in consistency, nor does high information produce consistency between attitudes whose objects are neither manifestly similar nor linked schematically. The principal exception is the very first finding presented, that is, the markedly increased consistency between general and group-specific values with greater information.

THE OPTIMAL LEVEL OF PROCESSING

One of the areas in which a simple symbolic politics theory clashes with other theories both of political behavior and social cognition concerns the effects of levels of abstraction. We saw earlier that it does not account perfectly for variations in consistency across attitudes both within and between a particular level of abstraction. As can be recalled, part of our goal in measuring attitudes at three levels of abstraction was to determine which, if any, was the optimal level of processing information about group equality. To be sure, there are moderately strong relationships within levels of abstraction. Interitem consistency within domains was fairly high. And there are fairly strong relationships between adjacent levels of abstraction. General political values contribute rather strongly to domain-specific values, and domain-specific values in turn contribute strongly to concrete issue positions. Can we say something about which level of processing information about equality is optimal if we probe these data further?

Group-Specific Values
as Optimal Level of Abstraction

On the face of it, group-specific values would seem to have been at a more optimal level of abstraction for processing information about equality in this study than were more abstract orientations. This can be seen in several ways. Group-specific values proved to be more important predictors of issue positions than were more abstract attitudes, such as general values or ideology, as shown in Table 8.2. Second, group-specific values retained their significant impact upon issue positions even with evaluations of their constituent symbols (general values and group affect) controlled (see Table 8.2, row 10). Third, the interitem reliabilities for group-specific values were considerably higher than those of attitudes at higher levels of abstraction (general values or group affect) as already indicated.[10] Fourth, group-specific values strongly influenced positions on group equality issues even when different groups were involved in the values and issues. Table 8.1 shows that racial values significantly influenced positions on the three women's issues and that gender values significantly influenced positions on racial issues (average beta = .28). In all these cases, general values and

---

[10]They prove to be slightly less reliable than still more concrete attitudes. Issue positions regarding equality for a particular group were intercorrelated slightly more highly than were the group-specific values for that group. For example, the Cronbach's alpha for all women's issue items was .76, whereas it was .71 for gender values; for all racial issue items it was .80, against .64 for racial values.

ideology had less effect (average betas = .16 and .18, respectively, with only two of eight effects significant). In all these respects, group-specific values had more weight and generated more affective consistency than their symbolic content would have warranted, and more than more abstract attitudes.

Some other kinds of evidence suggest, however, that the presence of the group symbol in group-specific values gave them their particular affective force. They do seem advantageous primarily when they share symbolic content with the dependent variable; when they do not, more abstract attitudes show that greater power. Consider equality-relevant issues that contain no references to specific groups, such as government spending. Group-specific values prove to be less potent than ideology in this case, as shown in Table 8.1.

Thus, within issue domains in which equality considerations matter (i.e., gender and racial equality), group-specific versions of equality are the most optimal. In other words, when questions about equality arise in connection with policy issues, they are concerned with group-specific equality, not general societal equality.

Neither general nor group-specific values play a large role when there is a long history of association between some other abstract attitude (e.g., ideology) and an issue, even when these latter two share no manifest symbolism. For example, Ronald Reagan has long been associated with partisan and ideological symbols. We have already seen in Table 8.2 (row 9) that these two political orientations are the primary determinants of evaluations of Reagan and that both general and domain-specific values add little explanatory power (an average of 4% of the variance, all told).

In short, a mixture of a simple symbolic politics theory with a more cognitive variant is suggested here. There is evidence for the symbolic politics notion that the optimal level of processing political information may be anything from the very abstract to the very concrete when the predictor attitude shares considerable manifest symbolism with the dependent variable. The same may be true when there has been an extended history of association between two manifestly dissimilar attitude objects. But beyond that simple symbolic politics outcome, it seems that group-specific values fall at some optimal level of abstraction for processing issues of equality. This optimality is due only in part to overlap in manifest symbolism with attitude objects that are more abstract or more concrete; part of it may be due to its being an appropriate level of abstraction in and of itself.

Expertise and the Optimal Level

Expertise is one potential determinant of which level of abstraction provides for optimal processing. As indicated earlier, some evidence indicates that the optimal level of processing may be more concrete and fine-grained for experts about the content area in question. This would suggest that highly informed individuals might be more likely to base their issue positions in more concrete predispositions (in this case, in group-specific values) than in ideology or general values. One way to test this is to compare the unstandardized regression coefficients of the high- and low-information groups at each level of abstraction. Table 8.3 shows that the *bs* for general political orientations or for general equality values are greater for the highly informed than for the less informed in 19 of 24 cases (78%); those for group-specific values are greater for the highly informed in 7 of 12 cases (57%). If anything, then, the better informed were more likely to use general values and ideology, and relatively less likely to use group-specific values.

Another way to test the hypothesis is to determine the level of abstraction at which the standardized regression coefficient is highest. For the highly informed, group-specific values had the highest beta in 5 of 12 cases (43%); for the less informed, they did so in 9 of 12 cases (75%). These data are not shown in the table. Either way of treating the data, then, produces conclusions contrary to the expertise hypothesis: Expertise is associated with using relatively more abstract orientations rather than with the more concrete group-specific values.

Gender Differences in Level of Processing

The expertise hypothesis suggests that women might process information in policy domains concerned with equality more concretely than men because of their greater experience with the negative consequences of sex-role stereotypes. Consistent with this hypothesis, group-specific gender values in fact did have greater effects for women than for men on the two principal equality issues: government involvement with women, and racial issues. In both cases, the more abstract general values were much more important for men. A pattern that was similar in certain crucial ways held for the two issues not concerned explicitly with groups, government spending and opposition to Reagan. Again, group-specific values were crucial for women but not for men (although in these cases party identification and ideology had important effects for both genders). These gender differences are shown in Table 4.

The expertise interpretation might be that group-specific gender values are at the optimal level of processing these issues for women, whereas men process at the more abstract level of general values. Consistent with this notion, other data seem to indicate that general values are more central in equality issues for men than women. Men tend to link general and gender values more strongly than do women ($r = .59$ and $.40$, respectively).

TABLE 8.4
Gender Differences in the Determinants of Issue Positions:
Unstandardized Regression Coefficients

	Male Respondents	Female Respondents
WOMEN'S ISSUES		
Government Involvement		
Political orientation	.44 (.23)	.24 (.19)
General political equality	.45 (.13)**	−.04 (.13)
Gender equality	.10 (.12)	.37 (.08)**
Adjusted R^2	.399	.222
Traditional Roles		
Political orientation	.15 (.16)	.09 (.17)
General political equality	−.01 (.09)	−.10 (.11)
Gender equality	.48 (.08)**	.39 (.07)**
Adjusted R^2	.574	.409
Collective Action		
Political orientation	.01 (.14)	.11 (.10)
General political equality	.00 (.08)	−.06 (.07)
Gender equality	.20 (.07)**	.21 (.05)**
Adjusted R^2	.152	.243
RACIAL ISSUES		
Political orientation	.05 (.27)	−.15 (.19)
General political equality	.57 (.15)**	.16 (.13)
Gender equality	.05 (.14)	.21 (.08)**
Adjusted R^2	.307	.217
RACIAL ISSUES		
Political orientation	.45 (.24)	.54 (.16)**
General political equality	.11 (.12)	.14 (.11)
Racial equality	.47 (.08)**	.35 (.07)**
Adjusted R^2	.523	.473
GOVERNMENT SPENDING		
Political orientation	.40 (.23)	.52 (.15)**
General political equality	.46 (.13)**	.08 (.10)
Gender equality	−.13 (.12)	.13 (.06)*
Adjusted R^2	.356	.334
OPPOSITION TO REAGAN		
Political orientation	.76 (.32)*	.97 (.23)**
General political equality	−.02 (.18)	.24 (.15)
Gender equality	.17 (.17)	.24 (.10)*
Adjusted R^2	.336	.350

Note. Entries are unstandardized regression coefficients with standard errors shown in parentheses. Separate regressions for men and women were calculated for each issue with gender equality as the group–specific value. An additional analysis was conducted for racial issues that included racial equality values.

*$p < .05$. **$p < .01$.

The factor structures for men's and women's attitudes also reveal this greater centrality of general values for men. Table 8.5 shows that for males, general values load heavily on both main factors, the first focusing on equality and government spending, the second on women's roles. Group-specific gender values have a more limited place, linked to women's roles but not to government policy. For women, on the other hand, group-specific gender values are linked closely to all issues of women's equality, and general values seem peripheral.

What is responsible for these gender differences in level of processing? To start with, women's processing of these issues at a more concrete level might reflect some content-free tendency toward more concreteness. However, women were not more concrete than men in applying racial values to racial issues, as shown in Table 8.4; the use of general values was similar for men and women ($b = .11$ and $.14$), as it was for racial values ($b = .47$ and $.35$). Similarly, racial values were just as closely connected to general values among women as among men ($r = .43$ and $.46$, respectively). Thus, the greater use of the more concrete group-specific values by women was specific to the use of gender values. Nor did women's use of more concrete categories seem to come at great expense to processing efficiency. The R^2 for these three nongender issues seems roughly comparable for men and women, averaging $.38$ and $.34$, respectively (see Table 8.4). Hence, the gender differences in processing seem specific to the use of gender equality values.

As indicated earlier, some evidence suggests that being an expert about a content domain leads to processing information about it that is more detailed and complex (Kinder et al., 1983). The reason presumably is that an expert has a more detailed category system than does a novice. This

TABLE 8.5
Gender Differences in Factor Structure

	Male Respondents		Female Respondents	
General equality values	**.51**	**.55**	.30	.28
Gender equality values	.28	**.77**	.20	**.75**
Issue positions				
Government involvement in women's issues	**.71**	.36	**.72**	**.42**
Traditional roles	.14	**.73**	.14	**.72**
Collective action	.08	**.56**	.26	**.59**
Racial issues	**.72**	.30	**.72**	.31
Government spending	**.85**	.00	**.70**	.01
Opposition to Reagan	**.51**	.14	**.48**	.25
Percentage variance	29.8	24.8	24.6	22.9

Note. Entries are factor loadings from orthogonal rotations. All factor loadings above .40 appear in bold type.

leads to the hypothesis that women process political information in these domains at a more concrete level because they are more expert in the matter of women in society. That is, for women the optimal level of processing may be at the group-specific level of gender values because of their special experience with problems of gender equality. This might be true even for issues with strong latent, but little or no manifest, gender symbolism. For men, according to this reasoning, more general values would be at the optimal level of processing unless the issue had some manifest gender symbolism; then, group-specific gender values might come into play. One could imagine women's greater expertise stemming from either or both of two independent sources. First is personal experience, such as working as a woman in what has been largely a male-dominated occupational world. Second is heightened political sensitivity to political issues involving women, which would perhaps lead to more detailed knowledge about women's issues and therefore to more refined thinking about them.

The next step was to test whether these two special types of expertise accounted for women's tendencies to process these three nongender issues at a more specific level than did men. We operationalized personal experience as having a working woman in the household. Knowledge about women's issues was operationalized in terms of familiarity with political candidates' positions on women's issues. To isolate it from more general political knowledge, both the women's issue familiarity and general political information scales were standardized, and the difference score was used in this analysis. As would be expected, women were higher than men on this difference score, on the average.

The key question then becomes which of these dimensions accounts for the tendency to process at the specific rather than at the general political level. Statistically, this would be revealed in an interaction between expertise and general equality values: general values would predict issue preferences among nonexperts, but would fail to do so among experts. We adopted a model analogous to an analysis of covariance, in which general equality values were treated as the covariate. The specific terms included in the model were interactions between general equality values and (a) personal experience, (b) knowledge of women's issues relative to general political information, and (c) gender itself.

The model was tested on the three nongender issues on which women appeared to process more concretely: racial issues, government spending, and opposition to Reagan. The interaction with gender was significant when entered first in a stagewise procedure on each of these nongender issues, confirming the earlier observation that men used general values more than did women, $F (2, 117) = 8.06, 2.96,$ and $9.35, ps < .001, < .10,$ and $< .001$, respectively.

Contrary to the hypothesis, none of the interactions with personal experience was significant. One piece of confirmatory evidence is that the interaction with knowledge of women's issues was significant for opposition to Reagan, $F(1, 117) = 4.28, p < .05$, but not for the other two issues (each $p > .10$). Even this interaction failed to reach significance when the main effect for gender equality values was included in the equation, however. Thus, even this mild support for the hypothesis that expertise produces more concrete processing must be regarded as very tentative.[11] These data do not provide any very conclusive explanations for the gender differences in processing, but hopefully they illustrate an approach that future research might take.

DISCUSSION

This paper had three main goals. The first was to develop a simple symbolic politics theory in more elaborate detail than had been the case in previous work. The second was to test its implications in order to identify data that would require a more cognitive, schematic variant of a symbolic politics theory. And the third was to shed light on the role that egalitarian values play in determining domestic policy preferences.

The key measures in the study fell at four levels of abstraction: general political ideology, general political equality values, group-specific equality values focusing on women and blacks, and issue positions regarding a wide variety of domestic matters. It was first necessary to establish that it is worthwhile to measure values at all, that is, that values are sufficiently independent of both general ideology and concrete issue positions to make it worth adding an entirely new level of measurement. This was the case: Equality values were only modestly correlated with political ideology and had considerable explanatory power independent of ideology for almost all of the issues considered, particularly for those dealing with government policy regarding group inequalities. The group-specific values had much stronger effects than did more general values, a phenomenon that later helped point to a more cognitive symbolic politics theory.

Next we explored the implications of the simplest form of a symbolic politics theory. This holds that political responses are a function of the learned affects associated with the particular symbols presented in the individual's informational environment. Consistency between attitudes thus depends on similarity in the manifest content of political symbols and/or

---

[11]This same analysis was performed on the government involvement with women's issue scale but yielded no significant interactions of general values with knowledge or personal experience.

repeated association of two symbols in the environment. Level of abstraction should not be an important factor.

Much evidence supported the value of such a parsimonious theory. Similarity of the symbols contained in pairs of attitude objects did frequently lead to greater consistency of affective response, whether the attitude objects were at the same or different levels of abstraction. First, affective responses to symbols of groups and of equality tended to be fairly consistent internally. The group-specific value scales and issue preferences regarding policies promoting each group's equality tended to be quite internally consistent, suggesting that the symbols of equality for a particular group evoked fairly constant affects. Somewhat weaker internal consistency held for general equality values and group affect when presented separately. Second, we tested the prediction that evaluations of composite stimuli would be a function of the evaluations of their separate constituent symbols; specifically, that affects toward such composite stimuli as either group-specific values or issue positions would be a function of general equality values and group affect. Indeed, general political equality values had quite strong effects upon both group-specific values and issue positions on equality for a particular group, and gender affect (though not racial affect) influenced both fairly strongly as well. Third, as would be expected, group affect and values concerning equality for any particular group strongly influenced issue positions concerning that group's equality, but not those concerning other groups' equality or nongroup issues (again, racial affect is an exception).

Other evidence for a simple symbolic politics theory came from examining the effects of information flow. It would assume that high levels of information flow would not be needed to produce consistency in these cases of manifest symbolic similarity, and this held true; even the poorly informed had highly consistent attitudes between manifestly similar objects, such as gender equality values and gender equality policy issues. Some of the data on processing attitude objects at different levels of abstraction also seemed to follow from a simple symbolic politics theory. When values and issues shared common group symbols, processing was at a concrete, group-specific level. When they shared only symbols of general equality, processing tended to be at that more general level. And when they shared only the most general symbols of ideology and partisanship, it tended to be at that level. Symbolic similarity, rather than level of abstraction, proved to be decisive in governing consistency.

Nevertheless, some data did not fit so readily with this simple version of a symbolic politics theory. One area of weakness was that affect toward blacks simply failed to have the effects a simple symbolic politics theory would have expected, explaining neither racial equality values nor issue positions. The notion that simple affects drive political attitudes is central to a symbolic politics formulation. One possibility is that the measures of racial affect may be suspect. Whites do often dissimulate when asked directly for their affects about blacks (e.g., Crosby, Bromley, & Saxe, 1980; McConahay, Hardee, & Batts, 1981), which would introduce high levels of unreliability and unpredictability into these measures. Alternatively, it is possible that group affect has its expected influence primarily when embedded in some appropriate cognitive structure, contrary to the simplest version of a symbolic politics approach. Kinder and Sears (1981) made this argument in their discussion of symbolic racism.

Beyond that, we sought data that would require a more schematic variant of a symbolic politics theory. Some positive evidence for schematic organization resulted from our search for an optimal level of abstraction for information processing. The internal consistency of attitudes toward multiple attitude objects (e.g., equality for a specific group) tended to be markedly higher than the consistency of attitudes toward their constituent symbols taken alone. In particular, general political values proved not to generate as much internal consistency or have as much power over issue positions as did group-specific values. Second, the group-specific values had rather strong direct effects upon issue positions apart from mediating the effects of their presumably constituent symbols, general equality and group affect. Even when manifest symbolic content was held constant, by considering both equality in general and affect toward the group in question, domain-specific values remained the most powerful determinants of issue positions. Hence, the greater influence of group-specific values on issue positions was not due solely to their greater manifest similarity with the issues (as long as one assumes that symbolic similarity works in an additive, rather than interactive, manner). This suggests that some more cognitive principles need to be added.

Why might group-specific values be a particularly useful level of abstraction? Very general values may be so abstract that they lend themselves too easily to changed meaning with minor changes of context. The meaning of more abstract symbols may be easily changed by being placed in a new context (Asch, 1948). Equality may mean something quite different depending on its context, and in the abstract, its meaning may not be very stable. Another possibility is that political values are more meaningful when embedded in a group context, rather than when presented in the abstract or in a self-oriented context.

We also tested the hypothesis that the optimal level of abstraction becomes more concrete as the individual becomes more expert. This did not hold for general political information; the highly informed were more likely to use ideology and general values, whereas the less informed depended more concretely on group-specific values. In some ways, this corresponds to Converse's (1964) observation that greater political sophistication makes ideology become more important, and group symbols less so (see also Campbell et al., 1960).

We then pursued the question of expertise in the issue-specific sense, within a given issue public rather than in this more global sense. Because women presumably have more experience with issues of gender equality than do men, we thought they might process these issues at a more concrete level. Indeed, women did tend to approach certain equality issues from the perspective of the relatively concrete gender equality values, whereas men tended to apply the more abstract general equality values of political orientations.

We then pursued the possibility that women may think differently about women's issues because they have more personal involvement with them. There is a little evidence that systematic, careful processing of information is more likely when personal involvement is high (Borgida & Howard-Pitney, 1983). We could not, however, find conclusive evidence that women's personal experience with women's issues or greater knowledge about them was related to their processing women's issues at a more concrete level.

The explanation for these gender differences in processing issues is therefore not altogether obvious. Another possibility is suggested by the finding that in-group members tend to look at each other in a more differentiated way than they look at out-group members (Brewer & Lui, 1983; Linville, 1982; Linville & Jones, 1980). We may have an analogous finding here; women think more complexly about issues that involve their group and thus are less likely to react to women's issues from an abstract stance about general political equality. Our analyses suggest that group membership per se affected level of processing, which would support findings from the in-group–out-group research. However, this conclusion also needs to be tested on other groups, particularly racial and ethnic groups.

Evidence of two other kinds supports the value of a schematic variant of the symbolic politics approach. It would propose that greater information flow plays a crucial role in increasing consistency of response to attitude objects with little manifest symbolic similarity when some underlying cognitive structure, or schema, already connects them. Like the simpler symbolic politics theory, it would suggest that strong information flow is unnecessary when the two attitude objects are already manifestly very similar because consistency will emerge in any case. And even strong information flow would have little effect when two attitude objects are manifestly dissimilar and no underlying linking schema exists that information can activate. This general proposition was tested in a number of ways and fits the data fairly well.[12]

We have suggested the extension of a symbolic politics theory into more cognitive realms in two rather different ways. One is that underlying schemata may exist rather widely in the mass public in certain domains and can be evoked by appropriate symbolic stimulation. In this form, a schema does bear considerable resemblance to Converse's notion of belief system (1964), though the schema concept bears a number of more specific implications about information processing.

Do we really have evidence for the existence of such schemata here? In order for the schematic variant of the symbolic politics theory to be tenable, certain minimal criteria must be met. The term "minimal" must be taken seriously. Because of the limitations faced in gathering the data for this study, many of the methods normally employed to test schema theories (e.g., requests for information, recall/recognition errors, reaction time, etc.) were rendered impossible. Therefore, our evidence for a schematic variant of the theory of symbolic politics, a variant that we suggest consists of a hierarchical ordering of symbols, may be considered provocative but by no means definitive. Schemata are characterized by the organization of information, but they also have dynamic functions. They are thought to affect information processing, retrieval, and inference (Fiske & Linville, 1980; Fiske & Taylor, 1984). Does the schema truly influence the processing of political information, information retrieval, and inferences made about associated symbols and issues? We have no direct evidence that equality schemata fill any of these latter functions, and this is obviously needed before we can confidently employ the schema concept.

We attempted to test for the evocation of schemata by high levels of information flow as a way of testing between a simple symbolic politics theory and a schematic variant. The notion was that schemata will be evoked given two necessary but individually insufficient conditions: high information flow and an underlying schema. In the absence of direct measurement of the latter and measurement of the former only in static terms, this test must be regarded as only suggestive. Moreover, evocation of a schema must ultimately be distinguished from passive reflection of an

---

[12]As indicated earlier, one could operationalize information flow directly by measuring transmission of information to the individual or indirectly by simply measuring the individual's volume of information. We opted for the latter because no measures of current interpersonal communication or media exposure were available on these respondents. However, doing so opens up the possibility that our index of information flow instead actually indexes the presence or absence of schemata. We are willing to tolerate this ambiguity in this exploratory venture, but resolving it would have a high priority in further work.

association of two symbols that have been systematically paired in the informational environment. Making this test convincingly in the absence of experimental controls on the environment may be difficult, as in earlier efforts to distinguish ideological structures from "ideology by proxy."

The second extension is the notion that processing efficiency may vary across levels of abstraction. Our finding that the politically knowledgeable process political information at a general, as opposed to a specific, level replicates Converse's earlier finding that links political sophistication to abstract thinking. However, some findings depart from that treatment. We found some suggestive evidence in the case of women and knowledge of women's issues that people may actually process at a more concrete level with greater knowledge. Moreover, much of our evidence emphasized that symbolic similarity is a more important factor than level of abstraction in determining information processing. This finding is more consistent with recent treatments of ideology that emphasize ideological labels as political symbols rather than as indicators of broad and abstract cognitive structures (Conover & Feldman, 1981; Levitin & Miller, 1979). Finally, there was no evidence that group symbols were more central for the less informed than for the best informed. Group symbols had a potent effect for all. This greater impact of group-specific values than of general values on issue positions holds for both the highly and less informed groups. For the highly informed, the mean unstandardized regression coefficients for the four equality issues are .34 and .07 for the group-specific and general values, respectively; for the less informed, the coefficients are .30 and −.01, respectively.

A schematic variant of symbolic politics also raises questions that might hopefully develop a fresh portrait of belief systems in the mass public. Do the most common schemata embody content from both political and personal lives, or are these normally compartmentalized into separate schemata? Do issue publics process information at a more, or less, abstract level in their own areas of special interest? Are group symbols generally central to the mass public's belief systems, or are schemata organized around a much wider variety of affectively charged symbols? Such questions might hopefully be addressed by further research.

Finally, we should return briefly to our concern with values about equality. We would assume that for most Americans, such values fall into the same general content domain as their feelings about such familiar political symbols as liberal or conservative, Democrat or Republican, or such groups as feminists, blacks, and so on. Most Americans' values about equality seem not to be part of a larger deductive structure headed by some abstract ideology. Rather, the affects people have toward symbols of equality are correlated with (but scarcely identical to) their affects toward the other major political symbols. It remains for further research to determine

APPENDIX
Item Wording for Equality Value Scales
at the General, Gender, and Racial Levels

	Mean	SD
General Political Equality		
1. If people were treated more equally in this country we would have fewer problems.[a]	3.97	1.42
2. Our society should do whatever is necessary to make sure that everyone has an equal opportunity to succeed.[a]	4.35	1.15
3. One of the big problems in this country is that we don't give everyone an equal chance.[a]	3.13	1.63
4. We should give up on the goal of equality since people are so different to begin with.	4.02	1.41
5. Some people are just better cut out than others for important positions in society.	1.87	1.28
6. Some people are better at running things and should be allowed to do so.	1.42	0.86
General Political Equality Scale	18.77	4.09
Gender Equality		
1. If men and women were treated more equally in this country we would have fewer problems.[a]	3.70	1.44
2. Our society should do whatever is necessary to make sure that women's opportunities to succeed are equal to those of men.[a]	4.30	1.18
3. One of the big problems in this country is that we don't give women an equal chance.[a]	2.95	1.54
4. We should give up on the goal of equality since men and women are so different to begin with.	4.15	1.24
5. Men are just better cut out than women for important positions in society.	3.81	1.50
6. Men are better at running things than women are and should be allowed to do so.	4.30	1.18
Gender Equality Scale	22.76	5.41
Racial Equality		
1. If blacks and whites were treated more equally in this country we would have fewer problems.[a]	3.77	1.52
2. Our society should do whatever is necessary to make sure that blacks' opportunities to succeed are equal to those of whites.[a]	4.30	1.12
3. One of the big problems in this country is that we don't give blacks an equal chance.[a]	3.14	1.58
4. We should give up on the goal of equality since blacks and whites are so different to begin with.	4.37	1.18

APPENDIX *(continued)*
Item Wording for Equality Value Scales
at the General, Gender, and Racial Levels

5. Whites are just better cut out than blacks for important positions in society.	4.52	0.91
6. Whites are better at running things than blacks are and should be allowed to do so.	4.29	1.07
Racial Equality Scale	24.38	4.45

Note. All items are based on a 1 (strongly disagree) to 5 (strongly agree) agreement scale.
[a]These items reversed to construct scale.

the full implications of our finding that group-specific values have the strongest impact on issue preferences.[13]

ACKNOWLEDGMENTS

We owe thanks to the staff of the Center for Political Studies, University of Michigan, and to the 1984 Study Committee, National Election Studies, for collecting and distributing the data. Financial support for data collection was provided by the National Science Foundation, for data analysis by the College of Letters and Science and the Office of Academic Computing at UCLA, and for manuscript preparation by the Cattell Foundation. Special thanks are also owed to Carolyn Drago, Reid Hastie, Stanley Feldman, and Jack Citrin for their help at various stages of the project. The project was conducted while the senior author was a Guest Scholar at the Brookings Institution.

---

[13]This finding does have some interesting implications for the measurement of values. It certainly cautions against measuring values at their most abstract. It also argues for a careful exploration of values within a context, particularly when the context is directly relevant to the group under investigation.

9 Partisan Cognitions in Transition

Arthur H. Miller
University of Iowa

The decline in public attachment to political parties, which occurred between the mid-1960s and 1980 (see Fig. 9.1), has been one of the most important attitudinal changes in recent decades. This shift has brought with it a reduction in political participation, increased ticket splitting, and electoral volatility, as well as the potential for partisan realignment. Nevertheless, despite the important political implications of declining partisanship, explanations for this trend remain controversial and less than conclusive; they are rarely examined with a multivariate approach or integrated into a general theoretical framework.

The American Voter (Campbell, Converse, Miller, & Stokes, 1960) focused on the maintenance of party identification rather than its decline. Socializing agents, particularly the family, aided in the subtle, almost unconscious transmission of partisan attachment across generations. Whether it was merely a sense of positive affect for a party that was transmitted or a cognitive awareness of the general policy orientations of the two parties is less than evident from a reading of *The American Voter*. However, Beck (1974, 1977) has extended the implicit argument of *The American Voter* by offering a socialization explanation for decaying party attachment. He suggests that the generation that came of voting age around the New Deal period clearly understood, from their experiences of the depression era, the policy differences between Democrats and Republicans. But this distinction was blurred in the subsequent transmission from generation to generation. The citizens who are two generations removed from the last partisan realignment are thus said to be uncertain of what the parties stand for, making them ripe for realignment.

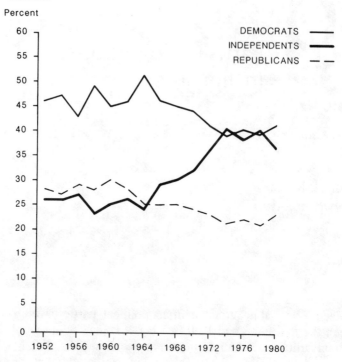

FIG. 9.1   Party Identification, 1952–1980.

Other competing explanations for declining party identification place more emphasis on conscious, rational assessments of the past policies and actions of political parties (Fiorina, 1981; Knoke, 1976). Many voters are said to see discrepancies between their own issue positions and those identified with their previously preferred or most preferred party; thus, they move toward independence because they feel that neither party represents them (Beck 1977; Ladd & Hadley, 1978). Others argue that people see no difference between the parties; hence, they are uncertain about which party to support (White & Morris, 1984). Some authors have extended this explanation by arguing that it leads to alienation from the party system per se (Black & Rabinowitz, 1980; Nie, Verba, & Petrocik, 1976). But Wattenberg (1981) has contradicted this explanation by demonstrating that the shift from parties represents a growth in neutrality toward parties rather than a negative rejection of them. Wattenberg's analysis, however, is based on shifts in marginal distributions rather than correlations of independent variables with the dependent variable (strength of party identification). Thus, the explanation for declining party identification remains controversial and inconclusive.

This paper attempts to synthesize these various explanations into a more integrated, information-processing framework. What is considered here are factors that reflect upon the acquisition, cognitive representation, and retrieval of party-relevant information, as well as the impact which these cognitions have on electoral decisions. Previously gathered evidence is reexamined and reinterpreted within this framework. Also, new data for the period 1952–1980 are introduced in an effort to resolve discrepancies between findings reported earlier by various researchers. However, given the limited scope of this paper, certain aspects of the overall explanation must go unaddressed. For example, I do not attempt to directly test the ability of an information-processing approach to incorporate a socialization interpretation by examining the data for different age cohorts. Such an undertaking must be reserved for a future paper.

INFORMATION PROCESSING
AND PARTY IDENTIFICATION

Many of the explanations that have been given for declining party identification involve the processing of political information. Explanations that hinge on perceived issue differences between parties, the absence of issue representation, and the intergenerational transmission of knowledge about what the parties stand for all rely heavily on an awareness of information regarding political parties. Theories that describe how people process social information may therefore be very helpful in providing an explanatory framework for understanding the decline in party identification.

In recent years, cognitive social psychologists have made major advances in their theorizing about social information processing (for a review of the relevant literature, see Taylor & Crocker, 1981). The most relevant concept from this work is the notion of schema, which helps us understand how people organize their thoughts about the world. Each day, the average citizen is confronted with information on a multitude of topics, including politics. People are more attentive to some of these items than to others. They take in information on those items to which they attend, storing it in a form that is readily accessible for use in the interpretation of similar events or topics in the future. The concept of schema provides a theoretical description of how people structure their knowledge of some social object and then utilize this cognitive structure to efficiently process subsequent information about the object or to guide future actions toward the object.

Stated more formally, the schema concept refers to cognitive structures of organized prior knowledge abstracted from experience with specific instances, which are subsequently applied to the encoding and comprehension of new information, as well as the retrieval of stored information (Fiske & Linville, 1980). Schema theories assume that each person has available a large number of schemata that can be used in interpreting experiences and in processing incoming information. Each of these schemata contains a number of elements that represent the person's accumulated knowledge, beliefs, and expectations relevant to that schema (Hamilton, 1981). When a new piece of information relevant to the schema is confronted in the environment, it will be encoded in memory, comprehended, and associated with other bits of knowledge in terms of the elements contained in that schema. Schemata exist at varying levels of abstraction. Newly formed or impoverished schemata can represent a narrow range of specific or morselized content (Lane, 1956; Tesser, 1978). Other schemata are more abstract; consequently, they have a richer set of associations with other schemata and a broader application to a variety of objects (Hamilton, 1981; Taylor & Crocker, 1981). Once formed, the schema is subsequently available for encoding and interpreting future information about the object or event. In addition, the schema is employed to fill in missing information or make inferences when an incoming stimulus is either incomplete or vague (Taylor & Crocker, 1981; see also Chapter 18 of this volume).

Although the schema concept does not directly suggest any specific hypotheses for explaining the decline of party identification, it does direct our attention to important aspects of information processing that will aid in understanding the decline. First, it suggests that we examine the content of the cognitions that citizens have of political parties as these provide clues to both the structure of party schemata and the encoding of party-relevant information. Second, it suggests an investigation of the interconnections among various elements in party schemata and the consistency of these cues. Third, it directs attention to the relative richness of the party schema. People with richer, elaborate, fully developed schemata are more likely to use their party schema in making political inferences and electoral choices. Declining party identification, therefore, may reflect an increasingly impoverished party schema for a significant segment of the population. These aspects of information processing and the concept of schema are employed in the remainder of this paper to guide the investigation and interpretation of the various explanations offered for declining party identification.

SORTING OUT THE EXPLANATIONS

A review of the literature dealing with the topic of declining partisanship reveals considerable confusion and overlap in the various explanations of the decline. Sorting out the several explanations, therefore, must be accomplished before proceeding to an empirical examination of them.

One of the most evident problems with the various explanations is that what could be interpreted as a distinct information-processing hypothesis has often been confounded with an alienation explanation. Nie et al., (1976) for example, have argued that "the parties offer no meaningful [issue] alternatives that might tie citizens more closely to them" (p. 283). As a result, citizens become disaffected and negative toward the parties, which subsequently reduces partisan attachment. Similarly, Black and Rabinowitz (1980) suggest that if neither party can solve important social problems, citizens will eventually view the parties unfavorably and lose faith in government. Wattenberg (1981) rejects the alienation explanation, but in the process, he provides the clearest statement of the hypothesis. He writes, "The alienation hypothesis depends largely on two assumptions . . . that voters no longer see important differences in what the parties stand for and that the decline in strength of party identification has been an outgrowth of the decay of public trust in the government" (p. 944).

Each of these statements confounds a number of potentially separable elements. For example, factors such as meaningful issue alternatives, the solution of important problems, and important differences in what the parties stand for are all relevant to a cognitive or information-processing interpretation. If citizens fail to receive informational cues regarding each of these factors, their partisan schema may not be activated either for the general comprehension of politics or for the electoral decision. The concept of alienation, on the other hand, potentially suggests an affective, negative rejection of parties. Thus, to reduce conceptual and empirical confusion, the different cognitive explanations need to be distinguished and treated separately from an alienation explanation.

Employing an information-processing framework suggests that the various explanations for declining partisanship can be synthesized into four major categories. Loosely defined, these categories deal with different levels of information processing. The initial step in responding to any object involves having sufficient informational cues to even attend to the object (Taylor & Fiske, 1978). Therefore, I first discuss those explanations that focus on the sheer absence or presence of partisan information. Next, I turn to explanations involving a somewhat higher level of information processing (i.e., the connection between bits of information) and discuss in particular the cognitive connection between candidates and parties. The third set of explanations all imply an even higher level of information processing, which involves drawing inferences that go beyond the immediate experiential information. For example, included among these explanations are judgments regarding the policy differences between the parties (see further discussion in Chapter 7 of this volume by Conover and Feldman). In addition to these three cognitively based sets of explanations, I reexamine the alienation hypothesis as involving affective information processing. Lastly, a multivariate analysis is employed to ascertain the relative direct effects of the competing explanations for declining strength of party identification.

THE ABSENCE OF PARTISAN INFORMATION

As previously mentioned, a number of researchers have suggested the absence of party-relevant information as an explanation for declining partisanship. For example, Beck (1974) pointed to the lack of understanding of what the parties represent among generations twice removed from the events of critical realignments. Similarly, A. H. Miller and Wattenberg (1983) argue that "no-preference" nonpartisans receive little personally meaningful information about parties; thus, they fail to attend to party cues that may be available. Likewise, one subset of respondents in the neutral category of Wattenberg (1981) included individuals who had absolutely nothing to say when asked in an unstructured way about political parties. Thus, we could reinterpret the growing neutrality toward parties cited by Wattenberg as an increase in the percentage of people who simply are not aware of or attentive to parties.

The processing of information generally involves scanning the stimuli available in the environment, attending to and storing certain of these items for later consideration or use. Which items get attention and how they are stored, however, depends on previously abstracted knowledge structures. Information has no relevance unless it fits into a cognitive context (i.e., a schema about the meaning of the stimulus). One of the first priorities, then, should be to determine how impoverished or how rich the cognitive representations are that citizens have of political parties. If individuals have no conception of a political party, they will not recognize available information as relevant to parties; in short, they will not attend to political parties. Citizens will understand and recognize parties only if they have a theory about what a party is (i.e., only if they have a party schema).

One potential explanation for the decline in attachment to political parties thus lies in the possibility that an increasing percentage of people have not developed schemata about parties because there is a dearth of information available about them in the social environment. Perhaps parents have talked less with their children about parties in recent years, or there may be fewer references to the parties as such in the media. The rise of candidate-based campaigns, the growth of political action committees, and the increased use of television, which focuses attention on individuals, not institutions, may have shifted the content of available information in a way that minimizes partisan cues. Regardless of the initial cause, the result of decreased information should be manifest through a reduced salience of parties and a lower level of party-relevant cognitions, especially among independents.

Empirical evidence bearing on this point can be found in responses to the unstructured, open-ended questions asking respondents what they like and dislike about the Democratic and Republican parties. These questions have been asked in the University of Michigan National Election Surveys (NES) since 1952. The absence of any comments in response to these questions can be interpreted as indicating the lack of a party schema. This interpretation is based on the assumption that schema-relevant information should be more readily recalled (Taylor & Crocker, 1978). Respondents who are aschematic should therefore have a minimal amount of information about political parties and provide few comments when asked to reflect upon the parties.

Indeed, these notions seem to fit quite well with the evidence from the party likes–dislikes questions. In each year, pure independents were less likely than stronger partisan identifiers to make any comments about either party, thereby implying that independents were more aschematic (see Fig. 9.2). After 1960, there occurred a rather dramatic increase in the percentage of respondents who had no information to convey when asked the likes–dislikes questions. By 1980, approximately three out of every four independents could be classified as a partisan aschematic on the basis of this criterion.

However, a decreased level of information about political parties was not solely restricted to independents. Indeed, even one quarter of the strong identifiers in 1980 were unable to recall anything they particularly liked or disliked about either party. Perhaps this decay in party-relevant information helps explain decreased partisan loyalty among those who remained identified with a party as well as the shift toward partisan independence.

I can only speculate on the various factors that might account for the decline in party-relevant information suggested by the data in Figure 9.2. Only one possibility appears fairly certain: It is definitely not the result of increased disinterest in politics. The same trend toward decreasing levels of party salience is found among both those who are highly interested, heavy media users and those who are less interested in politics. This implies that the quality and availability of informational cues regarding parties has diminished; otherwise, we would have expected the number of comments about parties to have remained high, at least for the better informed.

In short, the data in Figure 9.2 support the argument that independents are partisan aschematics (i.e., people with no party schemata), lacking all but rudimentary cognitions of the political parties. The decline in partisan

Percent Uninformed

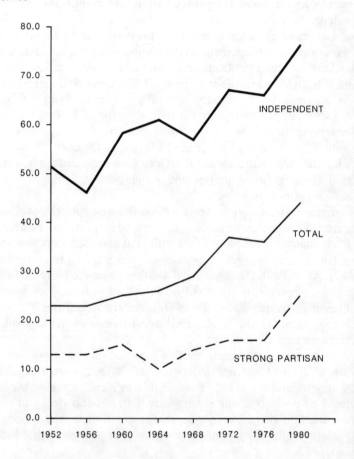

Figure entries are the percent of the respondents
who gave no substantive comments at all to the
NES party likes/dislikes questions.

FIG. 9.2   Percentage of respondents lacking party-relevant information.

identification, therefore, has apparently occurred because there is less
information or fewer informational cues in the social environment to
promote the development and use of party cognitions. This implies that
citizens, especially independents, are not particularly negative toward
parties; they are simply ignorant of them.

THE VANISHING OF CANDIDATE:
PARTY CONNECTIONS

An alternative explanation for declining partisanship assumes that people still have some understanding of parties, but their cognitions are not rich enough to form connections between judgments of different political objects, particularly candidates and parties. There appears to be some theoretical basis for this hypothesis in the cognitive literature. According to one theory of human information processing, information about objects is stored and later retrieved through a technique called *spreading activation* (J. R. Anderson, 1980), that is, new material is processed by being linked with previously established ideas. The less information that an individual has about an object, the more likely the information will be "morselized" (Lane, 1956), and the less likely there is to be a rich network of cognitive connections linking together information about separate but potentially interrelated objects and concepts.

One argument frequently seen in the dealignment literature, for example, is that decreased partisanship has resulted from a decline in the extent to which candidates are associated with parties. Some writers have suggested that this deterioration in the connection between candidate assessments and parties arises from a change in campaigns and political strategy in recent years (Seligman, 1978). Given the new style of campaigning, candidates no longer need parties; thus, they are less likely to emphasize their party or provide other cues that directly associate them with political parties. Other writers have argued that fewer party-candidate connections are available in the contemporary mass media relative to the past (Graber, 1976; Joslyn, 1980; Wattenberg, 1983).

Again, regardless of the actual mechanism that may be producing these changes, what we should expect by way of explaining declining partisanship is that independents make fewer party-candidate connections and that these linkages become less frequent over time. Although he did not examine the correlation with strength of party identification, Wattenberg (1981) contends that in the minds of voters the party-candidate link has in fact deteriorated. Indeed, empirical evidence, part of which Wattenberg himself reported, does show a decrease in the percentage of survey respondents making references to current or past presidential candidates when discussing their views of the parties (see Fig. 9.3).

However, the post-1964 decline in the percentage of respondents directly linking candidates and parties is not perfectly monotonic (see Fig. 9.3, nor do strong partisans appear to link candidates and parties substantially more than do independents. In short, the evidence provides only inconsistent support for the argument that the decline of partisanship has been caused

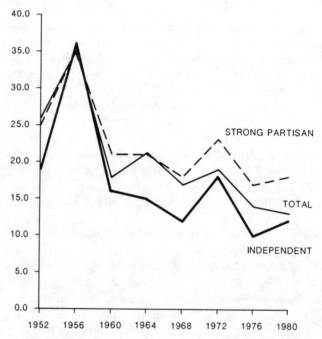

Percent
Mentioning
Candidates

FIG. 9.3   Percent mentioning candidates in response to party likes/dislikes.

by a deterioration in the cognitive association of parties and their standard-bearers.

Yet, there is an alternative, affective connection between candidates and parties that may be more promising as an explanation. One conceptualization of political parties, from the perspective of the mass public, is that they are the institutionalized embodiment of what specific leaders represent. Frequently, people do not have enough information regarding the details of the candidates' policy positions, and as a result, their thinking becomes more associative and affective. The information conveyed by the candidates about their issue positions becomes inextricably associated with feelings about the candidate. In the voters' minds, the policy maker and the policies become confounded, and politics thus becomes personified. Parties and candidates can become similarly linked in a way that is more accurately represented by a summary affective assessment than a detailed comprehension of issues and platforms. Under these circumstances, positive conceptions of political leaders would attract support for parties, whereas negative or neutral assessments would fail to foster partisan attachment.

Unlike judgments of political parties, public evaluations of the two presidential candidates, perhaps the most salient representatives of the parties, became significantly more negative from the mid-1960s to 1980 (see Miller, Wattenberg, & Malanchuk, 1982). Moreover, weaker identifiers were generally more negative toward both candidates than strong partisans, and the negative sentiments toward the candidates increased at a faster rate among independents than among the stronger identifiers (see Fig. 9.4). In brief, declining partisanship may have occurred because increasingly larger proportions of the public negatively evaluated both candidates, thereby undermining the previously positive affective association between candidates and parties.

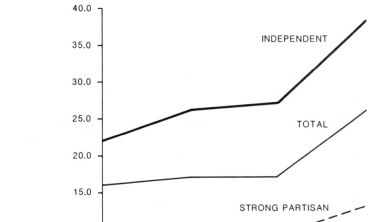

Figure entries are the percentage of respondents rating both the Democratic and Republican candidates below 60 degrees on the feeling thermometer after excluding neutral (50°).

FIG. 9.4   Percentage of respondents negative toward both candidates.

ACTIVE INFORMATION PROCESSING

The explanations for declining partisanship discussed thus far reflect rather passive, subtle processes: the loss of information or the deterioration in connections between cognitive elements. Another set of explanations found in the literature implies a more active, instrumental mode of information processing. These other explanations all assume that citizens have information about the parties, which they utilize to evaluate the parties, turning away from them if they do not satisfy their judgmental criteria.

Three separate explanations can be synthesized into this active information-processing mode. The first involves a comparison of the policy positions of voters and the parties. This explanation is based on the assumption that an increasing percentage of citizens perceives a sizable discrepancy between their own policy preferences and the positions taken by the parties (Ladd & Hadley, 1978; Nie et al., 1976; Pierce, Beatty, & Hagner, 1982). Because neither party is believed to promote their policy interest, a growing percentage of citizens feels unrepresented by either party; consequently, they think of themselves as independents. The available empirical evidence appears to lend some credence to this explanation. Unfortunately, the most appropriate evidence, which derives from the 7-point issue scales used by NES, is limited to the 1972–1980 period. Nonetheless, it shows an increase between 1972 and 1976 in the percentage of the NES sample who thought of themselves as equidistant from both parties and a reversal of that trend in 1980 (see Table 9.1), thus paralleling the trend in the proportion of independents.

There was in fact a divergence from this trend for strong identifiers who consistently shifted closer to one of the parties during the 6 years. Thus, the increased lack of issue representation from 1972 to 1976 occurred predominantly among the weaker identifiers. Moreover, the data in Table 9.1 reveal a moderately strong relationship between strength of party identification and feeling represented by one of the parties. Independents were substantially less likely than strong identifiers to perceive one of the parties as closer to them on the four different issues incorporated in the issue representation index. In brief, presumably they are independents because neither party best represents their interests.

The second active information-processing explanation also focuses on policy preferences. But this time, the emphasis is on the difference between the parties rather than a lack of policy representation. If the parties take inconsistent, ambiguous, or indistinguishable positions on issues, citizens may be unable to differentiate between the parties and consequently fail to identify with either of them (B. A. Campbell 1980; Wattenberg, 1981). Wattenberg (1981) actually found little support for this hypothesis in NES data from 1952 to 1980. During that period, he found that the proportion of

TABLE 9.1
Measures of Active Information Processing by Strength of Party
Identification

Issue Representation	1972	1976	1980
Independent			
% Equidistant from parties	29[a]	35	20
% Closer to a party	26	23	33
Strong Identifier			
% Equidistant from parties	20	16	13
% Closer to a party	49	61	66
Total			
% Equidistant from parties	22	25	15
% Closer to a party	46	42	57
Perceived Lack of Party Policy Difference			
Independents	32[b]	37	21
Strong identifiers	13	7	6
Total	18	15	8
Perceived Lack of Party Performance Difference			
Independents	70[c]	74	76
Strong identifiers	34	30	37
Total	47	49	52

[a]Issue representation was measured with the 7-point scales for guaranteed jobs, aid to minorities, equality for women, and liberal–conservative. Table entries give the percent equidistant or closer to a party across the four scales.

[b]The same four 7-point scales mentioned in footnote a were used, except here the measure is computed as the difference between the scale positions of the parties. Table entries are percent placing the parties at the same position across all four scales.

[c]The index combines perceived party performance on most important problem, inflation, and unemployment. Entries are percent seeing no difference between the parties.

survey respondents who thought that there were "important differences in what the Republican and Democratic parties stand for" (p. 942) remained quite stable. But again, he failed to report the cross-section correlations with strength of party attachment or the across-time trends in perceived party differences by level of partisanship.

A more precise measure of the perceived policy differences between parties (computed from the 7-point issue scales) reveals a significant correlation with strength of partisanship: Independents see less policy difference than stronger identifiers (see Table 9.1). Nevertheless, the distribution for the measure shows an overall population trend that runs counter to the increased percentage of independents. Contrary to what some have argued (see White & Morris, 1984), these data indicate that there was an increase in the percentage of people who perceived a difference in the parties' approaches to various policy issues during the 1970s although among independents the trend was more in line with shifting identification (see Table 9.1). Overall, however, the time-series evidence raises doubts about perceived policy differences as an explanation for declining partisanship.

On the other hand, the lack of support for the perceived policy differences explanation does not rule out the third active information-processing hypothesis. According to this explanation, a shift in the perceived performance differences between the parties accounts for decaying partisanship. During the 1980s, the United States was plagued with a number of difficult social problems, including racial strife, the Vietnam War, energy shortages, stagflation, and a host of other domestic and foreign problems. Neither the Democrats nor the Republicans appeared to deal with these concerns very successfully; thus, there was little reason to identify with either party.

This argument assumes that citizens pay more attention to the solution of problems (performance) than to the approach used by government to deal with the issue (policy). Presumably, a party (or perhaps, more appropriately, its leaders) perceived as capable of effectively handling problems will gain support and promote identification, whereas the opposite is true for incompetent, ineffective parties. Similarly, the failure of both parties over a period of time to provide solutions to society's concerns will result in a deterioration of support for the party system per se.

Fiorina (1981), building on the work of V. O. Key, has argued that party identification is formed and changed by retrospective evaluations of the parties' past performance. He puts it very concisely in stating, "As new evaluations form, an individual's identification may wax and wane" (p. 90). Wattenberg (1981), in contrast, rejects perceived differences in the performance of the parties as an explanation for declining partisanship. His dismissal of this explanation, however, appears to have arisen more from conceptual confusion than from the absence of supporting evidence. He first presents time-series data from 1952 to 1980 which show a large increase in the percentage of respondents who did not perceive any difference between how the parties would handle the most important problems confronting the United States. Next he attempts to see if the lack of perceived difference in performance is related to political cynicism, contending that it should produce alienation from both parties and government. He then rejects the hypothesis by concluding that respondents who see no difference in the performance of the parties are no more cynical than those who do see a difference. Unfortunately, in all of this he fails to test for the more direct correlation between assessments of party performance and strength of party attachment.

A good deal of available empirical evidence seems to suggest that the rise of independents has been related to questions of party performance (see Fiorina, 1981; White & Morris, 1984). For example, between 1972 and 1980 there was an increase in the percentage of people who saw no difference in how effectively the two parties would handle inflation, unemployment, and the "most important problem" facing the country (see Table 9.1). The trend was somewhat more apparent among independents than strong identifiers, and independents were much less likely to see performance differences.

In summary, a number of explanations for declining partisanship emphasize the active, instrumental processing of information. These arguments assume that people have information about the parties. Citizens are aware of either the parties' positions on policy questions or their past record of performance in office. Implicitly, these explanations assume even more. The citizens cognitively act on this information to make comparisons and draw inferences that go well beyond the initial information and experiences. They must, for example, infer from their knowledge of policy stands and preferences if there are significant differences between the policies of the two parties, if either party has done a better job over a lengthy time span, and if their interests will be better represented by one party or the other in the future.

These explanations describe a very different process for the development of party attachment than those earlier explanations based on the absence of party-relevant information. The active processing model maintains that people have information about the party's policies and performance which they use in judging the parties, and it is subsequently from these assessments that attachment to a party arises. The two sets of explanations leave the following question: Do independents fail to see a difference between the performance and policies of the parties because the cues they receive from the social environment indicate that there is no difference, or do they fail to see a difference because there is no information available which allows them to differentiate the two parties?

THE ALIENATION HYPOTHESIS REVISITED

Before entertaining a direct comparison of what we are calling the active and passive information-processing explanations, one further hypothesis must be addressed. The so-called *alienation hypothesis* has been referred to a number of times and, given its prominence in the literature, it deserves careful attention. As indicated earlier, this hypothesis frequently incorporates two elements: one cognitive and one affective. The argument, as presented by others, generally has combined one of the explanations already discussed, usually a lack of issue representation or the absence of a perceived difference between the parties, with a subsequent negative rejection of parties. However, theoretical confusion is often the result of combining these explanations (recall the difficulties Wattenberg encountered when considering these factors). Furthermore, the various cognitive explanations examined earlier posit a direct connection with partisan attachment, which is both logically and analytically distinguishable from an affective rejection of parties.

That people have an affective tie to parties, which may have waned regardless of cognitive changes, is a reasonable hypothesis grounded in work demonstrating that affective attachment is an important component of group identification (Gurin, Miller, & Gurin, 1980; Miller, Gurin, Gurin, & Malanchuk, 1981; Tajfel, 1982). Indeed, a positive feeling toward one of the parties gained through early family socialization was frequently assumed to precede a richer cognitive basis of partisan attachment (Campbell et al., 1960; Greenstein, 1965; Jennings & Niemi, 1981). In addition, Zajonc (1980) has suggested that cognitive and affective assessments of an object may be processed independently and in parallel. Given these arguments, it is important to separate conceptually the two elements that have been combined under the alienation hypothesis and which are thus often confounded in the empirical analysis of declining partisanship.

A related problem with some of the previous work aimed at testing the alienation hypothesis is that the measure of alienation frequently employed is the NES general trust in government index. This index may be useful for assessing alienation from the broader political system, but it is quite inappropriate as an indicator of alienation from parties. The attitudinal focus of the trust index is the federal government, not the political parties; thus, it provides an inadequate test of the alienation from parties hypothesis.

The best available measures for operationalizing divorcement from parties are the feeling thermometers used by the NES to obtain affective ratings of Democrats and Republicans. Combining the two ratings provides a single assessment of political parties per se. Two types of ratings are most interesting theoretically. Rating both parties negatively would surely provide evidence of rejection of the party system. Wattenberg (1981), on the other hand, has argued that it is neutrality toward the parties and not negativity that has increased over time. To a great extent, the thermometer ratings show a similar trend of increasing neutrality from 1964 to 1976, but then a significant decline occurs in 1980 (see Fig. 9.5 trend for total neutral). Even more in contrast to the evidence presented by Wattenberg is the steady growth in negative ratings of both parties that occurred from 1964 through 1980 (see Fig. 9.6). Feeling neutral toward the parties, however, appeared to be more strongly correlated with strength of party identification.

How do we explain the discrepancy between these findings and those reported by Wattenberg? The difference most surely arises from the operationalization of the measure for party affect. Wattenberg employed

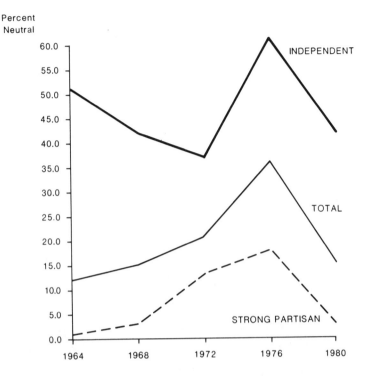

Percent
Neutral

Figure entries are the percent of respondents rating <u>both</u>
parties at 50 degrees (neutral) on the feeling thermometer.

FIG. 9.5   Percentage of respondents neutral toward both parties.

the NES open-ended likes–dislikes questions to build his measure of party
affect. This has an inherent limitation in that people may like or dislike the
parties but not be able to articulate any specific reasons for those feelings.
In addition, his neutral category incorporated two types of respondents
excluded from the thermometer categories reported in Figure 9.5, namely,
those who had nothing to say about either party and those who were
ambivalent in that they stated an equally balanced number of likes and
dislikes about the parties.

In summary, the data in Figures 9.5 and 9.6 provide some evidence
confirming Wattenberg's contention that declining partisanship has represented a growth in neutral sentiments toward parties. Yet the data also
reveal a separate significant increase in the proportion of people expressing
to some degree a negative repudiation of parties per se.

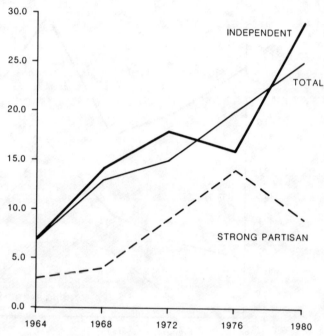

Figure entries are the percent rating both the Democratic and Republican parties below 60 degrees on the feeling thermometer excluding neutral (50°).

FIG. 9.6   Percentage of respondents negative toward both parties.

A MULTIVARIATE INQUIRY

Thus far, I have examined the various explanations offered in the literature for declining partisanship in a bivariate manner. The different explanations are not incompatible with one another; therefore, it is important to estimate their relative contributions to the growth in independents. As is often the case, there are a number of limitations to a multivariate analysis. For example, there are various causal lags and reciprocal relations among the several explanations that could be stipulated and examined. Some of these are discussed briefly, but a more complete specification of these inter-relationships goes well beyond the scope of this paper.

Furthermore, although a discussion of declining partisanship conjures up images of dynamic processes at the individual level, which should be addressed with panel data, I postpone this type of analysis also. Unfortunately, even the usable cross-section data are limited to a relatively short time span. It is only as of 1972 that indicators are available for measuring all of the theoretically relevant explanations. Despite these limitations, the results are quite interesting.

Certain explanations can be immediately excluded, as they have no direct effect on strength of partisan attachment. For example, the rise in independents appears to have little to do with either the absence of a cognitive connection between parties and candidates or the feeling that neither party represents one's policy interests (see Table 9.2). In addition, the perception of no policy differences between the parties was significantly related with being an independent in 1972 and 1976, but not in 1980; thus, it attains less general importance because of the inconsistency.

Among the remaining explanations, the relative importance of feeling neutral toward both parties, especially in 1976 and 1980, provides substantial confirmation of Wattenberg's (1981) earlier finding. However, the persistent and strong effects of negative sentiments toward both parties reveal that the negative rejection of the parties which occurred between the mid-1960s and 1980 has also contributed independently to the decline of partisanship in America for at least a significant subset of citizens. In addition, negative public assessments of the presidential candidates who have been selected to represent the parties in recent

TABLE 9.2
Regression Equations Predicting Strength of Party Identification

Predictors	1972	1976	1980
Neutral toward parties	.12**	.26**	.25**
Negative toward parties	.14**	.11**	.22**
Perceived performance difference	a	.17**	.12**
Party information	.21**	.15**	.12**
Negative toward candidates	.10*	.08*	.07*
Perceived policy difference	.12**	.06	.10*
Issue representation	.02	.07	.04
Candidate–party connections	.01	.02	.03
Multiple R	.44	.55	.51

Note. Entries are standardized coefficients. All variables have been reflected to produce positive relationships. For operationalization of the predictors see earlier Figures and Table.
[a]Not usable in 1972 because of split–half design of sample.
$*p < .01. **p < .001.$

years also promoted the slide in support for both parties.

The relatively strong impact that the lack of party-relevant information had in 1972 compared with 1976 and 1980 suggests that this was a particularly important factor in the earlier years of declining partisanship. In the later years, it appears as if the sheer absence of information led to both a growing neutrality and increasingly negative sentiments toward the parties. In many respects, this is what we might theoretically expect if there is a loss of familiarity with an object (Zajonc, 1968). Yet, the fact that the other variables remain significant even after controlling for lack of information reveals that declining partisanship is not simply the result of the absence of familiarity or the loss of information. The results suggest that a decline in partisanship also occurs among the informed, apparently because they have negative evaluations of the parties and their leaders and because they perceive no difference between the ability of the parties to solve the current major problems confronting society.

Most of the variables included in the equations of Table 9.2 have a straightforward substantive meaning. Feeling neutral toward the parties, on the other hand, could be interpreted as reflecting a number of different factors and causes. Wattenberg (1981), for example, maintains that neutral feelings result because voters no longer draw connections between the issue positions of candidates and the parties. Alternatively, feelings of neutrality might arise because of a dearth of information from which to judge the parties or because people are ambivalent about the parties or their leaders. Examining the intercorrelations among the independent variables used in the equations for Table 9.2 begins to provide a broader understanding of the forces promoting neutral feelings toward the parties. From a separate regression predicting neutrality toward parties, it was determined that those lacking information or perceiving no performance differences between the parties, and to a lesser extent those negative toward both candidates, were more likely to be neutral toward the parties. The policy variables and the variables measuring candidate-party linkages, on the other hand, had virtually no effect on feeling neutral toward parties.

We might similarly ask what information citizens are lacking today that may have produced a sense of partisan attachment in an earlier period. Is there some content or category of party cognitions that has faded over the years? These questions can be answered by focusing more closely on the content of the responses obtained in answers to the NES likes–dislikes questions.

Tables 9.3 and 9.4 present a revealing comparison of the partisan cognitions conveyed by the open-ended responses in 1952 and 1980. Some of these cognitive elements remained consistently prominent over the nearly 3 decades. For example, references to the social groups associated with each party were almost as prominent in 1980 as in 1952. Noting that the

TABLE 9.3
Substantive Content of Partisan Cognitions

	Images of the Political Parties, 1952			
	Like Democrats (%)	*Dislike Democrats (%)*	*Like Republicans (%)*	*Dislike Republicans (%)*
Because of:				
The groups they are for or against	33.1	4.7	3.2	20.3
Economic/welfare policy stands	31.9	16.3	22.1	22.4
Social issue stands	—	—	—	—
Stands on general philosophy of government activity	11.4	8.7	11.0	5.8
Their ability to manage the government	2.3	26.6	18.0	4.3
Foreign policy	4.1	17.1	12.3	3.4
Truman	1.0	7.6	—	—
Eisenhower	—	—	7.7	1.8
Stevenson	1.3	0.9	—	—

Note. Entries represent the proportion of the sample offering each given type of response. Source: SRC/CPS National Election Study, 1952; and Wattenberg and Miller, 1981.

Democrats are the party of the common man, whereas the Republicans are the party of the upper classes and big business, represents an enduring distinction that stems from the New Deal period.

Other cognitive categories, however, shifted quite markedly in the extent to which they were recalled. As suggested by Wattenberg, the mention of candidates in reference to the parties had changed noticeably between the two time points. Even more striking shifts, however, occurred in the proportions mentioning various political issues such as economic and welfare issues, foreign policy concerns, and the ability of the parties to manage the government. In 1952, for example, between 16 and 32% of the respondents said something positive or negative about the two parties and economic or welfare issues; in 1980, that figure had dropped to between 4 and 10%. Similarly, cognitions of what the parties represented in the areas of foreign relations and government management were less clearly defined and articulated in 1980 than they were earlier. In sum, neither party in 1980 had a very firmly entrenched positive or negative public image on such issues compared with 2 or 3 decades earlier.

Given the data in Tables 9.3 and 9.4, one might conclude that what had occurred over the years was a loss of information regarding the domestic

TABLE 9.4
Substantive Content of Political Cognitions

	Images of the Political Parties, 1980			
Because of:	Like Democrats (%)	Dislike Democrats (%)	Like Republicans (%)	Dislike Republicans (%)
The groups they are for or against	25.5	4.2	4.3	19.3
Economic/welfare policy stands	6.2	10.0	8.1	3.9
Social issue stands	0.8	0.7	1.0	1.1
Stands on general philosophy of government activity	8.1	8.2	11.1	5.1
Their ability to manage the government	2.5	9.7	7.2	2.0
Foreign policy	4.2	6.3	7.4	4.5
Carter	0.6	1.9	–	–
Reagan	–	–	1.1	1.5

Note. Entries represent the proportion of the sample offering each given type of response.
Source: SRC/CPS National Election Study, 1980; and Wattenberg and Miller, 1981.

and foreign policy positions of the two parties. But, the standard NES coding of the open-ended responses fails to make a theoretically critical distinction between issue responses, which refer to policy positions (the approach to problems), and responses that reflect upon performance (the outcomes or ability to solve problems). When this distinction is made by returning to the original protocols and coding anew all the responses, a very telling discovery is made (for a discussion of the coding, see A. H. Miller & Wattenberg, 1983).

What had deteriorated dramatically over the period of the mid-1960s to 1980 were not references to the policy positions associated with each party, but retrospective cognitions of how well each party had dealt with various problems (see Figs. 9.7 and 9.8). In the three surveys prior to 1964, an average of 46% of the respondents predominantly made performance comments about the parties, whereas in the final three surveys, only 18% did so on the average. This decline in performance cognitions was partly offset by a rise in policy comments after 1960. Note that in the three surveys for 1952–1960, compared with those for 1972–1980, the average proportion of respondents making policy comments was 22 and 34%, respectively. Moreover, prior to 1964, what had sharply differentiated strong identifiers from independents was the extent to which their cognitions focused on performance, not policy concerns. In the more recent surveys, in contrast,

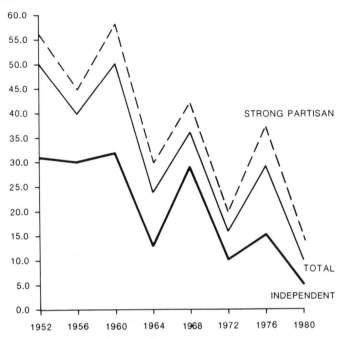

Figure entries are the percentage of respondents making predominantly performance statements about the parties when answering the NES party likes/dislikes questions.

FIG. 9.7   Percentage of respondents with cognitions focused on party performance.

the emphasis on policy cognitions has been a far more powerful discriminator between independents and stronger partisans. Thus, part of the decline in performance assessments of the parties was offset by increased attention among identifiers to policy differences between the parties. But most of the disappearance of performance cognitions resulted in the public simply not having much information about parties (recall from Fig. 9.2 the large increase in the proportion of respondents making no substantive comments at all about either party).

In summary, party identification declined during the 1960s and 1970s because an increasingly large proportion of citizens had no consistent expectations or schema of which party would handle the problems confronting society more effectively. Prior to the mid-1960s a number of beliefs about the abilities of the parties to deal with various difficulties had

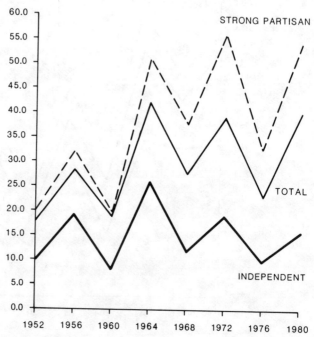

Percent Focused
on Policy

Figure entries are the percentage of respondents making
predominantly policy statements about the parties
when answering the NES party likes/dislikes questions.

FIG. 9.8   Percentage of respondents with cognitions focused on party
policy.

developed, largely influenced by the New Deal period. These cognitive
inferences were extrapolated from experiences and information that was
readily available. Thus, we find that the frequency of performance comments to the likes–dislikes questions is only weakly related to media usage
or attentiveness to politics, whereas policy comments are strongly correlated with attention to politics in the media.

However, with the rise of new social concerns in the 1960s and 1970s
(race riots, the Vietnam War, women's rights, energy shortages, environmental protection, stagflation, etc.), the cues that citizens began to receive
suggested that neither party was competent to handle these problems.
Moreover, there was a considerable amount of inconsistent information
available. Two examples might illustrate this point. Democrats were

traditionally known for dealing with unemployment, yet it rose significantly under the Carter administration. Similarly, Republicans were presumed better at controlling inflation, but both Nixon and Ford failed to win the war against rising prices. Such inconsistencies can be expected to foster beliefs that there is no difference between the parties. In addition, they undermine the individual's ability to predict and interpret the world of politics in terms of party labels.

Lacking consistent information to maintain their partisan schemata or for young people to develop schemata regarding which party would best solve various problems, people had to fall back on the cues that were readily available for political decision making. For the better informed, these cues still focused rather sharply on the policy distinctions between the parties. But many others came to rely more and more heavily on candidate-related information, especially on perceptions of how well they would perform in office or on policy promises (Miller & Wattenberg, 1983; Miller et al., 1982).

A number of political, psychological, and social factors helped focus attention on the candidates in recent years. Information about the candidates is readily available. It is more vivid and less abstract than references to parties, and in the absence of information clearly linking candidates and parties, it may be the only information available for political choices. Moreover, people have a psychological preference for person over group schemata (Tesser & Leone, 1977). In a period of dominant, appealing figures such as Franklin Delano Roosevelt or John Kennedy, the candidates are the parties, and their accomplishments convey an understanding of what the party represents.

A number of political and social changes have undermined this connection. The rise of television and the increase in primaries have resulted in the parties' factional disputes being aired in all the homes across the country rather than in the more confined quarters of party meeting rooms, caucuses, and conventions. The serious intraparty challenges to wrest the nomination away from a sitting President, such as occurred in 1968, 1976, and 1980, all helped to reduce the image of unitary parties reflecting a common interest. Subsequently, public schemata about parties became less cohesive and less reliable as a guide to organizing and predicting the political world. Lacking partisan schemata, what remains for decision making are cues that focus on the individual candidates. But even here we find more trouble for the development or maintenance of party schemata. During the 1960s and 1970s, a set of leaders who did not fit with prior partisan cognitions emerged. For example, many people felt that Goldwater, McGovern, Carter, and Reagan were less than adequate standard-bearers for their respective parties.

Clearly, then, leadership played a major role in the demise of partisanship.

From 1964 to 1980, a series of leaders failed to convey a consistent, positive, and enduring image of what the parties represented. Quite the contrary, their conduct in office helped undermine the performance-based schemata that formed the foundation of partisan attachment prior to the mid-1960s. Lacking these performance cues that were so important to the development or maintenance of a partisan schema, party identification declined.

CONCLUSION

At the outset of this paper, I stated that an information-processing framework would be used as a guide to the research reported. The usefulness of this approach may now be assessed. A critic might argue that the entire analysis, presentation, and conclusions would have been the same with or without the utilization of the information-processing approach. But that criticism seems highly unwarranted. Certainly, the paper provides neither confirmation nor disconfirmation for any specific hypotheses derived from schema theory. But then, that was not its purpose. The goal was to offer a more integrated and general explanation for the decline of partisan identification than could be currently found in the literature. Toward that end, the information-processing approach was quite helpful.

Starting from the information-processing framework provided a different perspective for the reinterpretation of previously offered explanations, the operationalization of measures, and the interpretation of results. Because of the approach, we examined the relative richness of partisan cognitions across time, the interconnection between different elements of partisan schemata, and various judgmental inferences about parties that go beyond the voters' immediate experience of the candidates, issues, or current events. The approach also focused attention on substantive explanations for partisan attachment that are different than those offered in previous work. For example, The American Voter (Campbell et al., 1960) emphasized the enduring effects of early socialization as the major source of partisan affiliation. The information-processing approach gives far more emphasis to cognitions that develop and change in response to real-world cues that occur over the life span.

Similarly, at one point in his analysis of partisanship, Fiorina (1981) included a dummy variable for those who respond "don't know" to questions measuring retrospective evaluations of the parties. Unwittingly, he incorporated a lack of information variable into his analysis. However, he passed over the variables without any discussion, except for a technical footnote indicating that the items had been included to "increase the number of useable cases" (p. 94). Because he was not using an information-processing approach and had no theory (i.e., no schema) for how the absence of information fit into a broader explanation for shifting partisanship, he failed to discuss these variables despite their strong statistical significance. In short, utilizing the information-processing approach has promoted a different perspective on the processes underlying the decline of party identification.

The analysis suggests that for many people party identification represents an accumulated set of judgments and evaluations based on the past performances of the incumbents of the two parties. If the leaders of one party are perceived over time to deal more effectively with the problems of concern to an individual, I would expect voters to identify increasingly with that party. If voters fail to receive consistent cues regarding performance differences, the party labels become less important as a cognitive guide to organizing thoughts and assessments of new candidates or current issues, and in turn, voters begin to see parties as irrelevant to the electoral choice.

The process of partisan decline suggested here is similar in many respects to the rational choice model presented by Fiorina (1981). However, my analysis places more emphasis on the absence of cognitions regarding party performance. Fiorina assumes that citizens have information about the performance of the parties, and they identify with the one they evaluate most highly over some period of time. My argument is that for some people those performance cognitions are absent or quite impoverished, and those lacking this information are just as likely to be independents as are those who believe that neither party has performed better.

Whether the process of change described here is any less rational than the model presented by Fiorina is open to debate. If we accept the argument that much of the impoverishment of performance-based partisan schemata originated with what appeared as inconsistencies in the behavior of political leaders, rather than some other shifts such as a change in family socialization patterns, then we could conclude that declining partisanship was the outcome of a "rational" process.

Another debatable point raised here focuses on the interpretation of the growing neutrality toward parties. Some may interpret this as a rather benign shift, less deserving of attention than a negative rejection of the parties. Yet, we should not dismiss this change too readily. The loss of positive identity with an institution represents at least a mild form of divorcement. The current belief expressed by many that the parties are no longer relevant to the political process and that party labels are unreliable political guides is reminiscent of the form of alienation that Seeman (1959) labeled *meaninglessness*. In addition, the evidence indicates that although the negative rejection of parties has been less prevalent than the growth in neutrality, it has nonetheless been significant. Indeed, in 1980 the proportion reacting negatively toward parties surpassed the proportion that was neutral. The 1960s and 1970s clearly witnessed a marked increase in alienation from parties as an institution.

What are the implications of these findings for the future of political parties? First, I would argue that the evidence runs counter to the conclusion of an inevitable long-term disintegration of the party system. Nevertheless, continued volatility in American electoral politics can be expected until public cognitions of consistent performance differences between the parties are reestablished. Given an inclination to focus on the individual rather than on something abstract, such as a group or institution (e.g., political parties), this is no mean task. Indeed, rather than spending so much time researching the decline of partisanship, perhaps we should be asking why parties and candidates ever get linked. Why should we expect them to be connected in the mind of the average citizen? From this perspective, the New Deal period may have been an aberration, and what we have witnessed since the 1960s may be a gradual return to something more normal. Whether or not it is more normal, it is clear that without retrospective party-performance judgments to guide electoral choices, voters will be more open to the short-term influences of specific issues, candidate appeals, and the vagaries of the media.

The results also suggest that much more than just party organizational activities or increased control over the candidate recruitment process is needed to reestablish parties as relevant political institutions. Part of this task involves renewing partisan schemata from which people can make party-relevant inferences about new candidates and new issues that emerge in the future. Consistent real-world cues are necessary for rebuilding and developing afresh those schemata. This means that the restoration of party labels as meaningful mechanisms for organizing our thoughts about the everyday world of politics and as guides for electoral decision making will come only by showing the public that it makes a difference which party wins an election. This does not only mean demonstrating a difference in party platforms or policy instruments. Rather, it depends on providing observable differences in policy outcomes, the solution of problems, and achieving results. This in turn requires a series of effective, successful, problem-solving administrations. This means reestablishing a positive attraction to parties by showing people that they are better off if one party rather than the other controls government. In short, restoring the relevance of party will depend on there being a real difference in the way parties perform in office.

ACKNOWLEDGMENTS

This paper was written while the author was a Visiting Professor on a Fulbright Fellowship at the Department of Sociology, University of Trondheim. It was prepared with the technical assistance of Hans Terje Mysen. Substantive suggestions from Oksana Malanchuk are also gratefully acknowledged.

10 Presidential Character Revisited

Donald R. Kinder
The University of Michigan

At about the time Richard Nixon and his loyal friends were preparing for the 1972 presidential contest, James David Barber was putting the final touches on *The Presidential Character* (1972). Barber argued that the best way to predict a President's success in office is to examine the development of his character in childhood. More than on ideas, organization, power, or historical accident, a president's performance depends, according to Barber, on character.

My purpose here is not to pick on Barber, but to use *The Presidential Character* as a point of contrast. Like Barber, I am interested in presidential character, conceptualized not as forces at work in the psyches of Presidents, however, but as cognitive categories at work in the minds of citizens. My interest is in perceived presidential character, where the perceiver is the ordinary citizen.

As such, my approach is consistent with general developments that have taken place in the last 15 years in the study of personality. A few years before *The Presidential Character* appeared, Mischel (1968) published his major assault on traditional conceptions of personality. Mischel argued that the fundamental assumption shared by both psychodynamic and trait approaches to personality (viz., that behavior is determined by generalized, powerful predispositions) is radically inconsistent with 5 decades worth of empirical research. Because people react to authority in one way at home and another way on the job, because moral behavior in one setting does not predict moral behavior in other ostensibly similar settings, because aggressiveness in one context is no guarantee of aggressiveness in other contexts, Mischel concluded that the traditional conception of personality in terms

233

of broad response predispositions must be abandoned.[1]

Whether or not psychologists should follow Mischel's advice and relinquish traditional conceptions of personality in their professional work (predictably, there is much disagreement about this; see, e.g., Epstein, 1984; Mischel, 1984), it is clear that people continue to cling to such conceptions in their everyday perceptions. That is, people regard others as consistent and stable, even if they apparently are not. As psychologists have pursued this curiosity, traits have undergone a subtle but important transformation. Whereas traditional personality theory, as in *The Presidential Character*, regards traits as the intrapsychic causes of behavior, the new view regards traits as cognitive categories that observers apply to behavior.

Without intending to endorse the wholesale abandonment of personality in the traditional sense, I pursue presidential character here in the "modern" style. For the most part, I ignore Presidents and concentrate on citizens. This chapter is about the analysis of presidential character undertaken not by professional psychologists equipped with formal and explicit theories but by ordinary people equipped, at best, with informal and implicit theories.

The first section of the chapter develops a theoretical framework for understanding the nature and function of the conceptions ordinary citizens hold regarding presidential character. This framework is then illustrated and tested in the next main section, drawing upon the results of a recent national survey designed with this purpose expressly in mind. In the chapter's final section, I both summarize what we have learned about presidential character from the citizen's point of view and suggest an agenda for future research.

THEORETICAL FRAMEWORK

To sustain popularity with the public and therefore power in Washington, Presidents must preside over a peaceful world, a healthy economy, a tranquil society, and a chaste administration. They must offer policy proposals on major issues that do not stray too far from the public's own ideas, champion virtuous causes, and oppose immoral ones (Kinder & Fiske, 1985). In addition, or so I argue here, they must convey admirable qualities of character. A President, like less celebrated people, is judged partly by the sort of person he seems to be. Why?

---

[1]Those familiar with the "attitude–nonattitude" debate in studies of public opinion will notice eerie parallels to the argument about the nature and very existence of personality (see, e.g., Converse, 1964; Kinder, 1983a).

One reason is that judgments of character offer citizens a familiar and convenient way to manage the avalanche of information made available to them each day about public affairs. As Heider (1958) argued more generally, one way people create meaning out of a complicated and changing social world is by attributing events to the stable internal dispositions of salient actors. In a political context, this may well mean the motives, intentions, and traits of the President. Americans may reduce the complexity of political affairs to manageable proportions by placing the President at the center of things. Keeping track of international and national events then reduces to the simpler task of keeping track of the President, a task that is consistent with the casual and intermittent attention Americans typically pay to politics (Kinder & Sears, 1985).

Judgments of a President's character may serve an instrumental function as well. If ordinary people agree with Barber's contention that a good way to predict a President's performance in office is to examine his character, then they will be motivated to examine the President's character partly for what it foretells about their future and the future of the country. This sentiment is captured nicely by Page's (1978) dramatic asertion that "in an age of nuclear weapons, no aspect of electoral outcomes is more important than the personality of the president, which might well determine how the United States would react in an international confrontation" (pp. 232–233).

Judgments of a President's character may also reflect an interest in the maintenance of public standards and the very special place of the President in public life. The presidency is not only an institution. It is, as Barber (1972) points out, "the focus for the most intense and persistent emotions in the American polity. The president is a symbolic leader, the one figure who draws together the people's hopes and fears for the political future" (p. 4). Because of their special symbolic significance, Presidents are venerated or villified partly by how well they live up to standards of character, among others.

All this suggests that character should figure prominently in Americans' thinking about the President, and indeed it does. When asked to describe what they like and dislike either about a particular President or an ideal President, many people mention aspects of character (Kinder, Abelson, & Fiske, 1979; Page, 1978), referring to such personal qualities as intelligence, honesty, warmth, and many more.

In deciding whether a President is intelligent, honest, or warm, I assume that people make use of an implicit theory they possess about presidential character more generally. I assume further that a person's theory is comprised of "a well-structured system of expectations about what behavioral signs go with what abstract dispositional qualities and about what abstract qualities, in turn, tend to cluster and co-occur" (Cantor & Mischel, 1979,

p. 45). That is, theories of presidential character enable citizens to move from evidence of malfeasance to judgments of dishonesty or from judgments that a President is knowledgeable to judgments that he is also intelligent. Put more generally, such theories permit citizens to go effortlessly and automatically beyond the information given about a particular President (Bruner, 1957).

But which aspects of presidential character are central? At the outset, I assumed, as Lane (1978) did, that "people seek in leaders the same qualities they seek in friends, that is, they simply generalize their demands from one case to the other" (p. 447). According to four autonomous lines of social psychological research, the demands of friendship seem to center on the largely independent dimensions of *competence* and *sociability*. These two dimensions emerge in investigations of leadership in small groups (task vs. socioemotional leadership; Cartwright & Zander, 1968); in attitude-change research on source credibility (expertise vs. trust; McGuire, 1969); in research on interpersonal attraction (respect vs. affection; Rubin, 1973); and in explorations of the tacit theories people apply in evaluating friends and acquaintances (intellectual competence vs. affection; Rosenberg, 1977).

Americans also seem to demand competence and sociability from their President as well, though the evidence to date is rather sketchy. References to competence and some version of sociability emerge frequently in voters' open-ended commentaries on presidential candidates (A. H. Miller & Miller, 1976; A. H. Miller, Wattenberg, & Malunchuk, 1982; Page, 1978). Moreover, structural analysis of trait inventories developed with the objective of identifying core aspects of presidential character generally reveal two correlated but distinct dimensions (competence and integrity) that are strongly reminiscent of the social psychological results (Kinder & Abelson, 1981; Kinder et al., 1979; G. B. Markus, 1982).

The purpose of the research reported here is to explore more deeply than previous efforts the American public's conception of presidential character. Previous work has identified two broad organizing themes in perceived presidential character: competence and integrity. Here we see whether Americans make still finer distinctions. One possibility is that citizens distinguish between two forms of competence, one represented by managerial, technical skills and the other by heroic, mythical leadership. Hereafter, I retain the label competence for the first and leadership for the second. Another possibility is that Americans also distinguish between a President's integrity and his empathy, that is, the degree to which he is regarded, on the one hand, as setting a good moral example for the country and, on the other, as compassionate and understanding.

My point of departure is thus to presume that citizens' thinking about the President's personal qualities is organized in terms of four key demands:

competence, leadership, integrity, and empathy.[2] Drawing on a national panel survey completed in the summer of 1983, I test this presumption in five ways. (The tests naturally concentrate on reactions to President Reagan, though evidence on Edward Kennedy and Walter Mondale is introduced at several points for comparative purposes). The first test is that of intelligibility. Do conceptions of presidential character, defined in terms of competence, leadership, integrity, and empathy, form recognizable, coherent patterns? Second, are judgments of character predictable? That is, are they related in sensible ways to other aspects of a citizen's political and social life? Third, are conceptions of presidential character stable over time? They must be reasonably stable if they are to serve as points of reference for citizens struggling to understand history as it happens. The fourth test gets directly at the question of structure. To what extent do competence, leadership, integrity, and empathy constitute separate and distinguishable demands? That the four can be distinguished conceptually does not, of course, guarantee that ordinary citizens will honor such distinctions in their thinking about the President. Fifth and finally is the test of consequentiality. Do citizens' conceptions of a President's character matter? In this case, we see whether such conceptions contribute independently to the judgments citizens make of a President's overall performance. If so, the consequences are both psychological and political. They are psychological for the individual citizen because judgments of character have consequences for other political beliefs; they are political for the society because the President's performance ratings partially determine the power he enjoys in Washington and therefore the success of his programs (e.g., Neustadt, 1960; Rivers & Rose, 1985).

EXPLORING THE PUBLIC'S CONCEPTION
OF PRESIDENTIAL CHARACTER

As preparation for the 1984 National Election Study, a national sample of adult citizens was interviewed in July 1983 by the Center for Political Studies and reinterviewed 1 month later. The 314 people questioned in 1983 are a random subsample of respondents to the 1982 National Election Study and thus constitute a national random sample of the 1982 voting age citizen population. (Each respondent's answers to the November 1982

---

[2]The survey actually investigated the possibility that a fifth central trait might exist for presidents: *stability*, operationalized as the degree to which a president was regarded as cautious, cool in a crisis, thoughtful, impulsive, loses his temper too easily, and reckless. The evidence regarding the existence of a stability trait in presidential judgment was overwhelmingly negative (for the grim details, see Kinder, 1983b).

survey are available for analysis; I capitalize on that opportunity later.) Midway through the interview, respondents were asked how well their impressions of three prominent national political figures (Ronald Reagan, Edward Kennedy, and Walter Mondale) could be characterized by a succession of 24 traits. The trait list encompassed the four key dimensions (competence, leadership, integrity, and empathy), each represented by six specific traits, three which were positive and three negative. (The 24 traits are listed in Table 10.2). Respondents were asked in the first interview for their impressions of Mr. Reagan and either Mr. Kennedy (one random half of the sample) or Mr. Mondale (the other random half); in the second interview, they were asked for their impressions of Mr. Reagan alone.

Regarding President Reagan's competence, leadership, integrity, and empathy, virtually all respondents answered all questions. On the average, 98.4% of the (first wave) sample delivered opinions on Mr. Reagan's personal qualities. The percentage diminished slightly, to 97.3%, when Edward Kennedy became the target, and a bit more, to 90.6%, in character judgments of Walter Mondale. The same gradient—from Reagan to Kennedy to Mondale—emerged in the proportion of respondents who replied that they "couldn't decide." Interviewers did not volunteer this category, but nevertheless made use of it when respondents seemed genuinely ambivalent. Such responses, which were coded into the middle of the scale in subsequent analysis, averaged just 1.6% of those who offered an opinion on Reagan's personal qualities, 3.3% for Kennedy, and 6.0% for Mondale.

Intelligible?

That Americans appear quite willing to offer character assessments of their most prominent political leaders says nothing about the depth and seriousness of such assessments. A first test of their quality can be had by seeing whether President Reagan and his challengers elicit distinctive and intelligible profiles. Figures 10.1 through 10.4 provide some first answers. The figures are arranged to enhance comparisons between the public's view of President Reagan and presidential hopefuls Kennedy and Mondale, with the traits grouped into four categories. They present Reagan's, Kennedy's, and Mondale's average score on competence (Fig. 10.1), leadership (Fig. 10.2), integrity (Fig. 10.3), and empathy (Fig. 10.4).[3] Together, these

---

[3]To compute these average scores, replies to the negative traits were first reflected. Then respondents were simply assigned their average score across the six items for each of the four central traits. To be assigned a score, respondents had to answer at least four of the six items. This requirement resulted in over 98% of the sample receiving a score in trait ratings of Reagan, over 96% in ratings of Kennedy, and over 88% in ratings of Mondale.

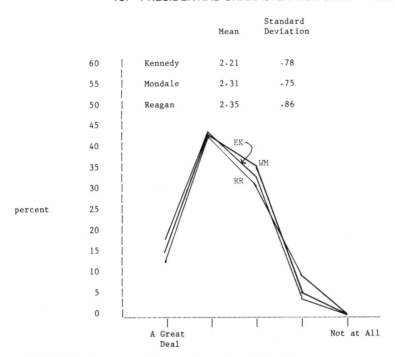

	Mean	Standard Deviation
Kennedy	2.21	.78
Mondale	2.31	.75
Reagan	2.35	.86

FIG. 10.1   Assessment of Reagan, Kennedy, and Mondale:
Competence Index.

results reveal whether, and in what ways, Reagan, Kennedy, and Mondale cut distinctive public profiles.

First, consider comparisons between Reagan and Kennedy. Overall, the public regards Edward Kennedy to be somewhat more competent than Ronald Reagan. The difference is small, but statistically reliable (t test for paired observations, $t = 1.58$, $p < .10$; Winkler & Hays, 1975).[4] Kennedy's advantage in this respect is due to his apparent superior intelligence, knowledge, and experience. On the other indicators of competence, Kennedy does no better than Reagan. In fact, the senator is regarded as somewhat less hard-working than the President, a difference that may have as much to do with public assumptions about the roles they occupy as with their "private" qualities.

Kennedy's edge on competence reverses on leadership, $t = -2.10$, $p < .05$ (see Fig. 10.2). This switch is important because it is the first hint that the public distinguishes between managerial and mythical aspects of leadership. Kennedy's disadvantage is especially pronounced on commanding respect and avoiding weakness, traces, perhaps, of Chappaquidick's legacy.

---

[4]All these candidate comparisons are based on roughly 150 cases. Remember that just one half the sample was asked about Kennedy with the other half asked about Mondale.

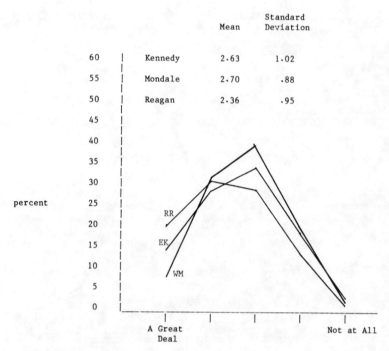

	Mean	Standard Deviation
Kennedy	2.63	1.02
Mondale	2.70	.88
Reagan	2.36	.95

FIG. 10.2   Assessment of Reagan, Kennedy, and Mondale: Leadership Index.

The stain of Chappaquidick is seen more clearly in the public's integrity judgments. As Figure 10.3 reveals, Kennedy runs far behind Reagan on integrity, $t = -6.02, p < .001$. Compared to Kennedy, Reagan is regarded by many more citizens as decent, moral, and as setting a good example, and by many fewer citizens as dishonest, likely to lie to the public, and power-hungry.

The public reverses again on judgments of empathy, now preferring Kennedy to Reagan, $t = 1.68, p = .10$. Kennedy's advantage is most apparent on fairness. Whereas one third of those interviewed said that "unfair" fit their impression of Ronald Reagan a great deal, only 11% said that of Kennedy. More generally, the public was more willing to deliver harsh judgments about Reagan's empathic sensibilities than Kennedy's. More people thought him not at all compassionate (15% for Reagan, 8% for Kennedy), regarded him as not caring at all about people like them (22% vs. 16%), as not understanding their problems (23% vs. 17%), and as generally out of touch (25% vs. 16%).

Comparing Reagan with Mondale also leads to some sharp contrasts. Overall, neither is advantaged on competence, $t = .04$, ns. Reagan is seen as the more experienced but also as more prone to make mistakes: the perquisites and liabilities of incumbency. On leadership, in contrast, Reagan

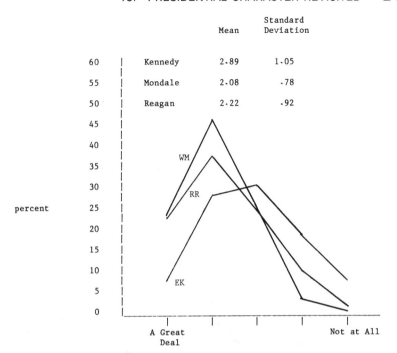

		Mean	Standard Deviation
60	Kennedy	2.89	1.05
55	Mondale	2.08	.78
50	Reagan	2.22	.92

FIG. 10.3   Assessment of Reagan, Kennedy, and Mondale: Integrity Index.

leads by a wide margin, $t = 3.51, p < .001$, and on all six indicators. Once again, this may reflect the perquisites of the office of presidency and also on Mondale's comparatively low profile. In any case, the fact of the difference, and its decisiveness, is important because it again signals that competence is not the same as leadership.

On matters of integrity, Mondale enjoys a slight advantage, $t = 1.53, p = .13$. Mondale and Reagan are judged to be more or less equal except on power-hungry and lies to the public, where Mondale leads. Mondale's advantage over Reagan widens on judgments of empathy, $t = -2.60, p < .01$. Although this contrast resembles the Kennedy–Reagan difference and runs in the same direction, it is substantially greater. Moreover, whereas the differences are modest to negligible on traits that capture Reagan's amiable ways (compassionate, kind, really cares about people like me), they are considerable on the more explicitly political versions of empathy (doesn't understand problems of people like me, out of touch with the people, and unfair). Later, we discover additional and stronger hints of this apparent split between personal and political manifestations of the President's empathy.

In these various comparisons, Reagan, Kennedy, and Mondale emerge as separate and distinct persons. Reagan appears as a leader of mythical

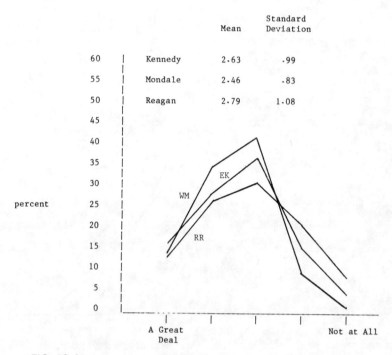

FIG. 10.4   Assessment of Reagan, Kennedy, and Mondale: Empathy Index.

proportions, commanding respect and setting high moral standards, but perhaps out of touch with the experiences of ordinary people. Kennedy's profile, in contrast, emphasizes competence, compassion, and a powerful and perhaps crippling strain of dishonesty. Mondale defines the least distinctive profile, although several qualities are suggested: capable, fair-minded, and in touch with ordinary people. That these profiles are distinctive, and that the distinctions make sense, supports in a general way the claim that Americans' thinking about presidential character is rather sophisticated. The public appears to reach sensible verdicts, and not about character in general, but about competence, leadership, integrity, and empathy in particular.

Predictable?

Judgments of presidential character should be related in predictable ways to the characteristics of those who do the judging. To a conservative corporate executive, President Reagan may seem intelligent and compassionate, whereas to a Democratic blue collar worker, the same President may appear thickheaded and cruel. Trait judgments should depend in some degree on the citizen's political outlook and social position.

To test this, judgments of Mr. Reagan's character were regressed against party identification, ideological identity, policy opinions, race, sex, age, and education. In this analysis, trait judgments were represented by the respondent's average reply over the six questions designed to measure each of the hypothesized four central traits (see footnote 3). Party identification is the traditional 7-point scale, ranging from strong Democrat to strong Republican. Ideological identity also takes the traditional 7-point form, from extreme conservative to extreme liberal, with the roughly one third of the sample who allowed as they never thought of themselves in ideological terms coded at middle-of-the-roaders. Policy opinions were measured by a single variable that again ranged from extreme conservative to extreme liberal, reflecting respondent's average position on nuclear arms control, money for defense, government aid to minorities, government guarantees of jobs, and cuts in government services. The three political variables (party, ideology, and policy) as well as the four measures of social location (race, sex, age, and education) were all taken from the 1982 National Election Study and therefore can safely be regarded as exogenous. All variables, including the trait judgment dependent measures, were coded to the 0 to 1 interval.

Table 10.1 presents the ordinary least squares estimates of the effect of party, ideology, policy, and social location on ratings of President Reagan's traits. They confirm the political outlook–social position thesis. In particular, judgments of President Reagan's traits depend heavily on citizens' policy preferences. Those who took conservative positions tended to regard Reagan considerably more favorably on all four traits, but especially on ratings of empathy, than did those who took liberal positions. The estimated impact of policy exceeded that due to either party or ideology. Moreover, the impact of policy was substantially greater on ratings of Reagan's traits than on trait judgments of Kennedy or Mondale, as revealed by parallel regression analyses.[5] Judgments of President Reagan seem to reflect in a distinctive way his conspicuously conservative policies.

Alongside the substantial effects of political outlook, the effects of social position pale. A small but reliable racial gap is apparent in Table 10.1. Blacks are consistently more critical of Reagan than are whites, with the widest gap coming, understandably, on empathy. Age is utterly unrelated to judgments of the President's competence or leadership, but it is quite sharply related to integrity and empathy. The elderly are less inclined to regard Mr. Reagan as setting a moral example for the country, and they are

[5]As indicated in Table 10.1, the estimated impact of policy on President Reagan's trait ratings was: −.236 (competence), −.319 (leadership), −.303 (integrity), and −.411 (empathy). For Kennedy, the respective coefficients are: .130, .276, .227, and .293; for Mondale: −.145, −.091, .160, and .122.

TABLE 10.1
Estimated Impact of Party, Ideology, Policy, and Social Location on
Reagan Trait Ratings (Ordinary Least Squares Estimates)

Equation	(1) Competence	(2) Leadership	(3) Integrity	(4) Empathy
Party	−.145	−.150	−.160	−.201
	(.039)	(.042)	(.039)	(.043)
Ideology	−.136	−.150	−.160	−.224
	(.071)	(.076)	(.072)	(.080)
Policy	−.236	−.319	−.303	−.411
	(.072)	(.077)	(.072)	(.080)
Sex	.027	.063	.013	.041
	(.024)	(.026)	(.024)	(.027)
Race	.065	.045	.090	.097
	(.043)	(.046)	(.043)	(.048)
Age	.001	−.032	−.164	−.193
	(.057)	(.061)	(.057)	(.064)
Education	.019	−.129	−.231	−.097
	(.076)	(.081)	(.076)	(.084)
R squared	.223	.271	.322	.389
Standard error of regression	.195	.208	.195	.217
N	280	280	280	280

much less willing to say that he understands their problems. As a rule, education is negatively related to trait ratings. This pattern also holds for Kennedy and Mondale, suggesting that the well-educated are generally more critical of the personal qualities of political leaders than are the less educated. In the case of Mr. Reagan, though not for Kennedy or Mondale, the education difference is most pronounced on matters of integrity. Finally, there are intimations in Table 10.1 of Mr. Reagan's notorious gender gap. Holding constant party, ideology, policy preferences, and other measures of social location, men evaluate Mr. Reagan's personal qualities more favorably than do women. The differences, though, were quite small, and particularly small where I expected them to be large, in ratings of the President's empathy.

However, a closer examination of empathy reveals that there is both strong support for this expectation and no support at all. In place of Reagan's overall empathy rating, I substituted in turn each of the six specific traits that supposedly stand for empathy in the regression equation just described. The results are striking. Men and women differ not at all in their ratings of Mr. Reagan's compassion, $b = .030$, $se = .040$, kindness

$b = -.044, se = .035$, or caring for people, $b = .021, se = .041$. But they do differ sharply in the more expressly political versions of empathy. Women much more than men believe that Reagan fails to understand their problems, $b = .132$, $se = .046$, that he is out of touch with the people, $b = .110$, $se = .044$, and that he is unfair, $b = .105, se = .041$. Thus, caring for people is not the same as comprehending their problems; compassion is not the same as being in touch; kindness is not fairness. Of course, these are not logical identities, but the sharpness of the gender differences they provoke is nevertheless remarkable. Such results are a further indication that citizens can be discriminating in their assessments of presidential character.

Stable?

Respondents were interviewed in July and in August. On both occasions, they were badgered for their assessments of President Reagan's competence, leadership, integrity, and empathy. Short of the intrusion of dramatic events, these assessments should be quite stable. The public should not have thought Reagan capable in July and a nincompoop in August. In fact, alterations in Reagan's profile in this aggregate sense were practically negligible. Judgments of the President's competence and leadership did not budge in any discernible way between July and August; his integrity ratings deteriorated slightly, $t = 1.86, p < .10$, and his empathy ratings improved slightly, $t = 1.37, p < .20$. These results both indicate a heavy inertial component to the President's trait profile and demonstrate that the different components of the profile can move simultaneously in opposite directions— another indication of the texture of the public's impressions.

Stable aggregate judgments are of course compatible with prodigious (but offsetting) vacillation in the trait judgments offered by individuals. But there was in fact rather little change of this sort as well. Raw continuity coefficients (Pearson correlations) for each of the four central traits are impressively high, ranging from .79 to .84. Respondents who thought about President Reagan in a certain way in July were very likely to think the same about him in August.

Structured?

Thus far, I have simply assumed that people can and do distinguish among the four aspects of presidential character. Here that assumption is put to a series of formal tests. To do so, I rely on confirmatory factor analysis, based on Joreskog's maximum likelihood model available in LISREL IV (Joreskog, 1969; Long, 1983a). Joreskog's model treats each particular trait judgment as if it were caused by a latent (or unobserved) factor. In the present instance, the latent factors are the four hypothesized generic presidential traits: competence, leadership, integrity, and empathy. The model generates estimates of the reliability of each trait judgment, how well each represents an underlying latent factor (factor loadings), relationships among the latent factors themselves, and an overall measure of fit. All parameters are maximum likelihood estimates based on the Pearson correlation matrix among the trait ratings (with negative trait ratings reflected).

In the model's initial specification, each of four correlated but distinct latent factors is assumed to cause only its own 6 trait judgments. That is, each of the 24 trait judgments was assumed to be due to one and only one latent factor. This model, which represents in the most straightforward way my starting assumption that there exist four distinct presidential generic traits, is quite clearly incorrect. Although the specification yields highly significant factor loadings, which range from .358 to .794, its overall fit to the observed correlation matrix is poor. Fit is assessed by the ratio of chi-square to degrees of freedom; ratios of 2 and less are customarily regarded as acceptable. The ratio here is an unacceptable 3.30, (Chi-square = 810.75; degrees of freedom = 246).

The trouble is located among the negative traits. This can be seen in two ways. First, negative traits are much less reliable, on the average, than are positive traits. The average estimated reliability of negative traits was .299; for positive traits, the corresponding average was .503. For just 3 of the 12 negative traits does the estimated reliability surpass .40; 11 of 12 positive traits' reliabilities do so. Second, the model systematically underestimates correlations between negative traits representing different latent factors. For example, the model estimates the correlation between thinking that President Reagan makes lots of mistakes and thinking that he is out of touch with ordinary people to be .317; the actual correlation is .549. Such underestimation is replicated throughout the correlation matrix in negative trait pairings. This pattern, plus the unreliabilities of the negative traits, implies that respondents encounter more difficulty making distinctions among Mr. Reagan's competence, leadership, integrity, and empathy when dealing in negative traits than when dealing in positive traits.

In response to this difficulty, I pursued two complementary tactics, hoping for convergent results. First of all, I reestimated the original model, making one change. The results from the initial model implied that when reaching judgments of the President's character, people to some degree ignore the connotative differences among the various negative traits. Such judgments seem to indicate, merely and with modest reliability, overall evaluations of the President. To take this into account, the new version of the model now includes a fifth latent factor (*negativity*) on which all negative trait judgments, regardless of connotation, are assumed to load equally. This specification thus assumes that any particular negative trait rating (e.g., makes lots of mistakes) has two underlying and unobserved causes: judgments of competence and overall evaluations.

The results are shown in Table 10.2. They indicate first of all that this specification fits the correlation matrix quite respectably, chi-square = 486.43, degrees of freedom = 241, ratio = 2.02. As the table shows, the model yields highly significant and generally hefty factor loadings. They range from .399 to .789. Negative trait judgments do load together on a single factor (with the equality constraint imposed, loading = .428 for all). In general, positive traits load more heavily on each of the four conceptual latent variables than do the corresponding negative traits. For competence, the average loading for positive traits is .732; for negative traits, it is .523; for leadership, .730 versus .473; for integrity, .708 versus .563; and for empathy, .771 versus .606. The estimated reliabilities for positive traits continue to surpass by a substantial margin the estimated reliabilities for negative traits (on average, .542 vs. .406).[6]

With some assurance that the model fits the data reasonably well, we can now turn to the estimated relationships between the core traits. These relationships, shown in Table 10.3, are Pearson correlations between the latent factors (i.e., with measurement error purged). Two are of special interest: that between competence and leadership and that between integrity and empathy. As indicated in Table 10.3, the model estimates the correlation between competence and leadership to be .876 (SE = .031) and

---

[6]Another interesting distinction can be extracted from Table 10.2. It so happens that the trait battery mixes two types of negative judgments. The first type asserts the presence of a negative quality (e.g., lies to the public), the second asserts the absence of a positive quality (as in has little experience). There are just four of the latter type on the trait list—has little experience, doesn't understand the problems of people like me, no sense of direction, and not qualified—and they are distinguished by their low reliabilities. Two of the four are the least reliable in the entire inventory; the other two are well below average.

The empirical contrast here is striking. It can be explained, I think, by noting the steps respondents are likely to go through in answering the trait questions. Consider the two questions: (a) How well does "lies to the public" fit your impression of Ronald Reagan? (b) How well does "has little experience" fit your impression of Ronald Reagan? In the first instance, respondents presumably simply match the trait phrase to their impression and then select the appropriate response category. In the second instance, the procedure is not so direct. People probably do not compare their impressions of Reagan against the phrase "has little experience." Rather they first translate the negative phrase into its affirmative counterpart (is experienced) and then ask themselves how well their impression fits the translated phrase. They ask themselves, in effect, whether Ronald Reagan has lots of experience. Having answered that question, they then have to back translate their answers in order to choose an appropriate response category. This question type can therefore go wrong at several junctures, and by the evidence assembled in Table 10.2, it did in fact go wrong. There may be a general measurement lesson here, and there certainly seems to be a specific one: In the assessment of negative presidential traits, ask respondents about the presence of negative qualities; do not ask about the absence of positive qualities.

TABLE 10.2
Maximum Likelihood Factor Analysis of Reagan Trait Assessments
(Estimates Based on Pearson Correlation Matrix)

	Loadings					Reliability
	Competence	Leadership	Integrity	Empathy	Negativity	
Hard-working	682					.465
Intelligent	.746					.556
Knowledgeable	.767					.588
Little experience	.399				.428	.189
Lots of mistakes	.558				.428	.438
Not qualified	.612				.428	.392
Commands respect		.661				.437
Inspiring		.778				.606
Strong		.750				.563
Weak		.458			.428	.344
No direction		.482			.428	.403
Easily influenced		.478			.428	.359
Decent			.641			.410
Moral			.698			.487
Good example			.784			.614
Dishonest			.589		.428	.360
Lies to public			.458		.428	.370
Power-hungry			.641		.428	.481
Compassionate				.768		.590
Kind				.757		.573
Really cares				.789		.622
Can't understand us				.417	.428	.330
Out of touch				.678	.428	.587
Unfair				.722	.428	.565

Note. Standard errors of loadings range from .029 to .092.
Number of cases = 282
Chi-Square = 486.43
Degrees of freedom = 241
Ratio = 2.02

between integrity and empathy to be .951 (*SE* = .020). Thus, competence and leadership are highly correlated but distinct elements of character, whereas integrity and empathy may be so highly correlated that the distinction is hardly worth making.

These results were corroborated by several additional analyses. As an alternative response to the initial model's difficulties, I simply reestimated it in two separate steps, first for positive traits alone and then for negative traits alone. In both instances, the initial model's specifications were maintained. Each of four correlated but distinct latent variables is assumed to cause a set of (now three) particular trait judgment; each trait judgment

TABLE 10.3
Relationships Between Latent Trait Factors: Pearson Correlations
(Standard Errors)

	Competence	Leadership	Integrity	Empathy	Negativity
Competence	1.0 ( )				
Leadership	.876 (.031)	1.0 ( )			
Integrity	.792 (.040)	.903 (.028)	1.0 ( )		
Empathy	.809 (.035)	.884 (.028)	.951 (.020)	1.0 ( )	
Negativity	– .281 (.160)	– .116 (.180)	– .177 (.176)	– .149 (.177)	1.0 ( )

$N = 282$

was assumed to be due to one and only one latent factor.[7] The results for positive traits indicate a good overall fit (chi-square = 96.78, degrees of freedom = 47, ratio = 2.06), substantial factor loadings (ranging from .637 to .797, averaging .724), and respectable reliabilities (ranging from .406 to .635, averaging .527). They also show that whereas competence and leadership are distinct elements of presidential character, $r = .895$, $SE = .042$, integrity and empathy may not be $r = .942$, $SE = .029$. The results for negative traits taken alone are quite similar. The model fits the overall data quite well (chi-square = 100.49, degrees of freedom = 48, ratio = 2.09), yields highly significant if somewhat erratic factor loadings (ranging from .396 to .795, averaging .635), and generates variable reliabilities, some respectable, some not (ranging from .167 to .638, averaging .415). On the major bone of contention, the model estimates faint distinctions between judgments of President Reagan's competence and leadership, $r = .920$, $SE = .055$, and between his integrity and empathy, $r = .931$, $SE = .041$.

Overall, these several analyses support the general claim that judgments of presidential character are structured around a small set of central traits. Americans clearly distinguish between presidential competence and leadership on the one hand, and integrity and empathy on the other. They also

---

[7]Across the various specifications, I have assumed covariances between the error terms to be zero. Inspection of the first order derivative matrices generally supported this assumption, with one conspicuous exception: The covariance between the error terms for judgments of President Reagan's intelligence and knowledgeability is very likely non-zero and positive. In this specific instance, but in no other, the assumption of non-zero covariances was relaxed.

appear to reach somewhat different conclusions about the private and public sides of competence; that is, they distinguish between the President's capacity to administer his office and to mobilize the public. The evidence here is not so clear as to whether people see any real difference between the President's integrity and his compassion.

Consequential?

We need, finally, to determine the extent to which citizens' assessments of the President's personal qualities influence their overall evaluations of the President's performance. To estimate this adequately requires taking into account plausible determinants of overall evaluation in addition to judgments of character. Here I assume that evaluation turns partly on character but also on party, ideological identity, policy options, and the particular affects the President evokes. The question then becomes the extent to which trait judgments influence overall evaluations independently of party, ideology, policy, and affect.

Ordinary least squares estimates of the impact of trait judgments on evaluations of President Reagan, as well as presidential hopefuls Kennedy and Mondale, are presented in Table 10.4. Overall evaluation was measured on a 100-point "thermometer scale," where 100 stands for a very favorable evaluation and 0 stands for an extremely unfavorable evaluation. For purposes of analysis, thermometer scale ratings were recoded to a 0 to 1 scale, as were all the independent variables. Party, ideological identity, and policy opinion were measured as described previously. Affect was assessed through a checklist procedure. Those interviewed were asked whether President Reagan (and later, whether Edward Kennedy or Walter Mondale) had ever made them feel angry, proud, afraid, or hopeful. Following precedents established in previous research (Abelson, Kinder, Peters, & Fiske, 1982; Kinder & Abelson, 1981), I formed two affect indices: a positive one, representing respondents' average reply to proud and hopeful, and a negative one, representing respondents' average reply to angry and afraid.

The unstandardized coefficients shown in Table 10.4 thus indicate the direct effect of trait judgments, independent of any direct effects due to party, ideology, policy, and affect. The major message of the table is that, indeed, judgments of character powerfully influence overall evaluations of the President and presidential hopefuls. The results are particularly striking for President Reagan, somewhat less so for Edward Kennedy, and least dramatic for Walter Mondale.

But the ordinary least squares estimates displayed in Table 10.4 suffer two limitations. One is that they are stained by measurement error and may therefore underestimate the real impact of character. The other is that the estimates may be corrupted by simultaneity. That is, judgments of charac-

TABLE 10.4
Estimated Impact of Trait Ratings on Overall Evaluations (Ordinary
Least Squares Estimates)

	Reagan	Kennedy	Mondale
Competence	.201 (.059)	.101 (.105)	.062 (.115)
Leadership	.077 (.058)	.163 (.086)	.052 (.092)
Integrity	.223 (.062)	.166 (.089)	.222 (.117)
Empathy	.191 (.061)	.097 (.093)	.024 (.101)
R squared	.736	.550	.561
Standard error of regression	.137	.162	.144
N	284	143	119

Note. Each equation also included party t-1, ideology t-1, policy t-1, positive affect index, and negative affect index.

ter may be both causes and consequences of overall evaluation. Someone who thinks President Reagan to be the nation's salvation for reasons of policy, values, philosophy, or merely because he is a Republican is probably more likely to regard him as competent, inspiring, honest, and so forth than is someone who thinks Reagan is a right-wing madman. The ordinary least squares estimates presume that the causal flow is unilaterally from particular traits to general evaluations. To the degree that this presumption is incorrect, the coefficients displayed in Table 10.4 may overestimate the impact of trait judgments.

In order to correct these two problems, the evaluation equations were reestimated, this time following a two-stage least squares procedure. In each equation, trait judgments were treated as endogenous variables. As before, party t-1, ideological identity t-1, policy t-1, and affect also appeared in each equation, treated as exogenous variables. Instruments came from a pool of variables included in the 1982 survey, including sex, race, education, income, age, region, marital status, urban-rural place of residence, and assessments of family and national economic conditions.

The two-stage least squares estimates of the impact of trait judgments on overall evaluation, shown in Table 10.5, generally strengthen the case for the importance of character. Once measurement error has been purged and simultaneity taken into account, the estimated effects of judgments of character typically increase. For Reagan, Mondale, and Kennedy alike, the most consequential aspect of character appears to be competence, a result

TABLE 10.5
Estimated Impact of Trait Ratings on Overall Evaluations
(Two-Stage Least Squares Estimates)

	Reagan	*Kennedy*	*Mondale*
Competence	.502	.324	.172
	(.257)	(.250)	(.301)
Leadership	—	—	—
	—	—	—
Integrity	.391	.150	—
	(.267)	(.226)	—
Empathy	.393	—	−.012
	(.219)	—	(.173)
R squared[a]	.687	.508	.530
Standard error of regression	.156	.170	.148
N	235	121	99

Note. Trait ratings were treated as endogenous. Party t-1, ideology t-1, policy t-1, positive affect index, and negative affect index also appeared in each equation, treated as exogenous. Instruments came from a pool of variables measured in the 1982 interview, including sex, race, age, education, income, region, marital status, rural–urban residence, and assessments of family and national economic conditions. Dashes in the table mean that the coefficient was set to zero, based on interim analyses.
[a]R squared is the squared correlation between predicted and observed evaluation.

in keeping with findings from earlier studies (Kinder & Abelson, 1981; G. B. Markus, 1982).

By far the strongest effects appear in the Reagan equation. Overall evaluations of Mr. Reagan are powerfully influenced by judgments of his competence, integrity, and empathy. By contrast, just one of the four traits (competence, once again) influences the overall evaluation of Senator Kennedy. This is something of a surprise because previous research had repeatedly uncovered the special importance of integrity for evaluations of Kennedy (Kinder & Abelson, 1981). In this instance, judgments of Kennedy's integrity and negative affective reactions to him were highly correlated: People who thought that Kennedy set a poor moral example for the country were also very likely to report negative feelings toward him, particularly anger. And it is the negative feeling state that appears to be the more consequential here. When the negative affect index is deleted from the equation, the estimated impact of integrity increases dramatically, $b = .506$, $SE = .184$. Finally, and consistent with other findings, the coefficients in the Mondale column suggest that the former Vice-President had not yet, by the summer of 1983, created a clear image with the public. Citizens' general evaluations of Mondale perhaps had a bit to do with their judgments about his competence. But in general, judgments of Mondale's character seem to be more the consequences than the causes of overall evaluation.

CONCLUSION

This chapter has been guided by the assumption that Americans understand and judge Presidents substantially by standards of character. As Presidents-to-be appear on the scene, win nomination and election, and then move through their term (dodging bullets, stirring up trouble in Central America, slashing the budget, railing against and then embracing the People's Republic), Americans repeatedly ask themselves (or so I claim): What sort of a person is this? I have assumed, furthermore, that they answer this question in a way analogous to the way in which they answer similar questions about their friends and neighbors, that is, partly by consulting their implicit theories regarding the organization and antecedents of character in general.

Although these assumptions are perfectly (and perhaps horrifyingly) general, the evidence presented here is quite specific, confined for the most part to judgments of President Reagan's character supplied by a representative sample of American citizens of voting age in the summer of 1983. In aggregate terms, the public's appraisal of Mr. Reagan's character resembled the public's appraisal of Mr. Kennedy and Mr. Mondale offered at the same time, but with several notable differences. Moreover, the differences seem grounded in real events and earned reputations. Such patterns suggest that judgments of presidential character reflect both (default) assumptions people make about political leaders in general, as well as particular and often distinctive things they know about particular leaders. Judgments of presidential character appear to be organized around a small set of correlated but distinct themes: competence, leadership, integrity, and (perhaps) empathy. Mr. Reagan's standing on these core traits depends a good bit on the political sensibilities of whoever is doing the judging. Republicans, self-styled conservatives, and advocates of the President's policy agenda tend to judge his character favorably; Democrats, self-styled liberals, and opponents of the President's policy agenda tend to be less generous. Perhaps because judgments of character are rooted at least partly in basic political orientations and perhaps because they are well-structured, they are quite stable over time. Finally, such judgments appear to be very consequential in shaping overall evaluations. The President's reputation depends powerfully on judgments of character.

At several points, the findings for President Reagan contrasted sharply, and perhaps instructively, with those for Senator Kennedy and Vice-President

Mondale. Of the three, Reagan's character left the deepest impression on the public's mind; Mondale's left the shallowest. In aggregate terms, Mr. Mondale's profile appeared to be the least distinctive. Factor analysis of Mondale's specific trait judgments produced a single general underlying factor rather than several correlated factors (in analysis not reported here). Finally, judgments of character appear to be the effects, not the causes, of respondents' overall evaluations of Mr. Mondale.

Mr. Mondale was, of course, no stranger to the national media in the summer of 1983, largely because of his presidential ambitions and prospects. Furthermore, he had completed a full term as Vice-President in the not so distant past. But this in no way approaches the attention and interest commanded simply as a matter of routine by an incumbent President. Whatever the President is up to, he is always on center stage, placed there by a relentless and untiring press (Gans, 1979; Robinson & Sheehan, 1983). Because Americans are ordinarily preoccupied first and foremost with their private lives, they will seldom notice the comings and goings of former Vice-Presidents. As a consequence, Mr. Mondale's character in the summer of 1983 remained mainly in the shadows.

Remember, though, that even in the summer of 1983, Americans were quite willing to offer their views on Mr. Mondale's character. Very few acknowledged that they did not know or could not decide the degree to which Mr. Mondale was hard-working, weak, and so on. What could the basis for such judgments be?

Some of it may have been pure guesswork, a reflection on the respondents' part that they ought to know about Mr. Mondale and that the interviewer very much wanted to know what they knew. Some of it surely reflects, however hazy and fuzzy, things that they knew and could recall about Mr. Mondale. But such judgments were also partly based on the assumptions people made about the general category to which they believed Mr. Mondale rightfully belonged. Knowing only that Mr. Mondale was a longtime prominent Democrat seeking his party's presidential nomination may tell people a good bit insofar as their understanding of this general type is rich. Then they will automatically "know" which groups Mondale likely favors, what policies he may advocate, and perhaps even what sort of person he may be (see Feldman & Conover, 1983).

Had Mr. Mondale actually made it to the White House and, as a consequence, become vastly better known, judgments of his character would no doubt have been gradually revised in light of the country's experiences, though which experiences would force what sorts of revisions is not at all obvious at present. This is a central question for democratic theory; it gets at whether the prominence of character in the public's view of the President should be celebrated or excoriated. Perhaps judgments of presidential character are both informed and realistic. Perhaps an erratic and incoherent foreign policy leads citizens to question the President's competence. Perhaps scandals in high places smear the President's integrity. Perhaps cuts in social services and tax benefits for the rich lead citizens to wonder about the President's compassion. Perhaps. Another, and sinister, possibility is that Americans never see the President's real qualities, blinded as they are by the dense fog of advertising that blankets the office. We have much to learn about the connections Americans make, and fail to make, between evidence and inference in appraisals of presidential character.

ACKNOWLEDGMENTS

Robert Abelson, Susan Fiske, and Mark Peters collaborated with me on earlier work on presidential character. Unfortunately, they cannot be held accountable for what is written here. Reid Hastie, Jon Krosnick, Gregory Markus, and Steven Rosenstone provided helpful and mostly polite comments on an earlier version of the chapter. Nancy Brennan, Pat Luevano, and Joyce Meyer prepared the manuscript with their customary competence.

11 Justice and Leadership Endorsement

Tom R. Tyler
Northwestern University

Past efforts to understand political behaviors and the political evaluations from which they flow have been heavily influenced by economic models of human judgment and action, an application that has been collectively labeled *public choice theory.* In recent years, an outpouring of writing has applied public choice theories to the political arena (Abrams, 1980; Barry & Hardin, 1982; Downs, 1957a, 1957b; Laver, 1981; Mueller, 1979; Riker & Ordeshook, 1973; Russell, 1979; Sugden, 1981).

The purpose of this paper is to argue that economic models are insufficient to describe political evaluations and behaviors because they ignore the important influence of concerns about injustice upon those evaluations and behaviors. My goal is to demonstrate that including concerns about justice into the study of political evaluation and political behavior leads to a substantially greater ability to understand both. In addition, this inclusion of concerns about justice leads to a substantially different view of the political actor than that which emerges from theories of public choice.

A major goal of economic models has been to provide a basis for understanding behaviors in people's personal lives, behaviors such as consumer choice decisions. Such behaviors are commonly referred to as *market decisions* (see Schoemaker, 1980). The purpose of this discussion is not to evaluate such uses of economic models (see M. J. Lerner, 1982), but to consider the economic study of nonmarket decision making (Mueller, 1979) embodied within public choice theories.

ECONOMIC MODELS

The core characteristics of the economic model seem elusive and hard to define because each writer using the model presents a somewhat different view of its key characteristics. As generally articulated within public choice theory, however, economic models are seen to have two key components: a theory of utility and a theory of judgment or choice.

The theory of utility embodied within economic models makes three assumptions about the nature of human values. The first is that political actors, whether citizens or leaders, will attempt to maximize their own personal gain from the political system. This is the key value assumption of public choice theory, and it provides the distinctiveness which sets that theory apart from other models of political evaluation and behavior. This concept of personal utility maximization has a long history within economics (Stigler, 1950) and has formed the basis of efforts to understand a variety of types of personal and political behaviors since the work of Smith and Bentham in the 1700s.

A second assumption of economic models is that actors are primarily motivated by a desire for material rewards. Although actions could conceivably be motivated by social utilities, such as a desire for prestige, this will only be the case if these secondary values are instrumental means ultimately linked to material gains (Laver, 1981).

Finally, the third assumption is that actors focus upon immediate (i.e., short-term) gains and loses. Although key assumptions in early economic models, the second and third assumptions have already been compromised in the economic arena by the recognition that social utilities such as power and prestige can take on a secondary value of their own and can be pursued following long-term strategies. Writers within the public choice literature differ greatly in their positions on these latter two assumptions.

The second aspect of an economic approach is a theory of judgment. Since the work of von Neumann and Morgenstern (1947), the major theory of judgment and action underlying economic models has been the familiar subjective expected utility model. According to that model, actions are governed by calculations involving the multiplicative combination of utilities and values (see Feather, 1964; Luce & Raiffa, 1957; Luce & Suppes, 1965; Savage, 1954). The theory of judgment underlying economic models has also undergone considerable modification from the original conceptions of the subjective expected utility model. In particular, a number of writers have followed the lead of Simon (1957, 1979c) and explored the heuristics and simplified strategies that individuals employ to make decisions that provide a satisfactory level of personal rewards, but which are not optimal (Arrow, 1982; Kahneman, Slovic, & Tversky, 1982; Lindblom, 1959; March, 1978). Underlying such research is the belief that citizens do not utilize a full or complete subjective expected utility decision-making strategy for all decisions (see Herstein, 1981, for an application of this heuristic approach to political judgment).

Theories of public choice have been important for two reasons. First, they have influenced the image of the political actor, which has dominated political science. The image of the political actor emerging from public choice theories is that of a self-interested agent whose actions are governed by a desire to maximize short-term material gains. According to this view, citizens decide to engage only in those political actions that will benefit them. The form of such actions is also determined by concerns of self-interest. This is true whether a citizen is deciding to vote or to riot, who to vote for, or what store to burn down.

Theories of public choice have also been important because they have had an influence on defining the problems that have occupied the attention of political scientists. In particular, attention has been directed at those political behaviors which appear paradoxical or problematic when viewed from an economic perspective. The fact that people vote, for example, appears unreasonable when voting is viewed in the context of subjective expected utility theories because the low probability of influencing election outcomes suggests that the expected gains from voting and not voting are very similar, whereas voting has clear costs. Similarly, the problem of noncompliance with government imposed burdens, the "free rider" problem, appears particularly likely to be troublesome if political actors are viewed as motivated by personal gain. When citizens are presented with a social obligation such as a tax, a personal utility perspective suggests that they will be motivated by the desire to avoid the obligation because the tax revenues will still be adequate if one person's contribution is held back. As a result, public choice theories suggest that society must develop other methods of insuring that social obligations are met. In other words, the issues that political scientists have studied, as well as the image of the political actor they bring to their examination of those issues, reflect their acceptance of the public choice perspective.

Alternative Models

Several previous efforts have been made to articulate models of political evaluation and behavior that differ from the economic view. One such effort is the "symbolic politics" literature principally associated with the work of David Sears. This literature suggests that political evaluations, policy support, and voting behavior are linked more strongly to general political predispositions than to concerns of immediate self-interest. This model has been confirmed in studies of public policy support involving the busing of students to desegregate schools (Sears, Hensler, & Speer, 1979), economic policies (Sears, Lau, Tyler, & Allen, 1980), the war in Vietnam (Lau, Brown, & Sears, 1978), and the death penalty (Tyler & Weber, 1982), but not support for tax policies (Sears & Citrin, 1982). It has also predicted voting behavior in local, state, and national elections (Kinder & Sears, 1981; Sears & Kinder, 1971; see Bobo, 1983, and Weatherford, 1983, for comments on this literature).

A second alternative model, developed within recent research, has emphasized the role of affect in political action. This line of research has suggested that political evaluations and actions are the result of feelings, not cognitive judgments. For example, in research on candidate evaluation, recent studies have found that affect is a key component of evaluation (Abelson, Kinder, Peters, & Fiske, 1982). Similarly, affect toward candidates has been found to be important in voting behavior (Maggiotto & Pierson, 1974; S. M. Margolis, 1977; G. B. Markus, 1982; Williams, Weber, Haaland, Mueller, & Craig, 1976; see Rasinski & Tyler, in press, for a review of this literature).

A JUSTICE-BASED MODEL

My purpose here is to outline and explore the importance of another potential input into political evaluations and behaviors which is not contained in the economic model or the previously discussed alternatives. That input is perceived injustice. I argue two basic points. First, judgments of the justice or injustice of government actions emerge as a key input into citizen evaluations and behaviors in the political arena. Second, a recognition of this fact should alter our view of the political actor. I do not argue that concerns about personal gains and loses are not important. Instead, I suggest that justice-related factors, not easily integrated into traditional economic models, are equally important in political settings. In other words, I want to argue that economic models are insufficient to describe the political actor, not that they are unnecessary.

Justice-Based Theories

Psychological theories of justice have identified two types of justice judgment: judgments of distributive justice and judgments of procedural justice. Judgments of distributive justice compare outcomes received to some standard of fairness or deservedness. Judgments of distributive injustice form the basis for feelings of relative deprivation (Crosby, 1976, 1982) and inequity (Walster, Walster, & Berscheid, 1978). According to these theories, those who receive low levels of outcome from the government will not evaluate government more negatively if they feel that such outcome levels are fair.

Judgments of procedural justice involve evaluations of the procedures by which outcome distributions are made, not of outcomes per se. For example, in the studies reported by Thibaut and Walker (1975), those whose cases were handled by the adversary trial procedure were found to be more satisfied, irrespective of the outcome of their case, than were those whose cases were handled via inquisitorial methods.

As was the case with the economic model, justice-based models make assumptions about personal utility. The major assumption is that individuals are motivated by a desire to receive fair outcomes, arrived at by using fair procedures, and that they evaluate their outcomes against such justice-based criteria, rather than simply in terms of personal gain and loss.

The model of judgment underlying justice-based views is the same subjective expected utility model that underlies economic approaches, except for the inclusion of terms reflecting the value attached to fair outcomes and fair procedures. Examples of this approach can be found in the work of Fishbein (Ajzen & Fishbein, 1980; Fishbein & Ajzen, 1975, 1981) and Leventhal (1976b, 1980). Each suggests an expanded subjective expected utility equation including terms reflecting fairness. Based upon the previous discussion of psychological models, it is clear that both distributive and procedural justice need to be independently represented within such a model.

The key concern here is the relevance of theories of justice to political evaluations and behaviors. The importance of justice-based theories has been explored within a variety of interpersonal contexts (Crosby, 1976, 1982; Eckhoff, 1974; Greenberg & Cohen, 1982; Mikula, 1980; Walster et al., 1978) and organizational settings (Martin, 1981; Sheppard, 1982) and, within such settings, concerns about justice are typically found to have an important influence upon outcome satisfaction and leadership endorsement. My concern here, however, is with political issues, that is, with the effect of judgments of the justice or injustice of political decisions or allocations upon the evaluation of political leaders and/or upon political behaviors. I do not want to assume that justice-based theories generalize to the political arena any more than I want to accept the public choice theory assumption that economic theories automatically explain political evaluations and behaviors. What is needed is empirical evidence.

Empirical Issues.   Two empirical issues concerning the role of justice in political settings need to be explored. The first is whether judgments of the justice or injustice of experiences or policies are distinct from judgments of the personal gain or loss arising from them. Economic analysts have suggested that ethical judgments are epiphenomenal, arising as socially appropriate justifications for evaluations and behaviors actually governed by concerns of self-interest. If this is true, then concerns about justice will not be separate from judgments of personal gain and loss in empirical research.

The second issue is whether judgments about justice or injustice, to the extent that they are distinct, exert an independent influence upon political evaluations and behaviors. People could conceivably distinguish between the justice or injustice of decisions and policies and their personal consequences, but react to such decisions and policies solely or largely in terms of personal consequences. In such a case, justice judgments would be distinct, but unimportant, because political evaluations and behaviors would be the result solely or largely of judgments of personal gain and loss.[1]

It is important to note that this definition of empirical issues is an oversimplification in two ways. First, it is not true that only the justice-based and the economic models explain political evaluations and behaviors. The symbolic and affect-based theories are also important to any full explanation. Further, it is not necessarily the case that the same one of these four models is superior to the other three in all cases. In fact, it may well be the case that each theory has some importance in many contexts and is a key factor in some settings. Ultimately, it seems most reasonable to adopt the approach of using an expanded expected utility model that includes factors operationalizing each of the four models outlined. Such an approach could then map the importance of each model across judgments, situations, and individuals. The goal of this paper is more modest. It seeks to show that the justice-based model is important in the case of one type of judgment: those involving the political arena.

RESEARCH

Before considering the literature on justice in the political arena, several conceptual distinctions, which are important within the literature on politics, need to be noted. The first is the distinction between political evaluations and political behaviors. Although my ultimate concern is with political behavior, past research suggests that such behavior is influenced by support for and evaluations of political leaders and institutions. As a result, both evaluations and behaviors have been studied in the past, and both types of research are considered here.

---

[1]It is clear that many economic theories of public choice are outcome focused and specifically exclude concerns about justice (see, e.g., Fishburn, 1973; Strotz, 1958). A similar outcome focus can also be found in many psychological theories of leadership endorsement (Hollander & Julian, 1970; Leventhal, Karuza, & Fry, 1980). But such psychological theories differ from economic models in that they include concerns about fairness. They argue, however, that such outcome fairness concerns are less central than are issues of outcome level.

Past studies of political evaluation have explored such evaluations on two levels. The first is the evaluation of particular political authorities. On the local level, this includes police officers, judges, aldermen, and mayors; on the national level, evaluations tend to focus on incumbent Presidents. Distinct from such evaluations are evaluations of the institutions of government (the court system; Congress) and of the rules or processes of government (often labeled "trust in government").

Past studies of political behavior have differentiated between positive behaviors, such as voting or writing to one's congressman (conventional behaviors), and negative behaviors, such as rule breaking (unconventional behavior). Such negative behavior can involve ignoring the rules, in cases such as speeding, and acts of antisystem behavior, such as riots, which are directed at changing the rules. Whether people engage in conventional behavior, and the form that such behavior takes, has been linked to evaluations of political candidates and their policies, as well as to a sense of civic duty. Similarly, engaging in unconventional behaviors has been tied to evaluations of the basic political system and its institutions.

Finally, two levels of concern with the issues outlined must be distinguished. On one level, political scientists have been concerned with citizen evaluations of national leaders and with citizen support for national government. Such evaluations and the behaviors responsive to them, especially voting behavior, have been widely examined. A second body of literature concerns citizen evaluations of local government and its agencies, such as the police and the courts. Because both of these literatures speak to the same empirical issues, although on different levels, both are considered here.

Past Research.   A number of political scientists have speculated that concerns about justice have an important influence upon political evaluations and behaviors. Support for political authorities has been linked both to distributive justice (Sarat, 1977) and to the belief among citizens that the procedures of government decision making are fair (Anton, 1967; Edelman, 1964; Engstrom & Giles, 1972; Murphy & Tanenhaus, 1969; Saphire, 1978; Scheingold, 1974; Wahlke, 1971). Behavior has been similarly linked to concerns about justice. In the case of conventional behavior, such as voting, the public choice literature itself has pointed to the important role of the moral sense of "civic duty" in decisions about whether to vote (Laver, 1981; Riker & Ordeshook, 1973), whereas unconventional behaviors, such as rioting, have been linked in the aggregate literature to violations in perceptions of distributive justice (Gurr, 1970; Levy, 1981).

This suggested importance of justice judgments has been supported by a variety of empirical studies of political evaluation and behavior. Several studies of overall justice judgments have suggested that beliefs about the justice or injustice of government decisions play an important independent role in political evaluations. On the local government level, this is suggested by studies of the police (Baker, Meyers, Corbett, & Rudoni, 1979); on the federal level, it is supported in research on citizen contact with federal agencies (see Tyler & Rasinski, 1982, for a secondary analysis of the Katz, Gutek, Kahn, & Barton, 1975, study), in research on support for government (see Tyler, 1984a, for a secondary analysis of the 1976 National Election Study data), and in several studies of voting behavior (Fishbein, Ajzen, & Hinkle, 1980; Fishbein, Bowman, Thomas, Jaccard, & Ajzen, 1980; Petrocik & Steeper, 1982).[2]

Fairness, in the form of judgments about the morality of laws, has also been found to be an important factor in obedience to the law. Economic approaches to the law stress the role of the perceived certainty and severity of punishment in shaping behavior (Becker & Landes, 1974; Stover & Brown, 1975). A number of direct comparisons of moral judgments and variations in the perceived certainty and severity of punishment have shown that, in fact, moral factors typically have about the same (Meier & Johnson, 1977; Tittle, 1980) or more influence upon compliance with the law than do instrumental concerns (Eiser, 1976; Grasmick & Green, 1980; Jacob, 1980; Paternoster, Saltzman, Waldo, & Chiricos, 1983; Silberman, 1976; also see Schwartz & Orleans, 1967).

There are also several more specific studies focusing on distributive justice. They suggest that concerns about distributive justice influence a variety of types of political evaluations and behaviors (see Crosby, 1976, for a review). Several studies have shown that this influence of fairness is independent of outcome concerns, both for evaluations (Casper, 1978; Curtin, 1977; Lawler, 1977; Michener & Lawler, 1975) and for behavior (Muller, 1980). Research has also supported the suggestion that judgments of procedural justice independently influence the evaluation of political and legal authorities (Tyler & Caine, 1981; Tyler & Folger, 1980).

Recent Studies.   These studies all suggest that justice has an important influence upon political evaluations and behaviors, but the difficulty with each is that none directly contrasts the influence of distributive justice, procedural justice, and outcome judgments within one study. Several recent studies have, however, included assessments of both distributive and procedural justice and have compared their influence upon political evaluations to the influence of outcomes. The first study (Tyler, 1984b) explored the endorsement of legal authorities. It examined defendants' generalizations

---

[2]In considering the Fishbein studies, it is important to note one limitation of their operationalization of moral concerns. Fishbein operationalizes subjective norms as beliefs about the views of one's reference group. Unfortunately, this confounds moral beliefs and peer pressures. As a result, the Fishbein findings provide only tentative support for a role of justice-based concerns in voting.

from personal experiences in court to views about the court system. The second study (Tyler, Rasinski, & McGraw, in press) examined the endorsement of political authorities. It considered the influence of two factors upon evaluations of President Reagan and government institutions (i.e., trust in government). These two factors were: (a) citizen agreement with the economic and social policies of the Reagan administration and (b) the level of benefits received and taxes paid under the Reagan administration.

In the first study, the influence of citizen experiences in court upon citizen views about the legal system was examined. The respondents in the study were 121 citizens who had been to traffic or misdemeanor court as defendants (see Tyler, 1984b). Respondents were interviewed by telephone following their appearances in court. In the interviews they were asked about the disposition of their case (i.e., their absolute outcomes), about that outcome relative to their prior expectations and to the outcomes of others, and about its fairness. They were also asked about the fairness of the trial procedures. The impact of these judgments upon three dependent variables was assessed. They were: outcome satisfaction, evaluations of the judge, and evaluations of the overall court system. These three dependent variables were highly interrelated, with a mean correlation of $r = .62$, $p < .001$. From the perspective of this discussion, the most important dependent variable was evaluation of the overall court system because it represents respondents' generalizations from their personal experience to broader political evaluations.

The first issue examined was the relationship between outcomes received and fairness judgments. The mean correlation between these two types of judgment was $r = .38$, suggesting that judgments about the quality of outcomes received were clearly distinguishable from fairness judgments, although the two types of judgment were not independent.

The second issue explored was the influence of outcome quality and distributive and procedural fairness upon views of the legal system. Regression analysis was used to assess this relationship (see Table 11.1). The analysis found that judgments of justice or injustice had an independent impact upon overall views of the court system, explaining 15% of the variance in such views beyond what could be explained by outcome judgments. Although case dispositions (i.e., absolute outcomes) and relative outcome judgments jointly influenced outcome satisfaction, $R^2 = 4\%$, they did not independently influence the impact of the courtroom experience upon views about the court system (explaining none of the variance beyond fairness judgments). In other words, only judgments of fairness uniquely influence views about the judge and the court.

If we look within fairness, the results suggest that the major independent influence upon views of the court system resulted from views about the justice of the procedures used to handle cases in court, beta $= .38, p < .05$,

TABLE 11.1
Justice and the Endorsement of Legal Authorities

	Outcome satisfaction		Evaluation of the judge		Evaluation of the court	
	Beta	R^2	Beta	R^2	Beta	R^2
Outcome level						
Absolute	.02	.13***	.03	.12**	.02	.03
Relative						
To prior expectations	.16	—	.02	—	−.01	—
To others in general	.21*	—	.10	—	.17	—
To specific others	.08	—	.09	—	.16	—
Total	—	.42***	—	.27***	—	.09*
Total	—	.44***	—	.30***	—	.09*
Fairness						
Distributional	.48***	.62***	.45***	.64***	.12	.19***
Procedural	.18	.47***	.41***	.61***	.38*	.24***
Total	—	.63***	—	.70***	—	.24***
Total	—	.67***	—	.70***	—	.24***
Usefulness analysis						
Outcome variables beyond fairness	—	.04***	—	.00	—	.00
Fairness beyond outcome variables	—	.23***	—	.40***	—	.15***

Note. Entries in the columns marked beta are standardized regression coefficients. Entries in the columns marked R^2 are the adjusted square of the multiple correlation coefficient. (From Tyler, 1984).
*$p < .05$. **$p < .01$. ***$p < .001$.

whereas neither judgments of distributive justice, beta = .12, ns, nor outcome judgments, beta = .02, ns, had an independent impact.

The second study (Tyler et al., 1984) examined political views among a random sample of 300 Chicago-area residents interviewed by telephone during the spring of 1983. The study examined inputs into national-level political evaluations (i.e., evaluations of President Reagan and of the political system itself). The first inputs examined were the respondents' judgments about the benefits they received from the federal government and the level of federal taxes they paid. For each issue, respondents were asked to indicate the absolute and relative level of benefits received and taxes paid, as well as the fairness of the benefits and taxes. They were also asked about the fairness of the procedures used to allocate benefits and determine tax rates. The second type of input was public policy evaluations in the economic and social arenas. Respondents were asked to indicate whether Reagan administration policies in each arena had helped or hurt them and about their distributive fairness. They were also asked about the procedural justice of the policy-making process.[3]

The first issue addressed was the relationship between outcome-based judgments and judgments of fairness. In the case of benefits and taxes, the relationship was low, with a mean correlation of $r = .17$. With policy issues, it was similar in magnitude to the results of the first study, with mean $r = .36$. As in the first study, the two types of judgment were distinct, but not independent.

When the influence of outcome and justice judgments upon government evaluations was considered, it was found both with policies and in the case of benefits received and taxes paid that the primary influence upon evaluations of political leaders and institutions was the judgment of justice or injustice in policy making and in the allocation of benefits and tax burdens (see Table 11.2). Judgments about personal gain or loss from the Reagan administration's economic or social policies or of personal gains or losses from the Reagan administration's allocation of benefits and taxes explained virtually no independent variance in support for Reagan or for the government, average R^2 less than 1%. In contrast, judgments of the fairness or unfairness of policies and/or benefits/taxes explained a substantial amount of independent variance, average $R^2 = 24\%$.

Within fairness, procedural justice was again found to be the key to both evaluations of President Reagan and government evaluations (for Reagan, beta $= .47$, $p < .001$; for government, beta $= .61$, $p < .001$). Although procedural justice was the major influence, a smaller independent influence of distributive justice judgments upon evaluations of President Reagan was also found, beta $= .11$, $p < .05$. No significant independent influence of outcomes was found.

DISCUSSION

Conclusions

This review of the empirical literature suggests two key conclusions. First, within political settings, judgments of justice or injustice are distinct from judgments of personal policy preference and personal gain and loss. At the same time, the studies reviewed typically suggest that judgments of fairness

---

[3]In this discussion, the focus is on personal gain and loss from policies. It is, of course, also important to consider group based judgments, that is, whether the groups to which one belongs are benefited by policies (see Rhodeback, 1981). Such judgments are considered in the larger study from which these data were drawn (Tyler, Rasinski, & McGraw, 1984). If these data were included in this analysis, it would not substantially modify the conclusions already stated.

TABLE 11.2
Justice and the Endorsement of Political Authorities

	Evaluation of President Reagan		Trust in the national government	
	Beta	R^2	Beta	R^2
Outcome level				
Absolute	.09	.08***	.11	.08***
Relative	-.04	.00	-.04	.00
Total	—	.08***	—	.07***
Fairness				
Distributional	.11*	.18***	-.01	.03**
Procedural	.47***	.41***	.61***	.34***
Total	—	.45***	—	.34***
Demographics				
Party	.20***	—	-.10	—
Liberalism	.16***	—	-.03	—
Age	-.07	—	.00	—
Education	.00	—	-.02	—
Race	.06	—	.00	—
Sex	.13**	—	-.05	—
Total	—	.30***	—	.00
Total	—	.54***	—	.34***
Usefulness Analysis				
Outcome level beyond fairness and demographics	—	.00	—	.01***
Fairness beyond level and demographics	—	.19***	—	.28***
Demographics beyond level and fairness	—	.09***	—	.00

Note. Entries in the columns marked beta are standardized regression coefficients. Entries in the columns marked R^2 are the adjusted multiple correlation coefficient. (from Tyler, et al., 1984).
*p < .05. **p < .01. ***p < .001.

are not independent of judgments of personal preference or of personal gains and loses. People are usually found to have some tendencies to view favorable outcomes as fairer and vice versa, even though they clearly distinguish between fairness and favorableness in outcomes. The two types of judgment are distinct, but not independent.

The second conclusion is that when the distinct influence of justice-based and outcome-based judgments concerning government decisions and policies is compared, justice-based judgments have an important, independent, direct impact upon political evaluations and behaviors. In fact, direct comparisons show that the impact of justice-based judgments is typically as large as or greater than that of outcome-based concerns. Within fairness judgments, those studies that distinguish between procedural and distributive injustice suggest that procedural injustice is the key judgment governing political evaluations and behaviors.

It is important to note that both studies do suggest that outcomes exert a smaller indirect influence upon political evaluations. Because respondents tend to see favorable outcomes as fairer and as arrived at using fairer procedures, outcomes exert some influence upon political evaluations through their influence upon justice judgments. It would be inaccurate, therefore, to suggest that there is no influence of outcomes upon evaluations. Both studies support the finding of indirect outcome effects.

These results suggest that economic models are insufficient to explain political evaluations and behaviors in that they ignore an important influence upon such evaluations and behaviors, namely, perceived injustice. The research reviewed here indicates that political evaluations and behaviors have an important moral component. In other words, citizens are not motivated simply by concerns of personal gain and loss in the political arena, as suggested by economic models. They are also motivated by concerns about justice. Our image of the political actor must incorporate the fact that citizens act as naive moral philosophers, evaluating government actions against abstract criteria of fairness.

One particularly important possibility suggested by the data examined here is that the results of other studies which have been attributed to outcome levels may actually be a spurious result of the joint association of outcome levels to justice judgments. In the studies considered here, outcome-level effects are typically found when zero-order effects are considered, but they disappear when controls for justice or injustice are introduced. Justice judgments, in contrast, remain when controls for outcomes are introduced. Because studies such as the National Election Study do not include justice judgments, the outcome effects they report may actually reflect the indirect influence of perceived injustice.

Of course, in considering these conclusions, it must be kept in mind that the data upon which they are based are not yet extensive. In particular, there have been more studies of political evaluation than of political behavior. This is especially a matter of concern in comparing the role of procedural and distributive justice because a study in organizational settings which directly compares the influence of the two types of justice judgment upon evaluations and behavioral intentions finds that procedural concerns predominate in evaluation, but distributive concerns predominate with behavioral intentions (Alexander & Ruderman, 1983).

A major reason for the lack of more complete data is the dominance of the economic model in political science thinking. For example, the principal study of voting behavior, the National Election Study, currently includes no questions examining either distributive or procedural fairness. As a result, national-level data are not available to examine the role of fairness in voting.

While acknowledging the limitations of currently available data, it is also important to note that the available research, whatever its limits, quite consistently suggests that fairness has an important independent impact upon political evaluations and behaviors. It should also be remembered that the alternative model, the economic model underlying public choice theory, rests largely upon assumptions about how people will behave (Laver, 1981), not upon data, good or bad.

Implications for the Image of the Public

Alteration of our image of the political actor to incorporate moral concerns has implications for three areas of political psychology: understanding of public dissatisfaction with government, predictions concerning the future of the American polity, and the study of policy implementation.

Public Dissatisfaction.   The first important implication of justice-based approaches involves our view of the nature of current public dissatisfaction with the political system. A number of social scientists and social commentators have expressed concern over recent evidence of public dissatisfaction with the political system and its leaders (Caddell, 1979; Lipset & Schneider, 1983b; Shaver, 1980). In the past, efforts to understand the nature of this dissatisfaction have followed a public choice approach and focused upon outcome-oriented issues such as whether leaders have followed citizens' preferred policies or solved their social and economic problems (A. H. Miller, 1974, 1979). A justice-based perspective would suggest a need to consider citizens' views about how government decisions are made and how government policies are arrived at. It would point to government practices such as the secrecy of decision making, public deception, or the perceived failure to consider public views (i.e., procedural injustices) as keys to declining public confidence.

Several more general questions about political dissatisfaction are also raised by a justice-based model. If dissatisfaction results from perceived injustice and, as suggested by recent public opinion polls, if dissatisfaction has grown over the past 20 years, it is important to determine the source of the increasing perceptions of injustice that are influencing this change. In particular, are more citizens personally experiencing injustice in their dealings with government, or are feelings of injustice the result of a general culture of estrangement which has developed from media portrayals of government and other indirect sources of knowledge about government leaders and institutions? In addition, it is important to determine the degree to which increases in the view that government is unjust mirror objective reality. In other words, to what extent are government decision-making procedures actually becoming more unfair? Although it is natural to wish that citizen support for political leaders would increase rather than decrease, it is unclear whether such an increase would have to be linked to some type of effort to improve the objective quality of government leaders and institutions.

The Future of the Polity.   A second area in which a justice-based perspective has different implications than public choice theory is in our image of America's political future. A number of writers have predicted a future era of heightened scarcity and increased social conflict (Blumberg, 1980; deCarufel, 1981; Deutsch, 1981; Greenberg, 1981; Lerner, 1981; Ophuls, 1977). If we view the political actor in economic terms, our visions of the future of the polity will be grim. As the level of resources available declines, political leaders will be less able to provide citizens with desired outcomes, leading inevitably to lessened public support. A justice-based view suggests that citizens will accept absolute decreases in their outcomes without lowering support for the political system, if they believe that those decreases are fair and are arrived at using fair procedures (Austin, 1979; Flacks, 1969; Friedman, 1975; Kelman, 1969). A justice-based perspective, in other words, suggests a more optimistic vision of the future.

Policy Implementation.   A third area in which a justice-based perspective has different implications than public choice theory is policy implementation. Within that area, a justice-based perspective suggests that citizens' acceptance or rejection of government policies will be influenced by fairness judgments more than by calculations of personal gain and loss. In the case of obedience to the law, for example, recent studies suggest that creating a moral climate supporting a law will increase compliance more effectively than will altering estimates of the certainty or severity of punishment. The implications of this suggestion are illustrated by the classic Schwartz and Orleans (1967) study of income tax payment. The study found moral appeals to be four times as effective as sanction threats in stimulating income tax payment. Similarly, perceived fairness in government decision making is more essential to public support of the government and its decisions than is personal agreement with government policies or the belief that one is personally benefiting from those policies.

The justice-based approach to policy implementation also has implications beyond the question of how to implement public policies. It suggests that policy implementation can be efficient and effective in situations within which a moral climate can be tapped. Previous discussions of policy implementation, focusing on the ability of democratic governments to manipulate rewards and punishments, have seen the ability of governments to implement policies as much more limited and costly than would be suggested by a justice-based perspective. Of course, this is only the case when a set of moral values exists to which the government can appeal.

In addition, a justice-based approach suggests much more optimistic implications concerning the ability of government to mobilize the polity in the face of crisis. Past treatments of crisis have noted that the government is least likely to be able to secure public compliance with its policies when such compliance is most needed. That is, in a crisis when government resources are less available, citizens will be less influenced by manipulations of rewards and punishments. A justice-based perspective suggests that the availability of rewards and punishments is likely to be less important than is the ability of government to make justice-based appeals. If a moral consensus exists concerning the political issues involved, citizen compliance should be securable without the need to utilize rewards and punishments.

Pessimistic Aspects of Justice-Based Approaches.   Although this presentation of the implications of justice-based models has stressed their positive, optimistic implications, it is also important to note that there are potentially pessimistic consequences of adopting a justice-based view of the political actor. If public satisfaction is linked to judgments of fairness, the government may find it much easier to create conditions of "perceived fairness" than to solve problems or provide benefits. In other words, arguing that citizens link satisfaction to abstract judgments of justice indicates a susceptibility to the type of government manipulation outlined by Edelman (1964) in his discussion of the use of symbols by government. Because citizens focus on procedural fairness, government may be able to induce greater "false consciousness" (satisfaction with an objectively poor situation) than would be possible if citizens focused on their own outcomes or on the ability of government to solve problems when evaluating government. Recent research on procedural justice effects suggests that such concerns are well-founded. It indicates that in some situations satisfaction with procedures is not linked to objectively high levels of control over decisions made through those procedures (Cohen, 1983; Lind, Lissak, & Conlon, 1983; Tyler, Rasinski, & Spodick, 1985).

Problems for Future Study.   Just as they have implications for our image of the political actor, these findings have implications concerning problems that should be the focus of attention within political psychology. It is here that this paper makes its most direct connection with the social cognition literature, which has formed the basis for most of the other papers in this volume. A justice-based approach suggests that attention should be focused on the structure of citizens' beliefs about political justice and injustice, on the childhood and adolescent origins of such beliefs, and on their development and change in response to adult experience.

A focus on justice-related beliefs of the type outlined earlier argues for attention to two distinct issues: utilities and judgments. Examining moral utilities involves a concern with the development of a set of values that leads justice-based evaluations and behaviors to be valued by political actors. An exploration of moral judgments focuses on the cognitive dynamics through which moral and nonmoral concerns are integrated together in an elaborated subjective expected utility model, as well as on the exploration of heuristics and biases in moral judgment (see Hastie, 1983, for a review of recent studies of this type). Elaboration of the justice-based approach must ultimately involve an exploration of both these issues.

Implications for Political Leaders

Although the discussion has focused on citizens up to this point, a justice-based perspective also has implications for the behavior of political leaders, an area discussed within theories of public choice (Downs, 1957b; see Laver, 1981, for a discussion of more recent research). It is important to distinguish between two distinct issues: how leaders ought to act, given what the public is like, and what leaders themselves are like. This discussion deals only with the implications of assuming that the public is concerned about justice and leaders are concerned about public views. The latter issue—the bases of leader behavior—is not explored. A justice-based view indicates that, instead of focusing on citizen outcomes, on the assumption that such outcomes drive citizen evaluations, leaders should give attention to the fairness of their decision-making procedures and of the outcomes they provide citizens.

To cite one example of how leader misperceptions might be counterproductive, Tyler (1984b) found that judges sometimes obscured trial verdicts, a practice which seems to reflect their view that being found guilty will lead to hostility toward the courts. In fact, however, poor outcomes do not lead to hostility if they are arrived at following fair procedures. Obscuring verdicts may, however, lead to feelings of procedural injustice, which would lead to negative feelings toward the court. An accurate knowledge of the psychology of the citizen would help judges emphasize the fairness of trial procedures.

Another example of how leaders' behavior would change if a justice-based perspective were adopted is found in government responses to the energy crisis. In responding to that crisis, government leaders were reluctant to impose life-style changes upon citizens, fearing the loss of their public support through association with material deprivations (Sears, Tyler, Citrin, & Kinder, 1978). A justice-based perspective suggests that such fears were exaggerated because the public should focus on the fairness of sacrifices, not on their absolute nature, when evaluating government leaders. In the case of energy conservation, there is evidence to indicate that the public did, in fact, focus on fairness in evaluating conservation measures (Montgomery & Leonard-Barton, 1977). Similarly, a recent review of conservation research concluded that "a sense of social duty can be as influential as financial considerations in motivating people to attempt to conserve energy" (Olsen, 1981, p. 126). Moral concerns have also been found to be important in stimulating other positive political actions (Tyler & McGraw, 1983). Recognizing this fact, leaders should focus on creating a moral climate conducive to change.

It is interesting to note that Tyler and Folger (1980) found fairness to be an especially important evaluation criterion for citizens in situations within which authorities imposed themselves upon the public. This is important because it is precisely such situations about which leaders have the greatest fears concerning adverse public reactions to government restrictions.

Of course, for leaders to cope effectively with increased conflict, they need to know which procedures citizens feel are fair. In the studies reported, this issue has typically been avoided by simply asking citizens whether the procedures utilized were fair. It is clear, however, that it is important to attempt to identify the nature of the procedures that citizens judge to be fair. Tyler (1984b) explored this issue within courtroom settings and found that citizens placed great value upon having the opportunity to state their grievances before a judge who listened and allowed them enough time to make their case.

A question of particular interest in future research involves the generality of fair procedures. Of concern here is the degree to which there are procedures that are universally viewed as fair—across people and across conflict/allocation/policy-making settings—as opposed to different procedures for different people and settings.

Implications for Public Choice Theory

These results also raise questions about the completeness of the public choice theories that have guided previous research into political evaluation and behavior. Although it is possible to develop explanations for the research examined that are consistent with outcome-focused models, a much more straightforward explanation is a simple recognition that citizens are concerned with the justice of the allocation decisions affecting them, independent of any concerns they may have about the level of outcomes they personally receive from the political system.

Of course, these results should not be taken as a suggestion that traditional outcome-based models are never an appropriate description of citizens' concerns. In the case of personal judgments, the importance of economic models has been widely documented. Similarly, the studies discussed here suggest that outcomes are important when the dependent variable of concern is outcome satisfaction. What the results reported suggest, however, is that citizens differentiate between types of judgments, utilizing outcomes and justice-based concerns to differing degrees with different types of evaluation and behavior. In the political arena, judgments of justice or injustice predominate, whereas in the personal arena, outcome judgments seem to be the key influence (a view recently disputed by M. J. Lerner, 1982).

As previously noted, it is possible to incorporate concerns about justice into an expanded expected utility model, following the conceptual approach of Fishbein and Ajzen (1975; Ajzen & Fishbein, 1980) or Leventhal (1976b, 1980). To do so would follow the pattern of recent studies of deterrence, which have incorporated both informal sanctions and moral concerns into models traditionally including only judgments of the certainty and severity of punishment. In this sense, it is important to realize that support for justice-based models does not in any sense invalidate subjective expected utility models. The mathematics of such models must be distinguished from the image of the political actor contained in the public choice theories that employ subjective expected utility approaches. That image is linked to the conception of utility employed by public choice theories. The research examined here has clear implications for that image. It suggests that citizens (i.e., political actors) are not primarily motivated by the desire for personal gains in their political evaluations and behaviors in the sense in which that concept is traditionally used within economic theory.

Once the concept of an expanded subjective utility model, which includes terms indexing moral concerns, is accepted, the issue becomes one of specifying when each of the terms in the equation will be important. One factor that this paper suggests will be important is the type of judgment being made, personal or political. Within the same situation, the same person may utilize justice-based criteria more heavily when making political judgments. Another factor is the situation itself. For example, it has been suggested that scarcity of resources within a situation will heighten concerns about personal gain, leading justice to be less important (Greenberg, 1981). Finally, individuals may differ in their general tendency to evaluate situations in terms of justice (Feather, 1979; Rohrbaugh, McClelland, & Quinn, 1980). Ultimately, it would be most helpful to specify the impact of each type of factor on the use of justice as an evaluation criterion (i.e., to focus on when justice matters rather than if it does).

A specification of the conditions under which justice is and is not an important evaluation criterion, though a necessary first step, will ultimately prove unsatisfying unless it can be linked to a psychological model that explains why such weighting differences occur. In the case of the difference in citizen concerns within the personal and the political arenas, which have been outlined in this paper, such differences may represent the recognition among citizens that they should be pursuing different goals within the two areas of their lives. That goals might influence the principles used in evaluations and behaviors is suggested both by theoretical statements (Lamm, Kayser, & Schwinger, 1982; Mikula & Schwinger, 1978) and by two lines of empirical work. First, a number of psychologists have shown that interaction goals shape the principles of justice that are used in allocation (Austin, 1980; Benton, 1971; Curtis, 1979; Deutsch, 1975; Leventhal, 1976a, 1976b; Leventhal, Michaels, & Sanford, 1972; Morgan & Sawyer, 1967, 1979; E. G. Shapiro, 1975). Second, Barrett-Howard & Tyler (in press) have found that interaction goals influence whether justice is an important factor in allocation decisions. Of particular relevance is their finding that heightened concerns about positive social relations and others' welfare, issues likely to be important in political judgments, increase both the general role of fairness in allocation decisions and the importance placed upon procedural justice.

Of course, examining factors that lead to an emphasis on fairness does not indicate why the research reported here finds that citizens focus on procedural, rather than distributive, fairness. An interesting suggestion concerning the reasons for this procedural focus has been made by Schwartz (1978). He argues that the pluralistic nature of American society leads to a lack of clear moral values concerning standards of distributive fairness. As a result, citizens focus on the manner in which allocation decisions are made. The assumption being made in such settings is that fair procedures lead to fair outcomes. The finding that there is greater consensus about what procedures are fair than about what distributions or allocations of outcomes are fair would lend support to Schwartz's hypothesis.

The recognition that justice-based concerns may influence political evaluations and behaviors is not one that has eluded all economists. Some discussions of political economy have suggested that traditional utility models are inadequate to explain observed behavior in the political arena and that citizens might be responsive to both distributive justice (Sen, 1973) and procedural justice (Diamond, 1967). This suggestion has received support in an experimental study by McClelland and Rohrbaugh (1978) in which subjects were found to violate utility rules out of a concern for equity. The economic perspective on fairness has been most recently summarized by Margolis (1982), who writes: "In the presence of public goods, the behavior of a self-interested 'economic man' conflicts with everyday observation. Indeed, it is positively bizarre" (p. 17). Margolis suggests that economists must incorporate fairness into their theories, and he attempts to create a theory that does so.

The difficulty with economic treatments of fairness is that such approaches have not been extensively developed and do not flow easily from the economic models underlying public choice. It is, in fact, difficult for public choice theories to invoke concepts of justice because they must ultimately relate such ideas back to the concept of individually self-interested actors. Similar difficulties can be found in treatments of justice within some areas of psychology. In traditional equity theory (Walster et al., 1978), in the literature on social dilemmas (Axelrod & Hamilton, 1981; Buckley, Burns, & Meeker, 1974; Dawes, 1980; Hardin, 1982; Russell, 1979), and in psychological studies of mixed motive games (Kelley & Thibaut, 1978; McClintock, 1972), fairness is also suggested to flow from personal utilities. In each case, concerns about justice are built upon a framework ultimately linked to a self-interested actor.

A contrasting perspective is provided by justice-based psychological models, which recognize ethical judgments and behaviors as a core feature of human concerns. Such approaches can more easily incorporate the ethical propensities of the political actor because they view ethical behavior as an intrinsic feature of the person. Two varieties of such theories have been offered. First, some writers have suggested that whatever their initial reason for being formed, moral values and concerns about justice take on a life of their own and become separate from self-interested concerns through the process of internalization (Hoffman, 1977). A second approach has argued that justice-based concerns are intrinsic to humans. Perhaps the best known theory of this kind is the cognitive developmental approach of Piaget and Kohlberg (Kohlberg, 1976). Within social psychology, a similar view has been proposed by Lerner (1977, 1982) in the context of his "justice motive" theory. Whether or not such theories are necessary to explain citizens' uses of justice in political evaluations and behaviors, the theories have the advantage of allowing such concerns to be explained within a framework that easily accommodates the influence of moral judgments because they view ethical judgments and behaviors as a core feature of human nature.[4]

---

[4]In his book *The Copernican Revolution* (1957), Thomas Kuhn details the efforts of Aristotelian astronomers to preserve their system of astronomy in the face of conflicting data. Their efforts went to the extreme of postulating small "epicycles" in which planets reversed orbit for brief periods of time. While such a complex system did continue to explain the movement of the planets accurately, it eventually so destroyed the conceptual simplicity that had made Aristotelian astronomy attractive that the theory became unsatisfying and was replaced. The situation we face in political psychology today is in some respects similar to that described by Kuhn. The extension of economic theory to the political arena was initially

In summary, support for justice-based models of the political actor is not an attack upon the economic model itself, but upon its extension to the political arena in theories of public choice. As the studies discussed here indicate, the justice-based public actor differs substantially from the image of the self-interested political actor, which is the key feature of public choice theory. Instead of viewing justice-based actions as paradoxes or problems to be explained away, they should be viewed as an intrinsic feature of citizens' political evaluations and behaviors. In addition, political scientists might profitably focus on the issues raised by the justice-based political actor: the development of conceptions of justice during political socialization; the structure of beliefs about political justice; the nature of justice-based reasoning; and the circumstances under which justice-based concerns exercise a larger or smaller influence upon political evaluations and behaviors.

ACKNOWLEDGMENTS

The author would like to thank Reid Hastie and Ray Soloman for their comments on a draft of this chapter.

---

attractive because the conceptual simplicity of economic models held out the promise of a more parsimonious explanation of complex political issues. Over the course of time, however, economic theories have been forced to attempt to explain findings such as those reported in this paper, which do not fit easily into traditional economic models. To do so, public choice theorists have developed increasingly complex conceptual frameworks which bear less and less resemblance to simple economic models. As a result, the simplicity that first made economic models attractive is disappearing.

12 Emotion and Political Cognition: Emotional Appeals in Political Communication

Ira Roseman
New School for Social Research

Robert P. Abelson
Michael F. Ewing
Yale University

What is the relationship of emotion to political cognition? The traditional view, with roots deep in Western philosophy, is that emotion is separate from or antithetical to cognition. Demagogues prey on popular passions, which the educated citizen is taught to master with reason.

Early psychological theories of emotion (e.g., James, 1890) maintained that emotions are at least in part noncognitive, and there are contemporary advocates of a separate systems view (e.g., Zajonc, 1980, 1984). But in recent years, many psychologists (e.g., Abelson, 1983; Arnold, 1960; deRivera, 1977; Kahneman & Tversky, 1982; Lazarus, 1968, Mandler, 1980; Ortony, Collins, & Clore, 1982; Roseman, 1979, Weiner, 1982;) have come to see emotion and cognition as intimately interrelated. Thus, the time seems right for a reconsideration of this question, particularly now that the dominance of "cognitive imperialism" (Tomkins, 1981) in social psychological theorizing has given way to a renewed interest in emotional phenomena.

That emotion is important to political attitudes and behavior is attested to by common lore and psychological research. Political issues are often debated heatedly, and many people seem emotionally attached to political beliefs. Political pollsters and media consultants place considerable importance on the emotional tone of their campaigns and on the feelings of the electorate (Raines, 1984). And well they might. In an analysis of survey data from the 1980 presidential election, Abelson, Kinder, Peters, and Fiske (1982) showed that respondents' feelings toward the candidates were highly predictive of candidate preferences. Respondents had been given a simple question frame, for example: Has Ronald Reagan, because of the kind of

279

person he is, or because of something he has done, ever made you feel: Proud? Uneasy? Afraid? And so on. These questions were asked of national samples gathered in 1980 under the auspices of the Center for Political Studies at Michigan, and they were asked again in 1984. As it turned out in 1980, positive and negative feelings toward the candidates were more predictive of candidate preferences than party identification or issue positions, and about equal in predictive power to trait ratings of the candidates. Results for the 1984 election are still being analyzed.

These results testify to the importance of the emotions of political respondents. But what of the emotions contained in political stimuli? For example, candidates communicate emotions nonverbally, particularly through facial expression and voice quality on the broadcast media. The effects of such emotional displays are presently being investigated by Masters, Sullivan, Lanzetta, McHugo, and Englis (1984) at Dartmouth. Emotions may also be present in the content or style of verbal appeals made by candidates or political organizations. Another possibility is that emotions may be aroused by events, as when one sees victims of some natural disaster (e.g., an earthquake) or heinous act (e.g., the taking of American hostages in Iran).

One not so obvious question raised by these possibilities concerns the relationship between the emotion in the stimulus and the emotion of respondents. The most straightforward assumption would be that they correspond and that the emotion in the stimulus creates or resonates with a corresponding emotional response. But there are many determinants of emotions in individuals other than political communications or events, for example, individual predispositions, transitory or enduring life events, and so on. Moreover, factors such as partisanship may transform the emotion in a stimulus into different emotional responses. American audiences could be made angry by exposure to pictures of sad hostages, and the emotion stirred in Democratic loyalists by a smiling Ronald Reagan might be sadness. It is also possible that complementarity rather than similarity of emotion would be preferred by political audiences. A depressed electorate, for example, might respond more favorably to a happy candidate than to a sad one. In this chapter, we report research exploring the relationship between emotion in political stimuli and emotion in political respondents, critically examining the hypothesis that the most effective appeals would be those with emotional content matching the emotional tendencies of the audience.

STUDIES OF EMOTIONS
AND POLITICAL COGNITION

Public Affairs Organizations

To investigate the role of emotions in political communication, we conducted three studies on public affairs appeals. Political groups interested in issues such as abortion, gun control, foreign aid, arms control, peace, and communism are in the business of recruiting members, soliciting donations, and encouraging actions consistent with their cause. Such groups try to win agreement and support with statements of who they are and what they stand for. The "statement of purpose" and "public education" materials or solicitations of public affairs organizations have both cognitive and emotional content. They include facts, arguments, and explanations about issues that are emotion-laden, and they are often laced with emotionally toned words and phrases. We began this research with the straightforward hypothesis that the attraction of an individual to an organization's appeal is, in part, a function of "resonance" to its emotional content. Resonance, in the simplest conceptualization, is a matter of good fit. Hopeful people should resonate to hopeful organizations, just as people who cognitively believe in the free market system should resonate to organizations supporting free markets. We were looking in these studies for an effect of emotion above and beyond cognition, and our preliminary model was that attraction to a cause is the result of an emotional as well as cognitive matching process.

Preparation of Stimulus Materials

We began by writing to 100 organizations drawn at random from the public affairs section of the *Encyclopedia of Associations* (Akey, 1978), asking for their self-descriptive brochures. About half replied, and after screening out some that were inappropriate for our purposes, we were left with 42 organizations. These included some well-known groups (e.g., Amnesty International, the Conservative party, and the National Coalition to Ban Handguns), some obscure causes (e.g., the Archonist Club, the American party, and the Initiators), and a wide variety of others.

Next, we scanned the appeals in the brochures for statements about each organization, its aims, and its methods. Table 12.1 shows two examples, heavily edited for conciseness. In both content and manner, the first sounds warmhearted, if not downright mushy. The second is testy and chip-on-the-shoulder.

TABLE 12.1
Examples of Emotion–Laden Appeals

Lutheran Human Relations Association (LHRA)

The purpose of LHRA is to train and equip Christians to express Christ's love and healing in today's world and to offer support as Christians combat racism, poverty, and injustice.

LHRA encourages the compassionate responses of effective human relations ministry through volunteer coordinators who organize projects to deal with specific local problems—housing and land use, prisoner concerns, home up-keep for the elderly, groceries–on–wheels for people in poor neighborhoods...

Atheist Association (AA)

The Association is for complete separation of church and state. We oppose giving any money in any form to any religious organization by government. We oppose the teaching of any kind of religion or prayers in the public schools.

We advocate the teaching of facts about religion, that it is a gigantic fraud, not based on reality or truth. We demand the right to the use of TV for time to air the atheist viewpoint, a right now denied.

Coding for Emotional Content

Surprisingly, an analysis of the variety of styles of emotional appeal in the political arena seems not to have been undertaken by social psychologists. The classic early study done by Hartmann (1936) simply contrasted rational with emotional appeals, without distinguishing different types of emotional appeals. The later literature on communication and persuasion is, of course, replete with experiments and discussions of fear appeals (Janis, 1967; Leventhal, 1970), mainly in health and safety contexts. We know also of one dissertation dealing with guilt appeals (Zemach, 1966) in connection with the civil rights movement. Other varieties of emotional appeal seem not to have been studied. One possible explanation for this state of affairs is that from the 1930s until the 1960s, many academic psychologists considered emotion to be a unitary phenomenon of arousal or activation (e.g., Duffy, 1934; Lindsley, 1951), varying only in intensity. When emotionality was studied, fear was typically taken as the paradigmatic case. Since the work of Ekman, Sorenson, and Friesen (1969), testing Tomkins' (1962) theory of distinct emotions manifest in pancultural facial expressions, this situation has been changing. The discrete emotion categories familiar to the layperson (e.g., anger, fear, sadness, and joy) are increasingly being recognized by psychologists (see, e.g., Izard, 1977; Plutchik & Kellerman, 1980), although there is disagreement about which categories are most fundamental.

The classificatory scheme we used was based on an application of Roseman's (1979, 1984a) structural theory of the antecedents of discrete emotions, applied to the organizational appeals that we solicited. Public affairs organizations seem to exist to solve perceived problems created by particular perceived agents. The emotions in such appeals might be focused on the problems or on the prospect of their resolution. Or the emotions might focus on the agents creating or resolving these problems.

Table 12.2 shows our taxonomy of public affairs appeals, the type of organization that might employ them, and the emotion associated with each type. This scheme guided our analysis of emotion in appeals by suggesting the emotions we should look for. Our analysis was also guided, however, by what we found in the appeals we had obtained. For example, Roseman's theory identifies a number of emotions experienced when goals have been attained or thwarted with certainty: joy, relief, sadness, discontent, and frustration. These emotions seemed uncommon in our sample of appeals in comparison to hope and fear, the emotions of *uncertain* goal fates. One explanation for this is that public affairs organizations, in motivating political action, tend to focus on the future: Problems, even those existing now, may get much worse unless we act (fear); and, if we act, the problems may be resolved (hope). Another example of selectivity in public affairs appeals concerns two types of love appeals, expressing the emotions gratitude and pity. Both are characteristic of "support" groups, but gratitude appeals express emotion toward others as agents of improvement (those who help us), whereas pity appeals express emotion toward targets of improvement (those whom we help). Although gratitude appeals exist within the American political arena, they typically focus transiently on leaders and potential benefactors, as in endorsements of political candidates. In our sample frame of public affairs organizations, candidate support groups did not occur. However, we found many groups with pity appeals addressing the resolution of the problems of worthy victims.

Our classification scheme is not meant to imply that combinations of emotions in appeals cannot occur. If, for example, an evil agent harms innocent victims, one may feel anger toward the agent and pity toward the victims; if circumstances threaten us and an indifferent agent fails to help, we may feel fear at the circumstances and anger at the agent.

TABLE 12.2
Classification of Public Affairs Appeals and Associated Emotions

Appeal Focus	Organizational Type	Associated Emotion
Dangerous problem	Prevention	Fear
Opportunity for resolution	Reform	Hope
Others as agents of problem	Opposition	Anger
Others as targets of resolution	Support	Pity
Self as agent of problem	Penitential	Guilt
Self as agent of resolution	Self-help	Pride

We excerpted from our sample of brochures four- to six-sentence summary statements about each organization and its aims and methods, such as those shown in Table 12.1. Then, on 7-point judgment scales, we coded these summary statements for degree of each of the six emotions listed in Table 12.2. We soon discovered that two of the six emotions were infrequent or overspecialized in our public affairs brochures. Guilt appeals were rare, perhaps because such appeals in effect require the organization to say that we (i.e., you and I) have done wrong, but will do better in the future. Such an apologetic tone may not constitute effective salesmanship. In a religious context, there is precedent for an appeal such as: We are all sinners, but it is not too late to be saved. In political contexts, however, guilt appeals are not popular. Note in this connection that if you say something like: Administration policy in Vietnam makes us guilty of war crimes, that is usually an anger appeal directed against the administration rather than a guilt appeal embracing America.

Meanwhile, pride appeals appeared to come predominantly from ethnic minority organizations such as the National Council for Puerto Rican Women and the Institute for Indian Affairs. The narrow target groups for such appeals made them difficult to study with our subject population. We therefore confined our preliminary investigation to the study of appeals based on the remaining four emotions: fear, hope, anger, and pity. Our coding of the degree of these emotions was based on holistic judgment, but one can get an idea of some of the piquant semantics associated with each emotion from Table 12.3 It gives a partial lexicon of appropriate words and phrases appearing in appeals judged to have at least some degree of anger, pity, fear, or hope.

Attraction to Appeals: Emotional Resonance?

Our Yale undergraduate subjects were presented with the set of organizational appeals, and were asked how favorable they felt toward each organization, how much money they would give the organization if they could afford to donate up to $1,000, whether they would join the organization if they received an appeal in the mail, and whether they would urge their friends to join. Responses to each question were assigned scores of 0, 1, or 2 (unfavorable, neutral, favorable; $0, $1 to $99, $100 to $1000; no, maybe, yes), yielding organizational attraction scores from 0 to 8, representing the degree to which each subject was attracted to each organization.

Our subjects were also asked questions about their own emotional tendencies. On the basis of the "emotional resonance" hypothesis, individuals who often experience particular emotions would tend to be especially attracted to appeals using those emotions. The self-report emotion tendency question was worded: In your everyday life, how frequently (compared

TABLE 12.3
An Emotional Appeal Lexicon

Some Words and Phrases Connoting Public Anger

---

mistaken priorities; injustice; unreasonable absurdity; unwholesome influence; pressure groups; we are being challenged; the truth is kept from us; revolt; sore point; crusade; encroachment; interference; conquest; stand on principle; torture; (to) combat; take a stand; harassed; (bad things) have become acceptable; oppose threats; undermined (good things); defend rights; (powerful people) ignore rights and wishes, fail to respond . . . ; repugnant; phony; deny relief; discrimination; deserve; our only crime was (innocuous thing); resisters; irate; recruit an army (in defense of good things); (rights) abridged; restore authority; (rights) surrendered; obsessed with power and violence; the right to demand X; intrude; assaults on rights; oppressed; oppressors; demonstrators; grievances; sell-out; mock trials; octopus control; agents; chauvinism.

Some Words and Phrases Connoting Public Pity

---

to give to ordinary men and women; express Christ's love and healing; compassionate responses; assist people to build a better life; give a hand; present award to (a deserving) person; make friends with other races; sponsor a refugee family; help to poverty-stricken; international friendship; they not only need (help), they *deserve* it; obligation to stand on the side of the poor; fundamental unity of the human family; sustain idealism of youth; need wise policies toward (good group); the world cares (for the deserving); support those who (oppose tyranny); work for the millions who deserve (better).

Some Words and Phrases Connoting Public Fear

---

hazards; crime; violence; alarm; troops; weaponry; tinderbox; alarming problem; victims in the millions; enemies (exist); erosion; urgent; potential (bad outcome); torture; death; (bad outcome) grows; control (of good things) is by enemies; (bad things) are acceptable; threats (exist); be vigilant; (good things) are eroding; impotence; lack of control; threat to survival; deterioration; nuclear war; challenges to (good things).

Some Words and Phrases Connoting Public Hope

---

trying to solve; overcome (problem); effectively heard; get the message to X; introduce (good things); new ideas; lead to healthier X; (policy) would allow (good things); working for (good); promote goals; building bridges; inspire change; cause for hope; campaign to change . . . ; decision makers will act; crusade to change . . . ; ideals; expanding; can mean (good things); strive for improvement; further development; seeks X; works to gain . . . ; (bad) will never triumph; plan; improve; assistance toward X; start; X would serve (good); create; (bad) is decreasing; offer support to combat; encourage compassion; help advance . . . ; truth will win!; establish; achieving; will flourish; bring back (good); blueprint; meet challenges; open up; give a sense (of good); goal is . . . .

---

to other people) would you say you feel the following emotions: anger, hope, fear, pity, etc. Response categories were: never, less than other people, about the same as others, more than others.

The test of the resonance hypothesis involved some fancy statistical footwork. First we regressed each subject's organizational attraction scores on the emotional content ratings of each organization's appeal. This was done separately for each of the four emotions, yielding us four "appeal attraction" regression coefficients (one for each emotion) for each subject.

Take anger, for example. For a given subject, a large anger appeal attraction coefficient would indicate that to the degree an organization's appeal was angry, this subject was more attracted to the organization. A small coefficient would indicate little or no relationship between anger appeals and attraction, and a negative coefficient would indicate an inverse relationship.

Once we had anger, hope, fear, and pity appeal attraction coefficients for each subject, correlations were computed between these coefficients and the subjects' self-reported emotional tendencies. The emotional resonance hypothesis predicts significant positive correlations between the appeal attraction coefficients and the corresponding emotional tendencies. For example, people who report themselves as angry more often than most other people would tend to be relatively more attracted to organizations with angry appeals.

STUDIES 1 AND 2

Our original study was done in the spring of 1979, with 41 subjects and 42 organizational appeals. A replication was carried out in the summer of 1983, with 59 subjects and 36 organizational appeals. (Eight generally unattractive organizations were eliminated in Study 2, and two new ones added).

Results

Table 12.4 presents the correlational results of the two studies. The correlations relevant to the resonance hypothesis appear on the main diagonals of the matrices. In Study 1, two of the four resonances were significant at the .05 level. Self-reported pity correlated .34 with attraction to organizations high in pity appeal, and self-reported anger correlated .33 with attraction to organizations high in anger appeal. Although these correlations are not huge, they still seem remarkable in view of the many factors contributing to organizational attractiveness and the naively straightforward character of the resonance hypothesis.

Note, however, that simple resonance did not obtain for hope or for fear. Those who accounted themselves hopeful were not especially attracted by hope-mongering organizations. In fact, the situation was the reverse: Those who considered themselves fearful tended to be moved by hope appeals. This correlation was .44 in Study 1. Meanwhile, fear appeals showed no correlations with emotional self-reports.

Study 2 showed somewhat weaker results than Study 1. The resonance hypothesis for pity obtained in slightly greater degree, a correlation of .41 instead of .34. But the anger resonance correlation shrank to .14, no longer

TABLE 12.4
Correlational Results on the Affect Resonance Hypothesis

Self-Reports	Study 1 (N = 41)			
	Appeal Attractions			
	Hope	*Fear*	*Pity*	*Anger*
Hope	−.26	.02	.07	.16
Fear	.44*	−.08	.18	−.17
Pity	.14	−.08	.34*	−.30
Anger	.03	−.16	−.14	.33*
Self-Reports	Study 2 (N = 59)			
	Appeal Attractions			
	Hope	*Fear*	*Pity*	*Anger*
Hope	−.16	.09	−.05	−.16
Fear	.14	−.08	.06	−.06
Pity	−.06	−.18	.41*	−.14
Anger	−.09	.15	.20	.14

*p < .05

significant. Again, hope and fear resonances did not occur. Finally, the notion that fearful people like hopeful appeals yielded a weaker correlation than in Study 1, a nonsignificant .14.

When data from the two studies are pooled together, the three significant correlations of Study 1 remain significant. The pity-pity correlation is .35, the anger-anger correlation .24, and the fear-hope correlation .28. The pity relation appears to be fairly robust. (We found it also in an otherwise messy study run prior to Study 2.) The other two relations must be regarded as more tentative.

We also found a slight hint of general emotional appeal effects. Pity and hope appeals were generally somewhat attractive to our subjects, and anger appeals generally somewhat unattractive. Pooling over the 78 organizations in the two studies, the correlation of mean organizational attractiveness with the degree of pity in the appeal was .20, with degree of hope .18, with anger −.28, and with fear −.08.

Discussion of Results

How are the correlations testing the resonance hypothesis to be interpreted? Do they really indicate an effect of emotion above and beyond that of cognition? Shouldn't the appeal of these messages depend on political *content,* that is, on who needs help and why; on who the bad guys are and what kind of abuse they're giving us; or on what the threatening circumstances are? In a word, yes. That may be one reason why the resonance correlations are not larger. It even might explain why pity resonance appears to be more robust than the other two results. Sympathy for the suffering of others may be a rather general tendency, whereas anger at wrongdoing seems more specifically targeted on who is doing what; similarly, fearing and hoping tendencies may be more or less content specific.

Concern with message content, apart from style, also raises questions about possible artifacts explaining our correlational results. Perhaps there are some general political dimensions associated both with a sympathetic (or tough) personality and attraction to tender-minded (or tough-talking) organizations. The ideological dimension of liberalism versus conservatism comes to mind. The pity resonance result could come from a liberal group of subjects, "bleeding hearts" as it were, and the anger results could come from a no-nonsense group of conservatives.

We tried in two ways to partial out the effects of ideology. In Study 1, we rated each of the 42 organizations along a left-to-right ideological dimension. Then we regressed this rating out of each of the emotion ratings of the organizational appeals. Thereby we could correct for emotional-ideological confounds such as angry appeals coming mainly from right-wing organizations. Repeating the previous statistical footwork using corrected attraction regressions gave essentially the same results as before. None of the critical correlations changed by more than .01.

In Study 2, we tried yet another correction. We asked subjects how favorable they felt toward Ted Kennedy, Walter Mondale, and Ronald Reagan, and formed a simple composite score suggestive of left-to-right placement on the political spectrum. This score was partialed out of the emotional resonance correlations, and again, no coefficient changed by more than .01. Thus, it does not appear that a simple ideological dimension can account for the resonant tendencies between emotional self-characterizations and organizational appeals—not in our data, at any rate.

On careful consideration, it is in fact not accurate to characterize pity as the exclusive property of the political left and anger as the province of the right. These stereotypical connections are reversed when an organization advocates pity for the victims of communism or rages against American militarism. It is also possible for emotion to be attached to apolitical causes, as in the fighting words of Tippers International, which wants to punish lousy service in hotels and restaurants by giving lousy tips.

An entirely different possible artifact is suggested by the work of Gilligan (1982) on gender-related differences in moral reasoning. According to Gilligan, the "male voice" uses the concepts of equity and justice, whereas the "female voice" speaks in terms of care and responsibility. Males, by and large, are concerned with the fairness of rules, and females with the preservation of social relationships. If these notions are correct, what would we predict the two voices to say about political problems? The male voice should complain about injustice, unfairness, and rule breaking (i.e., it should speak the language of indignation and anger). By contrast, the female voice should express concern about people being ill-cared for and set apart from one another (i.e., its language should be that of love and pity). Applied to nuclear weapons policy, for example, the male voice might insist that the Soviets not gain an "unfair" advantage, and the female voice that such deadly weapons not be used. Applied to welfare policy, the male voice might grouse about welfare cheats, and the female voice might express pity for the victims of poverty.

The possible artifact in our data should now be obvious. Perhaps females respond more favorably to pity appeals and also report themselves as often experiencing pity; meanwhile, males may respond differentially to anger appeals and also confess to more frequent anger. In other words, pity and anger resonances may not be the consequence of personality variables so much as of a general gender difference.

As plausible as this artifactual explanation sounds, it turns out to cut no ice in our data. Female Yale undergraduates report themselves to be no more pitying and no less angry than male Yale undergraduates, on the average. In any case, the pity and anger resonance correlations are virtually equivalent within both male and female subsamples, in the pooled data from Studies 1 and 2, as Table 12.5 shows.

STUDY 3: EFFECTS OF MOOD INDUCTION

Another direction in our research involves studying the effects of situationally induced moods on appeal attractiveness. Different induced moods might make different emotional appeals differentially attractive. To investigate this possibility, we ran a study in which Yale undergraduates were induced

TABLE 12.5
Affect Resonances by Gender

Female (N = 52)			Male (N = 46)		
	Appeal Attractions			Appeal Attractions	
Self-Reports	Pity	Anger	Self-Reports	Pity	Anger
Pity	.35	−.35	Pity	.34	−.10
Anger	−.09	.24	Anger	−.25	.25

to feel either pity or anger prior to the administration of an appeals questionnaire that contained either pity or anger appeals.

Mood was induced by having subjects remember a recent experience that made them feel extreme anger or pity toward a close friend or relative. As in a procedure used by Malatesta and Izard (1984), subjects first jotted down the highlights of the experience for 10 min. Then they were asked to re-create the episode emotionally for approximately 1 min. by relating the major details of the episode, concentrating on what caused the emotion and how they felt. Finally, subjects were asked to summarize the entire experience in one sentence, which was tape recorded along with the 1-min re-creation. Subjects in a "neutral" mood induction condition were asked to remember their most recent trip to the supermarket and relate the thoughts they had on their way.

Two forms of appeals questionnaire were used, each containing 12 different organizational appeals whose emotional structures were either all angry or all pitiful. That is, the appeals focused on combating wrong-doers or on helping victims, respectively. Within each set of 12 appeals, an attempt was made to vary the wording style so that some appeals were made more flamboyantly angry (or pitiful) than others. These style variations did not produce coherent results and need not be further discussed.

Subjects in the anger mood induction received the anger appeals, and those in the pity condition received pity appeals; those in the neutral condition received either the pity or anger form of the questionnaire. There were thus two crucial comparisons: the effects of a pity induction (relative to a neutral induction) on the attractiveness of pity appeals and the effects of an anger induction on the attractiveness of anger appeals.

The two comparisons yielded modest support for the proposition that mood induction increases the attractiveness of corresponding appeals. On a scale from 0 to 8, the mean attractiveness of angry organizations was 4.23 under angry mood induction and 3.46 under neutral induction. The mean attractiveness of the pitiful organizations was 4.66 under pity induction and 3.94 under neutral induction. Because of large variance between individuals, these two differential effects are statistically marginal when considered separately. When combined, however, organizational appeals are found to be significantly more attractive under corresponding mood induction than under neutral induction: over subjects, $F(1,42) = 4.51$, $p < .05$; over organizations, $F(1,22) = 6.67$, $p < .05$.

The anger result conceptually replicates and broadens the finding made some years ago by Weiss and Fine (1956) that subjects insulted by an experimenter subsequently were more persuaded by a communication advocating harsh treatment for juvenile delinquents. The pity result, to our knowledge, is new. Clearly, further studies along this line would be useful.

In particular, a fear mood induction should be tried to see if hope appeals become more attractive, contrary to a simple matching hypothesis.

GENERAL DISCUSSION AND CONCLUSIONS

What, then, do our first attempts to study the relationship between political cognition and emotion tell us?

First, it seems that understanding the persuasive effects of emotions in political communication requires taking into account the emotional tendencies of the audience as well as the emotional content of the stimulus. In our data, appeals to pity were most successful with subjects who reported being disposed to feel pity or who were induced into a pitying mood; appeals to anger were most successful with subjects disposed to feel angry or who were in an angry mood; and appeals to hope were most successful with subjects disposed to feel fear. Appeals to pity were not successful for subjects disposed to feel anger, hope, or fear, nor were appeals to anger successful for subjects disposed to feel pity, hope, or fear. As these findings indicate, it is not general emotionality that is important, but rather the specific relationships between particular emotional tendencies and particular emotional stimuli. Our results support the claims of recent emotions theories (e.g., deRivera, 1977; Izard, 1977; Plutchik, 1980; Roseman, 1984a; Tomkins, 1962, 1981), that emotion is not a unitary phenomenon, but may be differentiated into discrete varieties which have different antecedents and effects upon cognition and behavior.

Second, the varied effects of emotions in political communications are not completely captured by the resonance hypothesis. Although angry subjects were more persuaded by angry appeals and pitying subjects liked pitying appeals, fearful people did not like fearful appeals. Rather, fearful people liked hopeful appeals. This result has parallels in the previous literature on fear appeals in which researchers found that high levels of fear diminished the persuasiveness of health-related communications (Janis, 1967). It also suggests a reinterpretation of the finding from that literature (Leventhal, Watts, & Pagano, 1967) that fear appeals were more persuasive if the preventive measures recommended in the communication were perceived as efficacious. Perhaps the presentation of effective preventive measures generates hope, with the emotional content of successful communications on health behaviors being fear plus hope. (Hope is just beginning to be recognized as a distinct emotion, with important behavioral consequences; see Breznitz, 1983; Roseman, 1984a).

The more important implication of the finding that fearful people are not differentially persuaded by fearful appeals, but rather by hopeful ones, is that it changes the way we think about emotion in the political arena.

The effectiveness of an emotional appeal is not merely a matter of satisfying "expressive needs" (Smith, Bruner, & White, 1956). Expressive theories of emotions view people as seeking opportunities to express (or discharge) feelings, as one would exercise one's muscles. But people are not attracted to an emotional appeal because it gives them an opportunity to express whatever it is they feel. People don't just want to feel; they want to feel good or better. Successful appeals to fearful people are those that give them hope, and successful fear appeals are those that provide a way to reduce fear, even if it is the fear aroused by that communication. This is consistent with theories that view emotions as oriented toward coping (e.g., Lazarus, Coyne, & Folkman, 1982; Roseman, 1984a), rather than as irrational disruptive influences on behavior.

A third implication of this research, perhaps the most relevant for our topic, is that emotion is not divorced from political cognition and is certainly not antithetical to it. In Study 3 and in other unreported variations, we have attempted to manipulate the emotional style of some of our appeals while holding content constant. For example, using emotionally toned words and phrases, we tried, like emotional alchemists, to convert the angry feeling of the Atheists appeal to pity and the pitying feeling of the Lutherans' message to hope. The altered appeals were not appealing; subjects told us that they sounded odd and strained. At least part of the problem seemed to be that emotions inappropriate to accompanying cognitions appear bizarre. Political emotions are consistent with political cognitions. The atheists are angry because they think their rights have been denied; this does not lead to feeling pity.

With regard to the emotions literature, this point is consistent with theories that view emotions as following from cognitive appraisals (Abelson, 1983; Arnold, 1960; Lazarus, 1982; Roseman, 1984a), rather than theories that view emotion as a separate system from cognition (Zajonc, 1980, 1984). In the political arena, it is not generally feasible to tack the emotion of one appeal onto the cognition of another. You cannot easily take an organization promoting nuclear buildup and sell it with a love message. As a bumper sticker we saw recently states: You Can't Hug a Child with Nuclear Arms. Political propagandists and psychologists should not try to graft wings onto whales.

If emotion is sensibly and systematically related to cognition, then perhaps preferred political emotions reveal preferred political cognitions. Our analysis of the emotions in the organizations that we surveyed, represented in Table 12.4, suggests three basic kinds of political action messages: (a) People are suffering, and we've got to help them (pity); (b) We've been treated unfairly by the bad guys, and we're going to put an end to it (anger); (c) Something terrible might happen, unless we act now to avoid it (fear-hope). The first tends differentially to appeal to sympathetic souls, the second to angry souls, and the third to fearful souls.

Why are these particular emotions, and the political cognitions that underlie them, prevalent in political communications? That fear appeals do not necessarily work well, and that fearful people prefer hopeful appeals, may indicate that people do not like being told of dangers unless they can be coped with effectively. Anger, though a negative emotion, may be acceptable emotional content for an appeal to angry people because the cognitions that go with anger are those of power and moral legitimacy (Roseman, 1984a), which presage victory. A manifesto that told of some injustice and then went on to say that nothing could be done about it would never inspire a movement. Pity, like anger, may imply the power to transform a situation. Almost by definition, we can help those less fortunate than ourselves. Cognitive content, however, must not contradict the cognitions implicit in emotional messages. Thus pity-oriented fund-raisers seem to place considerable importance on communicating the effectiveness of each donation. If our support wouldn't save that child's life, would we help (see Bandura, 1977)?

Perhaps, then, preferred political cognitions are optimistic: They tell of problems that can be solved (see Roseman, 1984b, for an extended discussion of the content and structure of political issue schemata). This may apply to the messages of political candidates as well as public affairs organizations. In the 1980 and 1984 presidential elections, it seemed that Democratic candidates Carter and Mondale tried to run on fear appeals— fear that Reagan would start a nuclear war or would promote huge federal deficits and social malaise. Reagan, in contrast, seemed to run on hope appeals—hope that America would be Number 1 again in world affairs and that social and economic problems would disappear if only Americans had faith in the marketplace and in him. Clearly, hope won out over fear.

Why are preferred political cognitions optimistic? It is easy to generate at least one explanation. Political cognitions are developed in the marketplace. There are competitors for popular allegiance, votes, contributions, and participation. Ideologies that are not optimistic, that do not hold the promise of solving the problems they confront, would lose appeal in the face of competing ideologies promising success. Perhaps the only way to combat hope is with greater hope. Perhaps the Democrats in 1984 would have had to offer more than Ronald Reagan: not only prosperity, but also a balanced budget, rather than huge deficits; not only military might, but also peace, rather than lives lost in futile adventures. In the ideological competition, perhaps the most successful promises triumph.

A theme of this discussion is that emotions are not irrational forces that move people to political adherence or action irrespective of what they think. To the contrary, emotion is intimately related to the content of political cognition. As we have argued elsewhere (Roseman, 1984a), emotions follow from the fate of goals. Positive emotions indicate goal attainment; negative emotions indicate goal blockage. Hopeful political appeals are preferred to fearful appeals because they indicate successful resolution of problems.

This view of emotions in political cognition contrasts sharply with an older view. About 30 years ago, emotional attachment to politics was theorized to be strongly associated with psychopathology. To be passionate about politics was to be some kind of nut. Research on the authoritarian personality (Adorno, Frenkel-Brunswik, Levinson, & Sanford, 1950) and the writings of Lasswell (1960) and Hoffer (1951) come to mind. Even the somewhat more eclectic treatments by Smith et al. (1956) and Lane (1962) were heavily laced with a psychodynamic orientation. In recent years, however, with the coming of age of the cognitive emphasis within psychology, combined with the newer emergence of interest in emotions as universal, often adaptive processes, it has become possible to take a more relaxed view. It seems that emotional evocation is a normal part of the impact of the political process on normal people. Political issues have natural emotional structures that people can evaluate in terms of what they know and want, and identify with, partly through the resonance of these issues with their own emotions, in the form of permanent personal characteristics or of transient moods.

IV COMMENTS FROM POLITICAL SCIENCE

13

Candidate Evaluations and the Vote: Some Considerations Affecting the Application of Cognitive Psychology to Voting Behavior

Richard A. Brody
Stanford University

The study of individual voting behavior seems a natural area in which to explore the applicability of insights, models, and hypotheses from contemporary cognitive psychology. On the face of it, the case for applicability seems reasonable: Voters process information from the world of politics and use that information along with politically relevant memories to form judgments about the candidates. These judgments have been found to be a source of the vote (Brody & Page, 1973; Kelley & Mirer, 1974). Information processing, memory, judgment, affect, and choice are all important research themes in cognitive psychology; it seems reasonable to expect the product of this research to shed light on voting behavior.

The main argument of this brief commentary is that we cannot profit fully from cognitive psychology unless we understand the features of the system that affect political cognition, attitude formation, evaluation, and learning. Ideally, our knowledge of this system should permit us to structure experiments with maximum external validity, but our knowledge is insufficient to this task. We simply do not know enough to assert with any great confidence that this feature is indispensable, whereas that one is epiphenomenal and, as such, can be safely omitted in a laboratory setting in which information flows lead to externally valid voting behavior.

We can develop a structured catalog of features of the situation that may be relevant to political behavior. These features can serve to suggest the sorts of experimental manipulations that cognitive psychologists might employ. They can also suggest the types of considerations political scientists should review when looking at ideas from cognitive psychology as a source of models of political behavior. The catalog begins with a consideration of the effects of electoral context on information processing. The electoral behavioral repertoire available to most Americans is severely restricted. One can either vote or abstain. In recent elections for President and Congress, between 40 and 60% of the age eligible voters have abstained. If one votes, the choice is between one of the two major parties or one of the minor parties. Minor party voting is rare: In the presidential elections since 1840, the third party vote has averaged below 15% on the 9 occasions in which a nationally prominent figure headed a minor party ticket; in the other 26 elections between 1840 and 1980, the third party vote averaged below 2% (Rosenstone, Behr, & Lazarus, 1984).

With the options so restricted in practice, if not in principle, voting behavior is apt to be, in the aggregate, substantially overdetermined. Overdetermination in aggregate analyses can act like multicollinearity and bias our understanding of the effects of any given cause. Analyzing experiments and surveys designed to study individual voting behavior, unless the behavior at this level is also substantially overdetermined, we can expect any given independent variable to produce weak main effects. Individual voters use distinct information-processing routines in arriving at their candidate evaluations and vote. Aggregating across this heterogeneity can obscure strong causal patterns. Indeed, one of the challenges facing students of voting behavior is to discover interesting criteria for disaggregating the voting public on the expectation that different kinds of voters will use different kinds of information and different kinds of processing routines in arriving at their judgments of the candidates.

Our image of the voter is that of an individual "sampling" of candidate-related information from a widely available pool of information. The pool contains more information than most Americans will use. Voters' sampling routines are of direct relevance to our understanding of the vote, but so too is knowledge of the content of the pool of information. The character of information available to the voter is an important element of the context in which the voting decision is made.

Research on campaign media content (e.g., Robinson & Sheehan, 1983) gives a picture of the structure of information available to the voter: Different types of candidates get coverage that is vastly different in quantity and nature. Most basic is the distinction between incumbent and challenger, but important differences between challengers, between phases of the campaign, and across context areas have also been discovered.

From the end of August, with the completion of the nominating conventions, both major parties field their candidates. In American politics, the role of candidate is well-established. Most Americans have developed candidate role schema which aid in converting candidate-related information into evaluations.

Typically, however, one of the candidates is also the incumbent. In 9 of the past 12 elections (including 1984), the occupant of the White House has sought reelection. In 7 of these 9, the incumbent had no real opposition for the nomination (1976 and 1980 are the exceptions). For our purposes, these facts mean that for a large part of the election year the eventual challenger occupies a different role than the incumbent. His coverage is based on different criteria. And citizens, arguably, apply different role schema in the process of reaching their evaluations. After the incumbent is nominated, coverage moves on two tracks: incumbency and candidacy (Robinson & Sheehan, 1983). Does the public continue to employ information-processing routines consonant with these separate roles, do people favor one role or the other, or do they construct some hybrid role schema as the President becomes the nominee? The relevance of the question does not suggest an answer; it suggests that an answer is worth pursuing.

The question generalizes to the situations in which the incumbent's renomination is seriously challenged within his own party. In 1976 and 1980 (our contemporary examples), were Presidents Ford and Carter viewed exclusively from the perspective of their candidacies or were there blocks of information, bearing upon their evaluations, which were processed through an "incumbency-role" schema?

Without question, the sheer volume of information on the incumbent far exceeds that of any other candidate. For 3 to 4 years, the incumbent has been the central focus of news coverage (Gans, 1979; Grossman & Kumar, 1981); indeed, the President gets more coverage in the news media than any other individual and is the single American political figure whose routine actions are considered "news." This news quite definitely contributes to the public's evaluation of presidential job performance (Brody, 1982; Brody & Page, 1975; Haight, 1978; Haight & Brody, 1977; Stone & Brody, 1970). Public approval of presidential job handling changes in relation to news reflecting positively or negatively on political or policy outcomes desired by the President. In the aggregate, the public acts as if it processes this evidence of presidential success or failure along the lines of Norman Anderson's information averaging algorithm (1974), but we have no data with which to determine how individual citizens arrive at and alter their judgments of the incumbent.

Kinder has demonstrated experimentally that media attention or inattention can alter the centrality of policy topics to the public's judgment of the President (Kinder, Iyengar, Krosnick, & Peters, 1983). This research and the wider research program in which it is embedded (Iyengar & Kinder, in press; Iyengar, Peters, & Kinder, 1982) alert us to the role played by media in directing public attention to one policy area or another. This fact is of considerable importance in the structuring of the perception of candidates per se. The media may be less significant in perceptions of the incumbent because of the greater volume of information and the greater likelihood that the media act as neutral conduits on the types of stories with which the public adjusts its judgment of presidential performance. To be sure, the media retail this information to the public, but their organizational needs and their professional norms and practices appear to have less impact on these stories than on campaign and candidate-related stories.

The news media treat campaigns as contests: The vast bulk of news about candidates and campaigns is news about the contest as such. *The CBS Evening News* devoted some 90 min. to the election campaign during the average month in 1980; 65% of this was coded by Robinson and Sheehan (1983) as "horse race" news. Horse race news not only preoccupies the media, but it is virtually the only campaign topic on which reporters offer independent evaluative judgments (Robinson & Sheehan, 1983). Media borne evaluations of other features of a candidacy (e.g., judgments on the personality, competence, and character of the candidates and evaluations of their policy proposals) come from the candidates themselves and/or from their opponents.

It seems likely that reporters are a more "credible" source, in terms of the persuasive communications paradigm (McGuire, 1973), than are election competitors. This means, inter alia, that news about the candidates as potential leaders and news about their program proposals should be most persuasive to those predisposed to be convinced (e.g., fellow partisans). Those predisposed to be skeptical are less likely to find such news credible and persuasive. Of course, all of this communication is subject to the attention, comprehension, and the yielding mediators and individual differences through which they operate (McGuire, 1973).

Taken together, the studies of campaign coverage and the persuasive communication paradigm argue for a candidate evaluation dynamic with the following properties. Citizens who are predisposed to support one candidate or the other will have their support strengthened by news reports on candidate qualities and policy positions; the stronger the predisposition and the greater the volume of news on this subject, the more positive will become the evaluation of the candidate toward whom a prior attraction exists. This tendency is abetted by the lack of specificity in policies proposed by the candidates during the campaign (Page, 1978), and it is made evident in the tendency to correlate one's own policy position with that of the candidate to whom one is otherwise attracted (Page & Brody, 1972). News stories that raise questions about a candidate and his or her policy proposals are subject to being discounted on the basis of source credibility; they cannot for this reason substantially undermine a positive predisposition.

Positive predispositions can be undermined by "strategic" factors. Brady (1984) has developed models of the role played in candidate evaluations by perceptions of candidate *viability* (i.e., the likelihood of getting the nomination) and *electability* (i.e., the likelihood of being elected President). Brady's experiments have demonstrated that manipulation of evidence on viability and electability can change voters' candidate preferences. Outside of the laboratory, where information is media borne, news on the strength of a campaign and on a candidate's chances of success come to the voter from a most credible source, namely, a neutral observer. On Brady's evidence and on the logic of the persuasive communication paradigm, we would expect candidate evaluations to be sensitive to coverage bearing on viability and electability.

News reports of the success/failure of candidacies should have greater effect on evaluations during the nomination phase of the election year. During this period of intraparty contention, predispositions are less likely to be clearly formed and stable. By the same logic, the discounting of information on candidate and policy program quality should also be less during the nomination period. The volatility of trial-hear polls during the nomination campaign is consistent with the lack of firm predispositions but, of course, cannot be considered more than suggestive evidence for the stability/liability of candidate evaluations.

There are two potential sources of trial-heat volatility during the general election campaigns: candidacy and incumbency performance-related information, which reflect the dynamics of candidate evaluations. As I stated earlier, we know that candidacy and incumbency are covered differently by the media; what we do not know is whether, or for whom, these streams of information are kept separate or integrated in the process of updating evaluations of the incumbent.

Unfortunately, this is not the only piece of ignorance that clouds our understanding of the dynamics of candidate evaluations. The dynamics of attention and the form of predispositional effects are two large areas of ignorance surrounding the processes of political cognition.

For many years, we have known that the public attends to topic areas deemed important by the media. This has been demonstrated at the aggregate level (see MacKuen & Coombs, 1981, for an analytic summary of this work) and at the individual level in a series of experiments (Iyengar & Kinder, in press; Iyengar et al., 1982). Clearly, the news media direct public attention to the subject areas in which candidates and/or incumbents will be evaluated.

If 1980 was typical, there is a seasonality to media attention to coverage themes (Robinson & Sheehan, 1983). Horse race coverage gets above average attention in the middle of the primary season and during the fall campaign; issues get covered most heavily in January, before the primaries get underway, and late in the fall. The total volume of coverage is below average in the middle of the season (April through July) and way above average in September and October.

These findings suggest, inter alia, that citizens who begin to pay attention to the election at different times during the election season will be exposed to a different mix of information about the candidates. Individual differences will doubtlessly affect when people tune in to the election. But the geographical spread of primaries and their distribution across the election calendar may also affect the quantity and quality of attention paid to an election that is still months away or may have already taken place. The dynamics of attention would seem to be an area in which there is a high potential for work on "cognitive economy," the realities of the electoral setting, and individual differences relating to the attention mediator to inform each other.

Finally, the question of the form of the effects of predispositions is one to which cognitive psychologists can contribute a great deal. In discussing the role of predispositions in the processing of candidate and policy information, I modeled predispositions as necessary but not sufficient for the discounting of negative information about a candidate toward whom one is predisposed; source credibility must be taken into account as well. This model treats source credibility and prior commitment as interactive but causally independent. We need to know, but do not, the conditions under which these factors remain casually independent and the conditions under which predispositions help determine source credibility.

These brief comments will have served their purpose if they give cognitive psychologists and political scientists some questions to ponder in planning collaboration. Collaboration and cross-fertilization will be most productive if volumes such as this lead us to recognize how to best profit from our mutual concerns and separate interests.

14

What Are People Trying to Do with Their Schemata? The Question of Purpose

Robert E. Lane
Institution for Social and Policy Studies
Yale University

> A reasoning, self-sufficing thing,
> An Intellectual, all in all.
> — *Wordsworth, "A Poet's Epitaph"*

Without purposes, people and societies stand still; worse, they run down, dribbling away their energies into habit and ritual. For the most part, thinking is purposive, although like the process of thinking itself, the purposes are often obscure to the thinking individual. Without purposes, "nothing is left of him [the modern thinker] than the eternally same *I think . . .* " (Horkheimer & Adorno, 1972, p. 26). What is left out of political cognition, and perhaps cognitive psychology more generally, is purpose. To what ends these schemata, these concepts, and these ideational structures? For what purposes is information processed?

Some time ago, the discovery of "ends" was the main focus of attention. In these "gratification studies," we discovered, or so we thought, what subtle satisfactions were derived by listeners (not yet viewers) from daytime serials (Arnheim, 1944) and why people were willing, even eager, to believe that the Martians had invaded the earth (Cantril, Gaudet, & Herzog, 1940). Extending this concern, we sought to account for the functions an idea served in the psychic economy of the individual. The strength and weakness of functional analysis were that it specified ends: strength because it asked fruitful questions; weakness because the acts that were "functional" in serving those ends may not have been either necessary or sufficient. But it was in that spirit that I (Lane, 1969) asked my students: Of what use to you is your liberalism or conservatism? With candor and insight, they told me how their political views served to make them acceptable to their roommates, challenged their father's claims on their total allegiance, prepared them for the business worlds to which they were destined. Thus did they process the information offered in the classroom.

Released from the classroom, what is it that people try to do as they process political information during (and between) election campaigns? Which of their purposes are served by their development and use of schemata of parties, issues, candidates, groups? As the research in this volume illustrates, even among these standard schemata, people choose different features to emphasize. "Individual differences are likely to be substantial in schema availability and access, and in the strategies people use to process political information" (Conover & Feldman, this volume). Just as "one's likes and dislikes influence what and how information is encoded and retrieved from memory" (Hamill & Lodge, this volume), so do one's purposes.

A preview of the five purposes I intend to discuss should make the next few pages more intelligible. There are two broad classes of purposes: (a) those that may be called *consummatory* in the sense that political schemata of this kind serve no other purpose in the psychic economy of individuals than to give them pleasure (of a sort), and (a) those that represent *transactions* with the world by means of which individuals hope to understand or change something outside themselves. The difference between the use of schemata in consummatory politics and transactional politics is that in consummatory politics the purposes served are not mediated by any concern for the outside world, but rather are directly and immediately internal. The environment serves to provide material for these internal processes, but concern for the environment is lacking; gratification comes not from understanding and evaluating reality, but from reducing effort and pain in thinking, enhancing one's self-esteem by subjective means, winning internal battles against the imagos of significant others. In an important sense, consummatory politics follows Piaget's (1959) egocentric pattern: Only what is in "my" head is real and true. In another Piagetian (1950) sense, consummatory politics emphasizes assimilation, adjusting observations to prior schemata as contrasted to accommodation, adjusting schemata to fit observations.

Transactional politics, on the other hand, implies an exchange with others, where reciprocity is important. But more important, it implies, in Robert White's (1959) terms, "Dealing with the environment [which] means carrying on a continuing *transaction* [italics added] which gradually changes one's relation to the environment" (p. 322). The satisfactions yielded by purely mental transactions along these lines might be said to be the satisfaction of curiosity or of the need for orientation, but in line with White's argument, we may suppose that behind these motives there is satisfaction in a latent readiness for effective action, for "effectance."

Of the consummatory purposes, there are (a) those that represent internal adjustment, perhaps to conserve effort ("cognitive misers"), to relieve mental conflict (e.g., balance theory), or to achieve self-consistency or improved self-esteem, and (b) those that are served by treating politics as an observer sport, as entertainment. In neither case is a political schema an instrument for influencing others or changing outcomes. For the trans-actional purposes, one represents (c) the familiar effort to consider more favorably the opinions of others about the self, that is, impression manage-ment. Another (d) has to do with concern over the democratic process, serving the purpose of maintaining and improving, according to some set of values, the way the political business of the society is conducted, perhaps as a matter of procedural fairness (Tyler, this volume).

Finally, in this brief catalog, there are (e) those purposes aimed at understanding or changing policies, whether about tax or defense, welfare or abortion, and whether for the advantage of the self or others, or addressed to symbolic or material gains. What I claim is that a person's schemata and their uses are influenced by the person's selection among these purposes, recognizing of course that in practice, these purposes are confounded and the first (internal adjustments designed to ease effort and relieve conflict) will be present in all cases of schema formation and use.

THE LIMITS AND SPECIFICATION OF PURPOSE

One reason the gratification studies and the functional analyses gave way to other modes of analysis was their weak understanding of mental processes (e.g., the strategies and shortcomings of social judgment; Nisbett & Ross, 1980). The tradition reflected in the papers in this volume goes some distance in making good this deficiency. There are other limits to purposive analysis. People differ in their capacities for processing information quite irrespective of their purposes. In Hamill and Lodge's (this volume) study, "cognitive ability," especially as measured by a vocabulary test, proved to be the best predictor of "ideological sophistication," that is, the ability to categorize political leaders, groups, and policies correctly as liberal or conservative. More generally, we know that for the cognitively less complex, the concrete, presentational, perceptual stimuli tend to overwhelm the distant and the abstract. But beware! Lau (this volume) found that educa-tion is not correlated with a stronger issue schema (more abstract), but rather with a strong candidate personality schema (more concrete), a finding modified by the fact that "education is not a particularly good indicator of cognitive ability" (Hamill & Lodge, this volume). Whatever the particulars, cognitive ability makes possible the use of abstractions and logic unavailable without it, as contemporary studies (e.g., L. Bennett, 1975; S. Rosenberg, in press) in the Piagetian tradition confirm. Cognitive abilities do two things: They shape the cognitive representations or sche-mata that implement purposes, and they help to define purposes. But alas, this double capacity does not guarantee a match between purpose and thinking ability. The risk is not so much that a person may want to do more than he can do as that he does not understand how to get what he wants. As we see later, a person's political schemata may not fit his purposes.

The effect of purpose on thought is also limited by lack of knowledge, of exposure to the media, and of political experience, three factors that differ in their relation to political schema formation (see Hamill & Lodge, Fig. 5.2, and Lau, Table 6.9, this volume). The point to bear in mind is twofold: (a) purposive behavior has a personal history leaving a deposit of knowledge and experience useful in current conceptualization; recently acquired purposes, therefore, may be handicapped by the lack of such a history; and (b) some knowledge and more exposure are accidental, products of the milieu that is given to the individual quite independently of that individual's political purposes.

One might saturate oneself in the media and learn little about some particular aspect of political life if the media were silent on that aspect. When politics is treated in the media as a contest of personalities, starving interests in issues and parties, a purposive interest in these schemata will not achieve its purposes. More than that, the nature of politics itself may shift, as it has, so that party-candidate links are minimized, depriving the party partisan of material to nourish his party schemata (A. Miller, this volume). And of course, purposes are not given in some way independent of politics and their reflection in the media; they are shaped by them as well.

Gallup regularly asks: What do you think is the most important problem facing this country today? The answers change with threats of war, energy problems, perceptions of crime, rates of inflation, and rates of unemployment. If the purpose of one's political schemata today is to reduce inflation, tomorrow it may be to reduce the threat of war, but it is history, not the values of the public, that has changed. The fluidity or apparent instability of electoral schemata, then, may be properly regarded as a change of purpose, but not of values. Answers to the question, What are you trying to achieve with your political schemata? must take that into account.

Quite apart from their reflection of these historical changes, elections vary in the stimuli they present to the public. If Kennedy had run in 1984, the integrity issue would have been salient; with Mondale as the Democratic candidate, the issue of leadership was more important (Kinder, this volume). In 1972, roughly twice as many people used an issue schema in arriving at their electoral choices as in 1976, whereas in 1976, candidate schemata were used half again as frequently as in 1972 (Lau, this volume). In the first instance, if the purpose was to approximate the selection of an "ideal candidate," that purpose cannot be said to have changed when the schemata employed changed. In the second instance, if the larger purpose was to achieve some end state of security, peace, prosperity, or justice, again the shifting schemata do not reflect changing ultimate purposes, but only shifting proximate purposes.

People's ends come burdened with chains, the endless ends–means chains, infinite regress. Proximate ends are means to larger, more distant ends: To preserve the larger end or good, people's purposes change. Statements of purpose, then, come in various sizes, narrow and broad, to reflect the proximate and the more distant ends they have in mind.

Often we cannot tell from people's acts, or even from their statements of ends pursued, exactly what it is that they are trying to do because these observations and statements must be supplemented by knowledge of their theories of cause and effect, of how to achieve their ends. The answers to questions about what an individual is trying to do with his or her political schemata must embrace means: "I am trying to achieve a certain goal by a certain means." Purposes that refer only to goals or ends are insufficiently specified.

Ends, goals, and values are multiple and require trade-offs. Purposes at any given moment imply a selection among ends in a given situation. The specification of purpose is better than a specification of values or ends because it avoids the problem of listing goals without requiring acknowledgment of the necessary trade-offs.

Abstract values do constrain behavior, but the slippage is substantial. Those who support the abstract value of free speech often endorse policies limiting the speech of those they dislike (Nunn, Crockett, & Williams, 1978; Stouffer, 1955). In Sears, Huddy, and Shaffer's paper in this volume, we see that some who endorse the abstract value of equality do not support policies designed to promote equality. Two things flow from this relative weakness of the constraining power of abstractions: (a) the value-maximization assumptions of economists (Becker, 1976) are likely to prove unrealistic and should be minimized in interpretations of purpose; (b) statements of purpose are more reliable when stated in their relatively more concrete forms. For example, one would have more confidence in the answer to the question of what a person is trying to do with his or her schema if it stated, "I am trying to have the Equal Rights Amendment passed," than if it stated, "I am trying to maximize equality."

Finally, in his seminal article on "Motivation Reconsidered: The Concept of Competence," mentioned earlier, Robert White (1959) argued that many kinds of evidence lead to a theory of motivation for effectance, satisfied by a sense of having an effect on the environment. But, White noted that the motive favored general, as contrasted to specific, learning if the strength of the motive was only modest. According to White (1959), "Strong motivation reinforces learning in a narrow sphere, whereas moderate motivation is more conducive to an exploratory and experimental attitude which leads to competent interactions in general, without reference to an immediate pressing need" (p. 330). Following this line of thought, we would argue that although such specific purposes as a person might harbor would narrow his schema formation, a more general curiosity, possibly in the service of the effectance motive but with no particular act of control in mind, would also lead to schema formation when the uses of the schema might be quite obscure to the thinking individual.

Thus, a proper understanding of what an individual is trying to do as he or she frames and uses a set of political schemata implies recognition of: (a) general cognitive strategies, (b) individual cognitive limitations, (c) the individual's experiential and knowledge bases, (d) information presented in the media from which schemata may be formed, (e) the changing nature of politics, (f) the changing character of the historical problems presented, (g) the changing stimuli presented in each election, (h) the relationship between an individual's proximate and more distant goals, (i) the means the individual thinks appropriate to achieve his or her ends, (j) the trade-offs involved in pursuing ends, (k) the slippage between abstract values and more concrete policies related to those values, and (l) the fact that people learn without any specific purpose in mind. If purposive analysis were a royal road, it would not be so pitted with potholes.

HOW PURPOSES AFFECT SCHEMATA

It may be agreed that people are more likely to learn useful information, that is, information that serves their purposes. It is beyond our powers to discuss in detail how this purposive learning, retention, and use of schemata proceeds, but we might consider how the five purposes mentioned would likely affect the character of the schemata. In a broad sense, compared to accidental or casually learned schemata, purposive schemata should be better informed and better integrated into the general pattern of other schemata (because they have been thought about), more complex, more stable, more "dominant," or constraining when in conflict with schemata serving no particular or a lesser purpose, and more charged emotionally. But the nature of the purpose will shape the way these effects work out in practice.

Internal Adjustments:
The Cognitive "Pleasure Principle"

People seem to need to think (Cacioppo & Petty, 1982), partly because it is physiologically inspired (the synapses fire, as in dreams), partly because of a need for orientation (Leighton, 1959, lists it among 10 basic needs), partly because of the need to relate to people, and partly because people need to explain themselves to themselves (M. J. Rosenberg, 1979). Moreover, people are inveterate theorizers (Nisbett & Ross, 1980). They do not need to think about politics, of course, but if they do, they will likely follow the course of preferred modes of thinking, easing effort, relieving conflict, choosing pleasant thoughts, that is, following the cognitive pleasure principle. They ease effort by employing the most "available," rather than the most fruitful or cogent, schemata (Tversky & Kahneman, 1974), taking such shortcuts as will make thinking less effortful (Taylor, 1981). Avoiding internal conflict, people tend to reduce cognitive inconsistency or imbalance by a variety of devices not designed to improve veridical thought (Abelson et al., 1968) or to reduce affective inconsistency by averaging the affective loading of the emotionally charged symbols (Sears, this volume, and elsewhere). Seeking pleasure, people choose the positive over the negative (Sears & Whitney, 1973), embrace the "Pollyanna Principle" (Matlin & Stang, 1978), or follow a hedonic principle in reconstructing events (M. J. Rosenberg & Abelson, 1960).

If a person's schemata are primarily designed to satisfy these internal adjustments in pursuit of the cognitive pleasure principle, there is no corrective force, no penalty for error. The incentives to think these ways are clear enough; the disincentives must come, if they come at all, through internal monitors and training (the cognitive conscience) that are weak in most people, perhaps because they do not link such processes to the concept of dishonesty. (In Rokeach's, 1974, list of instrumental values, honesty consistently ranks first.) But, if the person has some transaction with the world in mind (or in the unconscious), there are penalties for indulging in the cognitive pleasure principle and correctives (rather stronger in the market than in politics) for unveridical and illogical thinking. The correctives vary with the transactional purposes: Concerned about democratic forms, one will closely observe the democratic process to adjust one's schemata to observed reality, but given only that purpose, one has no incentive to adjust, say, schemata of tax policy to similarly observed reality. The correctives, such as they are, are purpose specific. Perhaps, following Tyler's (this volume) analysis, one's procedural-fairness schema would be enlisted and monitored, but one might permit the cognitive pleasure principle to dominate other schemata without any apparent cost.

The second element among these internal adjustment purposes has to do with the enhancement of self-consistency and self-esteem, which are certain features of the self-schema that Conover and Feldman (this volume) refer to in their analysis. The self, writes M. J. Rosenberg (1979), is "usually the most important [attitude] object in the world" (p. 24); therefore, we should not be surprised if something of such surpassing value plays a part in the development of political schemata. Rokeach (1973) has shown that the reconciliation of discrepancies between values and attitudes is accomplished not by superordination of the value to the attitudes, but by adjusting either the one or the other so as to conform more closely with the individual's preferred self-image. Without strain, one can interpret Sears et al.'s evidence (this volume) of the power of symbols in political thinking as deriving in part from the desire to validate one's values as part of oneself. Consistency in argument (compatible schemata) often derives its appeal less from the attractions of logic and more from the desire to appear to the self as self-consistent: "If I am a liberal, then I must believe in minority rights." One preserves one's integrated identity with almost the vigor that one preserves one's self-esteem, sometimes at the cost of lower self-esteem (Erikson, 1956). These are universal principles, as salient in transactional politics as in consummatory politics, but again, in transactional politics, there are correctives in the responses of the outside world. One is not quite so free to indulge in a preferred self-image (e.g., as a popular leader) where the evidence tends to disconfirm that image. A long-treasured image of the self as concerned more with the public interest than with self-interest is immune from correction in consummatory politics, but it bumps up against possible mild (and, it must be admitted, easily rationalized) correctives when a tax cut with large, immediate, visible advantages is presented (Sears & Citrin, 1985). Conover and Feldman (this volume) show how a person's self-schema as a liberal or conservative supplies "information" on the positions a preferred candidate must favor; the self-schema has default values for transactional politics. In consummatory politics, the process is reversed: One uses the evidence from politics in such a way as to offer default values for the deficient self-schema.

A third branch of consummatory politics as internal adjustment deals with the way individuals salve old wounds and win old quarrels by using politics in their internal, often unconscious, dialogues. These are not only adolescent rebels "talking" to their fathers; Franz Alexander (1959) reports many instances of mature patients devising their political schemata to express and maintain their defensive mechanisms. For example, a liberal patient will not vote for a certain liberal candidate because the patient believes that the candidate shares with him his own distressing symptoms. When they lead to transactions with the world, these internal adjustments are only modestly vulnerable to corrections because their roots are not in politics but in the self. But without transactions, although the internal adjustments may erode with maturity, they are unlikely to be corrected by political consequences because there are no relevant political consequences in consummatory politics. Given the prominence of parental figures in this third branch of consummatory politics, one suspects that candidate imagery is especially likely to be prominent, not in any simple "benevolent leader" sense (Greenstein, 1965), but rather in selecting the dimensions of candi-

date evaluation congenial to internal dialogues with parents. These dialogues have a way of stressing moral and authority qualities; thus, one
suspects that here, at least, the leadership and integrity dimensions, rather
than the competence dimension, would be more important. In partial
confirmation, Kinder and Abelson (1981) report that the relative importance of competence rises and integrity declines as political sophistication
and involvement increase. That is, in my terms, as transactional politics
increases, those who use political schemata for internal adjustments and
dialogues are less likely to be politically informed and sophisticated.

Politics as an Observer Sport

The second general type of consummatory purpose is illustrated by analogy.
The term "observer sport" is better than drama because of the oppositional,
winning and scoring partisanship of audience qualities in sport; sport does
not require "the willing suspension of disbelief" requested by drama (cf.
Gusfield, 1975). It is consummatory, and not transactional, because the
schemata of the political observer have as their main purposes either
entertainment or being on the winning side, with entertainment more often
served by criticism than endorsement of the players in the game. But it
borders on transactions in two respects: (a) where it is not private, it invites
impression management (discussed later), and (b) where it leads to cheering,
as in other sports, people insensibly believe that their cheering is effective
(Langer, 1983). It is available to partisans and nonpartisans, to voters and
nonvoters; as with other sports, information improves entertainment values,
but as in "spectacles," information is not crucial. Yet political campaigns
are insufficiently spectacular, and no doubt, the loss of information on
parties reported by Miller (this volume) reduces some of the party partisan
entertainment values.

Schemata devised or selected to serve these sports observers will likely
be weak in issue content because the sporting contest is posed as a contest
between candidates and parties; they are the players, and it is rather more
than issues or "liberals" that are said to win or lose. It is candidates who
make the news, who appear on television, and who, at least in election
periods, score and are scored upon. But it is parties which, like one's
favorite team, represent longer term attachments so that a person can,
especially in congressional elections, believe that we won or lost. The
real-world corrections to schemata devised for their entertainment and
identification values are not great; those who like to be winners will find
corrections as unfavorable outcomes become apparent; those who seek
heroes or star players are vulnerable to correction as well, but unlike sport
heroes, political heroes can survive defeat. The play of the cognitive
pleasure principle is fully licensed, but more is involved because political

sports fans are, to serve their purposes, attending to the game more than to themselves. Their schemata will be loosely organized, for few of their purposes are served by consistency. They are likely to be taxic, stimulus bound, concrete because of their perceptual nature, and unless they are choosing winners, quite stable because they are invulnerable to transactional corrections.

Impression Management

In asking Yale students some 30 years ago to answer the question, "Of what use to you is your liberalism or conservatism?" I (Lane, 1969) naturally found that many of them made their political views useful in "fitting into" the Yale environment (which was conservative at the time of the student reports in the 1950s), in dealing with and sometimes provoking their roommates, and in enlisting the support of at least one parent, often in a quarrel with the other. Political schemata are counters in the game of interpersonal relations, useful in managing the impressions we make on others. With the decline of the near hysteria of the 1950s about conformity, new themes of individuation (Lane, 1978; Snyder & Fromkin, 1980) have altered the direction of discussion about social influence, but not its central position in social psychology. In the current context, however, the point is less that a person's schemata are vulnerable to the influence of others, but rather that an individual devises his or her schemata to impress others, to persuade them about some special feature that the person wishes publicly to enhance. One may wish to enhance one's image for ulterior purposes (e.g., to get a job) or for the intrinsic pleasure in imagining oneself well regarded for some act or statement.

The purpose is transactional, and not merely consummatory, because it requires the individual to seek some change in his or her environment—to be sure, not the political environment, but rather the interpersonal environment. As a consequence, the central schemata, the organizing features of one's schematic world, are of the self and others and their interrelationships. Until we know the features of the self that the person wishes to enhance in a particular situation, and the person's schemata about the individual(s) composing an audience, and the person's theory of the behavior that creates the desired impression, we fail to understand a person's learning, content, and uses of schematic representations. The sport of politics is not the game that interests him or her; it is only the equipment, the bats and clubs and especially the uniforms, for the game.

Even for the impression manager, however, the monitored self does not signal, as Fromm (1947) suggested, "I am as you desire me" (p. 73). Policy positions may indeed be fluid (Markus, 1984) because they are not part of the self-image, but party and group identifications and self-labeled liberalism or conservatism are part of the self-image, and they are relatively constant (Conover & Feldman, this volume). Furthermore, those whose political schemata are most useful as masks and costumes, as poker chips and cards, or as clubs and racquets, may have enduring purposes and enduring partners, giving a certain constancy to their political opinions. In the interpersonal games, the players create persona for themselves that fix or freeze their positions: crusty conservative, the cynic, the moralist, the idealist. Markus (1984) points out that some of the conservative drift from adolescence into early adulthood may stem from beliefs about age-appropriate political positions.

The failure of any one policy preference to imply another in Converse's (1964) analysis of political belief systems would be quite compatible with the purposes of the impression manager. For the impression manager, the source of constraint is neither ideology nor logic, but rather the effect of a statement on another person: What will he think of me if I say this or that? The process is *reflected appraisal* ("each to each a looking glass . . . "), and the criteria for impression management are guided by the principles of *psychological centrality,* choosing dimensions for appraisal that reflect the "best" qualities of the self, whether moral, critical acumen, worldly wisdom, or whatever (M. J. Rosenberg, 1979). This is quite a different form of centrality from the one Converse was looking for.

The Democratic Process

The purpose of the sports fan is entertainment and being on the winning side; his schemata are consummatory because, like the Dodger fan, he does not seek to change the outcomes—except, perhaps, by cheering his team or heroes. But political schemata also embrace transactional purposes whose aim is to defend, or improve, the democratic process, yielding pride when the process works well and shame when it is clumsy, corrupt, or unfair. Tyler's (this volume) analysis of procedural fairness reveals a facet of political schemata with substantial explanatory power: At least for purposes of evaluation, if not for actual voting or other consequential decisions, assessments of procedural fairness weigh more heavily than assessments of outcomes. Beyond that, there is a pride in the electoral process and in the Constitution that guarantees that process, a pride that goes far beyond the sports fan's entertainment and winning orientation. Over recent decades, as confidence in political leaders and belief in the efficacy of voting declined, the public's sense of "citizen duty" remained remarkably constant (Lipset & Schneider, 1983b, p. 26). In 1976, when only 30% of the public believed that "you can trust the government in Washington to do what is right . . . always [or] most of the time," 76% said, "I am proud of many things about our form of government" and only 19% agreed that "I can't find much in our form of government to be proud of" (Lipset & Schneider, 1983b, pp. 304–305).

These schemata of duty are stable, and they do affect behavior. Those with a high sense of citizen duty are almost certain to vote, whereas those with a low sense of citizen duty rarely do (Campbell, Converse, Miller, & Stokes, 1960), and those who see themselves as "civic minded," in the sense that they see themselves as doing a lot for their community, participate in politics in a variety of ways more often than do others (Verba & Nie, 1972). Constitutional-regime schemata are likely to dominate (constrain) other schemata because when attitudes toward leaders, parties, and perceived government effectiveness turn sour, these regime-related attitudes are a protection against alienation, as well as apathy (Lipset & Schneider, 1983a, 1983b; A. Miller, 1983).

Of what use to a person is concern for the democratic process? What purposes does it serve (setting aside the collective purposes served in protecting the democratic decision-making process)? For one thing, it serves the terminal value most Americans put first: freedom (Rokeach, 1974); it touches an individual's pride (overwhelmingly, Americans say that the feature of America in which they have most pride is freedom, *Public Opinion,* 1981, pp. 30–31) and so his or her self-esteem (pride and shame are emotional states uniquely associated with those things which are in some sense "mine"). And in certain circumstances, especially war but also under real or feigned "threats" of subversion, it mobilizes defensive action and justifies sacrifice.

What Should the Government Do?

Winning elections is only an intermediate purpose for the involved citizen; beyond that lies some preferred state that governments can bring about in the order of things. In this respect, the several schemata analyzed in this volume have different standing. Party and candidate schemata are more productive of the consummatory values of winning an election; as pointed out, these lend themselves to serving the sports fan's pleasure in scoring and winning. Issue and group benefit schemata do not "play" and "win" in the same sense; they look beyond the election to that change in the preferred order of things. But viewed instrumentally, party and candidate schemata are also important in producing that order, for they are the agents of policy, as well as the players in the political game. There are also gratifications that flow from identification with the party or persons in power, some of which are symbolic and some which offer contingent security, rather like an insurance policy.

In asking citizens what they are trying to do with their schemata, we would not be satisfied, for the reasons given earlier, with some set of abstract values that they are trying to maximize. That may be our language, but it is not theirs. Rather, looking beyond the intermediate purpose of winning an election, we would take our cues, as Conover and Feldman do in this volume, from people's issue positions, recognizing that their priorities will change with historical changes and with changes in their own circumstances. The purposes of elections, then, are served by government action to reduce the risks of war, perhaps made concrete by withdrawal from danger spots, by tariffs against Japanese goods that threaten jobs, by more affirmative action or by less, and so forth. But this specification of what people are trying to do is incomplete in at least three respects.

First, there is the implication that the government both should and can carry out the purposes implicit in the policies at issue. "Should" defines by the case method the proper scope of government leading to that particular American ambivalence about minimal government in general and expanded services and regulatory protections in particular (Lipset & Schneider, 1983b). It is particularly American in that more Americans than Europeans believe that their own economic fates are the products of their own doing (Katona, Strumpel, & Zahn, 1971) and that the market is, indeed, a self-regulating instrumentality (survey by Harris in Atlantic Institute, 1983) whose faults are often government induced. "Can" because the current neoconservative theme of government incapacity is echoed by many citizens, reinforced by persisting unresolved problems of inflation and unemployment (Lipset & Schneider, 1983b).

Second, as mentioned earlier, the statement of what people are trying to do with their schemata embraces a set of causal attributions with two facets: what causes a problem and what causes a solution, that is, a socioeconomic theory and a political theory. Although it used to be the case that business and government were equally blamed for inflation, in the late 1970s and in the 1980s government came to receive most of the blame (*Public Opinion*, 1982, p. 22). These attributes of blame are rudimentary socioeconomic theories. The political theories refer not only to policies, but also to who makes them. In the 1950s, the ordinary American citizen believed pretty much that the President proposed legislation and the Congress then passed it. Citizens also believed that legislation was effective (Lane, 1962). Great man theories of politics lead to an emphasis on party schemata. Electoral schemata on issues, candidates, and parties will reveal, as through frosted glass, blurred images of these socioeconomic and political theories.

Third, electoral schemata inevitably reflect concepts of justice and self-interest, the appropriate beneficiaries of government policy: Who should get what? Modifying more global doctrines of "the just world" (whatever is, is just; M. Lerner, 1980) and premises of American self-attribution (whatever happens to me is due to my own efforts or faults; Feldman, 1982; Gurin &

Gurin, 1976), Tyler's work (this volume) on assessments of procedural and distributional justice motives informs our understanding of what lies behind some of the electoral schemata. Perhaps these justice facets of electoral schemata would come to light most readily in cross-class party and ideological identifications, the working-class economic conservatives and the upper-middle-class economic liberals. But we turn here to the problem of self and others reflected in Kinder and Kiewiet's (1979, 1981) and Kiewiet's (1983) work on sociotropic politics, that is, the finding that people with individual stakes in a policy outcome are little more likely to support it than those with no such stakes. People seem to respond to national problems more than to (or instead of) personal problems. The findings are important, with widespread ramifications, but they lend themselves to ambiguous interpretations. Consider these possibilities:

1. Unable to see the personal implications of policies, people use the well-reported national news as evidence of their present or future well-being.
2. People's standards of their own well-being are inevitably comparative; the reports on national well-being are used for the purposes of social comparison.
3. People so identify with the good of others and national well-being that they take satisfaction in "good news" and evidence that the nation is doing well; in that sense, what happens to the nation happens to the self.
4. Because people cannot achieve the benefits of such collective goods as peace and low inflation without others also benefiting, their self-interest is served by policies benefiting others as well as the self.
5. In a world of uncertainties and unknown probabilities, the degree to which others are well off affects the probabilities that the self will be well off.
6. As William James (1892–1961) wrote, the self embraces everything to which "mine" applies: my brother-in-law, my wife's niece; a favorable national milieu serves my self-interest by serving these related others. Without using self-interest in the tautological sense, we can see that sociotropic politics serves a variety of self-interests including those of the altruistic version, caring about the fate of the nation.

What are people trying to do when they frame and use their schemata? By opening doors, the papers in this volume not only let in much light but also invite entry into exciting realms of purpose. People are doing more than trying "to organize the political world" (Conover & Feldman, 1984); they are making their thoughts more comfortable to themselves; they are watching with a sports fan's eye and passion, impressing others, evaluating a process that, in the end, they cherish; and they are trying to understand and achieve something beyond the election that requires them to enlist their theories, interpret government boundaries and capabilities, and decide who should get what, themselves included. Each of these purposes will give color and tone, transience or durability, shape and content to their political schemata.

15

Cognition and Political Behavior

Robert Jervis
Department of Political Science
Columbia University

It is hard to see how we can ever gain anything like a complete understanding of politics without understanding how people think. Whether we are interested in voting behavior, the legislative process, or international relations, we confront individuals who set goals, process information about their external environments, adjust to changes that are going on around them, and reach decisions. Furthermore, a cognitive approach cuts across many of the subfield boundaries in political science. Although context is important, we would expect some similarity in information processing and decision making whether we are looking at how a statesman decides who to ally with or how an individual decides who to vote for. Indeed, fundamental inference and decision processes should help explain not only political behavior but also much about how people act in their everyday lives.

None of this is to say, of course, that examining cognition is the only way to understand behavior. The fact that almost all actions must in some sense "go through" cognition does not mean that cognition is a powerful independent variable. The reasons for this are well known. Although many of us find explanations that tell us how people are thinking especially satisfying intellectually because they spell out in detail the causal links involved, such "high density explanations" have no privileged epistemological status (Hirschi & Selvin, 1955, 1967; Kaplan, 1965; for the contrary argument, see Greenstein, 1967; R. Snyder, Bruck, & Sapin, 1962). Furthermore, the relationship between what people think and how they behave is not unambiguous (for summaries of the earlier studies of the links between attitudes and behavior, see Abelson, 1972; Schuman & Johnson, 1976). In both political science and psychology, the question of the extent to which

319

and the conditions under which behavior is determined by factors internal to the individual or to the external situation is very much an open one. To the extent that the external situation dominates, beliefs may be irrelevant to explaining behavior. Furthermore, in at least some cases in which beliefs and behavior are consistent, the former may be an effect rather than a cause. This is Bem's (1972) self-perception theory, which argues that people often alter or establish their beliefs to make them consistent with their behavior. This explanation has been found to account partially for the development of the containment policy on the part of some American decision makers in the aftermath of World War II (Larson, 1985).

In international politics, the question of the importance of beliefs and decision making is known as the level of analysis question—the relative merits of seeking the sources of a state's foreign policy at the level of its external environment, the nature of its domestic system, or the characteristics of its decision makers (the seminal work is Waltz, 1959; more recent discussions are in Jervis, 1976; Waltz, 1979). In the field of political science as a whole, the question is often couched in terms of arguments about reductionism and the contrast between structural and behavioral approaches— the former proceeding from the top down, the latter from the bottom up. The relative merits of these positions and the possible syntheses are beyond the scope of this paper. It is sufficient here to note that the attempts to explore political behavior by means of cognitive processes must necessarily incur the cost of slighting systemic or structural features. This means that we will have to lose sight of some of the most basic questions about politics, for example, the causes if not the consequences of different distributions of power; possible transformations of the state system; the social and economic factors that increase or decrease the likelihood of democratic government; the ways in which political outcomes are formed by the often complex interactions among individual actions.

Because no one approach is best for answering all questions, it is important to realize the implications of adopting a particular perspective. With this in mind, I think it is useful to look at five questions: What is the social cognition approach? In what domains will it fruitfully apply? What is the contribution of this approach to understanding political behavior? What can our knowledge of political behavior contribute to the social cognition approach? What does this approach say about our understanding of culture, society, and human nature?

SOCIAL COGNITION AND ITS PROBLEMS

Although there are differences within the cognitive approach, several common features stand out. The starting point is Herbert Simon's (1957) view that our minds are so limited and our world is so complicated that numerous shortcuts or heuristics are necessary to make sense out of it. Belief systems and schemata then guide us in perceiving our environment, drawing inferences from evidence, and reaching decisions. It follows that to understand behavior, we need to investigate both differences among individuals in their cognitions and beliefs that are shared, if not by all human beings, at least by those in the same culture. We also need to understand the processes by which these beliefs are formed, change, and structure incoming information and the formation and choice among alternatives. The other papers in this volume provide more details about this approach, and full-length treatments are available (Fiske & Taylor, 1984). So rather than elaborate, I proceed with a number of questions and problems. However, these should be seen within the context of an overall favorable evaluation of this approach. I have used it in my own work, and I think the insights provided by the chapters in this book demonstrate its utility.

Other Psychological Approaches

The first cautionary note is that although it is appropriate for political scientists to learn the latest findings and arguments of psychology, they should not be too quick to assume that older ideas are invalid. Psychologists are sometimes amused by the psychological ideas that political scientists employ; political scientists often get annoyed with psychologists for changing the rules of the game just as they have learned how to play it. Indeed, one can almost tell whether an idea has run its course in psychology by whether it is beginning to be used by political scientists. Thus, a closer articulation between the two fields is certainly useful. Not only will the political scientists be able to gain the benefit of the latest psychological thinking, but they will be able to make criticisms and suggestions at a time when they can be utilized.

Nevertheless, there is a danger that political scientists will believe that only the latest ideas are worth working with. This danger is especially great because psychologists seem to have even shorter memories than political scientists. For example, I see few references in the current psychological literature to the earlier work of Clinton De Soto (1960; De Soto & Albrecht, 1968a, 1968b), although much that he has written is still central to the concept of schema. Furthermore, older ideas (e.g., cognitive dissonance) may not lack utility even though psychologists are no longer interested in them. The fact that political scientists applied the notion of cognitive dissonance too broadly, almost as a synonym for cognitive consistency, and that cognitive psychology has moved in other directions does not mean that more precise and careful formulations of the implications of dissonance do not shed light on important political phenomena (see Jervis, 1976, for applications of cognitive dissonance to foreign policy decision making).

Two more recent approaches, both related to social cognition, also have not found their way into much work in political science, including the chapters of this book. One is the set of notions associated with Kahneman and Tversky's (1973) demonstration that people pay insufficient attention to what are known as "base rates" (e.g., the inherent probabilities that certain things are true) and overweigh the significance of the apparent resemblance between the case at hand and the stereotype into which it might fit. There are problems with this approach (Jervis, 1985b), but it provides one way of getting at the important question of what information people use when drawing inferences.

A second perspective whose absence is even more noticeable is that of attribution theory, that is, arguments about how people decide what is causing others (and themselves) to behave as they do (for a good review, see Kelley & Michela, 1980). This task is often central to political inferences because statesmen need to determine the causes of others' behavior in order to predict how they are likely to behave in the future. Voters employ related mental processes when they try to apportion responsibility for political events, as Popkin and his colleagues brought out in their analysis of the 1972 election (Popkin, Gorman, Phillips, & Smith, 1976). Thus, a matter of recent interest has been what commentators have called "the teflon factor," that is, the fact that the public does not seem to blame the President for many misfortunes of public policy. Indeed, whether or not a person held Reagan responsible for the country's economic problems played a large role in determining how he or she voted in the 1982 congressional elections (Petrocik & Steeper, 1984).

Alternative Models

A second potential danger with a stress on social cognition is that we forget about alternative models, especially those less rooted in psychology. Findings consistent with social cognition are not automatically inconsistent with competing explanations. Tyler's (this volume) contrasting of the implications drawn from social cognition with those derived from an economic model is a good example of what can be done. Similarly, Sears, Huddy, and Schaffer (this volume) contrast the expectations generated by the social cognition approach with those generated by a simple model of symbolic politics. Without arguing for the existence of simple and unambiguous "crucial tests" (see the cogent critique by Lakatos, 1970), the generation of competing predictions is useful for checking the adequacy of an explanation, sharpening one's thinking about the implications and causal links in the favored explanation, and explicating the shortcomings of models we believe to be inappropriate.

Affect and Cognition

A third problem with the social cognition approach, and with most of our ideas about psychology, is an inadequate integration of cognition and affect. As Abelson and Roseman (this volume) note, we usually treat affect as an "add-on." Students of social cognition are aware of this problem (Fiske & Taylor, 1984; Izard, Kagan, and Zajonc, 1984) which is not unique to this approach. Furthermore, our inability to deal with affect may not be critical in understanding mass political cognition because political objects excite great emotion in only a few people, although most people's lack of deep concern may give those emotions free rein. For an understanding of political behavior in general, surely a better appreciation of how affect and cognition intermix is necessary.

An Approach, Not a Theory

A final problem is that social cognition is an outlook, not a theory. It consists of essentially untestable assumptions and a series of somewhat loosely connected demonstrations and propositions. But there is not enough in between these two levels. Thus, the approach remains disturbingly ad hoc and does not lend itself to the deductive generation of important hypotheses. In part, scholars have followed this path as a reaction to earlier lines of investigation, such as consistency theory, which gained a high degree of unity at the cost of descriptive accuracy. In addition, the lack of coherence may partly be a function of the relative youth of the approach; it may become more of a theory as more work is done.

CONDITIONS UNDER WHICH SOCIAL COGNITION APPLIES

No one thinks that we can move directly from the laboratory to an understanding of political cognition. The question of external validity is always present. One way to approach this is to try to identify the conditions that make social cognition a more or less useful tool of analysis. I suspect that the distinction between political and nonpolitical realms is not a useful one in this regard. We want to know the characteristics that set domains apart from each other. Although the content of the information and beliefs is likely to be important, we need to specify what it is that matters.

One obvious distinction is the importance of the subject to the person.

That is, we may process information quite differently depending on the priority to which we accord the matter. People sometimes react without much thought, using only the simplest modes of processing (Langer, 1978; Langer, Blank, & Chanowitz, 1978; Taylor & Fiske, 1978). Thus, differences may emerge between cognition in mass political behavior and in elite decision making because most people do not care a great deal about politics and leaders are making decisions on matters that are crucial to them. By the same token, there may be a great deal of similarity between foreign policy decision making and the way people reach decisions on the important things in their lives, such as what career to follow, where to live, and whether and whom to marry. The fact that the latter realms are nonpolitical and the former are political may not be of much theoretical significance. Unfortunately, at this point, we do not have many nonobvious expectations about the differences that would be generated by different levels of importance.

A second distinction is between matters that heavily involve affect and those that do not. Although these two dimensions are not unrelated, neither are they identical. Issues of the same importance can differentially involve affect, and when they do, our ways of thinking may well be different. Again, our knowledge of the expected and actual differences is sharply limited, and this is more an area to be explored than one in which we have theoretically derived propositions.

Another significant distinction is between information-poor and information-rich environments. In most experiments, subjects have few preconceived notions and largely proceed on the basis of the very little information that the experimenters provide. Few real-world situations are like this, however. Individuals usually hold a number of ingrained beliefs and find themselves confronting a great deal of information, much of which is ambiguous. Exploring behavior under these conditions is both important and difficult. The more one improves external validity by making the experiments more lifelike, the greater the threats to internal validity, and the greater the difficulties in drawing causal inferences and teasing apart competing explanatory hypotheses.

The conditions that affect social cognition are related to the question of the robustness of the approach. Are many of the fascinating findings the product of bizarre laboratory manipulations? Do people behave in unusual ways in these settings because they confront problems of a kind they rarely see in their everyday lives? What is the strength of the factors isolated by social cognition in comparison with other influences that purposefully are removed from the experiments? At this point, we do not have good answers. The papers in this volume have found intriguing parallels between experimental results and the responses people give to political surveys. My own work yields ambivalent results. On the one hand, a great many incidents in diplomatic history seem best explained by the dynamics of social cognition, but on the other hand, a close examination of some particular cases shows that the impact of cognitive factors is minor compared to the brute force of political imperatives and the workings of informal organizational norms and incentives (Jervis, 1976, 1985a). But if a conclusion is not yet possible, at least we can note the importance of learning how social cognition varies with the context.

CONTRIBUTIONS OF SOCIAL COGNITION TO POLITICAL BEHAVIOR

The proof of the pudding is in the eating. The central question is: What do we learn about political behavior by adopting the social cognition perspective? To start with, we should separate the question of what people are concerned with from the question of how they go about making the necessary assessments. We are interested in both the shortcuts to rationality that people use and the goals toward which the shortcuts are directed. The social cognition approach to political behavior has contributed to our knowledge in both areas and, in doing so, has shed new light on the old question of voter rationality.

   Several reinforcing strands lead to the conclusion that people are more rational than some previous analyses had lead us to believe. First, this approach, like earlier work both on cognition (Simon, 1957) and on voting behavior (Page, 1976), stresses how difficult it would be for voters to employ anything like full rationality given the complexity and ambiguity of the information they receive. Thus, the processes adopted by highly rational people will not resemble the standard model of rationality. Second, and linked to this, some previously noted phenomena, such as the apparent projection of one's preferences on to the perceived stance of the candidates, appear not as simple ignorance or wishful thinking but rather as an understandable and rationally based method of inference (Conover & Feldman, this volume; Jervis, 1976). Third, what seems like inconsistency or irrationality may be a difference between the beliefs of the investigators and the beliefs of the people being studied. For example, even though it was clear in 1968 that Hubert Humphrey was more critical of the war in Vietnam than was Richard Nixon, it would not necessarily have been irrational for someone who felt that ending the war was the most important goal to have voted for Nixon. Such a person could have reasoned that campaign statements were an inadequate guide to how the candidates would behave in office and that, for any number of reasons, Nixon was more likely to withdraw than was Humphrey. Similarly, someone might vote for President Reagan not because he or she was a Republican or agreed with Reagan's

issue positions, but because of the belief that it was important to have some
stability and demonstrate that a President could be reelected. In the same
way, Popkin and his colleagues (Popkin et al, 1976) demonstrated that
voters were concerned with candidates' competences and pointed out that
it made sense to vote against a candidate who you thought shared your
goals if you believed that he was not competent enough to reach them.
Focusing on cognition thus sensitizes us to the multiplicity of goals that
people can have and the diverse chains of reasoning they may follow.

In the same vein, Tyler (this volume) shows that people are more
concerned with issues of distributive and procedural justice than most
previous treatments had assumed. It is commonly argued that people judge
policies in terms of their direct effect on them (i.e., whether the outcomes
made them better or worse off, usually in economic terms). Indeed, the
lack of a strong correspondence between such outcomes and voting behavior has been a puzzle. But Tyler notes that such a priori reasoning is not
appropriate. We should instead determine what people value; when we do
so, it appears that outcomes may be less important than whether the
processes by which they were produced are perceived as just.

In highlighting the importance of the concepts that people hold, the
social cognition perspective can link psychology and intellectual history.
The two fields focus on the ideas that shape the perceptions of the
environment and argue that if we are to understand how people behave, we
must understand how they are thinking. On a much smaller scale, let me
provide one example drawn from my own work (Jervis, 1984). The dominant strands in American thought about nuclear strategy have been based
on what Hans Morgenthau called "conventionalization," that is, the attempt
to understand nuclear weapons and their implications in the older, established prenuclear frames of reference. To make a long story short, this
conceptualization leads to the conclusion that deterrence requires the
ability to deny the other side any military advantage, an argument that has
been the foundation of American nuclear doctrine over the past 15 years.
This conclusion, and many of the official arguments, makes a great deal of
sense if one employs the postulates of prenuclear military thinking. Thus,
the unintended irony in Paul Nitze's (1979) argument:

It is a copybook principle in strategy that, in actual war, advantage tends to
go to the side in a better position to raise the stakes by expanding the scope,
duration or destructive intensity of the conflict. By the same token, at
junctures of high conflict short of war, the side better able to cope with the
potential consequences of raising the stakes has the advantage. The other
side is the one under greater pressure to scramble for a peaceful way out. To
have the advantage at the utmost level of violence helps at every lesser level.
(p. 6)

But if the mutual vulnerability created by large numbers of relatively invulnerable weapons of mass destruction has led to a true "nuclear revolution," the copybook no longer applies. The attempt to use our prenuclear ideas to understand the role of nuclear weapons will only lead to intellectual incoherence and political disaster.

Social cognition's stress on the importance of the ideas people hold brings up three related questions. First, how are beliefs related to each other? Can we find structures and hierarchies in a belief system? For example, a decision maker presumably has an image of the Soviet Union, a schema for hostile and threatening countries, and perhaps a set of expectations about how a typical country will behave in a particular situation. But we need to know more about how these are related to one another. As the framework of scripts indicates (Abelson, 1981; Schank & Abelson, 1977), beliefs and schemata may be nested within each other, some being more general and abstract and others more bounded and particular. But our knowledge in this area is still sharply limited.

A second obvious question is how beliefs, images, and schemata form. Knowing that they are so potent increases the importance of understanding how they are established in the first place. In some instances, they seem derived from historical events in a fairly straightforward manner. Thus, the Depression established many people's beliefs about the Democratic and Republican parties, and a trauma such as World War I or II gives the statesmen of the day powerful models for how wars can start. But this dynamic cannot explain the origins of all schemata and beliefs. Lau (this volume) shows that voters differ in the extent to which they use group, issue, personality, and party schemata. But his discovery of the demographic correlates of these alternative perspectives is not a complete or entirely satisfactory explanation of why some people use one kind of schema and others use another kind. Indeed, the whole attempt to trace "backward linkages" between beliefs and objective external conditions raises an intriguing question (Gorman, 1970). If the attempt fails, we will be unable to explain how the schemata arise and will wonder whether we have missed the most important variables. But to the extent that such attempts succeed, the variance explained by the schemata themselves may be quite limited.

Linked to the question of how beliefs and schemata form is the puzzle of how they change. The emphasis of the social cognition approach is on stability, and I think data from foreign policy decision making bear this out. But beliefs do change; schemata do not entirely guide new information. Both the question of when the same framework is used but a different answer is reached (e.g., the shift from seeing a country as hostile to seeing it as friendly) and the question of how entirely new schemata develop are significant and, at this point, largely unanswerable. Indeed, on these points, the new perspective creates some new problems, a transformation that is not unusual in science (Kuhn, 1962). Previously, change in beliefs could be seen as an almost self-explanatory result of new information, but a stress on the power of schemata makes such changes puzzling.

A cognitive approach can help us understand political behavior not only by taking into account the individual's goals and beliefs, but also by helping us see how people process information. The facts people attend to are strongly influenced by their schemata, a point well brought out by Lau's study and the Hamill and Lodge experiments in this volume. Our understanding of how people process information also sheds light on international relations, the area I am most familiar with. Let me just mention a few of the most important findings. (In addition to my own work, I draw heavily on George & Smoke, 1974; Holsti, 1967; Lebow, 1981; Snyder & Diesing, 1977; Wohlstetter, 1962.)

Theory-Driven Inferences

Statesmen's perceptions of other countries are strongly theory-driven rather than data-driven. That is, once they have developed an image of another country, they will interpret ambiguous evidence (and most evidence they receive is ambiguous) as being consistent with that image. Furthermore, they do not realize that they are processing information in this way and so grow systematically overconfident. Because they think they are responding to the evidence rather than to their own preexisting beliefs, they believe that the incoming information not only is consistent with their views but actually confirms it (i.e., is inconsistent with alternative explanations).

Preexisting beliefs strongly influence perceptions and behavior. Let me give only one example: Cognitive predispositions could trigger a nuclear war not only through the well-known operation of spirals of tensions and hostility based on incorrect images of the other side, but also through the workings of either side's warning systems. Once the U.S. or U.S.S.R. believes that the other may be ready to launch an attack, both human and mechanical systems will operate in a way that could create a self-fulfilling prophecy. Analysts and decision makers are aware of the danger that each side might react to warning by taking actions that unintentionally menace the other and so make war more likely. What are of interest here are some less familiar dynamics involving perception. First, when a decision maker thinks that he may soon be under attack (and by definition, this would be the case after a warning has been registered), he will place more credit in new information indicating that a war is imminent than he would if the same information were received in a period of calm. This effect operates both at the conscious and the subconscious levels. The decision maker will explicitly think that what he has learned about the other side's behavior warrants accepting ambiguous evidence as showing that an attack is likely. Furthermore, the fact that he is now perceptually ready to accept such evidence means that he will credit it without full consideration of alternative interpretations. Actions of the other side, which in normal times would be missed or seen as innocent, will now be perceived as evincing hostile intentions. The possibility that the acts were taken in self-defense, out of the fear that the state might attack, is not likely to be given serious consideration (or any consideration at all) because the most salient schema is that of the other's unprovoked hostility.

A reinforcing dynamic is that, once alerted, the actor will scrutinize evidence especially closely, a process which is likely to produce additional support for his suspicions. Even if the other's behavior has not in fact changed, looking at it closely will usually lead the person to see things not previously noticed. Thus, intelligence officers and decision makers may notice details of troop movements which, although routine, are not recognized as such because they never before have been examined so carefully. The activities will then be seen as unusual and, given the context provided by the alert, as threatening. Furthermore, when these activities are examined, decision makers will give their attention to positive instances (i.e., evidence consistent with the other's plan to attack) and ignore or treat as insignificant the absence of behavior which, if present, would also indicate that an attack was likely. People generally fail to realize that their beliefs should be treated as hypotheses that can be undermined by the other side's inaction in situations where the belief implies it should act.

The central point of both this example and the more general view of foreign policy decision making is that the most important predictor of what a person sees usually will be the beliefs and expectations that he holds. When President Kennedy heard the conflicting reports of two officials he had sent to Vietnam on a fact-finding mission, he remarked: "You two did visit the same country, didn't you?" (quoted in Hilsman, 1967, p. 502). In a real sense, they didn't: They both visited their own minds, which held quite different beliefs.

People as Cognitive Misers

One explanation for why inferences are theory-driven is that people are cognitive misers (Fiske & Taylor, 1984). If they tried to give full consideration to every bit of discrepant information they received, they would be unable to form any stable beliefs or take any actions. Thus, this way of thinking is required in order to make sense out of the world. As Michael Polanyi (1965), who is both a scientist and a philosopher of science, points out:

The process of explaining away deviations is in fact quite indispensable to the daily routine of research. In my laboratory I find the laws of nature formally contradicted at every hour, but I explain this away by the assumption of experimental error. I know that this may cause me one day to explain away a fundamentally new phenomenon and to miss a great discovery. Such things have often happened in the history of science. Yet I shall continue to explain away my odd results, for if every anomaly observed in my laboratory were taken at its face value, research would instantly degenerate into a wild-goose chase after imaginary fundamental novelties. (p. 31)

Shortcuts to Net Assessment.   The same impulse to conserve cognitive resources leads to what can be called the pattern of the drunkard's search. People often select information to use because it is readily available, not because it is especially valid. Information is processed in ways characterized by simplicity, not adequacy for the task at hand. These propositions are nicely illustrated by the way in which British statesmen in the 1930s and American decision makers today go about what is known as *net assessment,* that is, the judgment of the military balance. (For information on the 1930s, see Gilbert, 1976; for current practices, see Baugh, 1984.)

First, the basic question asked in both eras was: "Who is ahead?" not "Do we have sufficient military force to support our foreign policy?" A glance at almost any article on the current strategic debate, and the charts which invariably accompany them, is sufficient to reveal a preoccupation with the question of whether or not the United States is behind the Soviet Union. This is also the question that British leaders asked about their airpower compared to Germany's. But this approach, although simple, is very misleading. Depending on the task and context, a state could have more military power than its adversary and still not have enough. Alternatively, it could be inferior and still have more than it needed. In the interwar period, air parity might have been sufficient to deter a direct attack on England, but not enough for "extended deterrence" against German aggression against France, let alone against German expansion to the east. Similarly, the analysis of many hawks today implies that a significant margin of superiority (perhaps what Herman Kahn (1960) called a "not-incredible first strike capability") is needed if the American commitment to NATO is to be credible. By contrast, the implication of the arguments of many doves is that significantly less than parity is needed, certainly to protect the United States, and probably to protect vital European interests as well. But most of the debate focuses on who is ahead because this is a much more manageable question than how much is enough to deter and how various configurations of forces could contribute to terminating a war.

When we look at how the details of the military balance are measured, we also find the drunkard's search. People have a preference for absolutes; they examine what is most easily quantified and assume that what they have most information on is most important. In the 1930s, the British judged comparative air strength by counting the number of planes each side had. Sometimes they distinguished the total number from what they called "first-line" aircraft (i.e., planes of the most modern design), but even this degree of complexity was often dropped. This was not because they treated the whole question of the comparison casually. There were long debates over how to calculate first-line strength, but the attempts to push beyond this measure were few and desultory. Little attention was paid to the composition of the forces on both sides; quality of the aircraft was also omitted from most calculations. Likewise, quality of personnel was given short shrift. Thus, although the Germans suffered from the "teething problems" associated with a young and expanding force, questions of training, morale, and maintenance were generally ignored. (In assessing their naval strength before World War I, the British also relied exclusively on numerical comparisons, without considerations of quality. As the battles later showed, seamanship, strength of armor, accuracy of fire, ship design, and the effectiveness of shells were very important, and the German superiority in the latter two categories cost the British dearly.)

In addition, the stress on numbers of planes usually excluded consideration of production capacity, which was vital for each side's ability to sustain its force in wartime. A country might be stronger with a smaller standing air force supported by large and flexible production facilities than with a larger force that could not be maintained in the face of wartime losses. But this factor rarely entered into British thinking. Furthermore, by implicitly assuming that both sides were planning to use their airplanes in the same way, which they could have known was not correct, they were able to simplify their calculations further by concentrating on only one dimension, just as experimental subjects do (see, e.g., Slovic & MacPhillmay, 1974). The yardstick the British employed was distinguished only by the extent to which it facilitated comparisons and decisions. It gave the decision makers manageable simplicity, summary numbers that they could hold in their minds and use easily.

The same pattern is apparent today. Heavy reliance is placed on what are called *static indicators,* that is, the numbers and sizes of each side's missiles and warheads and the extent of the damage that each can do to the other. (The indicators of latter capability are themselves derived from highly oversimplified estimates.) Calculations are facilitated by comparing both sides on the same dimension, but the cost is that the comparisons do not make sense. The accuracies of each side's missiles or the quantity and quality of its bombers are significant, but direct comparisons of these factors are not. Each weapons system has to be evaluated in terms of its ability to carry out its mission; an improvement in, say, the quality of Soviet bombers may have important implications for U.S. air defense, but it says nothing about the utility of American bombers. But people, in fact, do compare the abilities of Soviet bombers with those of their American counterparts and talk of the danger of falling behind the Russians in bomber development.

Similarly, decision makers often worry about reports that Russian missiles are more accurate than American ones or that there are more Soviet warheads than those possessed by the U.S. These comparisons are simply irrelevant to any sensible conception of military power. For example, the capabilities of American missiles are at most indirectly affected by changes in the quantity and quality of their Soviet counterparts. More relevant are changes in the number and vulnerability of the things that the U.S. might seek to destroy in war. Thus, what is important is the match between the number and capability of American weapons, on the one hand, and the number and characteristics of Soviet targets, on the other. Of course, under certain possible circumstances, Soviet missiles would be shooting at American ones and vice versa, but the static indicators are only one component of the likely outcomes. The calculations that would be relevant are complex and would vary with the details of the situation (e.g., Who initiated the war? How many missiles were fired? What were each side's goals?). As a result, they would be very involved, admitting a great deal of uncertainty, and not easy to summarize.

In the same vein, analysts often compare the damage either side could do to the other in a war. Leaving aside the fact that such calculations are plagued by enormous and unacknowledged uncertainties, the comparison itself, although cognitively simple, is beside the point. A country would not go to war because it would suffer less than its adversary, nor would a country be deterred because it might be hurt more; the decision presumably would turn on the comparison between the expected value of the war and that of refraining from attacking. Only on some very extreme and implausible assumptions would the comparison of expected damage enter in. A state could easily think it would suffer less than its adversary and still opt for peace because this suffering outweighed the likely gains; it could also expect greater loss of life but still believe that war was a preferable policy. We continue to use the comparisons, however, because trying to determine how statesmen would estimate the likely costs and gains of a war is so difficult.

The assessments that are made also fit the drunkard's search in the omission of many factors whose importance is matched only by the difficulty of measuring them. Thus, long-term casualties and the environmental effects of nuclear war are generally ignored. But probably the most important omission is that of command, control, and communications. Although this subject has received increased attention in the past several years, few discussions of military power try to integrate it into the calculations. The survival and efficiency of these systems will have an enormous impact on the way any war could be fought and terminated. Most experts agree that a significant advantage on this dimension would more than outweigh a major disadvantage in numbers of missiles. But we know so little about how these systems would function in wartime that we do not try to enter them in our assessments.

In the same way, political factors that would influence the outcome of a less than total war are left out of most analyses of the strategic balance. We hardly need to be reminded that the victor in Vietnam was incomparably weaker than its adversary on all the standard indicators of military power. In any limited war, the stakes each side has in the conflict, the willingness of each to bear pain, the fears that the war will continue and grow even more destructive, and each side's perception of how the other stands on these dimensions will be crucial. But because these factors, which may be quite situation-specific, are so hard to estimate, they too are neglected for matters that are more amenable to calculation.

In summary, our analyses concentrate on the areas in which we have quite full information, and they down play possible interaction effects and the large number of unknowns that characterize complex weapons systems which have never been used. Indeed, there probably are crucial questions which we do not even know enough about to ask. For example, a few years ago no one would have listed the effects of dust and soot on the atmosphere as relevant. These uncertainties are so enormous that they present insurmountable obstacles to complete analysis. However, what is striking from the standpoint of common sense, but expected by the model of the drunkard's search, is that they are rarely given more than perfunctory treatment. In trying to assess the military balance, the only questions we ask are those that are relatively easy to answer.

Tendency to Avoid Trade-Offs.   The tendency for people to avoid value trade-offs (Jervis 1976) also can be partly explained by the need to minimize cognitive strain. When people think that a policy is better than the alternatives on one value dimension, they usually think it is also better on other, logically independent, value dimensions. For example, in the late 1950s and early 1960s, those people who thought that nuclear testing posed a great health hazard also thought that a test ban treaty was in the security interests of the United States. Those who disagreed on one point usually disagreed on the other. But the value dimensions of health and security are logically unrelated. Why didn't some people believe that although testing did cause cancer, it had to be continued for security reasons? Why didn't others believe that, although a treaty would be good politics, testing was harmless? The processes that produce this consistency are not entirely clear and probably include an important motivational component (i.e., people find it unpleasant to face the costs entailed by the policies they favor), but cognitive miserliness almost certainly plays a role. It would be very difficult to reduce the divergent impacts of alternative policies on very different values to a common yardstick. It is much simpler to decide on the basis of how the policy seems likely to affect one value and then to bring the other perceptions into line with the choice. Presumably, the value that drives the decision, and the perceptions which follow, will be one that is either highly salient or one on which the alternatives can be measured with relative ease, but much more work is needed on this subject.

CONTRIBUTIONS OF POLITICAL BEHAVIOR TO SOCIAL COGNITION

If one side of the coin is the contribution of the social cognition approach to an understanding of political behavior, the other side is the impact of our knowledge of political behavior on our understanding of how people process information, draw inferences, and reach conclusions. At this point, there is less to be said under this heading. Political science tends to import its theories from other fields rather than develop ones of its own that can be applied to other realms. This is not surprising: The study of politics is characterized by a concern with a set of problems, not with a common methodology or abstract theory. However, I am enough of a disciplinary chauvinist to think that the trade between political science and psychology is not inherently one-way. Political decision making can shed light on cognitive processes. Indeed, in a related vein, Greenwald (1980) has used the concept of totalitarianism derived from political science as a model for the workings of normal personalities.

Looking to the political arena, especially in foreign policy, is extremely productive because we can examine how highly articulate (although often deceptive) people come to grips with questions that are vital to them. The documentation is often extensive, including papers that present careful trains of reasoning, explicit considerations of the implications of various bits of evidence, and rebuttals to conflicting points of view. Furthermore, diaries and verbatim transcripts are common. Although nothing we have found so far would completely startle a cognitive psychologist, some intriguing tendencies have been found. First, the lack of value trade-offs, discussed earlier, is one of the most salient characteristics of political decision making. This is consistent with the social cognition approach, but it has not been stressed by psychologists or examined carefully in the laboratory.

A second finding from international political behavior modifies one aspect of social cognition. Theory and research on the attribution process indicate that observers generally explain a person's behavior in terms of his or her internal characteristics and down play the importance of the external situation. Statesmen adopt this inference pattern when judging the behavior of other states only when the other behaves in ways they do not desire. When the other state acts as the statesmen wish, they believe that they have exerted influence, that is, that the other's behavior is to be explained by the external situation including, in large measure, the state's policy (for further discussion, see Jervis, 1976).

A third modification or extension of social cognition is the role played by affect. When statesmen see a certain course of action as necessary, they are likely to come to believe that the policy can succeed even if a great deal of evidence indicates that it cannot (Cottam, 1977; Janis & Mann, 1977; Jervis, Lebow, and Stein, 1985c; Lebow, 1981). The resulting effects are quite important. Most strikingly, statesmen engage in belligerent activities that have little chance of success. An implication of this is that the attempt to deter, even if done well, is likely to fail if the target state is driven by particularly strong impulses to undertake the prohibited action. The reason for this is not a rational cost–benefit calculus, but rather the target state's inability to see the likely results of its policy.

SOCIAL COGNITION, HUMAN NATURE, AND POLITICS

This final topic may be the most important, but it is one on which I can say little. What does the social cognition approach indicate about the broadest questions of human nature and political behavior? How has it modified (and how will it modify) our sense of the political, the relationships between public and private realms, the interactions between culture and politics, and the way in which we construct our political worlds? At first glance, it seems that social cognition operates on much too small a scale to say anything about these questions. Indeed, this may be the case. But I am not sure. Any new conception of the way people think, even when it concentrates on fine-grained detail, often has much broader implications that come out only as people become increasingly familiar with the ideas.

We may need to adjust our ideas of how people can be expected to deal with politics to take account of what we are learning about the ways in which all of us process information. Our concepts of what is normative, both in the sense of how people should think about politics and in the sense of how they usually do so, may be affected. When major problems can be attributed to our cognitive processes (e.g., intelligence failures in foreign policy or the use of overly simple standards in judging political candidates), we may have to ask whether anything can be done to change the dominant pattern of thinking, and if it cannot be, how other aspects of our system can be altered to ameliorate the unfortunate effects.

It is hard to divorce many of our conceptions of politics from our ideas, often implicit, about human nature. Changes in our picture of how people think must have some impact on how we conceive of ourselves. Granted that such conceptions are usually ill-defined and often employed for pernicious purposes, still they cannot be dispensed with. Although the recent research on cognition stays far away from such amorphous topics, we should not be bound by this restriction. The way people are surely influences what politics is and can be. As Lane (this volume) reminds us, we should not lose sight of the most important questions about people and politics while we are working on questions of how people think about politics.

16

Argumentation and Decision Making in Government

Richard A. Smith
Department of Social Sciences
Carnegie-Mellon University

This volume explores the utility of ideas about cognition for understanding mass political behavior, especially the behavior of American voters. However, I was asked to comment on how ideas about cognitive processes might prove useful in a different domain, specifically, the behavior of decision makers within legislatures and bureaucracies. The particular behavior I consider is the development and presentation of arguments by the advocates of policy proposals. The central research problem is to develop generalizations about how argumentation contributes to the success of advocates in building support among decision makers for various policy alternatives. Such generalizations are crucial to understanding governmental decisions. A key feature of the decision process within government is the frequent attempts by advocates to adjust creatively their opportunities to win. Argumentation is one of the major ways to make these adjustments. Understanding its impact on governmental decisions, therefore, allows more precise generalizations about regularities in political outcomes. It also provides some of the statements necessary for the development of dynamic theories of governmental decision making (for extended expositions of these views, see Riker, 1984; R. A. Smith, 1984).

Current research has only begun to understand how the arguments that are offered by the advocates of different policy proposals influence the decisions of both individual decision makers and the institution to which they belong. During the consideration of policy options, advocates of particular alternatives repeatedly develop, present, and revise arguments that attempt to influence how decision makers think about the problem of choice among alternatives. The central feature of these presentations is that they emphasize, for a given policy alternative, only a subset of the actual consequences that might occur if the alternative was really chosen. The intent of the advocates is to try to stress those consequences that are most likely to lead a decision maker to choose the alternative most preferred by the advocates.

Presentations of arguments can be effective because of two, well-known, cognitive characteristics of decision makers. First, decision makers are boundedly rational (March, 1978; March & Simon, 1958; Simon, 1957). They rarely come close to understanding all the complexities of the choices they are asked to make. Rather, they develop for each alternative under consideration partial representations or interpretations of the consequences that might occur if the alternative was actually chosen. Second, decision makers develop their interpretations after only a limited search (Simon, 1957). The personal goals of decision makers are typically expressed in the form of aspiration levels. Decision makers process information and develop interpretations of the consequences of different positions on an alternative until they believe a particular position will yield some acceptable level of accomplishment of their personal goals. Other positions may better achieve their particular mix of goals, but because of time and cognitive constraints, decision makers are satisfied with a position that appears good enough.

Because these interpretations are only partial representations and because they are the result of limited search, opportunities exist for advocates to influence the policy preferences and, hence, the decisions of decision makers. By carefully crafting their arguments, advocates can shape and perhaps alter the interpretations that decision makers develop, thereby structuring the ways in which they think about the policy alternatives that confront them. As an example, consider an incident reported by Eric Redman involving the Senate's consideration of an amendment offered by Senator Warren G. Magnuson of Washington to block a proposed shipment of nerve gas from Okinawa through the Pacific northwest. The amendment appears destined for defeat. Redman (1973) writes:

> I prepared another memorandum cataloging the arguments he [Magnuson] had marshalled against the shipment and took it to him at his desk on the Senate Floor. He surveyed the memo cursorily, then handed it back with annoyed "No, no, no!" Bewildered, I retreated to the staff couch and waited to hear what argument he intended to use instead of familiar ones of possible sabotage, dangerous sections of track along the proposed route, and populations that would have to be evacuated as a precaution against leakage. When the time came, he took a wholly novel and ingenious approach. The issue he told his colleagues, was not one of the people versus the Pentagon, as the news media seemed to assume. Instead, it was another case of the President versus the Senate. The Senator from West Virginia (Robert C. Byrd) had

recently offered a resolution, which the Senate had passed, stating that the Senate expected the President to keep it informed throughout the treaty negotiations with the Japanese government on the subject of Okinawa. The President's sudden decision to move the nerve gas off Okinawa must reflect some aspect of those treaty negotiations, Magnuson insisted—and the Senate had not yet been informed of, much less consented to, any such agreement. To allow the nerve gas shipment under such circumstances, he asserted, would be to abandon the Byrd resolution and to abdicate the Senate's rightful role in treaty-making generally. The President, Magnuson said, might get the idea that he could ignore the Senate and its Constitutional prerogatives whenever he wished. Jolted by this reasoning, the Senator from West Virginia and his Southern colleagues—friends of the Pentagon almost to a man, but vigilant guardians of the Senate's Constitutional responsibilities—voted down the line with Magnuson. The amendment, which had been doomed a few minutes earlier, passed overwhelmingly. (pp. 206–207)

Magnuson's arguments appear to have been influential because they identified a set of consequences previously overlooked by senators. Magnuson provided no new information. The senators all knew about the Byrd resolution; they all knew about the President's decision. What they apparently did not perceive, however, was the connection between the pieces of information. By making the connection, Magnuson stimulated the construction by southern Democratic senators of a President versus the Senate interpretation—one that apparently dominated their prior interpretations (for other examples, see Riker, 1983, 1984; R. A. Smith, 1980).

Unfortunately for theories about politics, the conditions under which advocates may influence interpretations are only beginning to be specified (for an extended example, see R. A. Smith, 1984). The absence of such knowledge prevents the development of explanations and predictions about how regularities in political outcomes depend on argumentation. What is needed in large part is the further elaboration of the cognitive processes involved in the formation and change of interpretations. More specifically, the research needs to focus on how individual decision makers notice, interpret, organize, and recall arguments and interpretations. Consider some of the central questions:

1. To what extent do decision makers develop new interpretations for each policy decision they make? To what extent do the interpretations they developed for previous decisions regarding related policy questions influence the construction of their current interpretations?

2. Are the policy decisions of decision makers repeatedly based on variants of a few well-established interpretations? Or are the interpretations policy-specific?

3. After decision makers have developed their initial interpretations,

how do those interpretations influence what arguments they notice and process? Under what conditions do decision makers pay attention to new arguments?

4. How are interpretations revised? Is the revision piecemeal? Or is there a wholesale replacement of the old interpretation with the new one suggested by the arguments of the advocate? Or under some conditions is the revision piecemeal and under other conditions wholesale? What are the conditions?

5. In what ways do the structures and procedures of the institutions in which the decisions are made influence the ways in which interpretations are constructed and revised? How do institutional factors interact with cognitive processes?

Some of the current research in social cognition, cognitive psychology, and behavioral decision theory may be helpful in addressing these questions, especially the first four questions. The research on schemata (e.g., Fiske & Taylor, 1984), problem representations (e.g., Hayes, 1981), and decision frames (e.g., Tversky & Kahneman, 1981) seems especially relevant. However, at present, applications of this work to institutional decision making are nascent. For further progress to be made, both psychologists and political scientists need to redirect their work. Psychologists need to focus their research more directly on questions concerning political phenomena, such as argumentation and interpretation. Political scientists need to utilize far more extensively than they have to date the research that is already available about cognitive processes.

This research is likely to provide far more insight into the relationship between argumentation and decision making than the less cognitively oriented perspectives that are now popular in political science. This is particularly true of the more stylized views of rational decision making, the most common of which are variants of expected utility maximization models (for a review of this literature, see Ordeshook & Shepsle, 1982). These models typically take a static view of decision making. The set of alternatives is usually assumed to be fixed; the task of defining the consequences of various alternatives is assumed to be nonproblematic; and the preferences of decision makers over the alternatives are assumed to be stable. As a result, such models are not capable of providing much understanding of the role of argumentation in decision making. Cognitively richer models are needed. Perhaps future volumes on political cognition will produce them.

17

The Relevance of Social Cognition for the Study of Elites in Political Institutions, or Why It Isn't Enough to Understand What Goes on in Their Heads

Paul A. Anderson
Department of Social Sciences
Carnegie-Mellon University

In his paper in this volume, Reid Hastie made an important point justifying the use of concepts like schema in the study of political cognition: The primary reason for political scientists to use a concept like schema is that it is the best way psychologists have developed for talking about what goes on in people's heads. There is a parallel point, which also deserves emphasis: What goes on in people's heads is only part of what it takes to understand the actions of political institutions. The basic point is a simple one. Only some political phenomena are cognitive phenomena, and only some political questions demand answers in terms of what goes on in people's heads.

One of the distinguishing characteristics of the study of politics is a concern with collective outcomes, and there is little reason to suppose that individual preferences add up to collective outcomes in any straightforward way. Arrow's theorem on the impossibility of a social welfare function (a device that produces an ordinal ranking of alternatives) demonstrates the general impossibility of any general simple summation procedure, and the impossibility of predicting the winner of a U.S. presidential election given only the number of votes cast for each candidate is a practical demonstration of the problem. Political institutions and what goes on inside them get in the way of any simple summation of individual preferences.

What, then, is the relevance of social cognition for understanding the actions of political institutions? To begin, it is clear that understanding what goes on inside people's heads is not generally sufficient to explain how those individual cognitions will combine to produce institutional action. Under very special circumstances, individual cognition directly produces institutional action: pure legislative decision process with independent

341

decision makers and explicit formal preference aggregation procedures, and pure dictator or command decision processes with a single central decision maker with the authority to commit the institution to action. But most decisions in most political institutions deviate from these two pure types in significant respects: (a) only rarely is institutional action the result of a command decision; (b) individuals are not independent decision makers; (c) the menu of alternatives is ambiguous; (d) preference aggregation procedures are rarely formal or explicit.

The image of the President commanding the full might and power of the government is a myth. The great majority of actions by the government take place without the direct knowledge or participation of the President, and when the President does become involved, he rarely is in a position to make command decisions on major policy issues. Government action is not the action of a single powerful commander but the product of an array of committees, groups, and large organizations. Although knowing what happens in people's heads is important in understanding their individual behavior, understanding the behavior of large institutions requires understanding the institutional context of decision making.

Decisions in institutions are public acts: They are frequently made by groups or committees; they must be communicated to others if they are to be effective; and invariably, they are accompanied by justificatory arguments. If individuals did not care what others thought of them or what signals their arguments or actions sent to others in the institution, then the fact that decisions are public would be less important. But individuals do care about what others think, and as a result, decisions in organizations are social acts influenced by social comparison processes and efforts at self-presentation. Decision making in political institutions cannot be understood without considering these social processes.

Because the world of politics and policy making is fundamentally ambiguous, a considerable part of the social process of decision making is consumed by efforts to define the problem and identify the alternatives. Even in a crisis situation like the Cuban missile crisis of 1962, there was considerable ambiguity about the nature of the problem and the available alternatives. Some argued that the missiles posed no direct military threat to the United States; others argued that Cuba rather than the Soviet Union was the appropriate target for U.S. pressure, and the set of alternatives changed from one day to the next. Understanding the ultimate institutional action requires understanding how the problem and the alternatives were represented, and understanding how individuals represent the problem situation requires examining the social process that defines the collective choice problem.

Understanding the preferences of every individual with respect to a particular policy issue isn't enough to understand institutional action because institutional action is not the product of a formal and explicit preference aggregation procedure. In a study of decision making in the Swiss Free Democratic party, for example, Steiner and Dorff (1980) found that only 12% of the decision conflicts were resolved by explicit majority vote. Of the decision situations in which there was public conflict in the group, 30% resulted in decisions not to decide, 21% resulted in amicable agreement where the contending parties explicitly agreed to accept a particular course of action, and 37% of the disagreements were resolved through a group member asserting a "sense of the meeting," which was not disputed by the contending parties. This later conflict resolution style differs from amicable agreement in that the contending parties do not make a public signal of their capitulation; they simply refrain from objecting to the outcome. Whether this decision-making process is the most frequent in all political institutions is not the critical issue. The point is that the process is fluid and implicit and that to understand the collective outcome requires understanding how the preferences of the individual decision makers are aggregated.

These four characteristics of decision making in political institutions suggest that political scientists need to pay as much attention to social psychology as they do to cognitive psychology in understanding individual behavior in political institutions. But beyond the fact that decision making is a social process, the characteristics suggest something of how insights from both social and cognitive psychology can be used to develop theories of the action of political institutions.

It appears unlikely that we will ever be in a position to take the results of theories of individual cognition and predict collective outcomes. Those who adopt a public choice perspective can imagine performing the task only because they assume away all of the psychologically (and politically) interesting phenomena: Preferences are assumed to be known and stable, and alternatives are assumed to be fixed and unambiguous. But if preferences are formed and manipulated through social interaction and if alternatives are ambiguous and open to diverging interpretations, then predicting the collective outcome presupposes well-developed theories that can predict the preferences over the effective set of alternatives for every relevant actor. We might agree there is no reason in principle why that task cannot be performed, but the data requirements and the complexity of the problem make such a strategy computationally infeasible. As Herbert Simon (1981) wrote, "in the face of complexity an in-principle reductionist may be at the same time a pragmatic holist" (p. 195).

But even a pragmatic holist can see ways that individual-level theories can usefully inform theories of collective action. The computational complexity of predicting collective outcomes can partially be overcome by adopting a distributional approach to prediction. If the data and computational requirements of full prediction make the task infeasible, it may still be possible to use individual-level theories to predict the expected frequency distribution of collective outcomes. Such a distributional theory would not make point predictions or attempt to identify the public choice theorist's equilibrium outcome, but would instead identify the likelihood over the range of possible outcomes. Although a distributional theory is weaker than a theory that predicts exact outcomes, its weakness must be judged against the infeasibility of a stronger theory.

A second approach to the problem is to focus on the implications of the limited information-processing abilities of individuals and the resulting biases and errors in individual choice behavior. Although individuals "satisfice because they have not the wits to maximize" (Simon, 1976, p. xxviii), neither are they blithering idiots. Individuals are intendedly rational, goal-directed beings who do the best with what they have. But precisely because they have limited cognitive capacity, the strategies they adopt in the face of decision complexity will be biased and error-prone. The second theory-building strategy is to attempt to exploit these systematic biases to predict the class of errors and failures that a collection of limited information processors is likely to produce. Like the distributional theory, this sort of theory will generate probability distributions over likely errors and failures, and although this is weaker than a strongly predictive theory, it is exactly the sort of theory which would be extremely useful in the design of institutions.

In summary, although there are many interesting and important phenomena in political institutions that can be illuminated with a cognitive perspective, not all political phenomena are cognitive phenomena. Understanding the action of political institutions requires an understanding of the social and institutional dynamics of the setting as well as the cognitive processes of individual decision makers. And although there is little reason to believe that individual preferences sum to collective outcomes in any straightforward way, there are reasons to believe that a cognitive perspective can provide insights that can inform a theory of the action of political institutions.

V CONCLUSION

18

Social Cognition and Political Cognition: The Past, the Present, and the Future

Richard R. Lau
Department of Social Sciences
Carnegie-Mellon University

David O. Sears
Department of Psychology
University of California, Los Angeles

In reviewing the different papers collected in this volume, we realized the extent to which most of them rely on the knowledge accumulated over the past decade in the area that has come to be known as social cognition. Even the review chapters by Hastie, by Fiske, and by Fischer and Johnson assume a good bit of prior knowledge. Our colleagues Susan Fiske and Shelley Taylor have recently published an excellent review of social cognition (1984), to which we point any readers seeking an extensive survey of the relevant literature. We can only sketch out the bare bones of such a review, focusing on the concept that has appeared more frequently than any other in the papers reported here, that of a cognitive schema. We begin by trying to place the current information-processing focus of social psychology in historical perspective.

LIMITATIONS OF SOCIAL AND POLITICAL COGNITION[1]

Social psychology has in recent decades been dominated by three general views of thought processes, depicting humans successively as consistency

[1]Surprisingly similar discussions were provided in the original papers presented at the symposium by Conover and Feldman, Hamill and Lodge, and Lau. To eliminate some redundancy, those discussions were removed from all three papers for the versions published here. The section that follows relies most heavily on Lau's original paper, but borrows freely from the other two papers to improve the arguments. Conover, Feldman, Hamill, and Lodge all share credit for whatever strengths are found in the following account. Note also a related discussion by Bennett (1982).

seekers, naive scientists, and cognitive misers (Taylor, 1981). The consistency-seeker view has its origins in field theory (Lewin, 1939, 1951), Gestalt theory (Heider, 1946), and research on attitude change conducted during World War II (e.g., Hovland, Lumsdaine, & Sheffield, 1949). Several related theories advanced during this time suggest that people find perceived inconsistencies (e.g., among their attitudes or between their attitudes and their behavior) to be unpleasant (Festinger, 1957; Heider, 1958). People are motivated by this unpleasantness to reduce the inconsistency, usually by revising the belief element (e.g., an attitude) that is easiest to change. So, if a voter perceives the candidate she supported in the previous election as adopting a new issue position with which she disagrees, the voter will be motivated to change some belief element to reduce the inconsistency. She could change her own stand on the issue, change her opinion of the candidate, or change her perception of the candidate's position on the issue. As noted in the introduction to this volume, the social psychological or Michigan approach to voting behavior (Campbell, Converse, Miller, & Stokes, 1960) was rooted initially in a very similar Lewinian view of human decision making, though not expressly invoking any cognitive consistency theory. Later research following that model was based more explicitly upon such consistency theories, however (see the review by Sears, 1969). Although consistency theories dominated social psychology for some time (see Abelson et al., 1968, for a comprehensive review), the fact that people apparently can tolerate a great deal of inconsistency in their daily lives underscored the need for a broader approach (Kiesler, Collins, & Miller, 1969).

The second general approach adopted by social psychologists views people as rational problem solvers. This approach came in numerous versions. Early renditions of attribution theory tested the possibility that people logically deduce the causes of their own and others' behavior (Jones & Davis, 1965; Kelley, 1967, 1971a, 1971b; see Jones et al., 1971, for a review). According to this view, people consider information in a rational, scientific manner and attribute causality to that entity with which an outcome covaries. Thus, if a voter notices that having a Republican President regularly covaries with being laid-off from his job, he may come to attribute his unemployment to Republican economic policies and presumably grow to dislike Republicans. Other decision-making paradigms, such as expectancy-value theory (Feather & Newton, 1982) or the theory of reasoned action (Ajzen & Fishbein, 1980), describe people as making decisions on quite logical bases. Most errors and biases in the rational decision process were presumed to come from a lack of information or the intrusion of motivational factors, not from flaws in the thinking process itself. Similarly, the "economic" approaches to voting behavior now popular in political science (e.g., Davis, Hinich, & Ordeshook, 1970; Downs,

1957a; Fiorina, 1981; M. J. Shapiro, 1969) are also based on "rational" models of human behavior. People are assumed to weigh the potential costs and gains associated with any behavior (e.g., voting) before deciding how to act. The problem with these normative, rational approaches, in the view of other psychologists, is that people are rarely so careful and calculating in their thought processes. Even when information is plentiful and there is no reason to suspect motivational biases, there are so many errors and inconsistencies in human cognition that these normative attribution theories may not be very precise descriptions of how people usually make decisions. Information processing is itself normally flawed in certain predictable ways (see Nisbett & Ross, 1980).

These shortcomings in human information processing have led to a third view of thinking and perceiving, that of people as cognitive misers. This view builds on the growing evidence from cognitive psychology and social cognition research mentioned throughout this volume (e.g., J. R. Anderson, 1983; Fiske & Taylor, 1984). People have well-defined cognitive limits. Their span of active memory is small (Simon, 1979b), and their attention to various aspects of their environment is narrowly focused (Norman, 1976). As a result, their processing of the information environment can be quite selective.

A major determinant of this selectivity is the structure of previously stored knowledge about the world. These preexisting knowledge structures have been called different things by different researchers. Throughout most of this book, the authors generally use the term *schemata* (Fiske & Linville, 1980; Rumelhart & Ortony, 1977; Taylor & Crocker, 1981). A schema is a hierarchical organization of knowledge in a particular domain, which includes a category label, generic descriptions of the stimulus domain, particular instances of it, and interconnections among these. For example, a politician schema could include general information about all politicians (they are elected; they are usually male; they are middle-aged or older; they have opinions on defense spending), higher level organizing categories (liberal politicians; foreign politicians; local politicians), more specific (lower level) examples of politicians (Ted Kennedy, Margaret Thatcher, Edward Koch), and a specification of the relationships of the various attributes of the schema (Kennedy is a liberal, is opposed to increased defense spending).

Several different classes of schemata have been identified, two of which are important here. *Role schemata* concentrate on broad social groupings such as sex, race, or occupation. A politician schema is an example of a role schema. *Person schemata* organize knowledge about individuals. One could have a schema for Ronald Reagan which includes knowledge that he is President, that he is from California, that he is old, that he favors the MX missile, that he wants prayer in school, and so forth. The schema is central and organizes the individual elements. Figure 18.1 illustrates what a person schema for Ronald Reagan might look like. Reagan is a specific instance of various role schemata such as politician, actor, and older person, and he also could be the subject of an elaborate person schema. The figure illustrates the Reagan instantiation of a politician schema, and it also includes connections to a conservative Republican schema. An individual might have schemata for ranchers or former actors or older persons, but for simplicity these are not depicted. The figure also includes the possibility (denoted by the question mark) that affect is associated with each schema. If a person has a well-developed schema for Reagan, or for politicians, or for conservative Republicans, then some positive or negative affect may be immediately available when these schemata are brought to mind. Thus, schemata organize an individual's knowledge, but that same knowledge can be organized in many different ways.

Sometimes the term *implicit personality theory* is used to describe widely shared generic assumptions about what traits "go together" (Bruner & Taiguri, 1954). For example, if we learn that a person is warm, we would also expect (without any additional information) that person to be kind and perhaps generous. This idea is quite similar to that of schemata about various personality types. Kinder's chapter in this volume could be discussed in these terms, although he does not use either the label "person schema" or "implicit personality theory" in his discussion.

Schemata serve two important functions. First, they guide the processing and storage of incoming information. People are not passive recorders of

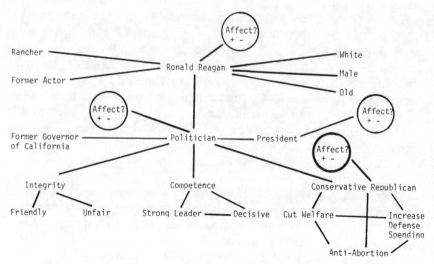

FIG. 18.1   Possible person schema for Ronald Reagan.

social action, accurately storing some objective trace of environmental stimuli. Instead, people actively process and interpret incoming information according to their preexisting knowledge structures—their schemata. For example, Zadny and Gerard (1974) showed subjects a video tape of two men walking around a friend's apartment. Subjects had been told either that the two men were planning to burglarize the apartment or that they had heard of a drug bust and were searching for any incriminating evidence in their friend's apartment. When later asked to recall as many things in the apartment as they could, subjects in the burglary condition had a bias toward remembering valuable items in the apartment, whereas subjects in the drug-bust condition were biased toward remembering drug-related paraphernalia.[2] Hence, the simple manipulation shifted the schema that was applied to the viewing of the video tape, thereby affecting what type of information was processed and stored in memory.

How might schematic processing affect political perception? Schemata determine what types of information are relevant, and therefore what information is noticed, stored, and consequently available for later recall and judgment. That a certain politician frequently gives speeches to the National Rifle Association is politically relevant information, which means that it might be part of many people's schema for that politician, and may therefore be processed and potentially recalled at some later date. Most observers would probably not process the fact that this same politician has brown eyes, however, because eye color is probably not part of most people's politician schemata. This same point becomes crucially important when one considers the possibility (discussed later) of individual differences in the structure of political schemata (i.e., that the same information is processed and stored by one individual and ignored by another).

The second major function of schemata is guiding the recall and interpretation of information in memory. Of course, recall is partially a function of the earlier processes of attention and interpretation. If information is irrelevant to the schema being applied (a politician has brown eyes), it will probably not be processed and stored. The other side of the coin is that information which is not only relevant to the schema but consistent with it (a liberal politician who opposes increased defense spending) will be very easily recalled.

One should explicitly distinguish between schema-inconsistent and schema-irrelevant information. Schema-inconsistent information is knowledge of a

---

[2]This bias is generally exaggerated when subjects receive the schema label before seeing the video tape, rather than after seeing it (Howard & Rothbart, 1980; Rothbart, Evans, & Fulero, 1979; Wyer, Srull, Gordon, & Hartwick, 1982; Zadny & Gerard, 1974).

trait or dimension that is part of a schema, but the particular value which that trait or dimension takes is contrary to the prototypic case. The fact that a particular back-room politician is honest is relevant to, but inconsistent with, the prototype of back-room politicians in general. On the other hand, the knowledge that he or she was born in April is neither consistent nor inconsistent with the schema, but simply irrelevant to it. As we see later, there are situations (or levels of schema development) in which both schema-consistent and schema-inconsistent information have an advantage in recall (Hastie & Kumar, 1979). Schema-irrelevant material, however, always has a disadvantage in terms of recall.

Perhaps more important, recall of schematically relevant material is often *reconstructive*. That is, recall of some specific instance of a schema is often guided by the generic principles of the schema rather than by the particulars of that specific instance (Rothbart, Evans, & Fulero, 1979; Snyder & Uranowitz, 1978). For example, once a person has been categorized as having a particular trait or as fitting into a particular category, people will falsely recognize traits which are prototypically associated with that trait or category because schemata provide "default values" to fill in the blanks (Minsky, 1975). If a politician is described as having just advanced to high office, he may be falsely remembered as being ambitious; if a person is categorized as a back-room politician, he may be falsely remembered as being corrupt, even if in each instance no information about the ambitiousness or honesty of the individual in question is available. Similarly, inferences about future behavior or probable past behavior will be made with considerable confidence once a person has been categorized into a particular schema.

In sum, the processing of schematically relevant material is often theory (or schema) driven rather than data driven. This is sometimes referred to as top down processing as opposed to bottom up processing. In similar vein, Fiske (this volume) contrasts schema-based processing with piecemeal processing.

Expert–Novice Differences

Thus far, we have discussed schemata in terms of knowledge structures about well-known social groups or categories of people. And this is certainly the thrust of most social cognition research. But having established that schemata often involve such consensual, stereotypic information, people nevertheless differ in how well their schemata are developed or in how easily they are activated (Fiske, Kinder, & Larter 1983; Lau, Coulam, & Sears, 1983; Lau & Erber, 1985; Lodge & Hamill, 1983). Experts in any field should have more elaborate, more hierarchically structured, and more easily activated schemata than novices in that field. Several researchers have applied this idea to social and political issues. For example, Linville (1982; Linville & Jones, 1980) has shown that people have more complex schemata about in-group members (i.e., members of their own group) than about out-group members; this greater complexity led to less extreme evaluations of the in-group than the out-group. Similarly, Fiske et al. (1983) found that people who were highly involved in politics (experts) processed information about a cued schema (about a communistic or democratic third world country) in a less simplistic, mechanical way than did people who were not highly involved in politics (novices). Experts remembered schema-consistent and schema-inconsistent information equally well and had more balanced predictions about the country's future, whereas novices remembered chiefly schema-consistent information and had more extreme prognoses for the country described. Lau et al. (1983) looked at expert-novice differences in attitudes toward Massachusetts' Proposition 2½. They found that the beliefs of experts were more tightly constrained and more hierarchically organized than those of novices, were less susceptible to selective misperception, and were more deeply embedded in social background characteristics and past political socialization (see Lau & Erber, 1985, for a review of expert–novice differences in politics).

It is instructive to think of the development of expertise in any area as an outcome of a sequential process of schema development or schema elaboration. Taylor and Winkler (1980) suggest that such development goes through four distinguishable stages. The schemata of rank novices involve only very rudimentary knowledge and specific, concrete examples of a general concept (e.g., a liberal is someone like Ted Kennedy; a conservative is like Barry Goldwater). There are very few interconnections (e.g., liberals and conservatives are orthogonal, not opposite). Such simple conceptual knowledge hardly fits our definition of schema because there is little or no hierarchy or structure.

Frequently, these specific examples are quickly extended to represent the general case. As people gain somewhat more expertise or gather more experience with the concept, they move into the second or stereotypic phase of schema development. Here the most representative attributes of a concept are known (e.g., liberals are for big government and social welfare; conservatives favor a strong military and individual initiative). More individual examples of the concept have been learned and are linked to it. Analogous to the earliest stage of schema development, the representative attributes are blindly assumed to characterize all specific examples of the concept. Hence, any new liberal or conservative is automatically assumed to hold the representative attributes of that type. Moreover, there is a bias for schema-consistent, as opposed to schema-inconsistent, information during the processing or reception of new information. That is, information that some specific liberal favors a larger military budget would not be processed.

As people progress toward the third stage of relative expertise (and most people never reach this stage of development in most areas of knowledge), they are much more aware of incongruities in new information or inconsistencies between data and a schema. For instance, only a relative expert would have noticed that Ronald Reagan (conservative, strong military) opposed draft registration in 1980. Such relative experts are somewhat more cautious in applying general attributes of a schema to specific examples. But these general attributes, when they are invoked, are applied more or less simultaneously as a group, whereas novices tend to deal with only one or two attributes at a time.[3] Relative experts not only have more structure or interrelations among the elements of their schemata, but they also undoubtedly have more elements, or more knowledge or concepts, associated with their schemata. For example, Lau and Erber (1985) found that political experts typically utilized their closeness to a candidate on multiple issues in forming evaluations of the candidate, whereas political novices utilized one issue at most in their impression formation.[4]

In the final stage of schema development, which we might call true expertise, processing becomes automatic. Many elements of the schema are so tightly linked internally that they become *unitized* (Hayes-Roth, 1977) and act as chunks. The individual elements of the schema do not enter awareness. Hence, in some cases, it would take absolute experts longer to process and make judgments on the basis of schema-inconsistent information, compared to relative experts, because the individual elements of the schema would have to be brought into active awareness.

This discussion of schema development of course simplifies reality. There are other factors that influence response time. For example, in some instances, experts may be motivated by self-presentational concerns to respond very rapidly and, in other cases, to respond very accurately (irrespective of time). And some types of expertise (e.g., a wine taster) require very fine discriminations for which large chunks of information would not be very useful. It is of course very difficult to study this process directly in any area as complex as politics because a longitudinal data set with quite elaborate measurement is required. But it is possible to make reasonable estimates of the process by comparing the schemata of people at different levels of expertise at any given time. All things being equal, political novices (rank and stereotypic) should differ from political experts (relative and absolute) in that: (a) experts should be faster than novices in

---

[3]These three stages have parallels in the learning of grammar rules by children (Brown, 1973) and in Schank and Abelson's (1977) work on the development of "scripts," which are in essence behavioral schemata.

[4]On the other hand, experts and novices alike utilized party identification, candidate traits, and feelings in the candidate evaluation process.

processing schema-relevant information, at least information which is consistent with the schema; (b) experts will be more aware than novices of incongruities between new data and an existing schema; (c) experts will less readily make "false recognitions" of schema-consistent information, compared to novices; (d) the schemata of experts will include more elements, and more tightly constrained elements, than those of novices. Lodge and Hamill (1983) provide confirmatory evidence for most of these hypotheses.

Idiosyncratic Schemata

An alternative approach to individual differences in social schemata looks for evidence of different types of schemata rather than differential expertise in the use of a consensually held schema. A well-known example of this type of schema difference is Hazel Markus' (1977) research on self-schemata. Markus has suggested that people differ in the content of their self-schemata. For example, some people think of themselves as being particularly independent or dependent, whereas others think of themselves as being introverted or extroverted. Such schematic differences are reflected (a) in how quickly different types of information about the self are processed and (b) in resistance to evidence about the self counter to the schema. Similarly, Markus, Crane, Bernstein, and Siladi (1982) have examined masculine, feminine, and androgynous self-schemata. Conover and Feldman's (1984) previous work with political schemata (on which their chapter in this volume builds) has also looked for individual differences in the structuring of political beliefs. Lau's chapter in this volume is another example of this general approach. The point is that people differ both in how well-developed their schemata are and in what sort of schemata they hold. Thus, certain information will be highly relevant to some people's schemata (and therefore easily processed, stored, and later recalled) and at the same time totally irrelevant to other people's schemata (and therefore not processed or remembered).

A NOTE ON TERMINOLOGY
AND COMMENTS ON THE PRESENT STATE
OF POLITICAL COGNITION RESEARCH

None of the papers in this volume attempts to provide a full-blown cognitive perspective on the vote choice; that step is still in the future, after much more about the dynamics of political cognition is learned. The empirical papers reported herein have more modest aims: examining political schemata per se (Hamill & Lodge; Lau; Sears, Huddy, & Schaffer); studying candidate (Kinder; Tyler), issue (Conover & Feldman), and party (A. Miller) perceptions; and studying emotional appeals (Abelson). What these papers have in common is an active awareness of cognitive variables in political information processing. They all provide new perspectives on issues that have long been studied by political behavior researchers.

Perhaps the most central concept in this collection is the notion of a schema, and it most likely will be the one to create the most disagreement. Application of this concept to political behavior data has been made in several quite different ways in the papers presented in this volume, and it might be advisable to make these differences explicit. All the papers are agreed in conceptualizing a schema as a knowledge structure. And all would concur that people with a schema can be called schematic and engage in the schematic processing of relevant information, whereas those without a schema can be described as aschematic. But when it comes to describing what knowledge is embodied in that structure and how it is to be measured, very major differences of approach emerge.

One general approach has been to identify individual differences in schematic thinking about standard political matters. Hence, Hamill and Lodge classify respondents as either ideological sophisticates, who think schematically about how conventional, liberal, or conservative ideologies relate to leaders, groups, and issues, or as individuals without such ideological schemata. They view such ideological schemata as being determined by a combination of more general cognitive ability with extensive political experience and as having the now familiar consequences of schematic thinking upon recognition, memory, and so forth. Conover and Feldman take a very similar approach. Some people have policy-oriented self-schemata and/or partisan schemata about the parties' issue positions, but others do not. Conover and Feldman contend that people with such schemata are more likely to use ideology to make inferences about ambiguous or complex political issues, as would be expected from the "gap-filling" function of schemata that has often been identified (see Taylor & Crocker, 1981).

Lau also takes an individual difference approach, separating respondents into those who process schematically and those who do not. But instead of essentially comparing sophisticates with nonsophisticates, as the prior two papers do, he compares people who have differing foci of attention. In his view, some people process politics in terms of candidates, some in terms of issues, and others in terms of groups. Thus, some people have a candidate schema, some an issue schema, some a group schema, some have a mixture, and others have none of these. The effect of having a schema is to focus one's attention upon a particular domain of politics. Hence, those with a candidate schema are likely to look for and process information primarily about candidates and so on. In this form, the schema serves more as a lens that focuses attention, and less as an indicator of superior information, structure, and so forth.

Sears, Huddy, and Schaffer pursue the presence or absence of schemata from a different vantage point. First, they are concerned with which attitude objects attract widespread schematic thinking in the general public and which ones do not, rather than with individual differences among citizens in schematic thinking about a given attitude object. Second, they assess the presence or absence of schematic thinking inferentially, rather than measuring schemata directly. Their analysis rests on the concept of schematic thinking because they are interested in knowing when people apply predispositions to forming policy positions. That is, when do people associate the symbols of a particular policy issue, such as affirmative action for women, to general predispositions, such as general equality values? They assert that affective consistency will result when the symbols to which both predisposition and issue refer are similar, whether or not widespread linking schemata exist in the general public. They suggest that high levels of information will enhance consistency, particularly when the two attitude objects have little manifest similarity and people are able to invoke underlying schemata. Hence, higher levels of information will produce more consistent attitudes toward dissimilar objects when the people have underlying schemata that link the two.

Miller brings a cognitive approach to the broad political question he has raised in other contexts: Why has partisanship been declining in the United States in the past 2 decades? He offers several alternative explanations: that information about partisan matters has been declining, that the connection between party and candidate is no longer seen as clearly as it once was, or that higher inferences are being made (e.g., that the parties do not differ much in policy or in performance). He finds the most promise in an approach that assumes active information processing on the part of the voter. His discussion does not explicitly evoke the notion of a schema, but he employs kindred concepts and locates the difficulty in the electorate squarely in the area of the active use of higher level inferences.

As our very brief review of the social cognition literature indicates, all of these approaches are quite direct applications of some generally agreed upon component of what social schemata are or what they can do, although each focuses on a somewhat different aspect. These differences spring not from ambiguity in the schema concept or from lack of precision in any of these authors' uses of the term, although these are issues that cannot be ignored. Instead, these differences are indicative of the breadth of applications of social cognition ideas in political behavior.

We could easily include Kinder's and Tyler's chapters in this discussion because their ideas fit readily within a political cognition framework, even though they do not write specifically about information processing. For example, Kinder could have discussed the role schemata voters have for Presidents or politicians, which they apply to specific candidates during an election. A politician by default might be expected to be competent, to have strong leadership ability, to have a great deal of empathy for constituents (if not the downtrodden more generally), and to have sterling integrity. Tyler would include some default values for justice and fairness. These default values are assumed to hold true for any particular politician unless specific information to the contrary about that politician is available. Information that is inconsistent with the schema (Kennedy's integrity, Reagan's favoritism) would especially be noticed and weigh heavily in the candidate evaluation process.

All of these applications are at the level of individual decision making in the mass public. These ideas could be readily extended to decision making by individual members of elites, as Jervis and Smith note. We should be careful to emphasize that much of political science deals with problems at a more aggregate level, however, and cognitive psychology and/or social cognition may be less valuable at that level. This is exactly Anderson's point. Individual perception is the core phenomenon that this book, and cognitive psychology more generally, addresses.

But even at the individual level, the more familiar concepts of attitudes and stereotypes may often suffice. This possibility was raised most strongly by Michael Ross during the Carnegie-Mellon Symposium. On the other hand, most areas of scientific research must periodically undergo a careful rethinking of basic premises and assumptions. As Warren Miller noted, the "political predispositions" that played such a large role in *The Voter Decides* (Campbell, Gurin, & Miller, 1954) and *The American Voter* (Campbell et al., 1960) would now be called, in the context of this book, political schemata. In these pioneering works, only the affective manifestations of these predispositions were measured in detail. The papers presented in this volume clearly indicate that both the affective and perceptual manifestations of these predispositions can be measured more directly. The difference is that cognitive theories not available during the 1950s now guide current operationalizations of political schemata. How future research will modify the conclusions of these classic studies of political behavior research as political predispositions (or political schemata) are measured more precisely can only be a topic of speculation. At the very least, an active awareness of the current state of knowledge about human cognitive processes will lead to cognitively more realistic models of candidate perception or political decision making. And hopefully, political behavior researchers will be led to new insights into some of our old problems, and perhaps to entirely new problems, by utilizing a political cognition approach.

THE FUTURE OF POLITICAL COGNITION:
A RESEARCH AGENDA

Affect

Traditional voting theories (e.g., *The American Voter*) and cognitive consistency theories alike were primarily theories about affect. They made no assumptions about cognitive processing, and when they searched for sophisticated thinking, they found "psychologic" rather than a more thoughtful variety, "nature of the times" voters rather than "ideologues." Rational voting, attribution, and decision theories have represented reactions against these pure affect views. They assume that voters are not fools but rather have rational thought processes that convert affective preferences into behavior. In turn, cognitive psychology and social cognition represent yet another reaction against these more rational views of human perception on the grounds that they are too calculating, too precise, and too veridical. Social cognition would propose more Gestalt-like information-processing mechanisms instead. Either way, however, these cognitive views drop affect altogether.

Both the rational decision theories and the cognitive information-processing theories are healthy correctives to an earlier preoccupation with affect. They have helped us see the true contributions of these other processes in political and social behavior more generally. But they both go too far: rational theories in ignoring all sources of irrationality and social cognition in ignoring affect. In the short run, it is useful to push these new approaches to the limit to see what new insights they create. But in the long run, they will need to build thoughtlessness and affect back in.

Political cognition, as illustrated by the papers in this volume, deals very heavily with memory (especially selective memory) and with perception (especially selective, or schematic, perception). All of the empirical papers in this volume struggle with affect, but none except chapter 12 by Roseman, Abelson, and Ewing confront affect directly. Whether their *emotional resonance* hypothesis could be combined with a model of cognitive representation and memory is a question for future research and theorizing. The inability of information-processing theories to handle affect with as much sophistication as they offer for memory and perception is, however, the biggest shortcoming of political and social cognition. We are not the first to make this observation, and an earlier symposium in the Carnegie series (Clark & Fiske, 1982) was convened specifically to deal with cognition and affect. It is no coincidence that the two chapters in this book that have the most to say about affect were authored (or coauthored) by researchers who were involved in that earlier symposium (Fiske and Abelson).

Measuring Schemata

Common early questions about a political cognition viewpoint were: How can I measure political schemata? How can I know when I've found one? There is no one answer to each of these questions.[5] Those researchers who have most actively tried to measure political schemata have chosen very different operationalizations. Lodge and his colleagues have tried to adopt the methods of cognitive psychology most faithfully, using reaction times and false recognitions of schema-consistent information as chief indicators of a political schema (see chapter 5). Conover and Feldman (1984) have used Q methodology to measure directly cognitive structures that presumably indicate underlying political schemata. Both of these procedures tap cognitive structures or functions fairly directly, which is the most precise way to infer the presence of a schema.

One problem is that such direct measurement of schemata may often be too cumbersome and time consuming to be used on large-scale surveys. Lau (chapter 6) employs a slightly more indirect procedure: open-ended responses to survey questions about the things the respondents liked and disliked about the major parties and candidates. Because the Democratic party or Richard Nixon is a cue to associated information in memory, Lau considered these responses "cued free recall" and used them as the basis for his measures of political schemata. Such open-ended questions are widely available in the type of surveys typically employed by political scientists. Hopefully, some convergence of methods will appear; someone needs to do the groundwork of comparing the more precise cognitive measures, such as reaction times and Q-sorts, to the type of measures that can easily be collected on a survey, such as free recall data and schema-specific knowledge (e.g., what position do most liberals/blacks/Republicans take on this issue? see Hamill & Lodge, and Conover & Feldman, this volume). Another intriguing possibility is to collect reaction-time measures during an interview. With the increasing use of telephone interviews and CATI (Computer Assisted Telephone Interviewing) systems, it should be fairly easy to adapt the programs and train interviewers to collect such information.

Trying to measure or operationalize political schemata is chiefly an issue when one is searching for individual differences in schemata. Another approach, and in fact the approach adopted much more frequently in psychology, is to look for the ramifications of consensually held schemata. In American politics, party is the one purely political factor that is almost impossible to avoid in any election, so it is a fairly safe assumption that

---

[5]This same problem, or lack of agreement on how best to measure schemata, also plagues cognitive psychology and social cognition; see Taylor and Fiske (1981).

most adults will have some sort of party schema.[6] This allows Miller to follow the line of reasoning he sets out in chapter 9. Similarly, certain values (e.g., equality and fairness) are widely shared by Americans and frequently applied to politics. Hence, Sears, Huddy, and Schaffer, and Tyler (this volume) did not feel that they had to distinguish between people who do and do not apply those values to politics. Likewise, Kinder safely assumes that people make trait inferences about politicians, just as they make such inferences about other people.

Whether one adopts the consensual approach or the individual difference approach to studying political information processing, one point cannot be emphasized too strongly. To reiterate what Fiske wrote in chapter 3: If the schema concept is going to be of use to political science, it must be applied rigorously. It must be carefully defined and operationalized. Most important, political schemata must be embedded in a specific information-processing model. If one does not precisely define the concept and lay out specific predictions about how it should affect some system or model, the concept is reduced to the status of a nonfalsifiable label.[7] A process model forces one to make specific predictions that can be empirically verified, and at least implicitly suggests alternative models to the one explicitly being tested.

All of the empirical models in this volume offer process models, though still in fairly rudimentary forms. Let us offer two examples of such models. Not surprisingly, we describe the two with which we are most familiar. Much of Lau's paper (chapter 6) addresses the reliability and validity of his operationalization of political schemata. Although these correlations were almost always statistically significant and in predictable patterns, in themselves they do not "prove" the existence of political schemata. The value of the approach rests most centrally on the tests of the specific information-processing model, which asserts that political schemata should influence the storage and recall of political information. This yielded some fairly strong confirmatory evidence. It predicted the finding that people with political group schemata would recall chiefly group-related information from the Ford–Carter debates, whereas people with issues schemata would recall chiefly issue-related information. It also predicted that candidate evaluations are determined primarily by information relevant to an available schema. In each case, the appropriate interaction terms were significant,

---

[6]Although with the widely documented "decline of party" (e.g., Wattenberg, 1982), this assumption may not be safe for long.

[7]In this sense, talking about political schemata is much like talking about self-interest or the functions of attitudes. Anything can be considered "in one's self-interest," even hitting yourself in the head with a hammer, because if it wasn't in your self-interest, why would you do it? Such a broad meaning of self-interest can never be falsified. For self-interest to be a testable concept, it must be defined more narrowly and precisely. The same is true of political schema.

lending considerable support to Lau's schematic model. The more general point, however, is that the schematic model is of value because it makes specific predictions and is inherently testable.

Sears, Huddy, and Schaffer (chapter 8) assume that people hold equality schemata. Based on this assumption, they sketch out an intricate theory of how information related to that schema must be hierarchically structured in memory. They test their theory by examining the intercorrelations of items directly tapping information presumed to be at different levels in the hierarchy. Their model allows them to predict not only the direction of these correlations (and that they should differ from zero) but also offers the prediction that certain correlations should be stronger than others. Moreover, Sears et al. offer an alternative (nonschematic) model of how these same data might be organized that predicts a different pattern of intercorrelations. Hence, they can evaluate their model not only in some absolute sense (are its predictions verified?) but also in a relative sense (does it fit the data better than an alternative model?).

When Are Schemata Cued?

One point that is repeatedly raised throughout these chapters is how we are to know what political schema will be "cued" or utilized at any given time. Even if we accept the notion of cognitive schemata as the way most knowledge is structured, surely people have multiple political schemata that they can apply to any political stimuli. How, then, do we know which political schema will be applied? This point is raised most forcefully by Conover and Feldman (chapter 7) when they discuss contextual factors that could lead to the cueing of different schemata; by Brody (chapter 13) when he argues that very different schemata must be applied to incumbents and to candidates, even when those two roles are filled by the same person in a short period of time; and by Lane (chapter 14) when he addresses the (multiple) purpose(s) of political schemata. At the individual level, particular schemata are cued or brought to mind in particular instances by exposure to explicit schema labels or to a set of attributes more closely linked to one schema than another (see Fiske & Pavelchak, in press, for more details on this point). When a particular attribute is closely linked to two different schemata, the frequency and recentness of activation of the schemata in the past will determine the probability of either one being activated in a particular instance (Wyer & Srull, 1981).

The answer for Conover and Feldman and for Brody, on the other hand, clearly lies not in individual factors but in the political environment. Remember that for the typical voter, most political perception is what Fiske (chapter 3) calls *mediated perception* in that it is almost all received indirectly through television or newspapers. During the Carnegie-Mellon

Symposium, Kathleen Frankovic of CBS news spoke of some of the standard operating procedures that the network news programs follow, which obviously must influence this mediation: only do a story if it is timely; don't repeat stories; simplify complex problems. Such biases in the nightly news have been noted earlier by researchers in political communication (e.g., Patterson, 1980; Patterson & McClure, 1976), and their influence on perceptions of the president have been closely studied by Iyengar, Kinder, and their colleagues (e.g., Iyengar & Kinder, in press; Iyengar, Peters, & Kinder, 1982; Kinder, Iyengar, Krosnick, & Peters, 1982). How (or whether) political schemata interact in this process has not been studied, but this is an obvious direction for future research.

The more general question is how successfully can politicians shape or influence the schemata that are applied to them? Worrying about a candidate's "image" is the chief job of a good campaign manager, but translating that into terms utilized in this volume, a candidate's image is equivalent to the schemata that are typically evoked by the candidate. This point is raised by Lau in chapter 6, and in a slightly different context (lobbying in Congress) by Smith in chapter 16. Politicians certainly adopt widely different campaign styles, just as lobbyists have different strategies for "framing" their bills. An important question for future research is whether the schemata held by the recipients of these influence attempts in any way affect their success.

What Can Political Science
Offer Cognitive Psychology?

If much of the information in this volume has been presented in a "look what cognitive psychology can teach political scientists" format, it is not because the editors or any of the psychologists represented believe that its contribution will occur in that direction alone. Important tests, extensions, and revisions of any theory cannot come until that theory is applied outside the narrow area and research paradigm in which it was originally developed. Information-processing theories should apply to the processing of all types of knowledge, not just to simple memory tasks and text comprehension. Neisser (1982) perhaps overstates the point when he writes that if a problem is interesting, cognitive psychologists have hardly ever studied it. But we can appreciate the spirit of this criticism. We do obviously believe that information-processing theories can be profitably applied to interesting political questions, and indeed to important, emotion-ridden questions of all kinds.

However, those theories may have to be revised in order to account for such phenomenon. We foresee three revisions that seem particularly crucial. The first has already been discussed: the need to incorporate affect more fully into any model of social, or political, cognition. A second revision would take cognition out of an individual, isolated mind and place it in a social context. Even the area of social cognition does not really do this because most social cognition research is basically cognitive psychology about social objects. Yet almost all political perception takes place in a social setting. Not only does political information almost always come through a secondary source (a television commentator, a newspaper writer, i.e., Fiske's mediated perceptions), but it is also frequently perceived in a social context (watching the nightly news with family or friends). The influence of other people on the information received, even when those other people are presumably unbiased (e.g., television commentators), is potentially great. And when the others in one's social environment make no pretensions of impartiality, the influence can be considerable. What schema is cued, and therefore what information is stored in memory, will certainly be a function of how that information is interpreted, which in turn is inevitably in part a function of the perceiver's immediate social environment. Studying social influences on an individual's cognitive structures will not only require revised theory but also revised or different research tools. As Murray Edelman warned during the Carnegie-Mellon symposium, both the typical experiment and the typical survey take the individual out of his or her social context. Social network analysis might provide one methodology for scientists attempting to study cognition in a social setting (e.g., Knoke & Kuklinski, 1982).

A third revision concerns the individual's own conscious or unconscious influence over cognitive processing. Lane's extended discussion of the purpose of political schemata raises this point and reminds us of the "functional" approach to attitudes (Katz, 1960; M. B. Smith, Bruner, & White, 1956). Here we are discussing not so much the influence of the social environment over cognitive processes but more the influence of an individual's motivational state. We must stretch our imaginations to think of situations in which individual motivations or goals would influence the perception of furniture, or of birds, or would affect simple text comprehension. Hence, cognitive psychology, with the problems it has chosen to study, is usually safe in ignoring any purposive influence from the individual over information processing. Such is not the case with most social perception, however. In social psychology, for example, attribution theorists have come to realize that quite frequently the attribution process is motivated not so much by the desire for a veridical understanding of the situation, as was originally assumed, but rather with the need to justify one's behavior (Kelley, 1976). The same is surely true for political perception. Even people who have identical political schemata available, then, may process and store the same political stimuli differently if their prejudices, biases, or needs are distinctive.

This third suggested revision or extension of current information-processing theories is more radical than the previous ones because it takes us into a realm for which cognitive psychology is not well suited. One might respond that two people with identical political schemata, but based on different needs, do not in fact have identical political schemata. However, then a new definition of schema, which includes something like purposes or goals, will have to be developed.

Behavioral Decision Theory

Fischer and Johnson (chapter 4) make a very convincing case for the application of behavioral decision theory to political behavior. Much political behavior research examines political decisions, after all. Information-processing theories deal primarily with the representation of knowledge in memory, not decision making per se. One can derive decisions from such representations only by including affect and by adopting some simple decision rule (e.g., vote for the candidate with whom the most affect is associated). However, behavioral decision theories consider decisions not as a sidelight but as the main point. Many political questions can be readily described as choices between alternatives (candidates, policies) that differ on multiple attributes (party, personality, policy outcomes, etc.). Hence, any multiple attribute decision theory would seem an obvious candidate upon which to build an elaborate model of vote choice. Fischer and Johnson suggest that when the task is evaluating a single candidate or making judgments about the performance of a specific incumbent in office, a simple linear statistical model is usually quite accurate. On the other hand, when people must choose between several alternatives, they are often forced to make value trade-offs. In such instances, few decision makers live up to our ideals of considering many different aspects of the problem before making a decision. This would certainly be the case for any person trying to decide which candidate to support in an election. Elimination by aspects (EBA) might accurately describe how a single-issue voter evaluates potential candidates, for example, eliminating from consideration any candidate who supports freedom of choice on the abortion issue. If all candidates (or no candidates) passed this test, the single-issue voter would be indifferent to the outcome and presumably would not vote.[8] Those who consider more than a single issue might still follow a similar

---

[8]We should point out that one theory that Fischer and Johnson offer as a prime candidate for a vote decision model, starting point plus adjustment theory (in which people form a first impression by considering a single attribute of the problem at hand), is basically incompatible with a schematic model that would assume more holistic perception and evaluation. It is closer to Fiske's piecemeal processing and, as such, might offer a good alternative to any schematic candidate evaluation model.

procedure as a reasonable way to simplify a hopelessly complex task. Voters might take the issue about which they are personally most concerned and eliminate from consideration any candidate who adopts an unacceptable position on that issue. Any remaining candidates would then be judged according to the acceptability of their position on the second most important issue, and so on, until only one candidate is left.

Information Processing and Political Science

In terms of political science, any theory is useful only to the extent that it stimulates us to confront interesting political questions. This is true of schema theory or any other information-processing theory. If political cognition is to have an important influence on political science, it is not enough merely to describe political perceptions accurately. This is a worthwhile goal in and of itself, but most of political science can get along quite nicely without this knowledge. For example, it will probably be impossible to create new models of the vote decision that predict the vote any more accurately than several currently available models (e.g., Brody & Page, 1973; Kelley & Mirer, 1974; G. B. Markus & Converse, 1979). A voting model based on some information-processing or behavioral decision theory may be a more veridical description of the actual process by which that decision is reached, but if one only cares about the outcome, the predicted vote, this may not matter at all.

Those of us now or soon to be working in the area of political cognition must seek out and try to address interesting political questions. Examples of such problems that political cognition seems best suited to deal with include: the pervasive effects of incumbency on congressional elections; the problem of attitudes and nonattitudes, and political ideologies more generally; the manner in which politicians are held accountable (or manage to avoid responsibility) for their deeds, and for circumstances more generally during their administrations;[9] the problem of information search in rational choice theories; strategies the problem of information search in rational choice theories; strategies and actual behavior, including coalition formation, in bargaining situations; and the reasoning or thinking processes of political elites. These and related problems are the challenge of the future.

---

[9]The "teflon" factor, by which some observers claim President Reagan has avoided personal accountability for the failures of his administration, is a recent example.

References

Abelson, R. P. (1972). Are attitudes necessary? In B. T. King & E. McGinnies (Eds.), *Attitudes, conflict, and social change* (pp. 19-32). New York: Academic Press.

Abelson, R. P. (1968). Simulation of social behavior. In G. Lindzey & E. Aronson (Eds.), *The handbook of social psychology,* (2nd ed., Vol. 2, pp. 274-356). Reading, MA: Addison-Wesley.

Abelson, R. P. (1976). Script processing in attitude formation and decision-making. In J. S. Carroll & J. W. Payne (Eds.), *Cognition and social behavior* (pp. 33-46). Hillsdale, NJ: Lawrence Erlbaum Associates.

Abelson, R. P. (1981). The psychological status of the script concept. *American Psychologist, 36,* 1715-1729.

Abelson, R. P. (1983). Whatever became of consistency theory? *Personality and Social Psychology Bulletin, 9,* 37-54.

Abelson, R. P., Aronson, E., McGuire, W. J., Newcomb, T. M., Rosenberg, M. J., & Tannenbaum, P. H. (Eds.). (1968). *Theories of cognitive consistency: A sourcebook.* Chicago: Rand McNally.

Abelson, R. P., Kinder, D. R., Peters, M. D., & Fiske, S. T. (1982). Affective and semantic components in political person perception. *Journal of Personality and Social Psychology, 42,* 619-630.

Abrams, R. (1980). *Foundations of political analysis: An introduction to the theory of collective choice.* New York: Columbia University Press.

Abramson, P. A. (1983). *Political attitudes in America: Formation and change.* San Francisco: Freeman.

Achen, C. H. (1975). Mass political attitudes and the survey response. *American Political Science Review, 69,* 1218-1231.

Adorno, T., Frenkel-Brunswik, E., Levinson, D., & Sanford, R. N. (1950). *The authoritarian personality.* New York: Harper & Row.

Ajzen, I., & Fishbein, M. (1980). *Understanding attitudes and predicting social behavior.* Englewood Cliffs, NJ: Prentice-Hall.

Akey, D. (Ed.). (1978). *Encyclopedia of associations.* Detroit: Gale Research.

Alba, J. W., & Hasher, L. (1983). Is memory schematic? *Psychological Bulletin, 93,* 203-231.

Aldrich, J. H., & McKelvey, R. D. (1977). A method of scaling with application to the 1968 and 1972 presidential election studies. *American Political Science Review, 71,* 111-130.

Alexander, F. (1959). Emotional factors in voting. In E. Burdick & J. Brodbeck (Eds.), *American voting behavior* (pp. 300-307). Glencoe, IL: Free Press.

Alexander, S., & Ruderman, M. (1983). *The influence of procedural and distributive justice on organizational behavior.* Paper presented at the annual meeting of the American Psychological Association, Anaheim, CA.

Allport, G. W. (1954). *The nature of prejudice.* Reading, MA: Addison-Wesley.

Anderson, J. R. (1980). *Cognitive psychology and its implications.* San Francisco: Freeman.

Anderson, J. R. (1981). *Cognitive skills and their acquisition.* Hillsdale, NJ: Lawrence Erlbaum Associates.

Anderson, J. R. (1983). *The architecture of cognition.* Cambridge, MA: Harvard University Press.

Anderson, J. R., & Bower, G. H. (1973). *Human associative memory.* New York: Wiley.

Anderson, N. H. (1972). *Information integration theory: A brief summary.* Unpublished manuscript, University of California, San Diego.

Anderson, N. H. (1974). Cognitive algebra: Integration theory applied to social attribution. In L. Berkowitz (Ed.), *Advances in experimental social psychology* (Vol. 7, pp. 1-101). New York: Academic Press.

Anderson, N. H. (Ed.). (1981). *Foundations of information integration theory.* New York: Academic Press.

Anderson, P. A. (1983). Decision making by objection and the Cuban missile crisis. *Administrative Science Quarterly, 28,* 201-222.

Anderson, R. C., & Pichert, J. W. (1978). Recall of previously unrecallable information following a shift in perspective. *Journal of Verbal Learning and Verbal Behavior, 17,* 1-12.

Anton, T. J. (1967). Roles and symbols in the determination of state expenditures. *Midwest Journal of Political Science, 11,* 27-43.

Arnheim, R. (1944). The world of the daytime serial. In P. F. Lazarsfeld & F. N. Stanton (Eds.), *Radio research 1942-43* (pp. 121-137). New York: Duell, Sloan & Pearce.

Arnold, M. B. (1960). *Emotion and personality.* New York: Columbia University Press.

Arrow, K. J. (1982). Risk perception in psychology and economics. *Economic Inquiry, 20,* 1-19.

Asch, S. E. (1946). Forming impressions of personality. *Journal of Abnormal and Social Psychology, 41,* 258-290.

Asch, S. E. (1948). The doctrine of suggestion, prestige, and imitation in social psychology. *Psychological Review, 55,* 250-276.

Asher, H. B. (1982). *Voting behavior research in the 1980's: An examination of some old and new problem areas.* Paper presented at the annual meeting of the American Political Science Association, Denver.

Atkinson, R. C., & Shiffrin, R. M. (1968). Human memory: A proposed system and its control structures. In K. Spence (Ed.), *The psychology of learning and motivation* (Vol. 2, pp. 90-195). New York: Academic Press.

Atlantic Institute for International Affairs, survey by Harris. (1983, May 16). Reported in the *International Herald Tribune.*

Austin, W. G. (1979). Justice, freedom, and self-interest in intergroup conflict. In W. G. Austin & S. Worchel (Eds.), *The social psychology of intergroup relations* (pp. 121-143). Monterey, CA: Brooks/Cole.

Austin, W. G. (1980). Friendship and fairness: Effects of type of relationship and task performance on choice of distributional rules. *Personality and Social Psychology Bulletin, 6,* 402-407.

Axelrod, R. (1972). Psycho-algebra: A mathematical theory of cognition and choice with an application to the British Eastern Committee in 1918. *Papers of the Peace Research Society (International), 18,* 113-131.

Axelrod, R. (1973). Schema theory: An information processing model of perception and cognition. *American Political Science Review, 67,* 1248-1266.

Axelrod, R. (Ed). (1976). *Structure of decision: The cognitive maps of political elites.* Princeton, NJ: Princeton University Press.

Axelrod, R., & Hamilton, W. D. (1981). The evolution of cooperation. *Science, 211,* 1390-1396.

Baker, R., Meyers, F. A., Corbett, A. M., & Rudoni, D. (1979). Evaluation of police services in medium-sized cities. *Law and Policy Quarterly, 1,* 235-248.

Bandura, A. (1977). Self efficacy: Toward a unifying theory of behavior change. *Psychological Review, 84,* 191-215.

Barber, J. D. (1972). *The presidential character.* Englewood Cliffs, NJ: Prentice-Hall.

Barrett-Howard, E., & Tyler, T. R. (in press). Procedural justice as a criterion in allocation decisions. *Journal of Personality and Social Psychology.*

Barry, B., & Hardin, R. (1982). *Rational man and irrational society.* Beverly Hills, CA: Sage.

Bastedo, R., & Lodge, M. (1980). The meaning of party labels. *Political Behavior, 2,* 287-308.

Baugh, W. (1984). *The politics of nuclear balance.* New York: Longman.

Beck, P. (1974). A socialization theory of partisan realignment. In R. Niemi (Ed.), *The politics of future citizens* (pp. 199-219). San Francisco: Jossey-Bass.

Beck, P. (1977). Partisan dealignment in the postwar South. *American Political Science Review, 71,* 477-496.

Becker, G. S. (1976). *The economic approach to human behavior.* Chicago: University of Chicago Press.

Becker, G. S., & Landes, W. M. (Eds.). (1974). *Essays in the economics of crime and punishment.* New York: Columbia University Press.

Bem, D. J. (1972). Self-perception theory. In L. Berkowitz (Ed.), *Advances in experimental social psychology,* (Vol. 6, pp. 1-61). New York: Academic Press.

Bennett, W. L. (1975). *The political mind and the political environment.* Lexington, MA: Heath.

Bennett, W. L. (1982). Rethinking political perception and cognition. *Micropolitics, 2,* 175-202.

Bentler, P. M. (1980). Multivariate analysis with latent variables: Causal modeling. *Annual Review of Psychology, 31,* 419-456.

Bentler, P. M., & Bonet, D. G. (1980). Significance tests and goodness of fit in the analysis of covariance structures. *Psychological Bulletin, 88,* 588-606.

Benton, A. A. (1971). Productivity, distributive justice, and bargaining among children. *Journal of Personality and Social Psychology, 18,* 68-78.

Berelson, B. R., Lazarsfeld, P. F., & McPhee, W. N. (1954). *Voting.* Chicago: University of Chicago Press.

Berman, J. S., Read, S. J., & Kenny, D. A. (1983). Processing social information. *Journal of Personality and Social Psychology, 45,* 1211-1224.

Black, M., & Rabinowitz, B. (1980). American electoral change: 1952-1972 (with a note on 1976). In W. Crotty (Ed.), *The party symbol: Readings on political parties* (pp. 222-256). San Francisco: Freeman.

Blumberg, P. (1980). *Inequality in an age of decline.* New York: Oxford University Press.

Bobo, L. (1983). Whites' opposition to busing: Symbolic racism or realistic group conflict? *Journal of Personality and Social Psychology, 45,* 1196-1210.

Bobrow, D. G., & Norman, D. A. (1975). Some principles of memory schemata. In D. G. Bobrow & A. Collins (Eds.), *Representation and understanding: Studies in cognitive science* (pp. 131-149). New York: Academic Press.

Boden, M. A. (1977). *Artificial intelligence and natural man.* New York: Basic Books.

Boles, J. K., & Durio, H. F. (1980). *Social stereotyping and females in elected office: The implications of an attitudinal study.* Paper presented at the annual meeting of the Midwest Political Science Association, Chicago.

Bolland, J., & Cigler, A. (1984). *The group participation decision: The role of belief system structure.* Paper presented at the annual meeting of the Midwest Political Science Association, Chicago.

Borgida, E., & Howard-Pitney, B. (1983). Personal involvement and the robustness of perceptual salience effects. *Journal of Personality and Social Psychology, 45,* 560–570.

Bower, G. H. (1978). Cognitive psychology: An introduction. In W. K. Estes (Ed.), *Handbook of learning and cognitive processes,* (Vol. 1, pp. 25–81). Hillsdale, NJ: Lawrence Erlbaum Associates.

Bower, G. H., & Cohen. P. R. (1982). Emotional influence in memory and thinking: Data and theory. In M. S. Clark & S. T. Fiske (Eds.), *Affect and cognition* (pp. 291–332). Hillsdale, NJ: Lawrence Erlbaum Associates.

Bower, G. H., & Hilgard, E. R. (1981). *Theories of learning* (5th ed.). Englewood Cliffs, NJ: Prentice-Hall.

Boyd, R. W. (1972). Popular control of public policy: A normal vote analysis of the 1968 election. *American Political Science Review, 66,* 429–449.

Brady, H. (1984). *Socio-political processes for nominating a president.* Paper presented at the Weingart-Caltech Conference on Institutional Context of Elections, Pasadena, CA.

Brent, E., & Granberg, D. (1982). Subjective agreement with the presidential candidates of 1976 and 1980. *Journal of Personality and Social Psychology, 42,* 393–403.

Brewer, M., & Lui, L. (1983). Categorization of the elderly by the elderly: Effects of perceiver's category membership. *Personality and Social Psychology Bulletin, 10,* 585–595.

Brewer, W. F., & Nakamura, G. V. (1984). The nature and functions of schemas. In R. S. Wyer, Jr., & T. K. Srull (Eds.), *Handbook of social cognition,* (Vol. 1, pp. 119–160). Hillsdale, NJ: Lawrence Erlbaum Associates.

Breznitz, S. (1983). Denial versus hope. In S. Breznitz (Ed.), *The denial of stress,* (pp. 297–302). New York: International Universities Press.

Broadbent, D. E. (1958). *Perception and communication.* London: Pergamon Press.

Brody, R. A. (1982). Public evaluations and expectations and the future of the presidency. In J. Young (Ed.), *Problems and prospects of presidential leadership in the nineteen-eighties,* (Vol. 1, pp. 189–212). Washington, DC: University Press of America.

Brody, R. A., & Page, B. I. (1972). The assessment of policy voting. *American Political Science Review, 66,* 450–458.

Brody, R. A., & Page, B. I. (1973). Indifference, alienation, and rational decision. *Public Choice, 15,* 1–17.

Brody, R. A., & Page, B. (1975). The impact of events on presidential popularity. In A. Wildavsky (Ed.), *Perspectives on the presidency* (pp. 136–148). Boston: Little Brown.

Brown, R. (1973). *A first language: The early stages.* Cambridge, MA: Harvard University Press.

Bruner, J. (1978). *Make your own Nixon: Projection of candidate issue stand as a fly in the ointment of issue voting.* Paper presented at the annual meeting of the Midwest Political Science Association, Chicago.

Bruner, J. S. (1957). Going beyond the information given. In J. S. Bruner, E. Brunswick, L. Festinger, F. Heider, K. F. Muenzinger, C. E. Osgood, & D. Rapaport (Eds.), *Contemporary approaches to cognition* (pp. 41–74). Cambridge, MA: Harvard University Press.

Bruner, J. S., & Taiguri, R. (1954). Person perception. In G. Lindzey (Ed.), *Handbook of social psychology,* (Vol. 2, pp. 634–654). Reading, MA: Addison-Wesley.

Buckley, W., Burns, T., & Meeker, L. D. (1974). Structural resolutions of collective action problems. *Behavioral Science, 19,* 277–297.

Cacioppo, J. T., & Petty, R. E. (1982). The need for cognition. *Journal of Personality and Social Psychology, 42,* 116-131.

Caddell, P. H. (1979, October/November). Crisis of confidence: Trapped in a downward spiral. *Public Opinion, 5,* 2-8.

Campbell, A., Converse, P. E., Miller, W. E., & Stokes, D. E. (1960). *The American voter.* New York: Wiley.

Campbell, A., Gurin, G., & Miller, W. E. (1954). *The voter decides.* Westport, CT: Greenwood.

Campbell, B. A. (1980). Realignment, party decomposition and issue voting. In B. A. Campbell & R. J. Trilling (Eds.), *Realignment in American politics* (pp. 82-109). Austin: University of Texas Press.

Cantor, N., & Mischel, W. (1979). Prototypes in person perception. In L. Berkowitz (Ed.), *Advances in experimental social psychology,* (Vol. 12, pp. 3-25). New York: Academic Press.

Cantril, H., Gaudet, H., & Herzog, H. (1940). *The invasion from Mars.* Princeton, NJ: Princeton University Press.

Carbonell, J. G. (1979). *Subjective understanding: Computer models of belief systems* (Research Report No. 150). New Haven, CT: Yale University, Department of Computer Science.

Carroll, J. S., & Payne, J. W. (Eds.). (1976). *Cognition and social behavior.* Hillsdale, NJ: Lawrence Erlbaum Associates.

Cartwright, D., & Zander, A. (1968). *Group dynamics: Research and theory* (3rd ed.). New York: Harper & Row.

Casper, J. D. (1978). Having their day in court: Defendant evaluations of the fairness of their treatment. *Law and Society Review, 12,* 237-251.

Chase, W. G. (1978). Elementary information processes. In W. K. Estes (Ed.), *Handbook of learning and cognitive processes,* (Vol. 5, pp. 19-90). Hillsdale, NJ: Lawrence Erlbaum Associates.

Chase, W. G., & Chi, M. R. H. (1985). Cognitive skill: Implications for spatial skill in large scale environments. In J. Harvey (Ed.), *Cognition, social behavior, and the environment* (pp. 111-136). Hillsdale, NJ: Lawrence Erlbaum Associates.

Chase, W. G., & Simon, H. A. (1973a). The mind's eye in chess. In W. G. Chase (Ed.), *Visual information processing* (pp. 215-282). New York: Academic Press.

Chase, W. G., & Simon, H. A. (1973b). Perception in chess. *Cognitive Psychology, 4,* 55-81.

Chi, M. T. H., Feltovich, P. J., & Glaser, R. (1981). Categorization and representation of physics problems by experts and novices. *Cognitive Science, 5,* 121-152.

Chi, M. T. H., & Koeske, R. (1983). Network representation of a child's dinosaur knowledge. *Developmental Psychology, 19,* 29-39.

Chiesi, H. L., Spilich, G. J., & Boss, J. F. (1981). Acquisition of domain specific information in relation to high and low domain knowledge. *Journal of Verbal Learning and Verbal Behavior, 18,* 257-273.

Clark, M. S., & Fiske, S. T. (Eds.). (1982). *Affect and cognition: The 17th annual Carnegie symposium on cognition.* Hillsdale, NJ: Lawrence Erlbaum Associates.

Cohen, C. E. (1981). Person categories and social perception: Testing some boundaries of the processing effects of prior knowledge. *Journal of Personality and Social Psychology, 40,* 441-452.

Cohen, R. L. (1983). *Participation as procedure: A critical examination of fair process and frustration effects in organizational settings.* Paper presented at the second annual Conference on Justice, Nags Head, NC.

Collins, A. M., & Quillian, M. R. (1972). Experiments on semantic memory and language comprehension. In L. W. Gregg (Ed.), *Cognition in learning and memory* (pp. 117-137). New York: Wiley.

Conover, P. J. (1980). The perception of political figures: An application of attribution theory.

In J. C. Pierce & J. L. Sullivan (Eds.), *The electorate reconsidered* (pp. 91–110). Beverly Hills, CA: Sage.

Conover, P. J. (1981). Political cues and the perception of candidates. *American Politics Quarterly, 9,* 427–448.

Conover, P. J. (1984). The influence of group identifications on political perception and evaluation. *Journal of Politics, 46,* 760–785.

Conover, P. J., & Feldman, S. (1981). The origins and meaning of liberal/conservative self-identifications. *American Journal of Political Science, 25,* 617–645.

Conover, P. J., & Feldman, S. (1982). Projection and the perception of candidates. *Western Political Quarterly, 35,* 228–244.

Conover, P. J., & Feldman, S. (1984). How people organize the political world: A schematic model. *American Journal of Political Science, 28,* 95–126.

Converse, P. E. (1962). Information flow and the stability of partisan attitudes. *Public Opinion Quarterly, 26,* 578–599.

Converse, P. E. (1964). The nature of belief systems in mass publics. In D. E. Apter (Ed.), *Ideology and discontent* (pp. 206–261). London: Collier-Macmillan.

Converse, P. E. (1970). Attitudes and non-attitudes: Continuation of a dialogue. In E. R. Tufte (Ed.), *The quantitative analysis of social problems* (pp. 168–189). Reading, MA: Addison-Wesley.

Converse, P. E. (1975). Public opinion and voting behavior. In F. Greenstein & N. Polsby (Eds.), *Handbook of political science,* (Vol. 4, pp. 75–170). Reading, MA: Addison-Wesley.

Converse, P. E. (1980). Comment: Rejoinder to Judd and Milburn. *American Sociological Review, 45,* 664–666.

Converse, P. E., & Markus, G. B. (1979). Plus ca change.... The new CPS election panel study. *American Political Science Review, 73,* 32–49.

Cottam, R. (1977). *Foreign policy motivation.* Pittsburgh, PA: University of Pittsburgh Press.

Crosby, F. (1976). A model of egotistical relative deprivation. *Psychological Review, 83,* 85–113.

Crosby, F. (1982). *Relative deprivation and working women.* New York: Oxford University Press.

Crosby, F., Bromley, S., & Saxe, L. (1980). Recent unobtrusive studies of black and white discrimination and prejudice: A literature review. *Psychological Bulletin, 87,* 546–563.

Curtin, R. T. (1977). *Income equity among U.S. workers.* New York: Praeger.

Curtis, R. (1979). The effects of knowledge of self-interest and social relationship upon the use of equity, utilitarian, and Rawlsian principles of allocation. *European Journal of Social Psychology, 9,* 165–175.

Davis, O. A., Hinich, M. J., & Ordeshook, P. C. (1970). An expository development of a mathematical model of the electoral process. *American Political Science Review, 64,* 426–448.

Dawes, R. M. (1980). Social dilemmas. *Annual Review of Psychology, 31,* 169–194.

Dawes, R. M., & Corrigan, B. (1974). Linear models in decision making. *Psychological Bulletin, 81,* 95–106.

DeCarufel, A. (1981). The allocation and acquisition of resources in times of scarcity. In M. J. Lerner & S. C. Lerner (Eds.), *The justice motive in social behavior* (pp. 317–341). New York: Plenum.

DeRivera, J. (1977). *A structural theory of the emotions.* New York: International Universities Press.

DeSoto, C. (1960). Learning a social structure. *Journal of Abnormal and Social Psychology, 60,* 417–421.

DeSoto, C., & Albrecht, F. (1968a). Cognition and social orderings. In R. P. Abelson,

E. Aronson, W. J. McGuire, T. M. Newcomb, M. J. Rosenberg, & P. H. Tannenbaum (Eds.), *Theories of cognitive consistency* (pp. 531-538). Chicago: Rand McNally.

DeSoto, C., & Albrecht, F. (1968b). Conceptual good figures. In R. P. Abelson, E. Aronson, W. J. McGuire, T. M. Newcomb, M. J. Rosenberg, & P. H. Tannenbaum (Eds.), *Theories of cognitive consistency* (pp. 504-511). Chicago: Rand McNally.

Deutsch, M. (1975). Equity, equality and need: What determines which value will be used as the basis of distributive justice? *Journal of Social Issues, 31,* 137-149.

Deutsch, M. (1981). Justice in "the crunch." In M. J. Lerner & S. C. Lerner (Eds.), *The justice motive in social behavior* (pp. 343-357). New York: Plenum.

Diamond, P. A. (1967). Cardinal welfare, individualistic ethics, and interpersonal comparisons of utility: Comment. *Journal of Political Economy, 75,* 765-766.

Downs, A. (1957a). *An economic theory of democracy.* New York: Harper & Row.

Downs, A. (1957b). An economic theory of political action in a democracy. *Journal of Political Economy, 65,* 135-150.

Duffy, E. (1934). Emotion: An example of the need for reorientation in psychology. *Psychological Review, 41,* 184-198.

Eckhoff, T. (1974). *Justice: Its determinants in social interaction.* Oslo, Norway: Rotterdam University Press.

Edelman, M. (1964). *The symbolic uses of politics.* Urbana: University of Illinois Press.

Edwards, W. (1954). The theory of decision making. *Psychological Bulletin, 51,* 380-417.

Einhorn, H. J., & Hogarth, R. M. (1981). Behavioral decision theory: Processes of judgment and choice. *Annual Review of Psychology, 32,* 53-88.

Eiser, J. R. (1976). Evaluation of choice-dilemma alternatives: Utility, morality and social judgment. *British Journal of Social and Clinical Psychology, 15,* 51-60.

Ekman, R., Sorenson, E. R., & Friesen, W. V. (1969). Pan-cultural elements in facial displays of emotion. *Science, 164,* 86-88.

Engstrom, R. L., & Giles, M. W. (1972). Expectations and images: A note on diffuse support for legal institutions. *Law and Society Review, 6,* 631-636.

Epstein, S. (1984). The stability of behavior across time and situations. In R. A. Zucker, J. Arnoff, & A. I. Rabin (Eds.), *Personality and the prediction of behavior* (pp. 209-268). Orlando, FL: Academic Press.

Ericsson, K. A., & Simon, H. A. (1984). *Protocol analysis: Verbal reports as data.* Cambridge, MA: MIT Press.

Erikson, E. (1956). The problem of ego identity. *Journal of the American Psychoanalytic Association, IV,* 58-121.

Estes, W. K. (1979). The information processing approach to cognition. In W. K. Estes (Ed.), *Handbook of learning and cognitive processes,* (Vol. 5, pp. 1-18). Hillsdale, NJ: Lawrence Erlbaum Associates.

Feather, N. T. (1964). Subjective probability and decisions under uncertainty. In W. G. Gore & J. W. Dyson (Eds.), *The making of decisions* (pp. 339-355). New York: Macmillan.

Feather, N. T. (1979). Value correlates of conservatism. *Journal of Personality and Social Psychology, 37,* 1617-1630.

Feather, N. T. (1982). *Expectations and actions: Expectancy-value models in psychology.* Hillsdale, NJ: Lawrence Erlbaum Associates.

Feather, N. T., & Newton, J. W. (1982). Values, expectations, and the prediction of social action: An expectancy valence analysis. *Motivations and Emotion, 6,* 217-244.

Feldman, S. (1982). Economic self-interest and political behavior. *American Journal of Political Science, 26,* 446-466.

Feldman, S. (1983). Economic individualism and American public opinion. *American Politics Quarterly, 11,* 3-30.

374 REFERENCES

Feldman, S., & Conover, P. J. (1983). Candidates, issues and voters: The role of inference in political perception. *Journal of Politics, 45,* 810–839.

Fenno, R. F., Jr. (1978). *Home style: House members in their districts.* Boston: Little, Brown.

Festinger, L. (1957). *A theory of cognitive dissonance.* Stanford, CA: Stanford University Press.

Fiorina, M. P. (1981). *Retrospective voting in American national elections.* New Haven, CT: Yale University Press.

Fischer, G. W. (1979). Utility models for multiple objective decision: Do they accurately represent human preferences? *Decision Sciences, 10,* 451–479.

Fischhoff, B. (1983). Predicting frames. *Journal of Experimental Psychology: Learning, Memory, and Cognition, 9,* 103–116.

Fishbein, M., & Ajzen, I. (1975). *Belief, attitude, intention and behavior.* Reading, MA: Addison-Wesley.

Fishbein, M., & Ajzen, I. (1981). Attitudes and voting behavior. In G. M. Stephenson & J. H. Davis (Eds.), *Progress in applied social psychology,* (Vol. 1, pp. 253–313). New York: Wiley.

Fishbein, M., Ajzen, I., & Hinkle, R. (1980). Predicting and understanding voting in American elections. In I. Ajzen & M. Fishbein (Eds.), *Understanding attitudes and predicting social behavior* (pp. 173–195). Englewood Cliffs, NJ: Prentice-Hall.

Fishbein, M., Bowman, C. H., Thomas, K., Jaccard, J. J., & Ajzen, I. (1980). Predicting and understanding voting in British elections and American referenda. In I. Ajzen & M. Fishbein (Eds.) *Understanding attitudes and predicting social behavior* (pp. 196–216). Englewood Cliffs, NJ: Prentice-Hall.

Fishburn, P. C. (1973). *The theory of social choice.* Princeton, NJ: Princeton University Press.

Fiske, S. T. (1980). Attention and weight in person perception: The impact of negative and extreme behavior. *Journal of Personality and Social Psychology, 38,* 889–906.

Fiske, S. T. (1981). Social cognition and affect. In J. Harvey (Ed.), *Cognition, social behavior, and the environment* (pp. 227–266). Hillsdale, NJ: Lawrence Erlbaum Associates.

Fiske, S. T. (1982). Schema-triggered affect: Application to social perception. In M. S. Clark & S. T. Fiske (Eds.), *Affect and cognition: The 17th annual Carnegie symposium on cognition* (pp. 55–78). Hillsdale, NJ: Lawrence Erlbaum Associates.

Fiske, S. T., & Kinder, D. R. (1981). Involvement, expertise, and schema use: Evidence from political cognition. In N. Cantor & J. F. Kihlstrom (Eds.), *Personality, cognition, and social interaction* (pp. 171–192). Hillsdale, NJ: Lawrence Erlbaum Associates.

Fiske, S. T., Kinder, D. R., & Larter, W. M. (1983). The novice and the expert Knowledge based strategies in political cognition. *Journal of Experimental Social Psychology, 19,* 381–400.

Fiske, S. T., & Linville, P. W. (1980). What does the schema concept buy us? *Personality and Social Psychology Bulletin, 6,* 543–557.

Fiske, S. T., Neuberg, S., Beattie, A. E., & Milberg, S. J. (1984). *Category-based affect: Stereotypic versus piecemeal processes in impression formation.* Unpublished manuscript, Carnegie-Mellon University.

Fiske, S. T., & Pavelchak, M. A. (1985). Category-based versus piecemeal-based affective responses: Developments in schema-triggered affect. In R. M. Sorrentino & E. T. Higgins (Eds.), *Handbook of motivation and cognition: Foundations of social behavior,* (pp. 167–203). New York: Guilford.

Fiske, S. T., & Taylor, S. E. (1984). *Social cognition.* New York: Random House.

Flacks, R. (1969). Protest or conform: Social psychological perspectives on legitimacy. *Journal of Applied Behavioral Science, 5,* 127–149.

Friedman, L. N. (1975). *The legal system: A social science perspective.* New York: Russell Sage.

Friedman, M. (1953). *Essays in positive economics.* Chicago, IL: University of Chicago Press.

Fromm, E. (1947). *Man for himself.* New York: Holt, Rinehart, & Winston.

Gans, H. J. (1979). *Deciding what's news.* New York: Pantheon Books.

Gant, M. M., & Luttbeg, N. R. (1983). *A comparison of ideology and political party as cognitive structures.* Paper presented at the annual meeting of the Midwest Political Science Association, Chicago.

Garner, W. R. (1962). *Uncertainty and structure as psychological concepts.* New York: Wiley.

George, A., & Smoke, R. (1974). *Deterrence in American foreign policy.* New York: Columbia University Press.

Gilbert, M. (1976). *Winston S. Churchill: Vol. 5.* 1922-1939. London: Heinemann.

Gilligan, C. (1982). *In a different voice.* Cambridge, MA: Harvard University Press.

Gillund, G., & Shiffrin, R. M. (1984). A retrieval model for both recognition and recall. *Psychological Review, 91,* 1-67.

Gorman, R. (1970). On the inadequacies of non-philosophical political science: A critical analysis of decision-making theory. *International Studies Quarterly, 14,* 408.

Graber, D. A. (1976). Press and TV as opinion resources in presidential campaigns. *Public Opinion Quarterly, 40,* 285-303.

Graber, D. A. (1980). *Mass media and American politics.* Washington, DC: Congressional Quarterly Press.

Graber, D. A. (1982). *Have I heard this before and is it worth knowing? Variations in political information processing.* Paper presented at the annual meeting of the American Political Science Association, Denver.

Graber, D. A. (1984). *Processing the news.* New York: Longman.

Granberg, D., & Brent, E. (1974). Dove-hawk placement in the 1968 election: Application of social judgment and balance theories. *Journal of Personality and Social Psychology, 29,* 687-695.

Grasmick, H. G., & Green, D. E. (1980). Legal punishment, social disapproval, and internalization as inhibitors of illegal behavior. *Journal of Criminal Law and Criminology, 71,* 325-335.

Greenberg, J. (1981). The justice of distributing scarce and abundant resources. In M. J. Lerner & S. C. Lerner (Eds.), *The justice motive in social behavior* (pp. 289-316). New York: Plenum.

Greenberg, J., & Cohen, R. J. (1982). *Equity and justice in social behavior.* New York: Academic Press.

Greenstein, F. L. (1965). *Children and politics.* New Haven, CT: Yale University Press.

Greenstein, F. L. (1967). The impact of personality on politics: An attempt to clear away underbrush. *American Political Science Review, 61,* 629-641.

Greenwald, A. G. (1980). The totalitarian ego: Fabrication and revision of personal history. *American Psychologist, 35,* 603-613.

Grether, D. M., & Plott, C. R. (1979). Economic theory of choice and the preference reversal phenomenon. *American Economic Review, 69,* 623-638.

Grossman, M., & Kumar, M. (1981). *Portraying the president.* Baltimore, MD: Johns Hopkins University Press.

Gurin, G., & Gurin, P. (1976). Personal efficacy and the ideology of individual responsibility. In B. Strumpel (Ed.), *Economic means for human needs* (pp. 131-159). Ann Arbor, MI: Institute for Social Research.

Gurin, P., Miller, A. H., & Gurin, G. (1980). Stratum identification and consciousness. *Social Psychology Quarterly, 43,* 30-47.

Gurr, T. R. (1970). *Why men rebel.* Princeton, NJ: Princeton University Press.

Gusfield, J. R. (1975). A dramatistic theory of status politics. In D. Brissett & C. Edgley (Eds.), *Life as theater.* Chicago: Aldine.

Hagner, R., & Pierce, J. C. (1982). Correlative characteristics of levels of conceptualization in the American public, 1956–1976. *Journal of Politics, 44,* 779–809.

Haight, T. (1978). *The mass media and presidential popularity, 1960–1976.* Unpublished doctoral dissertation, Stanford University, Stanford, CA.

Haight, T., & Brody, R. A. (1977). The mass media and presidential popularity. *Communication Research, 4,* 41–60.

Hamill, R., Blake, F., Finkel, S., & Lodge, M. (1984). *A cognitive model of ideological sophistication and attitude constraint.* Paper presented at the annual meeting of the American Political Science Association, Washington, DC.

Hamill, R., & Lodge, M. (1984). *Categorization and recall of political information: Consequences of a partisan schema* (Report No. 20), Stony Brook, NY: Laboratory for Behavioral Research, State University of New York at Stony Brook.

Hamill, R., Lodge, M., & Blake, F. (1985). *The breadth, depth, and utility of political schemas.* Paper presented at the annual meeting of the Midwest Political Science Association, Chicago.

Hamilton, D. L. (1981). Cognitive representations of persons. In E. T. Higgins, C. P. Herman, & M. P. Zanna (Eds.), *Social cognition: The Ontario symposium* (pp. 135–160). Hillsdale, NJ: Lawrence Erlbaum Associates.

Hardin, R. (1982). *Collective action.* Baltimore, MD: Johns Hopkins University Press.

Harris, R. J. (1981). Inferences in information processing. In G. H. Bower (Ed.), *The psychology of learning and motivation: Advances in research and theory,* (Vol. 15, pp. 81–128). New York: Academic Press.

Hartmann, G. W. (1936). A field experiment on the comparative effectiveness of "emotional" and "rational" political leaflets in determining election results. *Journal of Abnormal and Social Psychology, 31,* 99–114.

Hastie, R. (1981). Schematic principles in human memory. In E. T. Higgins, C. P. Herman, & M. P. Zanna (Eds.), *Social cognition: The Ontario symposium* (pp. 39–88). Hillsdale, NJ: Lawrence Erlbaum Associates.

Hastie, R. (1983). Social inference. *Annual Review of Psychology, 34,* 511–542.

Hastie, R., & Kumar, P. A. (1979). Person memory: Personality traits as organizing principles in memory for behaviors. *Journal of Personality and Social Psychology, 37,* 25–38.

Hastie, R., Park, B., & Weber, R. (1984). Social memory. In R. S. Wyer, Jr., & T. K. Srull (Eds.), *Handbook of social cognition,* (Vol. 2, pp. 151–212). Hillsdale, NJ: Lawrence Erlbaum Associates.

Hayes, J. R. (1981). *The complete problem solver.* Philadelphia, PA: Franklin Institute Press.

Hayes-Roth, B. (1977). Evolution of cognitive structure and processes. *Psychological Review, 84,* 260–278.

Heider, F. (1946). Attitudes and cognitive organization. *Journal of Psychology, 21,* 107–112.

Heider, F. (1958). *The psychology of interpersonal relations.* New York: Wiley.

Hemsley, G. D., & Marmurek, H. H. C. (1982). Person memory: The processing of consistent and inconsistent person information. *Personality and Social Psychology Bulletin, 8,* 433–438.

Herr, P. M., Sherman, S. J., & Fazio, R. H. (1983). On the consequences of priming: Assimilation and contrast effects. *Journal of Experimental Social Psychology, 40,* 843–861.

Higgins, E. T., & King, G. (1981). Accessibility of social constructs: Information processing consequences of individual and contextual variability. In N. Cantor & J. F. Kihlstrom (Eds.), *Personality, cognition, and social interaction* (pp. 69–122). Hillsdale, NJ: Lawrence Erlbaum Associates.

Hilsman, R. (1967). *To move a nation.* Garden City, NY: Doubleday.

Hirschi, T., & Selvin, H. (1955). *Survey design and analysis.* Glencoe, NY: Free Press. (Republished in 1967 as *Delinquency research.* New York: Free Press).

Hoffer, E. (1951). *The true believer.* New York: New American Library.

Hoffman, M. L. (1977). Moral internalization: Current theory and research. In L. Berkowitz (Ed.), *Advances in experimental social psychology,* (Vol. 10, pp. 85-134). New York: Academic Press.

Hollander, E. P., & Julian, J. W. (1970). Studies in leader legitimacy, influence, and innovation. In L. Berkowitz (Ed.), *Advances in experimental social psychology,* (Vol. 5 pp. 33-70). New York: Academic Press.

Holsti, O. (1967). Cognitive dynamics and images of the enemy: Dulles and Russia. In D. Finlay, O. Holsti, & R. Fagen (Eds.), *Enemies in politics* (pp. 25-96). Chicago: Rand McNally.

Horkheimer, M., & Adorno, T. W. (1972). *Dialectic of enlightenment* (J. Cumming, Trans.). New York: Herder & Herder.

Hovland, C. I., Lumsdaine, A. A., & Sheffield, F. D. (1949). *Studies in social psychology in World War II: Vol. 3. Experiments on mass communication.* Princeton, NJ: Princeton University Press.

Howard, J. W., & Rothbart, M. (1980). Social categorization and memory for ingroup and outgroup behavior. *Journal of Personality and Social Psychology, 38,* 301-310.

Inglehart, R. (1977). *The silent revolution: Changing values and political styles among Western publics.* Princeton, NJ: Princeton University Press.

Inglehart, R. (1979). Value priorities and socioeconomic change. In S. H. Barnes & M. Kaase (Eds.), *Political action: Mass participation in five Western democracies* (pp. 305-342). Beverly Hills, CA: Sage.

Iyengar, S., & Kinder D. (in press) *Media and mind.* Chicago, IL: University of Chicago Press.

Iyengar, S., Peters, M., & Kinder D. (1982). Experimental demonstration of the "not-so-minimal" consequences of television news programs. *American Political Science Review, 76,* 848-858.

Izard, C. E. (1977). *Human emotions.* New York: Plenum Press.

Izard, C., Kagan, J., & Zajonc, R. (1984). *Emotions, cognition, and behavior.* Cambridge, MA: Cambridge University Press.

Jacob, H. (1980). Deterrent effects of formal and informal sanctions. In J. Brigham & D. W. Brown (Eds.), *Policy implementation: Penalties or incentives* (pp. 69-88). Beverly Hills, CA: Sage.

James, W. (1890). *The principles of psychology,* (Vol. 2). New York: Holt, Rhinehart, & Winston.

James, W. (1961). *Psychology: The briefer course.* New York: Harper Torchbook. (Original work published 1892).

Janis, I. L. (1967). Effects of fear arousal on attitude change: Recent developments in theory and experimental research. In L. Berkowitz (Ed.), *Advances in experimental social psychology,* (Vol. 3, pp. 167-224). New York: Academic Press.

Janis, I., & Mann, L. (1977). *Decision making.* New York: Free Press.

Jennings, M. K., & Niemi, R. G. (1974). *The political character of adolescence.* Princeton, NJ: Princeton University Press.

Jennings, M. K., & Niemi, R. G. (1981). *Generations and politics.* Princeton, NJ: Princeton University Press.

Jervis, R. (1976). *Perception and misperception in international politics.* Princeton, NJ: Princeton University Press.

Jervis, R. (1980). Political decision making: Recent contributions. *Political Psychology, 1,* 86-101.

Jervis, R. (1984). *The illogic of American nuclear strategy.* Ithaca, NY: Cornell University Press.

Jervis, R. (1985a). Improving the intelligence process: Informal norms and incentives. In A. Maurer, M. Tunstall, & J. Keagle, (Eds.), *Intelligence: policy and process.* Boulder, CO: Westview.

Jervis, R. (1985b). Representativeness in foreign policy judgments. *Political Psychology,* (Forthcoming).

Jervis, R., Lebow, R. N., & Stein, J. (1985). *Psychology and Deterrence.* Baltimore, MD: Johns Hopkins University Press.

Johnson, E. J. (in press). Judgment under uncertainty: Process and performance. In M. Chi, M. Glaser, & M. Farr (Eds.), *The nature of expertise.* Hillsdale, NJ: Lawrence Erlbaum Associates.

Johnson, E. J., & Payne, J. W. (1985). Effort and accuracy in choice. *Management Science, 31,* 395-414.

Johnson, E. J., & Russo, J. E. (1984). Product familiarity and learning new information. *Journal of Consumer Research, 11,* 542-550.

Johnson, J. T., & Judd, C. M. (1983). Overlooking the incongruent: Categorization bias in the identification of political statements. *Journal of Personality and Social Psychology, 45,* 978-996.

Johnson, P. E., Duran, A. S., Hassebrock, F., Moller, J., Prietula, M., Feltovich, P., & Swanson, D. B. (1981). Expertise and error in diagnostic reasoning. *Cognitive Science, 5,* 235-283.

Jones, E. E., & Davis, K. E. (1965). From acts to dispositions: The attribution process in person perception. In L. Berkowitz (Ed.), *Advances in experimental social psychology,* (Vol. 2, pp. 219-266). New York: Academic Press.

Jones, E. E., Kanouse, D. E., Kelley, H. H., Nisbett, R. E., Valins, S., & Weiner, B. (Eds.). (1971). *Attribution: Perceiving the causes of behavior.* Morristown, NJ: General Learning Press.

Joreskog, K. G. (1969). A general approach to confirmatory maximum likelihood factor analysis. *Psychometrika, 34,* 183-202.

Joreskog, K. G. (1973). A general method for estimating a linear structural equation system. In A. S. Goldberger & O. D. Duncan (Eds.), *Structural equation models in the social sciences* (pp. 85-112). New York: Seminar Press.

Joreskog, K. G. (1977). Structural equation models in the social sciences: Specification, estimation, and testing. In P. R. Krishnaiah (Ed.), *Application of statistics* (pp. 192-240). Netherlands: North-Holland.

Joreskog, K. G., & Sorbom, D. (1978). *LISREL IV: Analysis of linear structural relationships by the method of maximum likelihood.* Chicago, IL: National Educational Resources.

Joslyn, R. A. (1980). The content of political spot ads. *Journalism Quarterly, 44,* 92-98.

Kahn, H. (1960). *On thermonuclear war.* Princeton, NJ: Princeton University Press.

Kahneman, D., Slovic, P., & Tversky, A. (Eds.). (1982). *Judgment under uncertainty: Heuristics and biases.* New York: Cambridge University Press.

Kahneman, D., & Tversky, A. (1973). On the psychology of prediction. *Psychological Review, 80,* 237-251.

Kahneman, D., & Tversky, A. (1974). Judgment under uncertainty: Heuristics and biases. *Science, 185,* 1124-1131.

Kahneman, D., & Tversky, A. (1979). Prospect theory: An analysis of decisions under risk. *Econometrica, 47,* 263-291.

Kahneman, D., & Tversky, A. (1982). The simulation heuristic. In D. Kahneman, P. Slovic, & A. Tversky (Eds.), *Judgment under uncertainty: Heuristics and biases* (pp. 201-210). New York: Cambridge University Press.

Kaplan, A. (1965). Non-causal explanation. In D. Lerner (Ed.), *Cause and effect* (pp. 145-155). New York: Free Press.

Katona, G., Strumpel, B., & Zahn, E. (1971). *Aspirations and affluence: Comparative studies of the U.S. and Western Europe.* New York: McGraw-Hill.

Katz, D. (1960). The functional approach to the study of attitudes. *Public Opinion Quarterly, 24,* 163-204.

Katz, D., Gutek, B. A., Kahn, R. L., & Barton, E. (1975). *Bureaucratic encounters.* Ann Arbor, MI: University of Michigan Press.

Kelley, H. H. (1967). Attribution theory in social psychology. In D. Levine (Ed.), *Nebraska symposium on motivation* (Vol. 15, pp. 192-238). Lincoln: University of Nebraska Press.

Kelley, H. H. (1971a). Attribution in social interaction. In E. E. Jones, D. E. Kanouse, H. H. Kelley, R. E. Nisbett, S. Valins, & B. Weiner (Eds.), *Attribution: Perceiving the causes of behavior* (pp. 1-26). Morristown, NJ: General Learning Press.

Kelley, H. H. (1971b). Causal schemata and the attribution process. In E. E. Jones, D. E. Kanouse, H. H. Kelley, R. E. Nisbett, S. Valins, & B. Weiner (Eds.), *Attribution: Perceiving the causes of behavior* (pp. 151-174). Morristown, NJ: General Learning Press.

Kelley, H. H. (1976). *Present research in causal attributions.* Address given to the annual meeting of the Western Psychological Association, Los Angeles.

Kelley, H. H., & Michela, J. (1980). Attribution theory and research. *Annual Review of Psychology 31,* 457-501.

Kelley, H. H., & Thibaut, J. (1978). *Interpersonal relations: A theory of interdependence.* New York: Wiley.

Kelley, S., Jr., & Mirer, T. W. (1974). The simple act of voting. *The American Political Science Review, 68,* 572-591.

Kelman, H. C. (1969). Patterns of personal involvement in the national system: A socio-psychological analysis of political legitimacy. In J. Rosenau (Ed.), *International politics and foreign policy* (rev. ed.), pp. 276-288. New York: Free Press.

Kelso, J. A. (Ed.). (1982). *Human motor behavior.* Hillsdale, NJ: Lawrence Erlbaum Associates.

Kessel, J. H. (1972). Comment: The issues in issue voting. *American Political Science Review, 66,* 459-465.

Key, V. O. (1961). *Public opinion and American democracy.* New York: Knopf.

Kiesler, C. A., Collins, B. E., & Miller, N. (1969). *Attitude change: A critical analysis of theoretical approaches.* New York: Wiley.

Kiewiet, D. R. (1983). *Macroeconomics and micropolitics: The electoral effects of economic issues.* Chicago: University of Chicago Press.

Kinder, D. R. (1978). Political person perception: The asymmetrical influence of sentiment and choice on perceptions of presidential candidates. *Journal of Personality and Social Psychology, 36,* 859-871.

Kinder, D. R., (1983a). Diversity and complexity in American public opinion. In A. Finifter (Ed.), *The state of the discipline* (pp. 47-68). Washington, DC: American Political Science Association.

Kinder, D. R. (1983b). *Presidential traits.* (Report prepared for the NES Board). Ann Arbor: University of Michigan, Center for Political Studies.

Kinder, D. R., & Abelson, R. P. (1981). *Appraising presidential candidates: Personality and affect in the 1980 campaign.* Paper presented at the annual meeting of the American Political Science Association, New York.

Kinder, D. R., Abelson, R. P., & Fiske, S. T. (1979). *Developmental research on candidate instrumentation: Results and recommendations* (Report prepared for the NES Board). Ann Arbor: University of Michigan, Center for Political Studies.

Kinder, D. R., & Fiske, S. T. (in press). Presidents in the public mind. In M. G. Hermann (Ed.), *Handbook of political psychology,* (Vol. 2). San Francisco: Jossey-Bass.

Kinder, D. R., Iyengar, S., Krosnick, J., & Peters, M. (1983). *More than meets the eye: The impact of television news on evaluations of presidential performance.* Paper presented at the annual meeting of the Midwest Political Science Association, Chicago.

Kinder, D. R., & Kiewiet, D. R. (1979). Economic discontent and political behavior: The role of personal grievances and collective economic judgments in congressional voting. *American Journal of Political Science, 23,* 495-527.

Kinder, D. R., & Kiewiet, D. R. (1981). Sociotropic politics: The American case. *British Journal of Political Science, 11,* 129–161.

Kinder, D. R., Peters, M. D., Abelson, R. P., & Fiske, S. T. (1982). Presidential prototypes. *Political Behavior, 2,* 315–337.

Kinder, D. R., & Sears, D. O. (1981). Prejudice and politics: Symbolic racism versus racial threats to the good life. *Journal of Personality and Social Psychology, 40,* 414–431.

Kinder, D. R., & Sears, D. O. (1985). Public opinion and political action. In G. Lindzey & E. Aronson (Eds.), *Handbook of social psychology,* (Vol. II, 3rd ed., pp. 659–741). Reading, MA: Addison-Wesley.

Kintsch, W. (1974). *The representation of meaning in memory.* New York: Wiley.

Kintsch, W. (1978). Comprehension and memory of text. In W. K. Estes (Ed.), *Handbook of learning and cognitive processes,* (Vol. 6, pp. 57–86). Hillsdale, NJ: Lawrence Erlbaum Associates.

Klapper, J. T. (1960). *The effects of mass communications.* Glencoe, NY: Free Press.

Knoke, D. (1976). *Change and continuity in American politics.* Baltimore, MD: Johns Hopkins University Press.

Knoke, D., & Kuklinski, J. H. (1982). *Network analysis.* Beverly Hills, CA: Sage.

Kohlberg, L. (1976). Moral stages and moralization: The cognitive developmental approach. In T. Lickona (Ed.), *Moral development and behavior* (pp. 31–53). New York: Holt, Rinehart, & Winston.

Kosslyn, S. M. (1980). *Image and mind.* Cambridge, MA: Harvard University Press.

Kuhn, T. S. (1957). *The Copernican revolution.* Cambridge, MA: Harvard University Press.

Kuhn, T. (1962). *The structure of scientific revolutions.* Chicago: University of Chicago Press.

Lachman, R., Lachman, J., & Butterfield, E. C. (1979). *Cognitive psychology and information processing.* Hillsdale, NJ: Lawrence Erlbaum Associates.

Ladd, E. C., Jr. & Hadley, C. D. (1978). *Transformations of the American party system.* New York: Norton.

Lakatos, I. (1970). Falsification and the methodology of scientific research programs. In I. M. Lakatos & A. Musgrave (Eds.), *Criticism and the growth of knowledge* (pp. 91–105). Cambridge: Cambridge University Press.

Lamm, H., Kayser, E., & Schwinger, T. (1982). Justice norms and other determinants of allocation and negotiation behavior. In M. Irle (Ed.), *Studies in decision making* (pp. 359–410). New York: Walter de Gruyter.

Lane, R. E. (1956). *Political ideology.* New Haven, CT: Yale University Press.

Lane, R. E. (1962). *Political ideology: Why the American common man believes what he does.* New York: Free Press.

Lane, R. E. (1969). *Political thinking and consciousness.* Chicago: Markham.

Lane, R. E. (1973). Patterns of political belief. In J. Knutson (Ed.), *Handbook of political psychology* (pp. 83–116). San Francisco: Jossey-Bass.

Lane, R. E. (1978). Interpersonal relations and leadership in a "cold society." *Comparative Politics, 10,* 443–459.

Langer, E. J. (1978). Rethinking the role of thought in social interaction. In J. H. Harvey, W. I. Ickes, & R. F. Kidd (Eds.), *New directions in attribution research,* (Vol. 2, pp. 36–58). Hillsdale, NJ: Lawrence Erlbaum Associates.

Langer, E. J. (1983). *The psychology of control.* Beverly Hills, CA: Sage.

Langer, E. J., Blank, A., & Chanowitz, B. (1978). The mindlessness of ostensibly thoughtful action: The role of "placebic" information in interpersonal interaction. *Journal of Personality and Social Psychology, 36,* 635–642.

Larkin, J. H., McDermott, J., Simon, D. P., & Simon, H. A. (1980). Expert and novice performance in solving physics problems. *Science, 200,* 1335–1342.

Larson, D. (in press). *The origins of containment: A psychological explanation.* Princeton, NJ: Princeton University Press.

Lasswell, H. D. (1936). *Who gets what, when, how.* New York: McGraw Hill.

Lasswell, H. D. (1960). *Psychopathology and politics: A new edition with afterthoughts by the author.* New York: Viking.

Lau, R. R. (1982). Negativity in political perception. *Political Behavior, 4,* 353–378.

Lau, R. R. (1983). *Reference group influence on political attitudes and behavior: The importance of the social, political, and psychological contexts.* Paper presented at the annual meeting of the American Political Science Association, Chicago.

Lau, R. R. (1985). Two explanations for negativity effects in political person perception. *American Journal of Political Science, 29,* 119–138.

Lau, R. R., Brown, T. A., & Sears, D. O. (1978). Self-interest and civilians' attitudes toward the Vietnam War. *Public Opinion Quarterly, 42,* 464–483.

Lau, R. R., Coulam, R. F., & Sears, D. O. (1983). *Proposition 2½ in Massachusetts: Self-interest, anti-government attitudes, and political schemas.* Paper presented at the annual meeting of the Midwest Political Science Association, Chicago.

Lau, R. R., & Erber, R. (1985). An information processing approach to political sophistication. In S. Kraus & R. Perloff (Eds.), *Mass media and political thought* (pp. 17–39). Beverly Hills, CA: Sage.

Laver, M. (1981). *The politics of private desires.* New York: Penguin.

Lawler, E. E., III (1977). Satisfaction and behavior. In B. M. Staw (Ed.), *Psychological foundations of organizational behavior* (pp. 90–109). Santa Monica, CA: Goodyear.

Lazarsfeld, P. F., Berelson, B., & Gaudet, H. (1944). *The people's choice.* New York: Columbia University Press.

Lazarus, R. S. (1968). Emotions and adaptation: Conceptual and empirical relations. In W. J. Arnold (Ed.), *Nebraska symposium on motivation,* (Vol. 16, pp. 175–266). Lincoln: University of Nebraska Press.

Lazarus, R. S. (1982). Thoughts on the relations between emotion and cognition. *American Psychologist, 37,* 1019–1024.

Lazarus, R. S., Coyne, J. C., & Folkman, S. (1982). Cognition, emotion, and motivation: The doctoring of Humpty-Dumpty. In R. W. J. Neufeld (Ed.), *Psychological stress and psychopathology,* (pp. 218–239). New York: McGraw-Hill.

Lebow, R. (1981). *Between peace and war.* Baltimore, MD: Johns Hopkins University Press.

Leighton, A. H. (1959). *My name is legion: Foundations for a theory of man in relation to culture.* New York: Basic Books.

Lerner, M. J. (1977). The justice motive: Some hypotheses as to its origins and forms. *Journal of Personality, 45,* 1–52.

Lerner, M. J. (1980). *The belief in a just world: A fundamental delusion.* New York: Plenum.

Lerner, M. J. (1982). The justice motive in human relations and the economic model of man: A radical analysis of facts and fictions. In V. J. Derlega & J. Grzelak, (Ed.), *Cooperation and helping behavior* (pp. 250–278). New York: Academic Press.

Lerner, S. C. (1981). Adapting to scarcity and change. In M. J. Lerner & S. C. Lerner (Eds.), *The justice motive in social behavior* (pp. 3–10). New York: Plenum.

Leventhal, G. S. (1976a). The distribution of rewards and resources in groups and organizations. In L. Berkowitz, (Ed.), *Advances in experimental social psychology,* (Vol. 9, pp. 91–131). New York: Academic Press.

Leventhal, G. S. (1976b). Fairness in social relationships. In J. W. Thibaut, J. T. Spence, & R. C. Carson (Eds.), *Contemporary topics in social psychology* (pp. 211–239). Morristown, NJ: General Learning Press.

Leventhal, G. S. (1980). What should be done with equity theory? New approaches to the study of fairness in social relationships. In K. J. Gergen, M. S. Greenberg, & R. H. Willis (Eds.), *Social exchange: Advances in theory and research* (pp. 27–55). New York: Plenum.

Leventhal, G. S., Karuza, J., Jr., & Fry W. R. (1980). Beyond fairness: A theory of allocation preferences. In G. Mikula (Ed.), *Justice and social interaction* (pp. 167–218). New York: Springer-Verlag.

Leventhal, G. S., Michaels, J. W., & Stanford, C. (1972). Inequity and interpersonal conflict: Reward allocation and secrecy about rewards as methods of preventing conflict. *Journal of Personality and Social Psychology, 23,* 88–102.

Leventhal, H. (1970). Findings and theory in the study of fear communications. In L. Berkowitz (Ed.), *Advances in experimental social psychology* (Vol. 5, pp. 119–186). New York: Academic Press.

Leventhal, H., Watts, J. C., & Pagano, F. (1967). Effects of fear and instructions on how to cope with danger. *Journal of Personality and Social Psychology, 6,* 313–321.

Levitin, T. E., & Miller, W. E. (1979). Ideological interpretations of presidential elections. *American Political Science Review, 73,* 751–771.

Levy, S. G. (1981). Political violence: A critical evaluation. In S. Long (Ed.), *The handbook of political behavior* (Vol. 2, pp. 163–224). New York: Plenum.

Lewin, K. (1939). Field theory and experiments in social psychology: Concepts and methods. *American Journal of Sociology, 44,* 868–896.

Lewin, K. (1951). *Field theory in social science.* New York: Harper & Row.

Lichtenstein, S., & Slovic, P. (1971). Reversals of preference between bids and choices in gambling decisions. *Journal of Experimental Psychology, 89,* 46–55.

Lind, E. A., Lissak, R. I., & Conlon, D. E. (1983). Decision control and process control effects on procedural fairness judgments. *Journal of Applied Social Psychology, 4,* 338–350.

Lindblom, C. E. (1959). The science of "muddling through." *Public Administration Review, 19,* 19–88.

Lindsley, D. B. (1951). Emotion. In S. S. Stevens (Ed.), *Handbook of experimental psychology,* (pp. 473–516). New York: Wiley.

Linville, P. W. (1982). The complexity-extremity effect and age-based stereotyping. *Journal of Personality and Social Psychology, 42,* 193–211.

Linville, P. W., & Fiske, S. T. (1985). *Political complexity and level of involvement as determinants of political judgment.* Unpublished manuscript, Yale University.

Linville, P. W., & Jones, E. E. (1980). Polarized appraisals of out-group members. *Journal of Personality and Social Psychology, 38,* 689–703.

Lippman, W. (1922). *Public opinion.* New York: Macmillan.

Lipset, S. M., & Schneider, W. (1983a, June/July). Confidence in confidence measures. *Public Opinion, 6,* 42–44.

Lipset, S. M., & Schneider, W. (1983b). *The confidence gap: Business, labor and government in the public mind.* New York: Free Press.

Lodge, M., & Hamill, R. (1983). *Some experimental effects of ideological sophistication on the processing of political information.* Unpublished manuscript, State University of New York, Stony Brook.

Loftus, G., & Loftus, E. (1976). *Human memory: The processing of information.* Hillsdale, NJ: Lawrence Erlbaum Associates.

Long, J. S. (1983a). *Confirmatory factor analysis.* Beverly Hills, CA: Sage.

Long, J. S. (1983b). *Covariance structure models: An introduction to LISREL.* Beverly Hills, CA: Sage.

Lopes, L. (1982). *Toward a procedural theory of judgment* (Tech. Rep. No, 17). Madison: University of Wisconsin, Wisconsin Information Processing Program.

Luce, R. D., & Raiffa, H. (1957). *Games and decisions: Introduction and critical survey.* New York: Wiley.

Luce, R. D., & Suppes, P. (1965). Preference, utility and subjective probability. In R. D. Luce, R. R. Bush, & E. Galanter (Eds.), *The handbook of mathematical psychology,* (Vol. 3, pp. 248–410). New York: Wiley.

Lukes, S. (1973). *Individualism.* Oxford: Basil Blackwell.

Maccrimmon, K. R., & Larsson, S. (1979). Utility Theory: Axioms versus 'paradoxes.' In M. Allais & O. Hagen (Eds.), *Expected utility hypothesis and the Allais paradox.* Dordrecht, The Netherlands: Riedel.

MacKuen, M., & Coombs, S. (1981). *More than news.* Beverly Hills, CA: Sage.

Maggiotto, M. A., & Pierson, J. E. (1974). Partisan identification and electoral choice: The hostility hypothesis. *American Journal of Political Science, 21,* 745–767.

Malatesta, C. Z., & Izard, C. E. (1984). Facial expression of emotion: Young, middle-age and older adults. In C. Z. Malatesta & C. E. Izard (Eds.), *Emotion in adult development,* (pp. 253–273). Beverly Hill, CA: Sage.

Mandler, G. (1979). Categorical and schematic organization in memory. In C. R. Puff (Ed.), *Memory organization and structure* (pp. 303–319). New York: Academic Press.

Mandler, G. (1980a). Categorical and schematic organization in memory. In C. R. Puff (Ed.), *Memory organization and structure* (pp. 219–243). New York: Academic Press.

Mandler, G. (1980b). The generation of emotion: A psychological theory. In R. Plutchik & H. Kellerman (Eds.), *Emotion, Theory, Research and Experience* (Vol. 1, pp. 219–343). New York: Academic Press.

March, J. G. (1978). Bounded rationality, ambiguity, and the engineering of choice. *The Bell Journal of Economics, 9,* 587–608.

March, J. G., & Simon H. A. (1958). *Organizations.* New York: Wiley.

Margolis, H. (1982). *Selfishness, altruism and rationality.* New York: Russell Sage.

Margolis, S. M. (1977). From confusion to confusion: Issues and the American voter 1956–1972. *American Political Science Review, 71,* 31–43.

Markus, G. B. (1982). Political attitudes during an election year: A report on the 1980 N.E.S. panel study. *American Political Science Review, 76,* 538–560.

Markus, G. B. (1983). Dynamic modeling of cohort change: The case of political partisanship. *American Journal of Political Science, 27,* 717–739.

Markus, G. B. (1984). *Recollecting and rationalizing of political attitude change.* Unpublished manuscript, University of Michigan, Ann Arbor.

Markus, G. B., & Converse, P. E. (1979). A dynamic simultaneous equation model of electoral choice. *American Political Science Review, 73,* 1055–1077.

Markus, H. (1977). Self-schemata and processing information about the self. *Journal of Personality and Social Psychology, 35,* 63–78.

Markus, H., Crane, M., Bernstein, S., & Saladi, M. (1982). Self-schemas and gender. *Journal of Personality and Social Psychology, 42,* 38–50.

Markus, H., & Sentis, K. (1982). The self in social information processing. In J. Suls (Ed.), *Social psychological perspectives on the self* (pp. 41–70). Hillsdale, NJ: Lawrence Erlbaum Associates.

Markus, H., & Smith J. (1981). The influence of self-schema on the perception of others. In N. Cantor & J. F. Kihlstrom (Eds.), *Personality, cognition, and social interaction* (pp. 233–262). Hillsdale, NJ: Lawrence Erlbaum Associates.

Marsh, A. (1975). Political socialization and intergenerational stability in political attitudes. *British Journal of Political Science, 5,* 509–516.

Martin, J. (1981). Relative deprivation: A theory of distributive justice for an era of shrinking resources. In L. L. Cummings & B. M. Staw (Eds.), *Research in organizational behavior,* (Vol. 3, pp. 53–107). Greenwich, CT: Aijai Press.

Martinez, M. D. (1984). *Projection and persuasion: Who does what?* Paper presented at the annual meeting of the Midwest Political Science Association, Chicago.

Masters, R. D., Sullivan, D. G., Lanzetta, J. T., McHugo, G. J., & Englis, B. (1984). *Facial displays and political leadership: An experimental approach to nonverbal leadership behavior based on ethology and social psychology.* Unpublished manuscript, Dartmouth College.

Matlin, M. W., & Stang, D. J. (1978). *The Pollyanna principle: Selectivity in language, memory, and thought.* Cambridge, MA: Schenkman.

McClelland, G., & Rohrbaugh, J. (1978). Who accepts the Pareto axiom? The role of utility and equity in arbitration decisions. *Behavioral Science, 23,* 446–456.

McClintock, C. G. (1972). Social motivation: A set of propositions. *Behavioral Science, 17,* 438–454.

McConahay, J. B., Hardee, B. B., & Batts, V. (1981). Has racism declined in America? *Journal of Conflict Resolution, 25,* 563–579.

McGuire, W. J. (1969). The nature of attitudes and attitude change. In G. Lindzey & E. Aronson (Eds.), *The handbook of social psychology,* (2nd ed., Vol. 3, pp. 136–314). Reading, MA: Addison–Wesley.

McGuire, W. J. (1973). Persuasion, resistance and attitude change. In I. Pool, W. Schramm, F. W. Frey, N. Maccoby, & E. B. Parker (Eds.), *Handbook of communication* (pp. 216–252). Chicago, IL: Rand McNally.

Meier, R. F., & Johnson, W. T. (1977). Deterrence as social control: The legal and extralegal production of conformity. *American Sociological Review, 42,* 292–304.

Michener, H. A., & Lawler, E. J. (1975). Endorsement of formal leaders: An integrative model. *Journal of Personality and Social Psychology, 31,* 216–223.

Mikula, G. (1980). *Justice and social interaction.* New York: Springer-Verlag.

Mikula, G., & Schwinger, T. (1978). Intermember relations and reward allocation: Theoretical considerations of affects. In H. Brandstatter, J. H. Davis, & H. Schuler (Eds.), *Dynamics of group decisions* (pp. 229–250). Beverly Hills, CA: Sage.

Miller, A. H. (1974). Political issues and trust in government: 1964–1970. *American Political Science Review, 68,* 951–972.

Miller, A. H. (1979). *The institutional focus of political distrust.* Paper presented at the annual meeting of the American Political Science Association, Washington DC.

Miller, A. H. (1983, August/September). Is confidence rebounding? *Public Opinion, 6,* 16–20.

Miller, A. H., Gurin, P., Gurin, G., & Malanchuk, O. (1981). Group consciousness and political participation. *American Journal of Political Science, 25,* 494–511.

Miller, A. H., & Miller, W. E. (1976). Ideology in the 1972 election: Myth or reality. *American Political Science Review, 70,* 832–849.

Miller, A. H., Miller, W. E., Raine, A. S., & Brown, T. A. (1976). A majority party in disarray: Policy polarization in the 1972 election. *American Political Science Review, 70,* 753–778.

Miller, A. H., & Wattenberg, M. P. (1983). Measuring party identification: Independent or no partisan preference? *American Journal of Political Science, 27,* 106–121.

Miller, A. H., Wattenberg, M. P., & Malanchuk, O. (1982). *Cognitive representations of candidate assessments.* Paper presented at the annual meeting of the American Political Science Association, Denver.

Miller, G. A., Galanter, E., & Pribram, K. (1960). *Plans and the structure of behavior.* New York: Holt, Rinehart, & Winston.

Miller, W. E., & Levitin, T. E. (1976). *Leadership and Change.* Cambridge, MA: Winthrop.

Minsky, M. (1975). A framework for representing knowledge. In P. H. Winston (Ed.), *The psychology of computer vision* (pp. 211–277). New York: McGraw-Hill.

Mischel, W. (1968). *Personality and assessment.* New York: Wiley.

Mischel, W. (1984). On the predictability of behavior and the structure of personality. In R. A. Zucker, J. Aronoff, & A. I. Rabin (Eds.), *Personality and the prediction of behavior* (pp. 269-305). Orlando, FL: Academic Press.

Mischel, W., Ebbesen, E. B., & Zeiss, A. M. (1976). Determinants of selective memory about the self. *Journal of Consulting and Clinical Psychology, 44,* 92-103.

Monroe, R. L. (1955). *Schools of psychoanalytic thought.* New York: Holt, Rinehart, & Winston.

Montgomery, D. B., & Leonard-Barton, D. (1977). *Toward strategies for marketing energy conservation* (Research Paper No. 372). Stanford, CA: Standford University, Graduate School of Business.

Morgan, W. R., & Sawyer, J. (1967). Bargaining, expectations, and the preference for equality over equity. *Journal of Personality and Social Psychology, 6,* 139-149.

Morgan, W. R., & Sawyer, J. (1979). Equality, equity, and procedural justice in social exchange. *Social Psychology Quarterly, 42,* 71-75.

Mueller, D. C. (1979). *Public choice.* New York: Cambridge University Press.

Muller, E. N. (1980). The psychology of political protest and violence. In T. D. R. Gurr (Ed.), *The handbook of political conflict* (pp. 69-99). New York: Free Press.

Murphy, W. F., & Tanenhaus, J. (1969). Public opinion and the United States Supreme Court: A preliminary mapping of some prerequisites for court legitimization of regime changes. In J. B. Grossman & J. Tanenhaus (Eds.), *Frontiers in judicial research* (pp. 273-303). New York: Wiley.

Navon, D., & Gopher, D. (1979). On the economy of the human processing system. *Psychological Review, 86,* 214-255.

Neisser, U. (1982). *Memory observed: Remembering in natural contexts.* San Francisco: Freeman.

Neustadt, R. E. (1960). *Presidential power: The politics of leadership.* New York: Wiley.

Newell, A., & Simon, H. A. (1972). *Human problem solving.* Englewood Cliffs, NJ: Prentice-Hall.

Nie, N. H., Verba, S., & Petrocik, J. R. (1976). *The changing American voter.* Cambridge, MA: Harvard University Press.

Nimmo, D., & Savage, R. L. (1976). *Candidates and their images.* Santa Monica, CA: Goodyear.

Nisbett, R. E., & Ross, L. (1980). *Human inference: Strategies and shortcomings of social judgement.* Englewood Cliffs, NJ: Prentice-Hall.

Nisbett, R. E., & Wilson, T. D. (1977). Telling more than we can know: Verbal reports on mental processes. *Psychological Review, 84,* 231-259.

Nitze, P. (1979). *Is SALT II a fair deal for the United States?* Washington, DC: Committee on the Present Danger.

Norman, D. A. (1976). *Memory and attention.* New York: Wiley.

Norman, D. A., & Bobrow, D. G. (1975). On the role of active memory processes in perception and cognition. In C. N. Cofer (Ed.), *The structure of human memory* (pp. 114-133). San Francisco: Freeman.

Norpoth, H., & Lodge, M. (1985). Political sophistication and the nature of attitude responses. *American Journal of Political Science, 29,* (pp. 291-307).

Norpoth, H., & Rusk, J. (1982). Partisan dealignment in the American electorate: Itemizing the deductions since 1964. *American Political Science Review, 76,* 538-560.

Nunn, C. Z., Crockett, H. J., Jr., & Williams, J. A. (1978). *Tolerance for nonconformity.* San Francisco: Jossey-Bass.

Olsen, M. E. (1981). Consumers' attitudes toward energy conservation. *Journal of Social Issues, 37,* 108-131.

Ophuls, W. (1977). *Ecology and the politics of scarcity.* San Francisco: Freeman.

Ordeshook, P. C., & Shepsle, K. A. (Eds.). (1982). *Political equilibrium: A delicate balance.* Boston: Kluwer-Nijhoff.

Ortony, A., Collins, A., & Clore, G. L. (1982). Principia pathematica. Unpublished manuscript, University of Illinois.

Osgood, C. E., & Tannenbaum, P. (1955). The principle of congruity and the prediction of attitude change. *Psychological Review, 62,* 42–55.

Ostrom, T. M. (1977). Between-theory and within-theory conflict in explaining context effects in impression formation. *Journal of Experimental Social Psychology, 13,* 492–503.

Ostrom, T. M., Pryor, J. B., & Simpson, D. D. (1981). The organization of social information. In E. T. Higgins, C. P. Herman, & M. P. Zanna (Eds.), *Social cognition: The Ontario symposium* (pp. 3–38). Hillsdale, NJ: Lawrence Erlbaum Associates.

Pachella, R. G. (1974). Interpretation of reaction time in information processing research. In P. Kantowitz (Ed.), *Human information processing: Tutorials in performance and cognition* (pp. 41–58). New York: Wiley.

Page, B. I. (1976). The theory of political ambiguity. *American Political Science Review 70,* 742–752.

Page, B. I. (1978). *Choices and echoes in presidential elections.* Chicago: University of Chicago Press.

Page, B. I., & Brody, R. A. (1972). Policy voting and the electoral process. *American Political Science Review, 66,* 979–995.

Page, B. I., & Jones, C. C. (1979). Reciprocal effects of policy preferences, party loyalties, and the vote. *American Political Science Review, 73,* 1071–1089.

Paternoster, R., Saltzman, L. E., Waldo, G. P., & Chiricos, T. G. (1983). Perceived risk and social control: Do sanctions really deter? *Law and Society Review, 17,* 457–479.

Patterson, T. E. (1980). *The mass media election.* New York: Praeger.

Patterson, T. E., & McClure, R. D. (1976). *The unseeing eye: The myth of television power in national politics.* New York: G. P. Putnam's Sons.

Payne, J. W. (1976). Task complexity and contingent processing in decision-making. *Organizational Behavior and Human Performance, 16,* 366–387.

Payne, J. W. (1982). Contingent decision behavior. *Psychological Bulletin, 92,* 382–402.

Pennington, N., & Hastie, R. (1981). *Juror decision making: Story structure and verdict choice.* Paper presented at the annual meeting of the American Psychological Association, Los Angeles.

Petrocik, J., & Steeper, F. T. (1982). *Economic issues and the local candidate in the 1982 congressional election.* Paper presented at the annual meeting of the Midwestern Association of Public Opinion Research, Chicago.

Petrocik, J., & Steeper, F. T. (1984). *The midterm referendum: The importance of attributions of responsibility.* Unpublished manuscript, University of California, Los Angeles.

Pettigrew, T. F. (1979). The ultimate attribution error: Extending Allport's cognitive analysis of prejudice. *Personality and Social Psychology Bulletin, 5,* 461–476.

Piaget, J. (1950). *The psychology of intelligence* (M. Piercy & D. E. Berlyne, Trans.). London: Routledge & Kegan Paul.

Piaget, J. (1959). *The language and thought of the child* (3rd ed.) (M. R. Gabin, Trans.). London: Routledge & Kegan Paul.

Pierce, J. C., Beatty, K. M., & Hagner, P. R. (1982). *The dynamics of American public opinion.* Glenview, IL: Scott, Foresman.

Pitz, G. F., & Sachs, N. J. (1984). Judgment and decision: Theory and application. *Annual Review of Psychology, 35,* 139–163.

Plutchik, R. (1980). *Emotion: A psychoevolutionary synthesis.* New York: Harper & Row.

Plutchik, R., & Kellerman, H. (Eds.), (1980). *Emotion: Theory, research, and experience,* (Vol. 1). New York: Academic Press.

Polanyi, M. (1965). *Science, faith and society.* Chicago: University of Chicago Press.

Pomper, G. (1972). From confusion to clarity: Issues and American voters. *American Political Science Review, 66,* 415–428.

Popkin, S., Gorman, J., Phillips, C., & Smith, J. (1976). Comment: What have you done for me lately? Toward an investment theory of voting. *American Political Science Review, 70,* 779–805.

Posner, M. I. (1978). *Chronometric explorations of mind.* Hillsdale, NJ: Lawrence Erlbaum Associates.

Posner, M. I., & McLeod, P. (1982). Information processing models: In search of elementary operations. *Annual Review of Psychology, 33,* 477–514.

Public Opinion (1981, June/July). Vol. 4, *3,* 30–31.

Raaijmakers, J. G. W., & Shiffrin, R. M. (1981). Search of associative memory. *Psychological Review,* 88, 93–134.

Raines, H. (1984, October 7). A chance to change psychology of election. *The New York Times,* pp. 1, 32.

Rasinski, K., & Tyler, T. R. (in press). Social psychology and political behavior. In S. Long (Ed.), *Political Behavior Annual.*

Redman, E. (1973). *The dance of legislation.* New York: Simon & Schuster.

Rhodeback, L. A. (1981). Group deprivation: An alternative model for explaining collective political action. *Micropolitics, 1,* 239–268.

Riker, W. H. (1983). Political theory and the art of heresthetics. In A. Finifter (Ed.), *Political science: The state of the discipline* (pp. 47–68). Washington, DC: American Political Science Association.

Riker, W. H. (1984). The heresthetics of constitution making: The presidency in 1787 with comments on determism and rational choice. *American Political Science Review, 78,* 1–16.

Riker, W. H., & Ordeshook, P. C. (1973). *An introduction to positive political theory.* Englewood Cliffs, NJ: Prentice-Hall.

Rips, L. J., Shoben, E. J., & Smith, E. E. (1973). Semantic distance and the verification of semantic relations. *Journal of Verbal Learning and Verbal Behavior, 12,* 1–20.

Rivers, D., & Rose, N. (1985). Passing the president's program: Public opinion and presidential influence in Congress. *American Journal of Political Science, 29,* 183–196.

Robinson, M. J., & Sheehan, M. A. (1983). *Over the wire and on TV: CBS and UPI in campaign '80.* New York: Russell Sage.

Rohrbaugh, J., McClelland, G., & Quinn, R. (1980). Measuring the relative importance of utilitarian and egalitarian values: A study of individual differences about fair distribution. *Journal of Applied Psychology, 65,* 34–49.

Rokeach, M. (1969). *Beliefs, attitudes, and values: A theory of organization and change.* San Francisco: Jossey-Bass.

Rokeach, M. (1973). *The nature of human values.* New York: Free Press.

Rokeach, M. (1974). Change and stability in American value systems, 1968–1971. *Public Opinion Quarterly, 38,* 222–238.

Rosch, E. (1975). Cognitive representations of semantic categories. *Journal of Experimental Social Psychology, 15,* 343–355.

Rosch, E. (1978). Principles of categorization. In E. Rosch & B. B. Lloyd (Eds.), *Cognition and categorization* (pp. 28–50). Hillsdale, NJ: Lawrence Erlbaum Associates.

Roseman, I. J. (1979). *Cognitive aspects of emotion and emotional behavior.* Paper presented at the annual meeting of the American Psychological Association, Washington, DC.

Roseman, I. J. (1984a). Cognitive determinants of emotions: A structural theory. In P. Shaver (Ed.), *Review of personality and social psychology,* (Vol. 5, pp. 11–36). Beverly Hill, CA: Sage.

Roseman, I. J. (1984b). *Psychology and ideology: Structures of belief about disarmament and defense.* Paper presented at general seminar, New School for Social Research, New York.

Rosenberg, M. J. (1979). *Conceiving the self.* New York: Basic Books.

Rosenberg, M. J., & Abelson, R. P. (1960). An analysis of cognitive balancing. In C. I. Hovland & M. J. Rosenberg (Eds.), *Attitude organization and change* (pp. 112-164). New Haven, CT: Yale University Press.

Rosenberg, S. (1977). New approaches to the analysis of personal constructs in person perception. In D. Levine (Ed.), *Nebraska symposium on motivation* (Vol. 24, pp. 179-243). Lincoln: University of Nebraska Press.

Rosenberg, S. (in press). The Structural developmental analysis of political cognition. In Dana Ward (Ed.), *Piaget and politics.* Durham, NC: Duke University Press.

Rosenstone, S., Behr, R., & Lazarus, E. (1984). *Third parties in America.* Princeton, NJ: Princeton University Press.

Rothbart, M., Evans, M., & Fulero, S. (1979). Recall for confirming events: Memory processes and the maintenance of social stereotyping. *Journal of Experimental Social Psychology, 15,* 343-355.

Rubin, Z. (1973). *Liking and loving.* New York: Holt, Rinehart, & Winston.

Rumelhart, D. E. (1984). Schemata and the cognitive system. In R. S. Wyer, Jr. & T. K. Srull (Eds.), *Handbook of social cognition,* (Vol. 1, pp. 161-188). Hillsdale, NJ: Lawrence Erlbaum Associates.

Rumelhart, D. E., & Norman, D. A. (1985). Representation in memory. In R. C. Atkinson, R. J. Herrnstein, G. Lindzey, & R. D. Luce (Eds.), *Handbook of experimental psychology.* New York: Wiley.

Rumelhart, D. E., & Ortony, A. (1977). The representative of knowledge in memory. In R. C. Anderson et al. (Eds.), *Schooling and the acquisition of knowledge* (pp. 99-135). Hillsdale, NJ: Lawrence Erlbaum Associates.

Russell, C. S. (1979). Applications of public choice theory: An introduction. In C. S. Russell (Ed.), *Collective decision making: Applications from public choice theory* (pp. 1-26). Baltimore, MD: Johns Hopkins University Press.

Sacerdoti, E. D. (1977). *A structure for plans and behavior.* New York: Elsevier North-Holland.

Saphire, R. B. (1978). Specifying due process values. *University of Pennsylvania Law Review, 127,* 111-195.

Sapiro, V. (1982). If U.S. Senator Baker were a woman: An experimental study of candidate images. *Political Psychology, 3,* 61-83.

Sarat, A. (1977). Studying American legal culture: An assessment of survey evidence. *Law and Society Review, 11,* 427-488.

Savage, L. J. (1954). *The foundations of statistics.* New York: Wiley.

Schank, R., & Abelson, R. (1977). *Scripts, plans, goals and universtanding: An inquiry into human knowledge structures.* Hillsdale, NJ: Lawrence Erlbaum Associates.

Scheingold, S. A. (1974). *The politics of rights.* New Haven, CT: Yale University Press.

Schneider, D. J., Hastorf, A. H., & Ellsworth, P. C. (1979). *Person perception.* Reading, MA: Addison-Wesley.

Schneider, W., & Shiffrin, R. M. (1977). Controlled and automatic human information processing: I. Detection, search, and attention. *Psychological Review, 84,* 1-66.

Schoemaker, P. J. H. (1980). *Experiments on decisions under risk: The expected utility hypothesis.* Boston: Kluwer-Nijhoff.

Schuman, H. S. (1983). Survey research and the fundamental attribution error. *Personality and Social Psychology Bulletin, 9,* 103-104.

Schuman, H. S., & Johnson, M. (1976). Attitudes and behavior. *Annual Review of Sociology, 2,* 167-207.

Schwartz, R. D. (1978). Moral order and sociology of law: Trends, problems and prospects. *Annual Review of Sociology, 4,* 577–601.

Schwartz, R. D., & Orleans, S. (1967). On legal sanctions. *University of Chicago Law Review, 34,* 274–300.

Sears, D. O. (1969). Political behavior. In G. Lindzey & E. Aronson (Eds.). *The handbook of social psychology,* (2nd ed., Vol. 5, pp. 315–458). Menlo Park, CA: Addison–Wesley.

Sears, D. O. (1975). Political socialization. In F. I. Greenstein & N. W. Polsby (Eds.), *Handbook of political science,* (Vol. 2, pp. 99–154). Menlo Park, CA: Addison–Wesley.

Sears, D. O. (1982). *Positivity bias in evaluation of public figures.* Paper presented at the annual meeting of the American Political Science Association, Denver.

Sears, D. O. (1983a). The persistence of early political predispositions. In L. Wheeler & P. Shaver (Eds.), *Review of personality and social psychology,* (Vol. 4, pp. 79–116). Beverly Hills, CA: Sage.

Sears, D. O. (1983b). The person-positivity bias. *Journal of Personality and Social Psychology, 44,* 233–250.

Sears, D. O., & Allen, H. M., Jr. (1984). The trajectory of local desegregation controversies and whites' opposition to busing. In N. Miller & M. Brewer (Eds.), *Groups in contact: The psychology of desegregation* (pp. 123–151). New York: Academic Press.

Sears, D. O., & Chaffee, S. H. (1979). Uses and effects of the 1976 debates: An overview of empirical studies. In S. Kraus (ed.), *The great debates, 1976: Ford s. Carter* (pp. 223–261). Bloomington: Indiana University Press.

Sears, D. O., & Citrin, J. (1985). *Tax revolt: Something for nothing in California* (Enlarged ed.). Cambridge, MA: Harvard University Press.

Sears, D. O., & Freedman, J. (1967). Selective exposure to information: A critical review. *Public Opinion Quarterly, 31,* 194–213.

Sears, D. O., Hensler, C. P., & Speer, L. K. (1979). Whites' opposition to "busing": Self-interest or symbolic politics? *American Political Science Review, 73,* 369–384.

Sears, D. O., & Kinder, D. R. (1971). Racial tensions and voting in Los Angeles. In W. Z. Hersch (Ed.), *Los Angeles: Viability and prospects for metropolitan leadership* (pp. 51-88). New York: Praeger.

Sears, D. O., & Lau, R. R. (1983). Inducing apparently self-interested political preferences: An experiment: *American Journal of Political Science, 27,* 223–252.

Sears, D. O., Lau, R. R., Tyler, T. R., & Allen, H. J., Jr. (1980). Self-interest vs. symbolic politics in policy attitudes and presidential voting. *American Political Science Review, 74,* 670–684.

Sears, D. O., Tyler, T. R., Citrin, J., & Kinder, D. R. (1978). Political system support and public response to the energy crisis. *American Journal of Political Science, 22,* 56–82.

Sears, D. O., & Whitney, R. (1973). *Political persuasion.* Morristown, NJ: General Learning Press.

Seeman, M. (1959). On the meaning of alienation. *American Sociological Review, 24,* 783–791.

Seligman, L. G. (1978). The presidential office and the president as party leader. In J. Fishel (Ed.), *Parties and elections in an anti-party age* (pp. 295–304). Bloomington: Indiana University Press.

Sen, A. (1973). *On economic inequality.* New York: Norton.

Sentis, K. P., & Burnstein, E. (1979). Remembering schema-consistent information: Effects of a balance schema on recognition memory. *Journal of Personality and Social Psychology, 37,* 2200–2211.

Shapiro, E. G. (1975). The effect of expectations of future interaction on reward allocations in dyads: Equity vs. equality. *Journal of Personality and Social Psychology, 31,* 873–880.

Shapiro, M. J. (1969). Rational political man: A synthesis of economic and social-psychological perspectives. *American Political Science Review, 63*, 1106-1119.

Sharp, C., & Lodge, M. (1985). Partisan and ideological belief systems: Do they differ? *Political Behavior, 7*, 167-191.

Shaver, P. (1980, October). The public distrust. *Psychology Today*, pp. 44-47.

Sheppard, B. H. (1982). Third party conflict intervention: A procedural framework. In L. L. Cummings & B. M. Staw (Eds.), *Research in organizational behavior*, (Vol. 4, pp. 141-190). Greenwich, CT: Aijai Press.

Shepsle, K. A. (1972). The strategy of ambiguity: Uncertainty and electoral competition. *American Political Science Review, 66*, 555-568.

Shiffrin, R. M., & Schneider, W. (1977). Controlled and automatic human information processing: II. Perceptual learning, automatic attending, and a general theory. *Psychological Review, 84*, 127-190.

Shively, W. P. (1979). The development of party identification among adults: Explorations of a functional model. *American Political Science Review, 73*, 1039-1058.

Shively, W. P. (1980). The nature of party identification: A review of recent developments. In J. C. Pierce & J. L. Sullivan (Eds.), *The electorate reconsidered* (pp. 219-236). Beverly Hills, CA: Sage.

Shoemaker, P. J. H. (1982). The expected utility model: Its variants, purposes, evidence, and limitations. *Journal of Economic Literature, 20*, 529-563.

Silberman, M. (1976). Toward a theory of criminal deterrence. *American Sociological Review, 41*, 442-461.

Simon, H. A. (1947). *Administrative behavior.* New York: Macmillan.

Simon, H. A. (1957). *Models of man: Social and rational.* New York: Wiley.

Simon, H. A. (1976). *Administrative behavior.* New York: Macmillan.

Simon, H. A. (1979a). Information processing models of cognition. *Annual Review of Psychology, 30.* 363-396.

Simon, H. A. (1979b). *Models of thought.* New Haven, CT: Yale University Press.

Simon, H. A. (1979c). Rational decision making in business organizations. *American Economic Review, 69*, 493-513.

Simon, H. A. (1980). Behavioral and social sciences. *Science, 209*, 72-78.

Simon, H. A. (1981). *The sciences of the artificial.* Cambridge, MA: MIT Press.

Slovic, P., & Lichtenstein, S. (1971). Comparison of Bayesian and regression approaches to the study of information processing in judgment. *Organizational Behavior and Human Performance, 6*, 649-744.

Slovic, P., & Lichtenstein, S. (1983). Preference reversals: A broader perspective. *American Economic Review, 73*, 414-422.

Slovic, P., & MacPhillmay, D. (1974). Dimensional commensurability and cue utilization in comparative judgment. *Organizational Behavior and Human Performance, 11*, 172-194.

Smith, E. E. (1979). Theories of semantic memory. In W. K. Estes (Ed.), *Handbook of learning and cognitive processes*, (Vol. 6, pp. 1-57). Hillsdale, NJ: Lawrence Erlbaum Associates.

Smith, E. E., & Medin, D. L. (1981). *Categories and concepts.* Cambridge, MA: Harvard University Press.

Smith, E. R. A. N. (1980). The levels of conceptualization: False measures of ideological sophistication. *American Political Science Review, 74*, 685-696.

Smith, M. B., Bruner, J. S., & White, R. W. (1956). *Opinions and personality.* New York: Wiley.

Smith, R. A. (1980). *Lobbying influence in Congress: Processes and effects.* Unpublished doctoral dissertation, University of Rochester, New York.

Smith, R. A. (1984). Advocacy, interpretation and influence in the U.S. Congress. *American Political Science Review, 78*, 44-63.

Snyder, C. R., & Fromkin, Howard L. (1980). *Uniqueness: The Human Pursuit of Difference.* New York: Plenum.

Snyder, G., & Diesing, P. (1977). *Conflict among the nations.* Princeton, NJ: Princeton University Press.

Snyder, M., & Uranowitz, S. W. (1978). Reconstructing the past. *Journal of Personality and Social Psychology, 36,* 941-950.

Snyder, R., Bruck, H., & Sapin, B. (1962). Decision-making as an approach to the study of international politics. In R. Snyder, H. Bruck, & B. Sapin (Eds.), *Foreign policy decision-making* (pp. 14-185). New York: Free Press.

Sorrentino, R. M., & Higgins, E. T. (Eds.) (1985). *Handbook of motivation and cognition: Foundations of social behavior.* New York: Guilford Press.

Srull, T. K. (1981). Person memory: Some tests of associative storage and retrieval modes. *Journal of Experimental Psychology: Human Learning and Memory, 7,* 440-463.

Steiner, J., & Dorff, R. H. (1980). *A theory of political decision modes: Intraparty decision making in Switzerland.* Chapel Hill: University of North Carolina Press.

Sternberg, S. (1969). The discovery of processing stages: Extension of Donders' method. In W. G. Koster (Ed.), *Attention and performance II* (pp. 276-315). Amsterdam: North-Holland.

Stigler, G. J. (1950). The development of utility theory. *Journal of Political Economy, 58,* 307-321, 373-396.

Stimson, J. A. (1975). Belief systems: Constraint, complexity, and the 1972 election. *American Journal of Political Science, 19,* 393-417.

Stone, P., & Brody, R. A. (1970). Modeling opinion responsiveness to daily news. *Social Science Information, 8,* 95-122.

Stouffer, S. A. (1955). *Communism, conformity, and civil liberties.* Garden City, NY: Doubleday.

Stover, R. V., & Brown, D. W. (1975). Understanding compliance and noncompliance with law: The contribution of utility theory. *Social Science Quarterly, 56,* 363-375.

Strotz, R. H. (1958). How income ought to be distributed: A paradox in distributive ethics. *Journal of Political Economy, 66,* 189-205.

Sugden, R. (1981). *The political economy of public choice: An introduction to welfare economics.* New York: Wiley.

Tajfel, H. (1982). Social psychology of intergroup relations. *Annual Review of Psychology, 33,* 1-39.

Taylor, S. E. (1981). The interface of cognitive and social psychology. In J. Harvey (Ed.), *Cognition, social behavior, and the environment* (pp. 189-213). Hillsdale, NJ: Lawrence Erlbaum Associates.

Taylor, S. E., & Crocker, J. (1981). Schematic bases of social information processing. In E. T. Higgins, C. P. Herman, & M. P. Zanna (Eds.), *Social cognition: The Ontario symposium* (pp. 89-134). Hillsdale, NJ: Lawrence Erlbaum Associates.

Taylor, S. E., & Fiske, S. T. (1978). Salience, attention and attribution: Top of the head phenomena. In L. Berkowitz (Ed.), *Advances in experimental social psychology,* (Vol. 11, pp. 249-288). New York: Academic Press.

Taylor, S. E., & Fiske, S. T. (1981). Getting inside the head: Methodologies for process analysis. In J. Harvey, W. Ickes, & R. Kidd (Eds.) *New directions in attribution research, Vol. 3* (pp. 459-525). Hillsdale, NJ: Lawrence Erlbaum Associates.

Taylor, S. E., Fiske, S. T., Etcoff, N. L., & Ruderman, A. J. (1978). Categorical and contextual bases of person memory and stereotyping. *Journal of Personality and Social Psychology, 36,* 778-793.

Taylor, S. E., & Winkler, J. D. (1980). *The development of schemas.* Paper presented at the annual meeting of the American Psychological Association, Montreal.

Tesser, A. (1978). Self-generated attitude change. In L. Berkowitz (Ed.), *Advances in experimental social psychology,* (Vol. 11, pp. 289–338). New York: Academic Press.

Tesser, A., & Leone, C. (1977). Cognitive schemas and thought as determinants of attitude change. *Journal of Experimental Social Psychology, 13,* 340–356.

Thaler, R. H. (1980). Toward a positive theory of consumer choice. *Journal of Economic Behavior and Organizations, 1,* 39–60.

Thibaut, J., & Walker, L. (1975). *Procedural justice: A psychological analysis.* Hillsdale, NJ: Lawrence Erlbaum Associates.

Tittle, C. R. (1980). *Sanction and social deviance: A question of deterrence.* New York: Praeger.

Tomkins, S. S. (1962). *Affect, imagery, consciousness.* New York: Springer.

Tomkins, S. S. (1981). The quest for primary motives. Biography and autobiography of an idea. *Journal of Personality and Social Psychology, 41,* 306–329.

Trabasso, T., Secco, T., & Van Den Broek, P. (1984). Causal cohesion and story coherence. In H. Mandl, N. L. Stein, & T. Trabasso (Eds.), *Learning and comprehension of text* (pp. 83–113). Hillsdale, NJ: Lawrence Erlbaum Associates.

Tulving, E. (1983). *Elements of episodic memory.* New York: Oxford University Press.

Tulving, E., & Donaldson, W. (Eds). (1972). *Organization of memory.* New York: Academic Press.

Tversky, A. (1972). Elimination by aspects: A theory of choice. *Psychological Review, 79,* 281–299.

Tversky, A., & Kahneman, D. (1974). Judgment under uncertainty: Heuristics and biases. *Science, 185,* 1124–1131.

Tversky, A., & Kahneman, D. (1978). Causal schemata in judgment under uncertainty. In M. Fishbein (Ed.), *Progress in social psychology* (pp. 49–73). Hillsdale, NJ: Lawrence Erlbaum Associates.

Tversky, A., & Kahneman, D. (1981). The framing of decisions and the psychology of choice. *Science, 211,* 453–458.

Tyler, T. R. (1984a). Justice in the political arena. In R. Folger (Ed.), *The sense of injustice* (pp. 189–225). New York: Plenum.

Tyler, T. R. (1984b). The role of perceived injustice in defendants' evaluations of their courtroom experience. *Law and Society Review, 18,* 51–74.

Tyler, T. R., & Caine, A. (1981). The influence of outcomes and procedures on satisfaction with formal leaders. *Journal of Personality and Social Psychology, 41,* 642–655.

Tyler, T. R., & Folger, R. (1980). Distributional and procedural aspects of satisfaction with citizen-police encounters. *Basic and Applied Social Psychology, 1,* 281–292.

Tyler, T. R., & McGraw, K. (1983). The threat of nuclear war: Risk interpretation and behavioral response. *Journal of Social Issues, 39,* 25–40.

Tyler, T. R., & Rasinski, K. (1982). *The influence of distributional and procedural injustice upon institutional and leadership endorsement.* Paper presented at the annual meeting of the American Political Science Association, Denver.

Tyler, T. R., Rasinski, K., & McGraw, K. (in press). The influence of perceived injustice on the endorsement of political leaders. *Journal of Applied Social Psychology.*

Tyler, T. R., Rasinski, K., & Spodick, N. (1985). The influence of voice upon satisfaction with leaders: Exploring the meaning of process control. *Journal of Personality and Social Psychology, 48,* 72–81.

Tyler, T. R., & Weber, R. (1982). Support for the death penalty: Instrumental response to crime or symbolic attitude? *Law and Society Review, 17,* 21–45.

Verba, S., & Nie, N. H. (1972). *Participation in America: Political democracy and social equality.* New York: Harper & Row.

Von Neumann, J., & Morgenstern, O. (1947). *Theory of games and economic behavior* (2nd ed.). Princeton, NJ: Princeton University Press.

Voss, J. F., Tyler, S. W., & Yengo, L. A. (1983). Individual differences in the solving of social science problems. In R. G. Dillon & R. R. Schmeck (Eds.), *Individual differences in cognition* (pp. 205–232). New York: Academic Press.

Wahlke, J. (1971). Policy demands and system support: The role of the represented. *British Journal of Political Science, 1,* 271–290.

Walster, E., Walster, G. W., & Berscheid, E. (1978). *Equity: Theory and research.* Boston: Allyn & Bacon.

Waltz, K. (1979). *Theory of international politics.* Reading, MA: Addison-Wesley.

Wattenberg, M. P. (1981). The decline of political partisanship in the United States: Negativity or neutrality? *American Political Science Review, 75,* 941–950.

Wattenberg, M. P. (1982). From parties to candidates: Examining the role of the media. *Public Opinion Quarterly, 46,* 216–227.

Wattenberg, M. P. (1983). *The decline of American political parties, 1952–1980.* Cambridge, MA: Harvard University Press.

Wattenberg, M. P. & Miller, A. H. (1981). Decay in regional party coalitions. In S. M. Lipset (Ed.), *Party Coalitions in the 1980s* (pp. 341–367). San Francisco: Institute for Contemporary Studies.

Weatherford, M. S. (1983). Voting and the "symbolic politics" argument: A reinterpretation and synthesis. *American Political Science Review, 77,* 158–174.

Weiner, B. (1982). The emotional consequences of causal ascriptions. In M. S. Clark & S. T. Fiske (Eds.), *Affect and cognition: The 17th annual Carnegie symposium on cognition,* (pp. 185–209). Hillsdale, NJ: Lawrence Erlbaum Associates.

Weiss, W., & Fine, B. (1956). The effect of induced aggressiveness on opinion change. *Journal of Abnormal and Social Psychology, 52,* 109–114.

White, J. K., & Morris, D. (1984, December/January). Shattered images: Political parties in the 1984 election. *Public Opinion, 7,* 44–48.

White, R. W. (1959). Motivation reconsidered: The concept of competence. *Psychological Review, 66,* 297–333.

Wilensky, R. (1983). *Planning and understanding.* Reading, MA: Addison-Wesley.

Williams, D. C., Weber, S. J., Haaland, G. A., Mueller, R. H., & Craig, R. E. (1976). Voter decision making in a primary election: An evaluation of three models of choice. *American Journal of Political Science, 20,* 37–49.

Winkler, R. L., & Hays, W. L. (1975). *Statistics: Probability, inference, and decision* (2nd ed.). New York: Holt, Rinehart, & Winston.

Winograd, T. (1975). Computer memories: A metaphor for memory organization. In C. N. Cofer (Ed.), *The structure of human memory* (pp. 133–162). San Francisco: Freeman.

Wohlstetter, R. (1962). *Pearl Harbor: Warning and decision.* Stanford, CA: Stanford University Press.

Wright, J. R., & Niemi, R. G. (1983). Perceptions of candidates' issue positions. *Political Behavior, 5,* 209–224.

Wyer, R. S., & Srull, T. K. (1981). Category accessibility: Some theoretical and empirical issues concerning the processing of social stimulus information. In E. T. Higgins, C. P. Herman, & M. P. Zanna (Eds.), *Social cognition: The Ontario symposium* (pp. 161–198). Hillsdale, NJ: Lawrence Erlbaum Associates.

Wyer, R. S., Srull, T. K., Gordon, S. E., & Hartwick, J. (1982). Effects of processing objectives on the recall of prose material. *Journal of Personality and Social Psychology, 43* 674–688.

Zadny, J., & Gerard, H. B. (1974). Attributed intentions and informational selectivity. *Journal of Experimental Social Psychology, 10,* 34–52.

Zajonc, R. B. (1968). Attitudinal effects of mere exposure. *Journal of Personality and Social Psychology Monograph Supplement, 9* (2, Part 2), 2-27.

Zajonc, R. B. (1980). Feeling and thinking: Preferences need no inferences. *American Psychologist, 35,* 151-175.

Zajonc, R. B. (1984). On the primacy of affect. *American Psychologist, 39,* 117-123.

Zemach, M. (1966). *Effects of guilt-arousing communications.* Unpublished doctoral dissertation, Yale University, New Haven, CT.

Author Index

Numbers in italic indicate the page on which the full reference appears.

A

Abelson, R. P., 3, 16, 19, 22, 26, 34, 37, 70, 133, 164, 235, 236, 250, 252, 260, 279, 292, 309, 311, 319, 323, 327, 348, 354
Abrams, R., 257
Abramson, P. A., 90
Achen, C., 146
Adorno, T., 294, 303
Ajzen, I., 5, 43, 261, 264, 275, 348
Akey, D., 281
Alba, J. W., 21, 71, 78, 84
Albrecht, F., 321
Aldrich, J. H., 127
Alexander, F., 310
Alexander, S., 269
Allen, H. M., Jr., 3, 159, 161, 162, 175, 260
Allport, G. W., 42
Anderson, J. R., 15, 17, 19, 20, 26, 27, 28, 31, 32, 70, 166, 211, 349
Anderson, N. H., 17, 43, 160
Anderson, P. A., 120
Anderson, R. C., 85
Anton, T. J., 263

B

Baker, R., 264
Bandura, A., 293
Barber, J. D., 12, 223, 235
Barrett-Howard, E., 276
Barry, B., 257
Barton, E., 264
Bastedo, R., 74
Batts, V., 197
Baugh, W., 330
Beattie, A. E., 47
Beatty, K. M., 214

Arnheim, R., 303
Arnold, M. B., 279, 292
Aronson, E., 309, 348
Arrow, K. J., 36, 258
Asch, S. E., 42, 43, 197
Asher, H. B., 140
Atkinson, R. C., 26, 130
Austin, W. G., 271, 276
Axelrod, R., 6, 20, 69, 277

395

Beck, P., 203, 204, 206
Becker, G. S., 36, 264, 307
Behr, R., 298
Bem, D. J., 320
Bennett, W. L., 92, 305, 347
Bentler, P. M., 87, 104
Benton, A. A., 276
Berelson, B., 118, 129
Berman, J. S., 84
Bernstein, S., 136, 335
Berscheid, E., 260, 261, 277
Black, M., 204, 207
Blake, F., 69, 72, 88, 89, 90, 133, 140, 141, 142,
    151, 152
Blank, A., 324
Blumberg, P., 271
Bobo, L., 260
Bobrow, D. G., 70
Boden, M. A., 16
Boles, J. K., 133
Bolland, J., 76
Bonet, D. G., 104
Borgida, E., 198
Boss, J. F., 72
Bower, G. H., 14, 17, 19, 28, 32, 70
Bowman, C. H., 264
Boyd, R. W., 3
Brady, H., 300
Brent, E., 129, 133, 147
Brewer, M., 198
Brewer, W. F., 19
Breznitz, S., 291
Broadbent, D. E., 28
Brody, R. A., 3, 4, 11, 117, 128, 129, 297, 299,
    300, 366
Bromley, S., 197
Brown, D. W., 264
Brown, R., 354
Brown, T. A., 129, 159, 260
Bruck, H., 319
Bruner, J. S., 129, 147, 234, 292, 294, 350, 364
Buckley, W., 277
Burns, T., 277
Burnstein, E., 84
Butterfield, E. C., 17

C

Cacioppo, J. T., 308
Caddell, P. H., 270

Caine, A., 264
Campbell, A., 3, 4, 19, 91, 112, 160, 162, 198,
    203, 218, 228, 314, 348, 358
Campbell, B. A., 214
Cantor, N., 70, 235
Cantril, H., 303
Carbonell, J. G., 26
Carroll, J. S., 6
Cartwright, D., 236
Casper, J. D., 264
Chaffee, S. H., 162
Chanowitz, B., 324
Chase, W. G., 25, 33, 63, 72, 164
Chi, M.R.H., 72, 164, 168
Chiesi, H. L., 72
Chiricos, T. G., 264
Cigler, A., 76
Citrin, J., 6, 159, 160, 161, 162, 163, 260, 274,
    310
Clark, M. S., 18, 34, 52, 359
Clore, G. L., 279
Cohen, C. E., 84
Cohen, P. R., 19, 32
Cohen, R. J., 261
Cohen, R. L., 272
Collins, A. M., 70, 279
Collins, B. E., 348
Conlon, D. E., 272
Conover, P. J., 6, 18, 72, 98, 129, 130, 132,
    135, 144, 160, 161, 167, 185, 200, 207, 254,
    304, 310, 313, 315, 316, 325, 360
Converse, P. E., 3, 4, 19, 75, 89, 90, 91, 106,
    112, 118, 121, 127, 129, 160, 162, 163, 181,
    198, 199, 203, 218, 228, 234, 313, 314, 348,
    358, 366
Coombs, S., 301
Corbett, A. M., 264
Corrigan, B., 60
Cottam, R., 335
Coulam, R. F., 6, 72, 135, 136, 352, 353
Coyne, J. C., 292
Craig, R. E., 260
Crane, M., 135, 355
Crocker, J., 21, 71, 131, 205, 206, 209, 349,
    356
Crockett, H. J., Jr., 307
Crosby, F., 197, 260, 261, 264
Curtin, R. T., 264
Curtis, R., 276

D

Davis, K. E., 348
Davis, O. A., 4, 5, 348
Dawes, R. M., 60, 277
DeCarufel, A., 271
DeRivera, J., 279, 291
DeSoto, C., 321
Deutsch, M., 271, 276
Diamond, P. A., 276
Diesing, P., 328
Donaldson, W., 70
Dorff, R. H., 343
Downs, A., 3, 4, 5, 43, 128, 130, 133, 257, 273, 348
Duffy, E., 282
Duran, A. S., 72
Durio, H. F., 133

E

Ebbeson, E. B., 70
Eckhoff, T., 261
Edelman, M., 263, 272
Edwards, W., 5
Einhorn, H. J., 55, 56, 60
Eiser, J. R., 264
Ekman, R., 282
Ellsworth, P. C., 43
Englis, B., 280
Engstrom, R. L., 263
Epstein, S., 234
Erber, R., 110, 352, 353, 354
Ericsson, K. A., 16
Erikson, E., 310
Estes, W. K., 15, 17
Etcoff, N. L., 134
Evans, M., 84, 351, 352

F

Fazio, R. H., 182
Feather, N. T., 5, 14, 258, 275, 348
Feldman, S., 6, 18, 72, 98, 129, 132, 144, 160, 161, 165, 166, 167, 185, 200, 254, 304, 310, 313, 315, 316, 325, 355, 360
Feltovich, P., 72
Fenno, R. F., Jr., 121
Festinger, L., 4, 348

Fine, B., 290
Finkel, S., 88
Fiorina, M. P., 3, 4, 5, 204, 216, 217, 229, 349
Fischer, G. W., 60
Fischhoff, B., 38
Fishbein, M., 5, 26, 43, 261, 262, 275, 348
Fishburn, B., 38
Fiske, S. T., 3, 6, 7, 18, 34, 41, 42, 44, 45, 46, 47, 48, 51, 52, 53, 63, 64, 70, 71, 72, 76, 91, 92, 100, 133, 134, 135, 136, 137, 138, 155, 160, 162, 163, 164, 168, 199, 205, 207, 234, 235, 236, 250, 260, 279, 321, 323, 324, 329, 340, 347, 349, 352, 353, 359, 362
Flacks, R., 271
Folger, R., 264, 274
Folkman, S., 292
Frenkel-Brunswick, E., 294
Friedman, L. N., 271
Friedman, M., 37
Friesen, M. V., 282
Fromkin, H. L., 312
Fromm, E., 312
Fry, W. R., 262
Fulero, S., 84, 351, 352

G

Galanter, E., 20, 34
Gans, H. J., 254, 299
Gant, M. M., 6
Garner, W. R., 17
Gaudet, H., 118, 303
George, A., 328
Gerard, H. B., 351
Gilbert, M., 330
Giles, M. W., 263
Gilligan, C., 288
Gillund, G., 15
Glaser, R., 72
Gopher, D., 29
Gordon, S. E., 351
Gorman, J., 130, 133, 322, 326
Gorman, R., 327
Graber, D. A., 6, 128, 133, 155, 211
Granberg, D., 129, 133, 147
Grasmick, H. G., 264
Green, D. E., 264
Greenberg, J., 271, 275
Greenstein, F. L., 218, 310, 319
Grether, D. M., 60

Grossman, M., 299
Gurin, G., 118, 218, 314, 358
Gurin, P., 118, 218
Gurr, T. R., 263
Gusfield, J. R., 311
Gutek, B. A., 264

H

Haaland, G. A., 260
Hadley, C. D., 204, 214
Hagner, P. R., 113, 214
Haight, T., 299
Hamil, R., 4, 18, 69, 72, 77, 83, 88, 89, 90, 98, 133, 140, 141, 142, 151, 152, 304, 305, 306, 355
Hamilton, D. L., 131, 134, 164, 206
Hamilton, W. D., 277
Hardee, B. B., 197
Hardin, R., 257, 277
Harris, R. J., 131
Hartmann, G. W., 282
Hartwick, J., 351
Hasher, L., 21, 71, 78, 84
Hassebrock, F., 72
Hastie, R., 15, 20, 21, 24, 32, 71, 84, 133, 273, 352
Hastorf, A. H., 43
Hayes, J. R., 340
Hayes-Roth, B., 354
Hays, W. L., 239
Heider, F., 4, 235, 348
Hemsley, G. D., 84
Hensler, C. P., 159, 259
Herr, P. M., 182
Herstein, J., 43, 47, 62, 95, 259
Herzog, H., 303
Higgins, E. T., 52, 131, 133, 134, 135, 136, 182, 183
Hilgard, E. R., 14
Hinich, M. J., 4, 5, 348
Hinkle, R., 43, 264
Hirschi, T., 319
Hoffer, E., 294
Hoffman, M. L., 277
Hogarth, R. M., 55, 56, 60
Hollander, E. P., 262
Holsti, O., 328
Horkheimer, M., 303
Hovland, C. I., 348

Howard, J. W., 351
Howard-Pitney, B., 198
Huddy, L., 180

I

Inglehart, R., 161, 167
Iyengar, S., 155, 193, 299, 301, 363
Izard, C. E., 282, 290, 291, 323

J

Jaccard, J. J., 264
Jacob, H., 264
James, W., 279
Janis, I. L., 282, 291, 335
Jennings, M. K., 218
Jervis, R., 13, 322, 325, 326, 333, 335
Johnson, E. J., 60, 62, 64
Johnson, J. T., 76, 84
Johnson, M., 319
Johnson, P. E., 72
Johnson, W. T., 264
Jones, C. C., 127, 132
Jones, E. E., 5, 64, 164, 198, 348, 353
Joreskog, K. G., 87
Joslyn, R. A., 211
Judd, C. M., 76, 84
Julian, J. W., 262

K

Kagan, J., 323
Kahn, J., 330
Kahn, R. L., 264
Kahneman, D., 6, 13, 37, 38, 56, 57, 58, 160, 258, 279, 309, 340
Kanouse, D. E., 5
Kaplan, A., 319
Karuza, J., Jr., 262
Katona, G., 315
Katz, D., 264, 364
Kayser, E., 276
Kellerman, H., 282
Kelley, H. H., 5, 6, 277, 322, 348, 364
Kelley, S., Jr., 43, 121, 297, 366
Kelman, H. C., 271
Kelso, J. A., 15

Kenny, D. A., 84
Kessel, J. H., 3
Key, V. O., 3
Kiesler, C. A., 348
Kiewiet, D. R., 316
Kinder, D. R., 3, 5, 18, 63, 72, 76, 92, 129, 133, 135, 136, 137, 147, 155, 159, 160, 164, 168, 193, 197, 234, 235, 236, 237, 250, 252, 260, 274, 279, 299, 301, 311, 314, 352, 353, 363
King, G., 131, 133, 134, 135, 136, 182, 183
Kintsch, W., 19, 32, 70
Klapper, J. T., 162
Knoke, D., 204, 364
Koeski, R., 72, 168
Kohlberg, L., 277
Kosslyn, S. M., 32
Krosnick, J., 193, 299, 363
Kuhn, T. S., 277, 328
Kuklinski, J. H., 364
Kumar, M., 299
Kumar, P. A., 20, 84, 352

L

Lachman, J., 17
Lachman, R., 17
Ladd, E. C., Jr., 204, 214
Lakatos, I., 322
Lamm, H., 276
Landes, W. M., 264
Lane, R. E., 3, 206, 211, 236, 294, 303, 312, 315, 336
Langer, E. J., 311, 324
Lanzetta, J. T., 280
Larkin, J. H., 64, 72
Larson, D., 320
Larsson, S., 36
Larter, W. M., 63, 72, 76, 135, 136, 164, 352, 353
Lasswell, H. D., 73, 294
Lau, R. R., 3, 5, 29, 48, 72, 107, 112, 114, 118, 129, 135, 159, 162, 260, 305, 306, 352, 353, 354, 355
Laver, M., 257, 258, 263, 270, 273
Lawler, E. E. III, 264
Lawler, E. J., 264
Lazarsfeld, P. F., 118, 129
Lazarus, E., 298
Lazarus, R. S., 279, 292

Lebow, R. N., 328, 335
Leighton, A. H., 308
Leonard-Barton, D., 274
Leone, C., 227
Lerner, M. J., 257, 275, 277, 315
Lerner, S. C., 271
Leventhal, G. S., 261, 262, 275, 276, 282, 291
Levinson, D., 294
Levitin, T. E., 128, 129, 151, 152, 200
Levy, S. G., 263
Lewin, K., 4, 348
Lichtenstein, S., 37, 60, 61
Lind, E. A., 272
Lindblom, C. E., 36, 258
Lindsley, D. B., 282
Linville, P. W., 51, 64, 138, 164, 168, 198, 199, 205, 349, 353
Lippman, W., 19
Lipset, S. M., 270, 313, 314, 315
Lissak, R. I., 272
Lodge, M., 5, 18, 69, 71, 72, 74, 76, 77, 83, 88, 89, 90, 98, 133, 140, 141, 142, 151, 152, 304, 305, 306, 352
Loftus, E., 70
Loftus, G., 70
Long, J. S., 87
Lopes, L., 60
Luce, R. D., 258
Lui, L., 198
Lukes, S., 161
Lumsdaine, A. S., 348
Luttbeg, N. R., 5

M

Maccrimmon, K. R., 36
MacKuen, M., 301
MacPhillmay, D., 331
Maggiotto, M. A., 260
Malanchuk, O., 118, 133, 136, 213, 218, 227, 236
Malatesta, C. Z., 290
Mandler, G., 21, 42, 279
Mann, L., 335
March, J. G., 258, 338
Margolis, H., 276
Margolis, S. M., 260
Markus, G. B., 118, 121, 124, 127, 129, 236, 252, 260, 312, 313, 366
Markus, H., 72, 87, 132, 135, 136, 163, 355

Marmurek, H.H.C., 84
Marsh, A., 167
Martin, J., 261
Martinez, M. D., 129
Masters, R. D., 280
Matlin, M. W., 309
McClelland, G., 275, 276
McClintock, C. G., 277
McClure, R. D., 115, 128, 363
McConahay, J. B., 197
McDermott, J., 64, 72
McGraw, K., 265, 267, 274
McGuire, W. J., 236, 300, 309, 348
McHugo, G. J., 280
McKelvey, R. D., 127
McLeod, P., 25
McPhea, W. N., 129
Medin, D. L., 19
Meeker, L. D., 277
Meier, R. F., 264
Meyers, F. A., 264
Michaels, J. W., 276
Michela, J., 322
Michener, H. A., 264
Mikula, G., 261, 276
Milberg, S. J., 47
Miller, A. H., 118, 129, 133, 136, 139, 208, 213,
    218, 223, 224, 227, 236, 270, 306, 311, 314
Miller, G. A., 20
Miller, N., 348
Miller, W. E., 3, 4, 19, 34, 91, 112, 128, 129,
    151, 152, 160, 162, 198, 200, 203, 218, 228,
    236, 314, 348, 358
Minsky, M., 131, 352
Mirer, T. W., 43, 121, 297
Mischel, W., 70, 233, 234, 235
Moller, J., 72
Monroe, R. L., 14
Montgomery, D. B., 274
Morgan, W. R., 276
Morgenstern, O., 35, 258
Morris, D., 204, 215, 216
Mueller, D. C., 257
Mueller, R. H., 260
Muller, E. N., 264
Murphy, W. F., 263

N

Nakamura, G. V., 21

Navon, D., 29
Neisser, U., 363
Neuberg, S., 47
Neustadt, R. E., 237
Newcomb, T. M., 309, 348
Newell, A., 15, 25, 26, 28, 34
Newton, J. W., 5, 348
Nie, N. H., 3, 13, 124, 204, 207, 314
Niemi, R. G., 150, 218
Nimmo, D., 129
Nisbett, R. E., 5, 13, 34, 305, 309, 348, 349
Nitze, P., 326
Norman, D. A., 15, 17, 70, 349
Norpoth, H., 71, 76, 124
Nunn, C. Z., 307

O

Olsen, M. E., 274
Ophuls, W., 271
Ordeshook, P. C., 4, 5, 263, 340, 348
Orleans, S., 264, 271
Ortony, A., 279, 349
Osgood, C. E., 166
Ostrom, T. M., 44

P

Pachella, R. G., 16, 81
Pagano, F., 291
Page, B. I., 3, 4, 117, 127, 128, 129, 132, 139,
    235, 236, 297, 299, 300, 325, 366
Park, B., 32
Paternoster, R., 264
Patterson, T. E., 115, 128, 137, 138, 363
Pavelchak, M. A., 42, 44, 45, 46, 51, 163, 168,
    362
Payne, J. W., 6, 56, 59, 62
Pennington, N., 24
Peters, M. D., 3, 19, 133, 155, 193, 250, 260,
    279, 299, 301, 363
Petrocik, J. R., 3, 124, 204, 207, 214, 264, 322
Pettigrew, T. F., 13
Petty, E. E., 308
Phillips, C., 130, 133, 322, 326
Piaget, J., 304
Pichert, J. W., 85
Pierce, J. C., 113, 214
Pierson, J. E., 260

Pitz, G. F., 56
Plott, C. R., 60
Plutchik, R., 282, 291
Polanyi, M., 329
Pomper, G., 3, 138
Popkin, S., 130, 322, 326
Posner, M. I., 25, 29
Pribram, K., 20, 34
Prietula, M., 72

Q

Quillian, M. R., 70
Quinn, R., 275

R

Raaijmakers, J. G. W., 15
Rabinowitz, B., 204, 207
Raiffa, H., 258
Raine, A. S., 129
Raines, H., 279
Rasinski, K., 260, 264, 265, 267, 272
Read, S. J., 84
Redman, E., 338
Riker, W. H., 257, 263, 337, 339
Rips, L. J., 70
Rivers, D., 237
Robinson, M. J., 254, 298, 299, 300, 301
Rohrbaugh, J., 275, 276
Rokeach, M., 161, 165, 167, 309, 314
Rosch, E., 18, 70, 74, 77, 164
Rose, N., 237
Roseman, I. J., 19, 37, 279, 282, 291, 292, 293, 294
Rosenberg, M. J., 309, 313, 348
Rosenberg, S., 236, 305
Rosenstone, S., 298
Ross, L., 5, 13, 34, 305, 309, 349
Rothbart, M., 84, 351, 352
Rubin, Z., 236
Ruderman, A. J., 134
Ruderman, M., 269
Rudoni, D., 264
Rumelhart, D. E., 15, 17, 21, 349
Rusk, J., 124
Russell, C. S., 257, 277
Russo, J. E., 60, 64

S

Sacerdoti, E. D., 27
Sachs, N. J., 56
Saltzman, L. E., 264
Sanford, C., 276
Sanford, R. N., 294
Saphire, R. B., 263
Sapin, B., 319
Sapiro, V., 133
Sarat, A., 263
Savage, L. J., 258
Savage, R. L., 129
Sawyer, J., 276
Saxe, L., 197
Schaffer, L., 180
Schank, R., 22, 26, 34, 37, 327, 354
Scheingold, S. A., 263
Schneider, D. J., 43
Schneider, W., 15, 270, 313, 314, 315
Schoemaker, P. J. H., 257
Schuman, H. S., 13, 319
Schwartz, R. D., 264, 271, 276
Schwinger, T., 276
Sears, D. O., 3, 4, 18, 48, 72, 107, 110, 129, 135, 136, 159, 160, 161, 162, 163, 175, 180, 197, 235, 259, 260, 274, 309, 310, 348, 352, 353
Secco, T., 21
Seeman, M., 229
Seligman, L. G., 211
Selvin, H., 319
Sen, A., 276
Sentis, K. P., 84
Shapiro, E. G., 276
Shapiro, M. J., 4, 5, 62, 349
Sharp, C., 4, 74
Shaver, P., 270
Sheehan, M. A., 254, 298, 299, 300, 301
Sheffield, F. D., 348
Shepsle, K. A., 128, 340
Sherman, S. J., 182
Shiffrin, R. M., 15, 26, 30
Shively, W. P., 133, 140
Shoben, E. J., 70
Shoemaker, P. J. H., 14, 35
Siladi, M., 136, 355
Silberman, M., 264
Simon, D. P., 64, 72
Simon, H. A., 15, 16, 25, 26, 28, 33, 34, 36, 61, 63, 64, 70, 72, 120, 258, 320, 325, 338, 344, 349

Slovic, P., 4, 37, 60, 61, 160, 258, 331
Smith, E. E., 18, 19, 32, 70
Smith, E.R.A.N., 113
Smith, J., 72, 130, 132, 136, 322, 326
Smith, M. B., 292, 294, 364
Smith, R. A., 337, 339
Smoke, R., 328
Snyder, C. R., 312
Snyder, G., 328
Snyder, M., 352
Snyder, R., 319
Sorbom, D., 87
Sorenson, E. R., 282
Sorrentino, R. M., 52
Speer, L. K., 159, 259
Spilich, G. J., 72
Spodick, N., 272
Srull, T. K., 20, 84, 133, 134, 183, 351, 362
Stang, D. J., 309
Steeper, F. T., 264, 322, 326
Stein, J., 334
Steiner, J., 343
Sternberg, S., 28
Stigler, G. J., 258
Stimson, J. A., 164
Stokes, D. E., 3, 4, 19, 91, 112, 160, 162, 198, 203, 218, 228, 314, 348
Stone, P., 299
Stouffer, S. A., 307
Stover, R. V., 264
Strotz, R. H., 262
Strumpel, B., 315
Sugden, R., 257
Sullivan, D. G., 280
Suppes, P., 258
Swanson, D. B., 72

T

Taiguiri, R., 350
Tajfel, J., 218
Tanenhaus, J., 263
Tannenbaum, P., 166, 309
Taylor, S. E., 5, 7, 29, 41, 44, 52, 53, 70, 71, 91, 130, 131, 134, 137, 138, 160, 162, 168, 199, 205, 206, 207, 209, 309, 321, 324, 328, 340, 347, 349, 353, 356, 360
Tesser, A., 71, 168, 206, 227
Thibaut, J., 261, 277
Thomas, K., 264

Tittle, C. R., 264
Tomkins, S. S., 279, 282, 291
Tulving, E., 24, 29, 70
Tversky, A., 6, 13, 37, 38, 56, 57, 58, 61, 160, 258, 279, 309, 322, 340
Tyler, T. R., 3, 35, 159, 162, 260, 264, 265, 267, 272, 273, 274, 276, 305, 313, 316, 322

U

Uranowitz, S. W., 350

V

Valins, S., 5, 348
Van Den Broek, P., 21
Verba, S., 3, 13, 124, 204, 207, 214, 314
Von Neumann, J., 35, 358
Voss, J. F., 72

W

Wahlke, J., 263
Waldo, G. P., 264
Walker, L., 261
Walster, E., 260, 261, 277
Walster, G. W., 260, 261, 277
Waltz, K., 320
Wattenberg, M. P., 5, 133, 136, 204, 207, 208, 211, 213, 214, 216, 218, 219, 221, 222, 223, 224, 227, 236, 361
Watts, J. C., 291
Weatherford, M. S., 260
Weber, R., 32, 260
Weber, S. J., 260
Weiner, B., 5, 279, 348
Weiss, W., 290
White, J. K., 204, 215, 217
White, R. W., 292, 294, 304, 307, 364
Whitney, R., 309
Wilensky, R., 26, 37
Williams, D. C., 260
Williams, J. A., 307
Winkler, J. D., 353
Winkler, R. L., 239
Winograd, T., 19
Wohlstetter, R., 328
Wright, J. R., 150

Wyer, R. S., 133, 134, 182, 362

Z

Zadny, J., 351

Zahn, E., 315
Zajonc, R. B., 19, 34, 91, 170, 218, 222, 279, 292, 323
Zander, A., 236
Zeiss, A. M., 70
Zemach, M., 282

Subject Index

A

Accessibility, 133-135, 144
Acquisition, 78, 205
ACT system, 30-33
Affect, 18, 31, 42, 46-51, 91, 97-98, 104, 106, 117, 159-163, 165, 170, 177, 179, 212, 250, 260, 297, 359, 365
Algebraic models, 43, 47
Alienation, 217
Anger, 250, 283-291
Artificial intelligence, 16-17, 25
Aschematic, 50, 72-73, 75, 77, 79, 81, 84-85, 106-107, 109, 136, 141, 163, 209, 356
Assimilation, 304
Attention, 349
Attitudes, 49, 71, 104, 106, 112, 159, 161, 176, 178-179, 297, 310, 348, 358, 366
   attitude change, 348
   attitude constraint, 109, 110
Attribute Lists, 17, 18
Attributions, 43-44, 46-48, 60, 64, 81, 109, 362
   attribution theory, 5, 13, 322, 334, 364

B

Balance theory (cognitive balance), 131-132, 304
Base-rate information, 13, 322
Behavioral decision theory, 55, 63, 65, 365
Belief system, 91, 112, 199, 321, 327
Biases, 349, 363
   in attributions 85
   in perception 363
Bounded rationality, 338

C

Candidate perception, 4, 111, 118, 127-131, 133, 135, 137
Carter, Jimmy, 117, 122, 133, 138, 143, 144, 147-149, 153-156-158
Category (cognitive) (categorize in memory), 41-42, 44-45, 48, 51, 91, 104-105, 163, 352
Central trait, 42, 236-237, 263
Character, 233, 235-236, 238, 242-243, 250, 253-255
Cognitive algebra, 12, 15
Cognitive consistency, 4, 129, 348, 358
Cognitive dissonance, 321-322

405

Cognitive economy, 29, 91, 112, 302
Cognitive limitations, 5, 36, 89–91, 95–96, 110, 120, 349
Cognitive miser, 29, 53, 63, 130, 136–137, 150, 304, 329, 348–349
Cognitive psychology, 5, 6, 26, 41, 63, 98, 120, 297, 302, 340, 358–359, 367
Cognitive representation, 205, 359
Collective outcomes, 341
Competence, 236–243, 245–249, 251–253, 326
Concept node, 17, 18
Conservatives, 74, 77, 81, 87, 90, 128, 138–139
Contextual effect, 134
Conventionalization, 326

D

Data-driven, 50–352
Decision-making (in general), 36, 56, 58–59, 324, 338–343
    decision-making (political), 47, 55–57, 62, 92, 121, 314, 324, 334, 337–339
Default value, 22, 131, 352
Democrats, 75, 83, 87, 103, 110–111, 122–123, 140–143, 227
Distributive justice, 50, 260, 263–265, 267–274, 276

E

Economic decision theory, 12
Economic theory (economic models), 12, 43, 58, 130, 257–258, 261–269
Education effects, 106, 124, 244
Electability, 301
Election campaign, 254–255, 300–301
Elimination by aspects, (EBA) 61, 365
Elites, 69, 77, 91, 358
Emotion, 13, 279–286, 288, 291–294
Emotional Resonance, 284, 286–288, 291, 294, 359
Empathy, 237–238, 240–243, 245–249, 251–253, 358
Encode (encoding), 63–64, 70, 78, 84–85, 87, 91, 206
Equality, 49, 175, 178–179, 185, 190, 196–197
    gender equality 49, 165–167, 171, 173, 182, 188, 198

racial equality 49, 165–167, 171, 173, 182, 187, 188
Equal rights ammendment, 76, 135, 172
Expectancy-value theory, 5, 348
Expected utility theory, 35–39, 258, 259
Experts, 76, 136, 142, 151–152, 154, 193, 198, 353–355

F

Fear, 280, 283–287, 291–292
Field theory, 4, 348
Ford, Jerry, 133, 138, 143, 147–150, 153, 156–158
Frames (framing), 57–58, 63, 69, 92, 363
Free rider, 259
Fundamental attribution error, 13

G

Gender, 146, 171–172, 175, 178, 180, 191–192, 194, 198, 244
Generation, 203
Goals, 24, 26, 31, 37, 124, 294, 307
Group identification, 117
Guilt, 284

H

Heuristics, 14, 15, 62, 91, 258, 321
    availability heuristic 13
Hierarchy (hierarchical ordering), 19, 20, 26, 37, 49, 95, 163, 165–166, 170, 327, 352, 362
Hope, 250, 283–287, 291–292
Horserace, 128
Humphrey, Hubert, 138, 143, 144, 147–149, 153, 156–158

I

Ideology, 3, 91–92, 138, 145, 148, 151, 159, 168, 173, 195, 190–191, 197, 244, 250, 288, 313
Income, 106, 146
Independents, 210, 212, 225
Individual differences, 53, 71–73, 135–136, 151–152, 352–355

Information search, 6, 366
Information-processing, 12–17, 19, 21–31, 34, 37, 39, 51, 64, 70, 72, 76–78, 82, 92–93, 95, 112, 120, 129, 136, 144, 191, 193–194, 207, 211, 214–216, 228, 297–298, 303–304, 324, 338, 344, 350–341, 363, 365
Injustice, 269–270, 273
Integrity, 236–243, 245–249, 251–253
Interpretation, 95, 351
Intuitive inference, 56
Invariance principle, 56
Issue distance (issue losses, issue proximity), 117, 122
Issue voting (policy voting), 3, 124

J

Joy, 283
Judgment, 12, 50–51, 60–62, 98, 132, 133, 235–237, 242, 245–253, 258, 260–269, 275, 298, 351
Justice, 11, 260–268, 307, 316, 326

K

Kennedy, Edward, 138, 143, 144, 147–149, 153, 156–159, 237–244, 250–253

L

Leadership, 171, 227, 236–243, 245–249, 251–253
Learning theory, 14, 16, 26, 297
Levels of conceptualization, 91, 92, 112, 113
Liberals, 74, 76–77, 81, 87, 138–139, 288
Limited capacity, 29
Limited search, 338
LISREL, 70, 87–88, 103–104, 245

M

Market decisions, 257
Mass media, 128, 145, 150, 211, 298–301
Mediated perception, 51, 362
Memory, 15, 19, 23, 24, 44, 47, 71–73, 83, 95, 297, 349
    long-term memory, 26, 28, 33

short-term memory, 26, 27, 28, 60
Michigan voting model (*The American Voter*), 3, 4, 203, 228, 348, 358–359
Mondale, Walter, 238–244, 250–254
Moral values, moral reasoning, 52, 242, 273, 276, 288
Morselize, 211
Motivation, 13, 37, 130, 307
Motivational factors (motivational biases), 34, 52

N

National election study (NES), 99, 120, 125, 170, 173, 209, 214, 218–219, 222, 224, 237, 243, 269–270
Network, 20
Non-compensatory choice, 62
Novices, 142, 152, 193, 353–355

P

Party identification, 3, 4, 47, 49, 69, 110, 117, 122–124, 140, 146, 161, 173, 175, 191, 203–206, 211, 228, 242, 250, 314, 357
Perceptual Screen, 3
Personality, 233–234
Personality traits, 43, 234–235, 238, 241, 244–249
Phased rules, 62
Piecemeal-based processing, 42–44, 46–48, 50–51, 105, 352
Pity, 283–287, 290–291
Political behavior, 98, 189, 257, 261–264, 269, 297, 334, 356
Political communications, 201, 293
Political evaluations, 91
Political science, 34, 35, 39, 71, 120, 269, 319, 340, 343, 366
Political socialization, 4, 353
Political sophistication, 49, 64, 71, 79, 91, 112–113, 164, 170
Pride, 280, 314
Probability, 35–38, 55
Procedural justice, 260–261, 264–265, 267–270, 271–274
Production systems, 28
Projection, 147–148
Prospect theory, 38, 58

R

Race, 89, 92, 146, 175, 178-181, 242, 251
Rational choice theory, 3, 4, 35-38, 59, 229,
  344
Rationality, 3, 36, 235, 348-349, 359
Reaction time, 81
Reagan, Ronald, 31, 33, 74, 237-344, 249-253
Recall, 33, 85, 95-96, 99, 351-352
Recognition, 28, 70, 78-81, 84, 87, 91
Republicans, 75, 83, 87, 110-111, 122, 140-143,
  227
Retrieval, 24, 33, 70, 81, 85, 87, 91

S

Sadness, 283
Salience, 47, 84
Satisfice (satisficing), 29, 61, 344
Schema, schemata, schematic, 6-7, 20-22,
  34-35, 42-51, 63, 69-76, 78, 81, 84-85, 89,
  91-92, 103-104, 106, 108-111, 112-113,
  117-122, 130-131, 133-136, 139-141, 144,
  150, 152, 154-155, 159, 162-166, 168, 170,
  175, 182-183, 186-188, 195, 197-201,
  205-206, 208-209, 227, 304, 306, 308-309,
  312-315, 321, 327-328, 340-341, 349-366
causal schema, 6
equality schemata (*see also* equality), 42,
  49
groups schema, 101, 103-104, 106-108, 113,
  120, 122-123, 314, 356
ideology schema, 72, 76-77, 79, 89, 92, 135,
  138, 149-152
issues schema, 97, 101, 103, 108-109, 111,
  113-115, 122, 124, 133, 305, 314, 356
party schema, partisan schema, 42, 72, 83,
  85, 92, 101, 103-104, 110, 113-115,
  117-122, 124, 135, 138-140, 142-148,
  150-151, 206, 227, 314, 361
person schema, 16, 349-350
personality schema, 42, 101, 103-104, 109,
  111, 113-115, 120, 122, 124, 305, 350
political schemata, 6, 71-72, 91, 93, 96-101,
  103-104, 109-118, 120-125, 135-137,
  139, 154, 165, 306, 309, 312, 317, 350,
  353, 358-360, 364-365
role schema, 98, 133, 298-299, 349, 358
schema accessibility, 135
schema-based processing, 87, 98, 352

schema-consistent information, 45, 352-353
schema-inconsistent information, 45,
  351-353
schema-irrelevant information, 45, 351-352
schema-relevant information, 96
self-schema, 131, 136, 138-139, 142, 150,
  154, 163, 309-310, 355
social class schema, 42
Script, 63, 69
Self-esteem, 309, 314
Self-interest, 159, 277, 316
Self-perception, 320
Self-presentation, 342, 354
Serial processing, 27, 60
Social cognition, 5, 6, 7, 41, 51-52, 70, 72, 84,
  127, 138, 163, 187, 322-327, 334-335,
  340-341, 347, 364
Social comparison, 342
Social psychology, social psychological
  theories, 4-5, 7, 52, 84, 120, 128, 205, 236,
  343, 347, 348, 358-359, 364
Socialization (general), 203, 205, 218, 228
Socializing agents, 203
Sociology, sociological theories, 4
Sociotropic beliefs, 316
Spreading activation, 211
Stereotypes, stereotypic, 350
Sunk cost, 58-59
Symbolic politics, 159-163, 165-166, 168, 170,
  177-183, 185, 187, 189-190, 195-199, 259

T

Theory of reasoned action, 5, 15, 43
Theory-driven, 87, 329, 352
Transactions, 304

V

Value function, 58
Value trade-offs, 333, 365
Vote choice, vote decision, 4, 5, 62, 127,
  365-366

W

Wallace, George, 138, 143, 144, 147-149, 152,
  153, 156-158